Tl

With thanks for your
generosity and friendship.

Jay

October, 2003

CHARLES DICKENS IN CYBERSPACE

Jay Clayton

Charles Dickens
IN CYBERSPACE

The Afterlife of the Nineteenth Century in Postmodern Culture

OXFORD
UNIVERSITY PRESS

2003

OXFORD
UNIVERSITY PRESS

Oxford   New York
Auckland   Bangkok   Buenos Aires   Cape Town   Chennai
Dar es Salaam   Delhi   Hong Kong   Istanbul   Karachi   Kolkata
Kuala Lumpur   Madrid   Melbourne   Mexico City   Mumbai   Nairobi
São Paulo   Shanghai   Taipei   Tokyo   Toronto

Copyright © 2003 by Oxford University Press, Inc.

Published by Oxford University Press, Inc.
198 Madison Avenue, New York, New York, 10016

www.oup.com

Oxford is a registered trademark of Oxford University Press

Library of Congress Cataloging-in-Publication Data
Clayton, Jay, 1951–
    Charles Dickens in cyberspace : the afterlife of the nineteenth
century in postmodern culture / Jay Clayton
        p.   cm.
    Includes bibliographical references and index.
    ISBN 0-19-516051-7
    1. English literature—19th century—History and criticism—Theory,
    etc. 2. Dickens, Charles, 1812–1870—Appreciation—United States.
    3. Criticism—United States—History—20th century. 4. English literature—
    Appreciation—United States. 5. United States—Civilization—British influences.
    6. United States—Civilization—20th century. 7. Great Britain—Civilization—
    19th century. 8. Postmodernism (Literature)—United States. 9. Literature
    and science—United States. 10. Literature and science—Great Britain.
    11. Romanticism—Great Britain.   I. Title.
    PR451. C58 2003
    823'.8—dc21   2002011755

9 8 7 6 5 4 3 2 1

Printed in the United States of America
on acid-free paper

TO JIM AND JOHN

ACKNOWLEDGMENTS

I am grateful to the numerous people who have helped me by suggesting sources and responding to questions: Joseph Bizup, Christy Burns, Janice Carlisle, Margaret Darby, Lynn Enterline, Eileen Gillooly, Gregg Hecimovich, Kurt Koenigsberger, Laurence Lerner, Alan Liu, Robert O'Malley, Leah Marcus, Jaya Mehta, Eric Rothstein, Garrett Stewart, Ronald Thomas, Cecelia Tichi, and Joseph Witek. My colleagues at Vanderbilt University were enormously supportive, particularly a group of unselfish friends who read portions of this manuscript at crucial stages: Jerry Christensen, Carolyn Dever, Jim Epstein, Deak Nabers, Mark Schoenfield, and Mark Wollaeger. Others who have guided me with their clear-sighted responses include Alison Booth, Marianne Hirsch, Margaret Homans, Andrew Miller, Dianne F. Sadoff, Valerie Traub, and Priscilla Wald. Several friends in Nashville and elsewhere have stimulated me by their wide-ranging engagement with literature, science, and society: George Bradley, Robert J. Coffey, Marie Griffin, Keith Meador, and Craig Smyser.

Lisa Niles has been an exemplary research assistant, as knowledgeable as she is professional. Jamie Adams, who took the photos reproduced here, was a pleasure to work with. Elissa Morris, my editor at Oxford University Press, encouraged this project and helped shape it in valuable ways. Barry Varela suggested several points during the editing process.

I would also like to thank the John Simon Guggenheim Memorial Foundation and Vanderbilt University for fellowships that gave me time to work on this study. Audiences at a number of institutions have provided me with valuable responses to early versions of this material: The Center for Aesthetics and Logic at Aalborg University, Denmark; Cornell University; CUNY— Graduate Center; Emory University; The English Institute; INCS—Interdisciplinary Nineteenth-Century Studies; Indiana University; The Modern Language Association; The Society for the Study of Narrative Literature; The National Human Genome Research Institute; The Northeast Victorian Studies Association; The Society for Literature and Science; Southern Methodist University; Tulane University; Vanderbilt Medical School; and The University of Washington.

Finally, I give thanks to Ellen Wright Clayton, companion in the pleasures of scholarship as in all other things, and to our two children, who have waited long to have this work dedicated to them. Now that it has arrived, it cannot possibly express all they have meant to me.

Portions of various chapters appeared, in altered form, in the following places and are reprinted with the permission of their publishers: "Dickens and the Genealogy of Postmodernism," *Nineteenth-Century Literature* 46 (1991): 181–95; "Is Pip Postmodern? or, Dickens at the End of the Twentieth Century," *Case Studies in Contemporary Criticism: Charles Dickens's "Great Expectations"*, ed. Janice Carlisle (Boston: Bedford Books, 1995), pp. 606–24; "Concealed Circuits: Frankenstein's Monster, the Medusa, and the Cyborg," *Raritan* 15 (1996): 53–69; "The Voice in the Machine: Hazlitt, Hardy, James," *Language Machines: Technologies of Literary and Cultural Production,* ed. Jeffrey Masten, Peter Stallybrass, and Nancy J. Vickers (New York: Routledge, 1997), pp. 209–32; "Hacking the Nineteenth Century," *Victorian Afterlife: Postmodern Culture Rewrites the Nineteenth Century,* ed. John R. Kucich and Dianne F. Sadoff (Minneapolis: University of Minnesota Press, 2000), pp. 186–210; "Genome Time," *Time and the Literary,* ed. Karen Newman, Jay Clayton, and Marianne Hirsch (New York: Routledge, 2002), pp. 31–59; "Cultural Patchwork in the Classroom: Shelley Jackson, Tom Stoppard, William Gibson, and Bruce Sterling Rewrite the Romantics," *Romanticism and Contemporary Culture,* online, http://www.rc.umd.edu/features/rcc/papers.html, February 2002; "*Frankenstein*'s Futurity: From Replicants to Robotics," *The Cambridge Companion to Mary Shelley,* ed. Esther Schor (Cambridge: Cambridge University Press, 2003), pp. 111–31; and "Convergence of the Two Cultures: A Geek's Guide to Contemporary Literature," *American Literature* 74 (2002): 807–31.

CONTENTS

CHARLES DICKENS IN CYBERSPACE

Dickens Browses the World Wide Web

I magine a Victorian novelist sitting before a computer browsing the World
Wide Web. Watch this author click through research databases, follow
links to commercial sites, send an e-mail to one of a multitude of corre-
spondents, tap out an Instant Message, and enter an appointment in an electronic calendar. If you could picture such a thing, who would the novelist
be? My choice is Charles Dickens.

More than any other writer of the nineteenth century, Dickens would
have been fascinated by the Internet. Throughout his long career, he exhibited a passion for new technology and eagerly exploited every innovation in
the communications and transportation networks of his day. He published
admiring articles on the London Post Office, the railroads, and steam engines. When away from London, he composed on mail coaches and railway
cars, dashed off letters by every post, and dispatched messages by telegraph.
He was not merely a believer in the Victorian gospel of progress but was a
hugely successful entrepreneur himself. Like today's Internet pioneers, he
showed genius in creating new channels of distribution for his writing. He
had a hand in inventing such major breakthroughs as publication by
monthly numbers, serialization of new fiction in weekly journals, and uniform editions of a living author (himself). Moreover he was never averse to
commercializing these enterprises: his serials carried advertising from al-

most the beginning, and he took pleasure in noting the spinoff products from his imagination, such as the Little Nell Cigar and the Gamp Umbrella, even though he received no royalties from their sale. He understood their publicity value, just as he later realized the marketing value of his public readings (another of his firsts). If Dickens did not invent a publishing technology, he was invariably what is known in computer circles as an "early adopter." One could think of his journal *Household Words,* with the banner across every page reading "Conducted by Charles Dickens," as an information outlet as close to a corporate home page as nineteenth-century print media could devise.

Dickens's coauthored article "Valentine's Day at the Post-Office," which appeared in the first issue of *Household Words* on March 30, 1850, will provide a glimpse of the enthusiasm this Victorian writer had for the inner workings of the communications system. The article marvels at the volume of messages the system can handle, the speed of transmission, the coordination of the sorting room, the convenience of the mail tunnels and conduits, the global reach of the system, and the cost effectiveness of the whole operation. He provides a careful description of the routing grid, which to a contemporary eye resembles the division of a Web address into domain name, server, and individual address. The wonder of this network prompts Dickens to compare the entire enterprise to something in a "fairy tale" and himself and his fellow explorer to "knights-errant," journeying through dark passages and enormous halls "illumined by myriads of lights" ("Valentine's Day" 1.73). Hence Dickens becomes the unlikely predecessor of gamers who imagine the inner spaces of the communications system in terms of knights and quests, bright halls and dark passageways. This is how it feels to enter cyberspace, nineteenth-century style.

Fast forward to September 1995. That was the month when a professor at Nagoya University in Japan set up *The Dickens Page,* one of the first Web sites devoted to Charles Dickens. Now there are more than a thousand that touch on his life or career.[1] Professor Mitsuharu Matsuoka created his site in the early years of the Web, when the protocol developed by Tim Berners-Lee began to make the Internet accessible to people other than academics, Defense Department personnel, hackers, and geeks. Matsuoka's continuing commitment to Dickens online is a nice example of the worldwide appeal of this nineteenth-century writer at the turn of the millennium. As I write these words, *The Dickens Page* has been accessed 2,721,124 times, and that number is increasing rapidly. According to my calculations, Dickens has one of the largest Web presences of any literary figure.[2] Thus if the title of this book, *Charles Dickens in Cyberspace,* has a metaphoric dimension, suggesting the ways in which a nineteenth-century writer might have anticipated some of the technological experiences of today, the title also has a literal meaning. Dickens *is* in cyberspace, right alongside MOOs, MUDs, computer games, gambling sites, and Amazon.com.

Speaking of this book's title, I should disclose that the work that follows is not primarily about Dickens. The Inimitable appears in fewer than half of the chapters, and in those chapters, he often stands as a representative of larger cultural patterns rather than as a center of attention in his own right. Instead, this book focuses on the often hidden connections between nineteenth-century culture and today. Moving among science, technology, literature, film, popular culture, and digital media, spanning the last two hundred years, my analysis spends as much time on contemporary figures as on their nineteenth-century predecessors. Recent cultural figures such as Andrea Barrett, Greg Bear, Peter Carey, Hélène Cixous, Alfonso Cuarón, Rick Geary, William Gibson, Donna Haraway, Shelley Jackson, David Lean, Roger McDonald, Andrew Niccols, Richard Powers, Salman Rushdie, Ridley Scott, Susan Sontag, Neal Stephenson, Bruce Sterling, and Tom Stoppard share equal time with nineteenth-century writers such as Jane Austen, Charles Dickens, Benjamin Disraeli, Thomas Hardy, William Hazlitt, Henry James, Thomas Love Peacock, and Mary Shelley. Current developments in communications technology and the Human Genome Project share space with the scientific and engineering achievements of nineteenth-century figures such as Charles Babbage, Samuel Bentham, Isambard Kingdom Brunel, Charles Darwin, Ada Lovelace, Joseph Paxton, Mary Somerville, and Charles Wheatstone.

The sometimes surprising juxtapositions that occur in the following pages are meant to illustrate the value of combining history with current modes of cultural studies. The implicit postmodern assumptions of cultural studies, especially as it is practiced in the United States and on contemporary society, have encouraged critics to sever yesterday from today and deny the validity of long historical perspectives. This book participates in three counter trends. The first, which has gained force over the course of the last decade, during which this book was composed, should be regarded as a necessary premise: that postmodernism has a hidden or repressed connection with nineteenth-century culture. The second, which is also gaining adherents, is the effort to add a historical dimension to cultural studies. The third is the least widespread, but it still claims important adherents: the effort to heal the gap between what C. P. Snow called the "two cultures," literature and science.

I first became interested in the links between the nineteenth century and postmodernism back in 1990, when I composed an article titled "Dickens and the Genealogy of Postmodernism." There I noticed how predictably the same historical pattern was traced in foundational works of postmodernism. In keeping with the logic of *post-*, theories of postmodernism usually constructed an account of the periods that preceded it. This history had three major stages and one glaring gap. The first stage was the Enlightenment, which was seen as the source of the philosophical and political projects of modernity, the origin of its faith in reason, individualism, and science. The second stage came some hundred and fifty years later, in the early decades of the twentieth century, when the Enlightenment project was seen as culminating in the technocratic rationality of modern life. The third stage involved some definition of the present, which was variously identified with the coming of advanced capitalism, a postindustrial society, or an information age.

What was missing from this neat historical scheme was Romanticism—and often the rest of the nineteenth century too. Postmodern theorists tended to ignore the many complex relationships between Romantic culture and the contemporary world. Three of the principal names associated with this theory—Baudrillard, Lyotard, and Foucault—were serious students of the eighteenth century but devoted little attention to writers usually termed Romantics. On the first page of his influential book *The Postmodern Condition* (1979), Lyotard positioned postmodernism as a rejection of the grand Enlightenment metanarratives of rationality and progress. Jürgen Habermas responded that, "in the name of a farewell to modernity," postmodernists "are merely cloaking their complicity with the venerable tradition of counter-Enlightenment" (*Philosophical* 5). The ensuing debate between Lyotard and Habermas set the tone for numerous subsequent writers: if modernity was equated with Enlightenment values of rationality, secularization, empiricism, and individualism, then postmodernism was defined as a rejection or revision of one or more of those terms. This strategy had several interesting effects, not the least of which was the erasure of Romanticism. It was as if Romanticism could have no conceivable connection with the present, as if the circuit that led from the Enlightenment, to the high modern era, to postmodernity would be disrupted by any mention of the Romantic movement.

One of Foucault's last essays was a lecture, which he never lived to deliver, that returned to the topic of the Enlightenment as a way of replying to Habermas. Foucault took as his title the same words Kant had used nearly two hundred years before as the name of a provocative essay: "What Is Enlightenment?" Foucault argued that Kant's seven-page essay, published in 1784, marked a genuine "point of departure," the beginning "of what one might call the attitude of modernity" (38). For Foucault, this attitude consisted of a dual imperative, still operative today: to reflect on the meaning of progress and on the struggle for freedom. But Foucault departed from Habermas and other admirers of the Enlightenment by calling for renewed attention to "whatever is singular, contingent, and the product of arbitrary constraints," to whatever "takes the form of a possible transgression" (45). In making this call, he implicitly aligned himself with Kant and over against Habermas, for Kant had maintained that "An age cannot bind itself and ordain to put the succeeding one into such a condition that it cannot extend its . . . knowledge, purify itself of errors, and progress in general enlightenment. That would be a crime against human nature" (Kant 266). Any attempt to restrain postmodern modes of philosophical inquiry would be a crime against human nature, Foucault implied, and untrue to the Enlightenment itself. This attempt to lay claim to the heritage of the Enlightenment differed from the more common strategy of posing contemporary thought as a total departure, but it had the same effect of eliminating Romanticism entirely from the historical narrative.

There were connections between Romanticism and postmodernism, however, junctures that formed a concealed circuit within the walls of the vast structure of contemporary theory. Romanticism and postmodernism share the distinction of being the two most significant counter-Enlightenment discourses produced in the West.[3] Indeed, they represent this society's only sustained internal oppositions to Enlightenment. Romanticism's challenge came at the very beginnings of that project, while postmodernism's challenge arises at the other end, when some believe that the project has run its course; but the two discourses are united not only in many aspects of their critiques but also in some of the utopian alternatives they propose. Important figures from both eras share counter-Enlightenment attitudes such as an opposition to the hegemony of sight, a critical attitude toward instrumental reason, a preference for undisciplined modes of inquiry, an interest in ad-hoc practices, a relish for hacking, and a reliance on self-reflexive modes of thought.

Since 1990 significant work has been done to establish the relationship between the nineteenth century and postmodernism—and studies are continuing to emerge as this book goes to press. The most important contribution to this project, which influenced my research from the very beginning, was Fredric Jameson's series of articles that culminated in his massive summary statement, *Postmodernism, or, The Cultural Logic of Late Capitalism* (1991). I will have occasion to discuss Jameson's ideas, and air my points of disagreement, at several junctures in the work that follows. For now, let me mention some of the other valuable critical texts that have helped dispel the notion that postmodernism has no relation to the nineteenth century. Two people whose ideas have continually stimulated and challenged my own thinking are Alan Liu and John McGowan. Liu's 1990 article, "Local Transcendence: Cultural Criticism, Postmodernism, and the Romanticism of Detail," was among the first to propose that postmodernism "aggressively sublated romanticism" (87), exhibiting an "amnesia" that "characteristically attempts to find its identity by asking the claustrophobic, historically foreshortened question 'Is postmodernism continuous or discontinuous with modernism?'" (104n26). Similarly, McGowan proposed "that postmodernism can best be defined as a particular, if admittedly diminished, version of romantic dreams of transformation" on the first page of his indispensable study *Postmodernism and Its Critics* (1991). In his most recent work McGowan has continued to pose this issue in highly sophisticated terms. His contribution to *Victorian Afterlife: Postmodern Culture Rewrites the Nineteenth-Century*

(2000) not only demonstrates the debt of postmodern thinking to the nineteenth century but proposes that cultural studies too needs to be seen in relation to the Victorians.[4]

If these parallel allegiances did not prompt the initial theorists of postmodernism to consider the movement's relationship to the nineteenth century, then perhaps one should ask: What work was performed by this absence, what difficulties were evaded? One preliminary answer has become clear: by ignoring the Romantic critique of Enlightenment (wiring around the nineteenth century, as it were), postmodernism concealed its own affinities with Romanticism. But like all repressed knowledge, this problem came back to haunt contemporary theorists. Romanticism looms as a dark presence within postmodernism, something like its cultural unconscious.

Another answer is that such period-bound thinking has made it difficult to perceive the full implications of developments that do not conform to postmodernism. My chief example will be the changing relations of literature, science, and technology. Today a convergence is underway in these domains as important as any transformation proposed by postmodern theory, but the shift is largely obscured by habits of thought that continue to interpret contemporary culture in terms of the dialectic of modernism/postmodernism. Greater insight may be obtained by looking further back, to the early decades of the nineteenth century, the last period before modern disciplinary formations were solidified. Two centuries ago science was not separated off from the larger literary and intellectual culture. In the chapters to come, I point to intriguing signs that a related (although not identical) state of affairs may now be coming to pass. There are odd parallels between the two times, conjunctions that share a weird, long-hidden logic. Some of the most notable of these parallels include: the telegraph and the Internet; Babbage's Analytical Engine and the digital computer; nineteenth-century sound technology and virtual reality; Frankenstein's monster and genetic clones; automata and artificial-life research.

The largest common structure shared by the figures in this book is their similar investment in what I am calling "undisciplined culture." In looking at the fortunes of an early scientist such as Mary Somerville, I discovered that she thrived in an atmosphere that might be described as predisciplinary, a world in which the professional characteristics of science as a discipline had not yet been codified. The same was true, in different ways, of other hybrid scientists, engineers, and figures of general learning such as Charles Babbage and Joseph Paxton. These men and women had an irreverent attitude toward boundaries and an impatience with anything resembling intellectual restraint. They mixed science, engineering, and the arts as they pleased. Without too much exaggeration, they might be described as the nineteenth-century equivalent of hackers.

The 1990s culture of Silicon Valley and Redmond, in which techies roam freely across boundaries that once separated engineering, technology, hard science, popular culture, visual arts, multimedia, and virtual reality, seems undisciplined in a different but related way. I will demonstrate why in much of what follows. But the perplexing thing about these parallels is that nothing leads directly from one time to another. No traditional linear history can plausibly link them in terms of influence, causality, or unbroken development. Moreover the various schemes of periodization familiar to most literary scholars and historians of science actually serve to conceal the existence of any relationship between these two times. Hence it is necessary to work toward a new understanding of cultural parallels in history, one that is as sensitive to disjunction as to recurrence, as careful in delineating gaps, discontinuities, and altered meanings as in making the comparisons that urgently need to be made.

The conjunctions examined here chiefly lie between nineteenth-century England and the United States at the turn of the millennium. In part this emphasis stems from an effort on my part to bring together two strands of research that have shaped my career: the analysis of nineteenth-century British literature, which was the topic of my first book, *Romantic Vision and the Novel* (1987), and contemporary culture, which I explored in *The Pleasures of Babel: Contemporary American Literature and Theory* (1993). There are other reasons, however, which have to do with the construction of literary theory in the academy today. Postmodernism has been theorized as the culture of advanced technological society, and nowhere is this culture more developed than it is in the United States. At the same time, theorists of the postmodern formulate their positions by rejecting an Enlightenment and modernist heritage that comes principally from Britain and the continent. For this reason some of the most prominent critics of contemporary culture tend to draw on a similarly disjunct archive: recent U.S. consumer culture, film, architecture, and literature, on the one hand, and European theorists, on the other hand, whether they are Enlightenment figures such as Kant and Hume or poststructuralists such as Derrida and Lacan. The great absent landscape in this discourse, however, is the terrain covered by this book. Nineteenth-century England—the nation that symbolized in its time the forces of industry, science, engineering, realism, progress, capitalism, and empire—has been largely missing from the historical discourse surrounding postmodernism.

Why were the connections between today's culture and something as crucial to modern society as nineteenth-century England ignored for so long? Why have critics now begun to explore these very connections? What in that earlier time and place caused its strongest links with the present to be obscured, and its most quaint and clichéd features to be revived ad nauseam in nostalgic movies, neoconservative diatribes on Victorian values, and faux-elite consumer marketing? The key lies in the nineteenth-century word "culture" that is buried in the postmodern phrase "cultural studies." For all too many critics, nineteenth-century England has come to symbolize the exclusive Arnoldian tradition of "high" art and literature, which cultural studies aims to dismantle. The reality, as I will demonstrate, is more complex.

If Dickens were sitting before a computer screen today, he would not be surprised at what his browser revealed. The global network, the commercial crassness, and the dizzying pace of both technology and the imagination were all discernible in the nineteenth-century world of cyberspace.

One

THE PAST IN THE FUTURE OF CULTURAL STUDIES

Crystal Palace to Millennium Dome

On December 31, 1999, Greenwich, England, was the site of an equivocal gathering. Queen Elizabeth II officially opened the Millennium Dome in a ceremony that paid homage to the glorious past of her country and nervously promised a transformed future. The rhetoric leading up to this event was a strange mixture of elation and anxiety, as was the news coverage of the actual ceremony. While the latter focused obsessively on the danger of terrorism and the inadequate heating inside the Dome, the former treated the question of history as a troubling burden. From the moment the government convened a special Panel 2000 to oversee the planning of the nation's millennium celebrations, the issue of how to deal with England's decline from her former glory loomed large. History could not be suppressed, for everyone knew it was one of England's most marketable commodities. Yet the panel worried about dwelling too much on the past. Perhaps they had been reading Julian Barnes's novel *England, England* (1998), in which a corporation buys the Isle of Wight and turns it into a historical theme park, replete with replicas of every major tourist attraction from Big Ben and Buckingham Palace to Stonehenge and Sherwood Forest. At any rate, they were frank about their anxiety. One promotional document admitted: "Some still see Britain as it was two decades ago: in decline. Others as no more than a relic of the past, a theme park of castles and villages" (*Towards a Cool Bri-*

tannia), and the official report confessed: "The world does not always think us quite as wonderful as we think we are" (*Consultation Document*).

The solution was to erect the world's largest dome—with an "area more than twice that of Trafalgar Square" and "tall enough to house Nelson's column"—on the site of an abandoned gasworks by the Thames (*Millennium Dome Building*). Coordinated with this project was a nationwide competition to reward inventors who came up with "2000 world beating new products and services" that would help Britain compete in a global market they no longer came close to dominating (*Tony Blair*). These products were to be on display for a full year as part of a tourist attraction featuring interactive exhibits, multimedia performances, virtual reality, live entertainment, food, drink, and other amenities—all the wonders that visitors have come to expect at a world's fair or at Disney's Epcot Center. To dispel the notion that Britain was nothing but a historical theme park, the panel decided to build—what else?—a theme park, albeit in an upscale, architecturally daring pavilion. The favorable media exposure that would supposedly be generated by this year-long "Millennium Experience," brought to consumers by a specially chartered corporation, aimed to "replace a myth of an old Britain" with a new "Cool Britannia" (*Towards*).[1]

What could be more postmodern, more turn of the twenty-first century, more in tune with the new global market for services and images, glitz and glitter? For those who have followed the critical debates about today's culture, there is no need to rehearse Baudrillard's lessons about the world of simulacra standing in for reality or Jameson's reflections on the penetration of capital throughout every aspect of life, so that no one has experience anymore but instead purchases a Millennium Experience. Even without the theoretical discourse, it is easy to see how the forces of marketing and media relations attempt to repackage Britain's national identity. Nothing escapes. History returns, now made virtual in the form of a "History Zone" on the Greenwich Web site. There one may take *A Literary Tour of Charles Dickens's Greenwich* or browse three millennia of English history on the *Millennium Time-lines* page. No fear about being a relic of the past if consumers get their history mediated electronically. Even the ambition to become a "Cool Britannia" participates in the Web's dominant aesthetic of cool, which Alan Liu has brilliantly anatomized as the cultural logic of the information age ("Future Literary").

What could be more postmodern? And yet the Millennium Dome bears an uncanny resemblance to another mass spectacle staged in London nearly a hundred and fifty years ago, the Great Exhibition of 1851.[2] Both events were opened by a Queen; both were housed in dazzling translucent structures that highlighted dramatic advances in engineering and construction; both were conceived as displays of England's glory; both were focused on products and technology; both generated concern over the risk of foreign terrorism; and both attracted massive crowds, requiring the construction of special railway, hotel, and eating facilities, as well as the implementation of controversial ticketing and policing procedures to ensure the orderly processing of spectators. The Great Exhibition took place in Joseph Paxton's iron-and-glass pavilion known as the Crystal Palace. Covering fourteen acres in Hyde Park, the Crystal Palace had room under its glass ceilings to accommodate the towering elms that had been growing on the site. Up to a hundred thousand visitors a day streamed through its aisles, and a total of over six million people gaped at its overwhelming displays during the six months of the exhibition. It was an immense success, a showcase of England's glory exceeding even the most optimistic projections. Surely this exposition, the first and most influential of all international fairs, must have haunted the planners of the Millennium Dome.

Millennium Dome publicity, however, omits any reference to its once-famous predecessor. This omission is hardly surprising, given the panel's anxiety about history, yet the absence helps conceal the very different national temper that prevailed a century and a half ago. When the Great Exhibition opened its doors, London was the center of an unrivaled empire, and English manufacturing confidently viewed itself as second to none. The drawing by George Cruikshank "All the World Going to See the Great Exhibition of 1851" captured the sense Londoners had that England ruled the globe and that the Crystal Palace was her crown (Figure 1.1). By contrast, the Millennium panel worked with an uneasy consciousness of their country's faded power. To claim London as the center of world capitalism today would be even more implausible than to suggest any foreign city during the reign of Queen Victoria. Even though nineteenth-century Paris and New York had reasons to boast, Londoners were certain of their own preeminence. As one contemporary publication put it, the Great Exhibition "implies a conscious greatness, on the part of our country sufficient to warrant such a bold and unprecedented step. It would be presumptuous and idle for an inferior state to ask her potent neighbors thus to honor her" (qtd. in Andrew Miller 76). In year 2000 choosing London as the premier place to welcome the new millennium needed (and received) considerable justification. Cleverly, the panel made Time itself their principal qualification. Billing Greenwich as the "Centre of Time and Space" because of its position on the prime meridian, they urged the world to focus on their atomic clock as it counted down to what they proclaimed to be the true beginning of the new millennium (*Millennium Dome*). The center of Time, if not of global capitalism, London hoped to extend its moment of glory into a renewed future.

Juxtaposing the Millennium Dome with the Crystal Palace raises one of the central questions of this book: What is the place of the past in contemporary culture? *Charles Dickens in Cyberspace* takes up this question by focusing on contemporary transformations of nineteenth-century literature, science, and technology. The discussion often must consider the startling gaps in this heritage, the missing awareness of something that should be inescapable, like Paxton's Palace. Just as often, the book confronts a be-

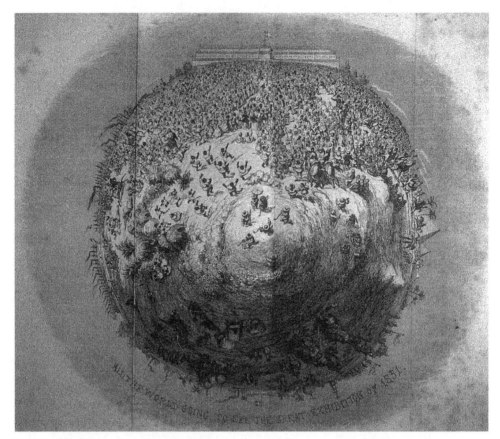

FIGURE 1.1
George Cruikshank, "All the World
Going to See the Great Exhibition
of 1851." *1851, or, The Adventures of
Mr and Mrs Sandboys and Family*
(London: D. Bogue, 1851).

wildering array of allusions to the earlier century, a hodgepodge of trivia
and clichés, as well as more illuminating images in novels, films, advertising,
consumer products, and the Web. From Jane Austen in Hollywood to Charles
Dickens Christmas celebrations, from neo-Victorian novels by A. S. Byatt
and Peter Carey to lingerie from Victoria's Secret, from discussion lists rev-
eling in Regency fashion to Web sites selling Gaslight bric-a-brac—nostalgic
trips back to the earlier century are a major growth industry today.

When it comes to gaps in historical consciousness, the most surprising
failures occur not in the popular media but in the very critical discourses designed to account for our times: postmodernism and cultural studies. Postmodernism has been defined in many different ways in its nearly 45-year

career as a critical term. Here let me offer the preliminary observation that postmodern theory is a discourse of historical rupture that initially came into being only by suppressing its many continuities with nineteenth-century culture. Postmodern scepticism about reason, objectivity, and universalism has striking affinities with positions taken by the English Romantics. For example, I shall have occasion to compare postmodern and Romantic attitudes toward subjectivity, the sublime, formal fragmentation, science, technology, and the environment. Lately, a few critics have begun to talk about these affinities in theoretical and philosophical terms.[3] The discussion here takes a different tack. Rather than offering another survey of postmodern philosophers, this book analyzes specific areas of conjunction between nineteenth-century experience and today's culture. It reads works of literature, recovers neglected historical moments in science, and explores a diverse range of popular media. Although informed by literary theory, this book explores a crowded intersection—a crossroads where cultural studies meets literature, science, and history.

Cultural studies is an increasingly prominent critical practice that attends not only to popular media but also to everyday life and material culture. This movement takes all aspects of culture as its province, eclectically using methods derived from sociology, literary theory, gender studies, and postcolonial criticism. But like postmodernism it has had a vexed relation to history. In its first incarnations in the United States, it commonly produced political critiques of contemporary practices, media, or discourse situated in specific, local contexts, informed by the personal experience of the author, and shaped by "bricolage," or the willingness to employ whatever theoretical tools come to hand. (In keeping with my focus on the United States when dealing with contemporary culture, my reflections on cultural studies apply chiefly to the way it has been practiced in the States.[4]) The best early examples of American cultural studies were penetrating in their social analysis and animated by engaging narratives, but they seldom contained a historical dimension. As in the fanfare surrounding the Millennium Dome, parallels from the past hardly ever came up.

This point was often overlooked because of a widespread tendency to confuse the *social* with the *historical.* Since cultural studies enormously expanded the canon of acceptable topics of study, moving far beyond the sphere of high literature and art to encompass such topics as Madonna, hiphop culture, Barbie dolls, and the aesthetics of cigarettes, it was easy to equate its perspective with that of social history. Focusing on what once used to be thought of as context, however, is not the same thing as taking a historical approach.[5] The two have come to be conflated for a number of reasons. To begin with, in the United States this conflation largely stems from the struggle between formalist and contextualist methods in literary studies over the last several decades. From the 1970s onward, various formalisms such as the New Criticism and poststructuralism were increasingly contested by contextual methods such as feminism, the New Historicism, and postcolonial studies.[6] One result was that any decision to concentrate on political and social issues outside the text came to be seen as a historicist gesture. Much of this "historicist" work, however, was resolutely synchronic in its focus, examining a cross-section of social relations in a particular period rather than the transformation of relations through time. The fact that New Historicism first came to prominence in the field of Renaissance studies, and shortly thereafter in Romanticism and nineteenth-century American studies, further helped to disguise the absence of a diachronic dimension in much of the research produced under its banner. Sociological perspectives, drawn from the work of Pierre Bourdieu and Michel de Certeau, tended to emphasize mechanisms of cultural reproduction rather than temporal development, while the infusion of ideas from Horkheimer and Adorno of the Frankfurt school—a prominent aspect of U.S. cultural studies—tended to concentrate attention on the dominance of the culture industry after World War II. As a result, most work in cultural studies came to deal with "Western societies from the 1960s on" (Gitlin 77).

The absence of history in U.S. cultural studies has been attributed to the field's orientation toward the present.[7] But the problem runs deeper. There was a fundamental tension between history and cultural studies, at least as each field initially conceived of the other. In what might be called the "first wave" of cultural studies in the United States (roughly the mid-1980s to early 1990s), this tension had two sources. First, the resistance of many critics to Marxist versions of historical determinism made them chary of all arguments about historical causality. Opposition to models of society that saw the economic base as primary and culture as derivative was common in this phase of cultural studies. Instead critics tended to emphasize the forces of consumption rather than production and to give weight to the social construction of the material world. "In its zeal to escape from historical determination," historian Michael P. Steinberg observed, "cultural studies has proved able to sacrifice the historical dimensions of present cultural reality" (110). Second, the implicit postmodernism of cultural studies appeared, from some perspectives, to render historical inquiry difficult, if not impossible. The postmodern critique of metanarratives and totalizing modes of knowledge made any effort to draw long historical connections appear suspect. This suspicion relied on a simplistic equation of history with linear schemes and developmental narratives, but it was pervasive nonetheless. Equally, the postmodern critique of objectivity and universalism made history's apparent claim to uncover the Truth about the past suspect. Again, this suspicion applied only to a limited conception of history, which was belied by the actual practice of many contemporary historians. Other models of historical thinking existed, as I shall show, but they were—and perhaps still are—too little known among literary and cultural critics.

In the 1990s the rise of the new cultural history as practiced by Lynn Hunt, Peter Burke, and others offered attractive models to cultural studies.[8] Within the field of nineteenth-century British history, impressive examples of this new cultural history appeared in the writings of James Epstein, Catherine Hall, Patrick Joyce, Carolyn Steedman, James Vernon, and Judith R. Walkowitz.[9] Literary critics working on earlier centuries were quick to adopt such models. Thus one finds something like the kind of historical cultural studies I am calling for emerging in the work of important critics of nineteenth-century literature such as Mary Poovey and Deborah Nord. But similar models have not spread to the majority of cultural studies critics focusing on the present, which is to say to the majority of those in U.S. literary circles.

Making historical connections is crucial to the next stage of research on contemporary culture. What the historian Carolyn Steedman called for in 1992 still remains true: "cultural studies needs to think about what it will *do* with history, and what kind of historical thinking it will ask its students to perform" (620). Even when analysis focuses on contemporary life, one cannot afford to neglect the way in which earlier cultural formations are sedimented in today's latest fashion. How, then, can the study of the present contain a viable sense of history? Or, to rephrase the question, what is the role of the past in the future of cultural studies?

To begin answering these questions, let me turn to Peter Carey's Booker Prize–winning novel of 1988, *Oscar and Lucinda*. This novel comes to mind because its story of colonial Australia is deeply haunted by the Crystal Palace. The novel also serves a strategic function: I want to demonstrate how literature can aid the project of a historical cultural studies.

In recent years, there has been a return of interest in the question of the literary.[10] This concern scarcely resembles the older preoccupations of critics who viewed literary works as unified autonomous objects, verbal icons, or well-wrought urns. Rather it stems from a desire to specify the distinctive cultural work performed by different forms, genres, and media. Hence literature returns as one element among others—no longer privileged, perhaps, but not discredited, forgotten, or dissolved into "textuality," either. Literature returns as the name for a specific formal domain, with its own unique social coordinates, in a diverse and competitive world filled with rival signifying practices. Peter Carey, who has worked in other media and who frequently transgresses the boundary between fiction and history, exploits the advantages of this new dispensation.

Narrated by a nearly anonymous figure writing in the present, *Oscar and Lucinda* tells the story of a defrocked Anglican priest named Oscar Hopkins who transported an iron-and-glass church across the Australian wilderness a hundred and twenty years before. Although virtually no trace of the Crystal Palace's influence remains visible in the 1980s, its peculiar cultural legacy—at once inspiring and grotesque—mangles the lives of the novel's nineteenth-century characters and survives in the narrator's quest to understand his own time. The novel's glass church was inspired by a visit to the Crystal Palace by a woman Oscar loved to madness, Lucinda Leplastrier. The scheme to transport this prefabricated gothic fantasy in glass across hundreds of miles of uncharted territory leads to tragic consequences, including the massacre of an Aborigine tribe, physical and sexual abuse of expedition members, the murder of the expedition's leader, the loveless act of conception that made Oscar the narrator's great-grandfather, and Oscar's own death in a grotesque mishap the night after arriving at his destination. In the twentieth century all that is left of the church is a faded wooden building on an iron frame. On the last pages of the novel even this pitiful reminder of Oscar and Lucinda's struggle is carted away on a flatbed truck. Nothing remains to mark their passing but wheel ruts and thistles—nothing except for the narrator's painful reconstruction of his own and his nation's past.

Carey's novel illustrates the bizarre ways in which nineteenth-century culture can live on, almost undetected, in the contemporary world. This hidden afterlife often takes forms very different from those found in official memory. The Crystal Palace, for example, had meanings for a solitary Australian woman that few today would guess. These meanings, moreover, were strangely at odds with its public symbolism at the time. Where the great pavilion incarnated for London its imperial mastery of the globe, for Lucinda it symbolized incongruous things, hard to put in words. It was bound up with her unresolved desires, her oddity, her improper behavior, her restless inarticulate feminism, her strength of will, and her preference for engineering wonders instead of the high art and culture of the English capital. All of these inchoate feelings came together and received their only expression in her fascination with glass. After visiting the Crystal Palace on her one trip to England, "Her head was burning with dreams of glass" (240). Seeing it inspired her "to build something Extraordinary and Fine from glass and cast-iron. A Crystal Palace, but not a Crystal Palace. . . . Glass laced with steel, spun like a spider web—the idea danced around the periphery of her vision, never long enough to be clear" (305). Oscar, in his passion for Lucinda, understood her vision, even though he misunderstood almost everything else about her, including the fact that she returned his love. Hence Oscar conceived the idea of building a glass church and taking it as a gift to the man he wrongly supposed she preferred:

> "You could transport an entire cathedral and assemble it across the mountains," [Oscar said]. "Can you imagine a glass cathedral?"
> She could. She saw its steeples, domes, its flying buttresses, motes of dust, shafts of light. "Mr. Hopkins, we are mad to think of it." (326)

Mad, yes. But ecstatic too, transfigured and defiant, driven against the grain by fiercely independent wills. This combination makes it hard to assimilate these characters into normative cultural narratives. They are odd, and their oddity receives great stress. Oscar, called "Odd Bod" by his only friend, is a total misfit at Oxford: poor, from a dissenting background, addicted to gambling, a gangly weakling, terrified of water, and plagued with as many bodily tics as Dr. Johnson. Oscar is even more out of place after emigrating to Australia with the harebrained idea of converting the Aborigines. Lucinda, for her part, is an orphan, also addicted to gambling, who has never mastered the social codes of Australian society and who confronts even greater prejudice against colonials during her unrewarding trip to England. When she tries to run a factory in Sydney, she is continually thwarted by barriers against women in business. Ultimately she is ostracized for what everyone assumes to be her immoral behavior, even though she and Oscar live together in complete chastity. They are odd people out.

The characters' oddity exemplifies something beyond the merely personal; it stands for more general forms of discordant experience, which are often culturally invisible. These odd, disjunctive lives have had a shaping force on the narrator's world, but their traumatic experiences have vanished from history. The theme of history's omissions is a prominent motif in the novel. At the very beginning, the narrator reveals: "I learned long ago to distrust local history," and adduces as an example a cliff named Darkwood, which had been changed from Darkies' Point to disguise the genocide that occurred when white settlers "pushed an entire tribe of aboriginal men and women and children off the edge" (2). The narrator's father, too, used to become enraged whenever he heard his wife's sanitized account of how her ancestor had transported the church to this frontier outpost. Most important, the novel laments the erasure of Aboriginal culture, the loss of "sacred stories more ancient than the ones [Oscar] carried in his sweat-slippery leather Bible" (416).

Carey's novel uses multiple perspectives, temporal layering, and intertextuality to restore some of these vanished narratives. A historical cultural studies must do the same if it is to register the diverse ways in which the past resonates in the present. Critics need to find techniques that respond to the often incompatible cultural meanings the past may possess, particularly for figures who are marginal to mainstream society. Literature models a way of seeing these partial and incompatible perspectives as meaningful, not arbitrary or relativistic. Literature offers modes of response and comprehension that do not have to be reconciled with the dominant ideology in order to be considered valid and ethically significant.

Seen through the eyes of outsiders like Oscar and Lucinda, nineteenth-century culture becomes strange, decentered. The difference may be little more than a shift in emphasis, but the shift can be hard to assess if it does not happen to line up with any of the identity categories recognized today. Take Lucinda's preference for Joseph Paxton over George Eliot. Current identity politics would not suggest that an intellectual, free-thinking woman with literary tastes would prefer a gardener-turned-builder to her mother's revered friend, Marian Evans.[11] The attraction lies in a realm of culture to which contemporary critics have lost the key: engineering. Lucinda finds herself drawn to Paxton and other engineers, although they are intolerant of her sex and terribly patronizing, because of affinities that should properly be seen as cultural, even aesthetic. They share her sense of the beauty of tech-

nology and industrial manufacture; they understand her pride in collaborative endeavors and anonymous creation. Such affinities are out of sync with
contemporary expectations. Understanding their logic requires historical
work. Understanding their legacy requires something more: a flexible, multifaceted awareness of how a diverse present relates to an equally various
past. This requirement is perhaps why novelists and playwrights have been
the first to explore the odd interrelations between science and literature in
nineteenth-century culture: witness the marine biology and entomology in
A. S. Byatt's *Possession* (1990) and *Angels and Insects* (1992); the mathematics
in Tom Stoppard's *Arcadia* (1993); the natural history in Andrea Barrett's
Ship Fever (1996) and *The Voyage of the Narwhal* (1998).

Lucinda's passion for the aesthetics of engineering was already under
attack by 1863, the time the novel has her visiting the Crystal Palace. The attack came from architectural critics, who were committed both to the modern trend toward professional specialization and to the Modernist project of
separating art from all merely mechanical activities. Paxton's building contradicted both of these impulses, for he had no formal training in architecture and his prefabricated, modular design made it possible to assemble and
disassemble the structure like a giant Erector set. The Crystal Palace provoked
an extended debate over whether it could be considered architecture, a debate that was resolved, even by admirers of the building, in the negative. The
reason paradoxically lay in its engineering achievements. One professional
journal was up front about its disciplinary agenda: Paxton could not be considered an architect because he lacked the "education and training for a
profession," any profession. Another publication distinguished between the
"science of building," which was engineering, and "the art of *beautifying*
building," which was architecture (qtd. in McKean 41). This conclusion
echoed John Ruskin, who attacked the Crystal Palace for its lack of orna-
mentation and its ungainly size. Others felt its modular construction and
prefabricated parts disqualified it: "the infinite multiplication of the same
component parts . . . appears to us to be destructive of its claim to high architectural merit" (qtd. in Chadwick 123). By 1863 the consensus in professional and artistic circles on Paxton's building was: "it is engineering—of the
highest merit and excellence—but not architecture" (qtd. in McKean 41).

Lucinda's cultural tastes, then, were as odd as everything else about her.
Carey helps readers both sympathize with her position and grasp its oddity
by embedding her story, and Oscar's too, in a dense set of allusions to other
nineteenth-century writers. This intertextual network gives their oddity the
exemplary quality I mentioned before, and it provides terms by which to interpret eccentricities that might otherwise remain opaque. As several commentators have noted, Oscar's youthful rebellion against his father, a stern
religious dissenter and naturalist, is patterned after Edmund Gosse's Victorian autobiography, *Father and Son*.[12] Lucinda's difference from English
norms is emphasized by the contrast her life offers to the British novels she

loves to read: Trollope's *Barchester Towers,* Scott's *Waverley,* Dickens's *Bleak House,* and other nineteenth-century bestsellers (188, 241).

Less visible but even more significant intertexts for their lives are three novels by Fyodor Dostoevsky: *The Gambler, The Idiot,* and *Notes from Underground.* Oscar and Lucinda's shared obsession with gambling is at first hard to fathom—hard to reconcile with other aspects of their characters or to recuperate in terms of the novel's themes.[13] Late in the book, however, the decision to risk everything on the glass church suddenly brings gambling into focus as a Dostoevskian wager with their very souls. Oscar asserts that God's "fundamental requirement of us is that we gamble our mortal souls, every second of our temporal existence" (218); their grand wager on the church will make them "gamblers in the noble sense" (325). At this juncture, the reader might recall that Dostoevsky is mentioned as one of the volumes Lucinda inherits from her mother, right alongside books by Carlyle, Dickens, John Stuart Mill, and George Eliot (63).[14] With this hint, Oscar's unworldly innocence begins to make sense as a variation on Prince Myshkin from *The Idiot.* Lucinda is "so moved by his goodness that her eyes watered" (207). During the time spent on the *Leviathan,* a long ocean crossing aboard a steamship based on Isambard Kingdom Brunel's *Great Western,* a "rude and contemptuous" fellow passenger "was made, at least temporarily, into something fine" by Oscar's guileless character (206–7). Like the divine fool in Dostoevsky's novel, Oscar raises selflessness to a religious pitch. Deciding to transport the church to the man he thinks Lucinda loves instead of him is an idea "born out of habits of mind produced by Christianity. . . . It was a knife of an idea, a cruel instrument of sacrifice, but also one of great beauty, silvery, curved, dancing with light" (324).

Notes from Underground (1864) has a more complex relevance to Carey's text. Dostoevsky, who visited the Crystal Palace in 1862 (the year before Lucinda's imaginary trip), uses the glass building to symbolize all that is sterile and deadening in modern existence. Mocking a fellow Russian writer, N. G. Chernyshevsky, who had portrayed the Crystal Palace as a utopian symbol in his novel *What Is To Be Done* (1863), Dostoevsky's antihero proclaims that a future spent in a crystal palace would be "dreadfully boring" (27) and that he is "afraid of this edifice just because it is crystal and forever imperishable" (40). What disturbs him the most is that "suffering is inadmissible. . . . In a crystal palace it's unthinkable; suffering is doubt, negation, and what kind of a crystal palace would it be if doubt were possible in it?" (39). Nothing could be further from Carey's use of the symbol. Not only does the Crystal Palace inspire rather than bore Lucinda, it also proves anything but imperishable, since the glass church in the novel shatters to ruins and sinks in the river on the very night of its arrival. Further, the building causes immense suffering, doubt, and negation. Oscar's last thoughts as he drowns inside the crystal edifice are of religious despair and negation: "All he could think was that the glass church was the devil's work, that it had been the agent of murder and fornication" (424). Through these antithetical interpretations, Carey's text enters into dialogue with Dostoevsky's novel.

Notes from Underground illuminates much that is troubling about both Oscar and Lucinda. Oscar's excruciating humiliations at the hands of school friends and strangers alike mirror the underground man's repeated humiliations by his school friends. So extreme is Oscar's degradation that it is hard to know how to read it in psychological, ethical, or political terms, but the reflections of the underground man offer some guidance. Dostoevsky's character articulates a psychology of limits, of the freedom that comes from knowing one has reached the nadir. "This pleasure comes precisely from the sharpest awareness of your own degradation; from the knowledge that you have gone to the utmost limit; that it is despicable, yet cannot be otherwise" (Dostoevsky 7). Oscar feels this kind of release at all the chief turning points in his story. Lucinda's character also reflects elements in Dostoevsky's text. Her ecstatic willingness to embrace an apparently mad desire is clarified by the underground man's belief that what makes one human is the courage to commit oneself to "one's own free, untrammeled desires, one's own whim, no matter how extravagant, one's own fancy, be it wrought up at times to the point of madness" (Dostoevsky 28).

It is symptomatic of the thin, ahistorical approach to the cultural issues this novel raises that none of the criticism it has received discusses the Crystal Palace in any detail; none analyses Joseph Paxton or I. K. Brunel; none considers nineteenth-century engineering or architecture; none discusses Dostoevsky at any length; and only one piece conveys the sense to the reader that the two central figures would have been complete misfits in their own time.[15] Reading the assembled criticism of this text, one would get the impression that it treats postcolonial issues and metafiction solely in terms of today's models and debates, an approach that turns the novel's play with history into an elaborate postmodern game. Admittedly, Dostoevsky appears as the merest trace in the text, an eccentric link to a past that seems almost incidental to the main action. This eccentricity, however, makes a telling point for a historical approach to culture. In a diverse contemporary world, the past that matters is not always obvious or inescapable. Dostoevsky appears as a trace or sediment of a nearly lost history, a past perspective that is almost as difficult to discern as that of the eradicated Aboriginal tribe. Dostoevsky's counter-reading of the Crystal Palace haunts the text the way these damaged remnants from Australia's past haunt the present.

The Crystal Palace's ability to generate antithetical interpretations may ultimately be Carey's point in invoking Dostoevsky. It is certainly my point. *Oscar and Lucinda* adopts Dostoevsky's symbol only to transform it completely. The very properties of glass are taken to authorize such contradictory uses of a cultural icon. From the age of nine, Lucinda "knew already the lovely contradictory nature of glass"; "glass is a thing in disguise, an actor . . . invisible, solid, in short, a joyous and paradoxical thing" (111). The presence of the underground man's view of the Crystal Palace, shimmering behind

Oscar and Lucinda's vision, testifies to the contradictory nature—the para-doxical quality, not always joyous—with which a historical cultural studies must contend.

Four general attitudes toward the past stand out in the current vogue for nineteenth-century culture. Each expresses an implicit cultural politics and thus reflects a larger position in contemporary debates. Let us call these attitudes the neoconservative, liberal, identitarian, and postmodern. Neo-conservative Victorianism produces a linear historical narrative of degener-ation. Ethical in tone and intent, it holds up the nineteenth century as an ad-monishment to our wayward times and calls for a return to once-cherished ideals. Claiming philosophical lineage from Edmund Burke, it has a learned exponent these days in Gertrude Himmelfarb, who promotes a neocon-servative agenda by celebrating nineteenth-century political thinkers from John Stuart Mill to William Gladstone.[16] In the wider popular culture, its influence is manifested in phenomena ranging from Margaret Thatcher's advocating the Victorian values of hard work, self-reliance, and frugality to the former Republican Speaker of the House Newt Gingrich's praising Vic-torian Poor Laws; from William J. Bennett's promoting traditional virtues in his anthologies, tapes, calendars, and illustrated children's books to Rene Denfeld's attacking feminism in her nonfiction bestseller *The New Victori-ans* (1995).

Liberal admirers of the nineteenth century follow a different but related pattern. Rather than a story of decline, they invoke a universal conception of culture as a repository of timeless truths that retain their importance regard-less of the historical period. The liberal position uses culture as a touchstone with which to measure out praise or blame impartially to both yesterday and today. Matthew Arnold is its tutelary spirit, and thoughtful contemporary avatars include Eugene Goodheart and Martha Nussbaum. The latter, for example, employs Dickens's *Hard Times* to instruct public policy wonks—whether nineteenth-century utilitarians or twenty-first–century cost-benefit analysts—in the importance of imagination and love. Nussbaum's *Poetic Justice* (1995) conducts a sustained debate with the ideas of Richard Posner, a prominent jurist and leader of the Law and Economics movement, over her contention that reading Dickens can help policymakers more than studying abstract economic formulas can, because his novels treat problems in terms of "certain views about human freedom and human functioning that I take to have universal significance" (8).[17] In the same year Oscar Hi-juelos's fine novel *Mr. Ives' Christmas* celebrated Dickens in much the same liberal spirit, turning to *A Christmas Carol* for insights into the consequences of urban poverty no matter what its time period. In some respects, the lib-eral view of culture is the mirror image of the neoconservative. Despite their opposed agendas, both end up relying on similar conceptions of the histo-rian's task, which they see as that of producing a continuous, unified ac-count of how the present has emerged from the past.

Neither stance is well suited to a historical cultural studies. Unified visions of history work against what I am recommending: an awareness of the contradictory legacies cultural objects can bestow. One of the most important lessons for cultural studies is that apparently similar, even identical, phenomena can have hugely variable meanings for different people and at different times. The critic who attempts to compare past and present must be alert to these differences, not merely to the analogies that make comparison possible in the first place.[18] Putting the Millennium Dome side by side with the Crystal Palace will not suffice, for the functions of exhibitions change not only across time but also across spatial and social distance. Analogy, like repetition, contains difference within a structure of similitude. While this difference often has a social dimension, it is always temporal as well, which means that, in historical writing more than any other, noting resemblance is not enough. In a historical cultural studies, the purpose of comparing works from widely separated times will inevitably be to measure the distance traveled, the forces that made the journey possible, and the consequences of arriving, burdened with memory and forgetfulness, at a new place and a new hour.

Gertrude Himmelfarb's writings on contemporary society provide a good example of how *not* to include history in cultural studies. Himmelfarb has published important studies of poverty in the nineteenth century, but her critique of contemporary politics illustrates some of the consequences of neglecting historical difference. In *The De-Moralization of Society: From Victorian Virtues to Modern Values* (1995), she accuses feminists who confront issues of pornography, hate speech, sexual harassment, and date rape of "moralistic paternalism" (259). Although she protests that one should not confuse these "New Victorians" with honest-to-God Victorians, her own practice betrays the typifying and analogizing strategy behind her social criticism. For example, Himmelfarb turns to Dickens's *Bleak House* (1852–53) to find an analogue for today's crusading feminists. She claims they resemble nothing so much as Dickens's character Mrs. Jellyby, a mother who was too busy with charity work on behalf of the "Borrioboola-Gha" in Africa to pay attention to her children at home. "Today's moralists," Himmelfarb writes, "have that same far-away, fanatical glint in their eye" (261).

One could scarcely ask for a more inappropriate parallel. The comparison ignores both the diversity of positions in contemporary feminism around all the issues she names and the complex historical undercurrents present in Dickens's caricature. Activists involved in issues of sexual harassment today face a tangled skein of legal definitions, changing mores, doubts about unconscious motivations, worries about freedom of expression, fears that emphasizing victimization will deny agency to women, and the knowledge that views on sexual roles can vary across class, race, religious heritage, and more. Yet Himmelfarb collapses the many different positions that activists espouse on these topics into a comparison with Mrs. Jellyby's "telescopic philanthropy" (261). More troubling in a historian, Himmelfarb ignores the complex cultural associations that are woven into Dickens's satire of female philanthropists. Dickens's mockery of Mrs. Jellyby's mission to help Africans brings his own social attitudes into view. Few today remember that readers in 1852, including Lord Chief Justice Denman, saw Dickens's satire of Mrs. Jellyby as an attack on English antislavery efforts.[19] Perhaps Himmelfarb forgot as well while she was engaged in using Dickens's caricature to pummel feminists with whom she disagrees. Although Dickens was no supporter of slavery, his views of race and colonialism were shaped by the commonplace assumptions of his day, and his portrait of Mrs. Jellyby reflects those assumptions.

Identitarian and postmodern approaches to the nineteenth century reject the unified vision of history found in the first two models, neoconservative and liberal, although for different reasons. The identitarian position sees the past not in terms of unity but of division and conflict. Nourished by the new social movements and identity politics of recent decades, this approach portrays the nineteenth century as divided by multiple fissures, carved up along fault lines of race, nationality, class, gender, sexuality, age, disability, religious conviction, and more. It stresses conflict rather than consensus and explores scenes where new social groups coalesce. The end result was the construction of alternative traditions or counterhistories of Victorian outsiders. In *The Pleasures of Babel* (1993) I analyzed the advantages of this multicultural view in the context of contemporary American society, although my approach to culture differs, in ways that I will make clear below, from the identitarian model.

Postmodern attitudes toward the nineteenth century are a special case. Although postmodern theorists reject unified accounts of the past, they generally are not interested in tracing alternative traditions. Instead, they challenge the very project of history itself. In recent years critics have interpreted the ideas of Foucault and Derrida to signal the "end of history," both in the sense of the professional study of the past and in the more idiosyncratic usages of Francis Fukuyama and Jean Baudrillard, who argue, for different reasons, that contemporary experience no longer possesses a historical character. For example, Elizabeth Ermarth asserts that postmodernism subverts "historical time," bringing about the "disappearance of history" (7), and Keith Jenkins recommends "letting history and ethics go because postmodern thinking has provided all the intellectual resources we now need to think in future-oriented, emancipatory and democratising ways" (*Why History?* 2). Given this position, it is no surprise that few postmodern approaches to nineteenth-century history exist. What one finds instead is a great deal of polemic, both pro and con, typified by Keith Windschuttle's hyperbolically titled *The Killing of History: How Literary Critics and Social Theorists Are Murdering Our Past* (1996).[20] The neglect of the nineteenth century in postmodern thought, however, stemmed from more than simply an antipathy to historical modes of inquiry. As I demonstrate in chapter 5, the absence of nineteenth-century culture from the discourse of postmodernism, at least until recently, was part of a deeper logic in postmodern theory itself. Here I want to take up the more limited question of whether the identitarian or postmodern visions of history can serve the project of cultural studies.

Again, neither approach is entirely satisfactory. Identitarian assumptions pose the risk to cultural studies of a misplaced reliance on personal experience as a foundation or ground of knowledge. In current practice, cultural studies is frequently underwritten by its connection with the personal experience of the critic. Marianna Torgovnick highlights the role of the autobiographical in her introduction to a collection of new work in the field: "Something in the writer's background or experience took hold in the imagination, so that the essay grew from the core of experience—often from an important bit of family or personal history" (1). The essay on "Cultural Studies" in the 1992 guide to scholarship issued by the Modern Language Association traces this "emphasis on experience as the starting point for social analysis" to the Birmingham School and quotes Stuart Hall as saying that "the question of the status of the experiential moment in 'lived' cultures [is] an irreducible element of any explanation" (Bathrick 331).

Part of the novelty and iconoclasm of cultural studies is its openness to the lived experience of the writer, and I do not want to suggest that the field should re-embrace scholarly conventions of a neutral, impersonal stance. As Patricia Williams says in *The Alchemy of Race and Rights* (1991), an important study of legal culture, "much of what is spoken in so-called objective, unmediated voices is in fact mired in hidden subjectivities and unexamined claims" (11). Drawing on personal experience, however, does not mean enshrining subjectivity as a privileged source of insight or truth. That way lies a new essentialism. Critics need to be wary of turning the personal into a foundation for a monolithic counterhistory. Writing history from the perspective of formerly excluded subjects has done much to challenge received versions of the past. It has helped remedy one-sided, even discriminatory historical accounts. Ultimately, though, many alternative histories mirror, in their essentialism and their assumption of unproblematic referentiality, the very normative discourse that they aim to contest.

The feminist historian Joan W. Scott has suggested that modes of history that make epistemological appeals to experience limit the value of their accounts. This limitation becomes especially troubling for historians intent on documenting the lives of people omitted from traditional histories. Assumptions about the transparency of experience make it hard to analyze the social conventions that excluded certain kinds of subjects from history in the first place. According to Scott, "When experience is taken as the origin of knowledge . . . questions about the constructed nature of experience, about how subjects are constituted as different in the first place, about how one's vision is structured—about language (or discourse) and history—are left aside" (25). Scott's analysis applies equally to the field of cultural studies. An unproblematic reliance on experience can imply that the critic is idealizing a particular behavior or form of life, that of the subculture being studied.

The challenge is to remain alert to the possible otherness of experience without falling back into a new form of foundationalism.

The fourth position, postmodernism, raises passions not only because of its perceived assault on the disciplinary norms of history but also because of its frequent claim that there is no difference between history and fiction. The first concern is more parochial and perhaps should be left to professional historians, although my discussion of genre, narrative, and periodization necessarily trespasses on the historians' debate. The second claim arouses strong reactions in people across a wide spectrum of fields and even beyond academia, where journalists, educators, politicians, novelists, moviemakers, and readers at large have occasionally felt moved to enter the fray. Since I frequently discuss novels and film in the context of nineteenth-century history, I need to be clear about the status of different genres in my argument. Let me approach the question of history and fiction by returning to *Oscar and Lucinda.*

Carey's book is a work of fiction with postmodern literary characteristics, prompting some critics to describe it as a metafiction, others as a postcolonial response to narratives of empire. All, however, contend that Carey's novel provides authentically "historical" insights into Australia's colonial past—paradoxically because of the way it calls into question the reliability of historical knowledge. In one critic's words, the novel subverts history's naive faith in "sequentiality, inevitability, purpose, authority" (Ashcroft 194). Here is another version of this widespread idea: In *Oscar and Lucinda* "history is viewed, not as a fixed and given series of events and motives, but as a text itself, which is as subject to the whims and needs of historians as the literary text is to those of the writers" (Petersen 108).

This postmodern position is so commonplace as to have become banal, which is a shame, because it only matters when it matters urgently. History in the service of dominant ideology, history in the hands of bigots and demagogues, can deny or conceal what most needs remembering. At such times it is imperative to accuse history of being a lie. One effective way to expose the power of history to lie on behalf of a dominant ideology is to deconstruct its claims to comprehensive truth. But to equate history with fiction in a banal sense is to obliterate the value of this critical position. Both genres have distinctive intellectual, social, and political functions, and to critique one in terms of the other requires a keen sense of how these functions intersect. Further, critiquing history as fiction requires an account of how these roles have changed over time and how they can vary from one place to another, one group to another. To say "history is a fiction" means very little indeed without a rigorous specification of the cultural work each activity is performing in the particular case at hand.

In the case of *Oscar and Lucinda,* to say the novel is history actually blunts its cultural force. Carey fully understands this point. In interviews he admits to making factual errors about the nineteenth century, but he distinguishes between a "historian's objection" to these mistakes and a "storyteller's" (qtd. in Tausky). Historians feel an obligation to be as accurate as possible, but novelists do not, and this novelistic freedom actually enhances his power as a postcolonial writer. As he remarks in another interview: "*Oscar and Lucinda* is—not so much saving history as inventing it, re-shaping it, creating ways of looking at it. . . . [I]n young countries it seems more important to find ways to look at your past. . . . You can do anything. The page is still blank. We really can make ourselves up" (qtd. in Ruth Brown 135).

The freedom to "make ourselves up," to write on the blank page, to imagine possible futures, depends on Carey's position in the culture as a writer of fiction. The anachronisms in the text—such as the Dostoevsky volume, having electricity on the *Leviathan,* and talking about celluloid before it could have been produced—distress Carey on one level, as signs of carelessness, but they do not vitiate his fictional vision of Australia's heritage. These anachronisms were caused, he confesses, because he "changed the dates half-way through and forgot that [he] had done it" (qtd. in Tausky). He does not go on to mention that his date change resulted in numerous internal inconsistencies in the novel's chronology. On the first page of the book Oscar's death is given as 1866, but according to many passages later in the text, the events culminating in his death occurred in 1867. Oscar could not have been at Oriel when Lucinda was nursing her mother, as one passage asserts (74), nor could Lucinda be working in the Druitt Street pickle factory two years after 1859, as another passage suggests (125). Lucinda's age is incorrect on page 167, and Oscar's on page 298. These chronological inconsistencies are just the tip of the iceberg, and they would have devastating effects on a work of history. The fact that only one of the numerous critics who have written on this novel has noted any of these problems (and that one only in passing [Woodcock 80]) says something about their ahistorical approach. More important, it shows how little such anachronisms matter to the text's postcolonial themes. Some readers might regret that Carey is a sloppy writer, but that would not stop them from reflecting on the profound questions his novel raises about Australia's history of genocide and colonialism. *Oscar and Lucinda* succeeds in deconstructing history only by remaining fiction.

Preserving an acute sense of the different functions of genres is essential for a historical cultural studies. To some, this statement may come as a surprise, for the movement is known for mixing genres, treating romance fiction, say, or slasher movies, or (as I shall do in other chapters) science fiction, television ads, comic books, and hypertext with the same serious attention bestowed on the monuments of "high" culture. This practice may appear to have abolished generic boundaries, but the effect has actually been more complex. At its best, cultural studies interrogates the nature of such boundaries, asks what work these categories perform, why they change over time, how they organize aspects of experience far removed from the aesthetic. In refusing to take the boundaries of genre as natural, cultural studies accords more importance than ever before to understanding how they operate.

If neoconservative, liberal, identitarian, and postmodern approaches to history all have their drawbacks, what is left? A great deal actually. A sophisticated body of historical theory exists that could help define the place of the past in cultural studies. I have in mind aspects of Paul Carter's spatial history, Paul Gilroy's transnational studies, Carlo Ginzburg's microhistory, and Judith Walkowitz's feminist cultural history.[21]

Paul Carter's *The Road to Botany Bay* (1987) may provide a preliminary glimpse of how some theorists of history are moving beyond the limits of the four categories discussed above. I choose Carter's innovative essay on Australian exploration narratives because Peter Carey read this book in manuscript while working on *Oscar and Lucinda* (the historian thanks the novelist for helping him get his book published). Carter organizes his spatial history in terms of an opposition between what he calls "travelling," which he sees not as a physical activity so much as a particularized, immediate way of knowing the world, and "imperial history," which he associates with an Enlightenment goal of mastering the world from the perspective of an "all-seeing spectator" (xv–xvi). Carter stresses the importance of attending to genre in historical inquiry. He finds a world of difference between forms that are often conflated by historians, flattened into undifferentiated primary sources. For example, he contrasts singular or ad hoc forms such as the traveler's journal and the explorer's field map, which convey the specificity of historical experience, with totalizing forms such as the botanist's taxonomy and the geographer's map, which reduce the world to static categories—Linnaeus's system or the grid of longitude and latitude.[22] Similarly, Carter views the explorer's act of naming not as a generalizing or classifying procedure but as a gesture that "denoted particulars alone"; the traveler's narrative "was a genealogy of particulars, a horizontal disposition to mark things where they occurred locally, rather than to organize them hierarchically or thematically" (8). The narrative remains open to other journeys, to being contested by later ad hoc enterprises. Hence Carter tries to model his project on the act of traveling: "like the traveller whose gaze is oriented and limited, [spatial history] makes no claim to authoritative completeness. It is, must be, like a journey, exploratory. It suggests certain directions in historical texts, leaves others for others to explore" (xxiii).

This openness puts the past and future in a dialectical relationship rather than in the causal relation of organic growth that structures most history. That is, individual, partial histories are rediscovered because of their futures. This dialectical relationship is not an invitation to construct the past as one sees fit but rather an incitement to look again at the record of material traces for the sediment that must be *there* if one is *here*. Carter's detractors have called his history "postmodern," but it is his repudiation of the skeptical, relativistic conclusions of postmodernism that attracts me. His attention to the "material hereness and nowness" (22) provides him with a contingent foundation for knowledge and aligns his work with the project of cultural studies. As James Epstein puts it in a valuable review of new kinds of history: "Such studies may indeed help us to ground historical reasoning in something beyond the purely textual. . . . Paying close attention to spatial practice and imagining might move us towards a qualified re-engagement with the terms of 'the social,' sustaining a cultural materiality in our interpretation of historical and literary texts" (296). Epstein's point is similar to one I made before: History may forego "authoritative completeness" without also sacrificing materiality or the possibility of historical truth.

Finally, Carter distinguishes rigorously between fiction and history. The explorer's journals resembled novels or poems in being built around governing metaphors and symbols, but "they also fulfilled the factual demands of history and even science" (Carter 72).[23] They meet these "apparently antithetical conditions" not by effacing their subjective involvement in the interest of neutrality but by the reverse, by highlighting their "phenomenological" investment in the world described (72, 82). Like Gilroy, Ginzburg, and Walkowitz, historians whom I shall discuss at greater length below, Carter makes a dual commitment: on the one hand, he portrays a discontinuous, heterogeneous past, and on the other, he believes in the possibility of determinate historical knowledge.

Joseph Paxton played his own small part in the history of exploration narratives. Twice during his career he was involved in sending out botanical expeditions to discover and collect new species of plants for the conservatories at Chatsworth. One mission traveled to India at his employer's expense and brought back rare specimens that contributed to Paxton's growing reputation among horticulturists. The other, for which he raised the funds himself, ended in disaster when the two plant collectors Paxton had trained were drowned in river rapids in the Pacific Northwest. After this disaster Paxton decided to concentrate his gardening skills on what he did best: cultivating the exotic plants brought back by others.

A feat of gardening, combined with an innovation in glass architecture, brought him his first widespread fame. An article in Dickens's journal *Household Words* about the origins of the Crystal Palace harks back to this earlier triumph.[24] "The Private History of the Palace of Glass" begins with a vivid narrative of the events of New Year's Day, 1837, when the botanist Sir Robert Schomburgk discovered an immense water lily, fully five feet across, in the Amazon.[25] Schomburgk sent seedlings of the lily back to England, where by permission of the Queen it was given the name *Victoria regia* (today it is known as *Victoria amazonica*). Despite the attention of England's most renowned horticulturists, it had never grown to its full size or flowered. Paxton was the first to succeed. Once he had achieved this feat, the lily continued to grow at such a tremendous rate that he had to design a special glass Lily House with a tank over thirty feet in width, which reproduced as closely as possible the lily's native habitat. Paxton's success in flowering the lily drew a flurry of attention, and his design for the Lily House decisively influenced his plans for the Crystal Palace. Delicacy and lightness of construction, combined with strength and stability, were the hallmarks of all Paxton's engineering breakthroughs. The water lily episode incarnated both. Showman that he was, Paxton demonstrated these qualities of the lily by posing his daughter Annie on a leaf, a scene captured by a drawing in the *Illustrated London News* of November 17, 1849 (Figure 1.2).

This image is as bizarre as it is quaint. The lily's remarkable strength, the girl's unsettling passivity before the adult gazes, make the scene both evocative and disturbing. Feminist critics have employed the image to dramatize Victorian assumptions about women as "hothouse lilies."[26] I want to pursue a complementary path, which leads into some odd recesses of Victorian conceptions of masculinity. Paxton possessed many of the traits most often associated with the Victorian male character: indomitable energy, fortitude in the face of reversals, resourcefulness, a can-do spirit, and supreme confidence in his own opinion. He was the nominal head of a large, bustling family, complete with a scapegrace son and six devoted daughters, but his wife did all the household work. He professed the deepest obligations to this woman, who seemed to have been the person who taught him to write and

FIGURE 1.2
"The Gigantic Water-Lily (Victoria Regia), in Flower at Chatsworth."
Illustrated London News (November 17, 1849), 328.

who managed his business affairs with skill, but he left her alone for long periods as he traveled on the continent and was lionized in London. In short, it would be easy to find Paxton insufferable were it not for some other qualities of character that do not surface in the standard tale.

These qualities are not those usually associated with Victorian masculinity. They are evanescent, darting, as light yet resilient as his glass constructions. He took such an unexpected delight in inventing outlandish things. He could be frolicsome. His buildings were fantasies; his fountains, fireworks, and light shows were like something out of Virginia Woolf's *Orlando*. I like the story of his bribing the guards at Cassel to let him climb fully dressed into the great fountain there to measure the size of its jets. What fun he must have had holding Annie's hand as she stepped gingerly out onto the surface of—a leaf! It is like a missing adventure from *Alice in Wonderland*. The spirit of science fiction ran through many of his creations. For the Crystal Palace he imagined a raised trolley, running just under the roof, that would carry spectators from one end of the pavilion to the other. This precursor of the monorails at Disneyland was never built; I have not been able to discover if his plan for an automatic sweeping robot was. After the exhibition ended, he submitted a proposal to build an elevated railway and shopping arcade that would circle all of London like a ring road, suspended thirty feet above ground and covered in glass. He planned a subway system linking all the boroughs of London forty years before the first subway was dug anywhere.

This independence of mind extended to the way in which he conducted his private life. Although he was at ease in the official masculine world of board meetings and clubs, for thirty- two years his life centered on one abiding—if wholly unexpected—relationship, the deep bond of affection he shared with his employer, patron, and devoted friend. The story of Paxton's relationship with the sixth Duke of Devonshire, who hired him when he was a mere garden boy and who eventually entrusted him with the management of all his vast estates and business affairs, is a strange and affecting tale. It was hardly usual for a celebrated society figure, born into a more exalted family than the Queen's own, a close companion of the emperor of Russia, well educated, refined, and possessing the worldly resources to do whatever he pleased—it was hardly usual for such a man to grow intimate with his gardener. The Duke, however, chose Paxton as his companion on continental tours, where they lived in each other's company for nearly a year at a time. The Duke taught Paxton personally about art and culture, introduced him to the titled heads of Europe; the Duke wrote to Paxton constantly when they were apart, and grew to admire and love and trust him beyond all other people.

There is no modern biography of Paxton, only the admiring portrait by his granddaughter Violet R. Markham, but her suggestively titled book, *Paxton and the Bachelor Duke* (1935), testifies to the odd dimensions of this friendship. She takes as her epigraph a passage praising her grandfather from the Duke's privately printed *Handbook of Chatsworth*, which ends with the words: "To me a friend, if ever man had one" (Markham vi). In the Duke's diary one finds more intimate avowals: "O! Paxton, my kind deliverer from all ills, how good and kind to-day" (Markham 201). The letters Markham quotes from her grandfather are more public and thus necessarily restrained, but one can still discern the strength of his regard. Here is one laying all the glory of the Crystal Palace to the Duke's credit: "It owes its erection to a nobler work of nature, the noble Duke. . . . It is to his fostering hand I owe all I possess; he took me when quite a youth and moulded me according to his tastes and wishes" (Markham 201). Most telling of all is the outpouring of sympathy Paxton received on the Duke's death. By everyone, even by the Duke's own family members, Paxton is recognized as the chief mourner. They write to him of his "peculiar sorrow," of his "trying affliction, for it is a greater one perhaps to you than to almost any one" (Markham 304).

Were Paxton and the Bachelor Duke lovers? Did Paxton intend the innuendoes that sound suggestive to contemporary ears? Given the available evidence, there is no way to know and little need for an answer. Definite knowledge is hardly necessary in such a case. The intense character of their bond is clear without any further probing. I am reminded of a film by John Madden called *Mrs. Brown* (1997), which presents a similarly enigmatic relationship in a heterosexual context. This movie imagines what Queen Victoria's feelings might have been toward her Scottish servant John Brown, whose presence seemed to have comforted her after her husband's death. Like Madden's more popular *Shakespeare in Love* (1998), this story challenges easy assumptions about gender, but it also adds issues of class disparity of the sort that are so striking in Paxton's case. Judi Dench's fine portrayal of the Queen leaves in doubt the exact nature of their relationship, but she clearly conveys the depth of Victoria's feelings. That is where I am left when I explore the biography of Paxton and his bachelor Duke. Even without knowing more, one has been brought in contact with structures of feeling that unsettle the accepted picture of the past.

Throughout this book I focus on the historically odd to stress the importance of reconsidering things that do not fit within normative categories (literary and scientific as well as the class, gender, and educational boundaries transgressed here). As a structure of feeling the *odd* may or may not possess a sexual dimension (like its critically more prominent cousin *queer*), but the word's connotations resonate in many contexts. According to the OED, the transferred senses of *odd* define a range of concepts that are vital to my project. Something may be odd because it "stands alone" or is "singular"; because it is not "accordant, or conformable" to existing categories but is "discrepant, diverse, different"; because it is "extraneous or additional to what is reckoned or taken into account"; and hence, because it "is not, or cannot be, reckoned, included, or co-ordinated with other things." Paxton is the first of many figures who, judging from the paucity of published reflections, may have struck some people as too odd for words.

Paxton's departure from Victorian stereotypes has ramifications that are not confined to the personal. Like the oddities of Oscar and Lucinda, it exemplifies experiences that leave their traces in today's culture. The Crystal Palace and *Victoria regia* have provoked such divergent interpretations in subsequent years because they are rich, ambiguous sites of cultural invention, like their creator. Marshall Berman, in a brilliant reading of the architectural legacy of the Crystal Palace, is the only critic I know of to have responded to this multiplicity of cultural meanings. He charts two of the main currents to emerge from this site, calling one "modernization as *adventure*" and the other "modernization as *routine*" (243). Paxton's sense of adventure was what made the Crystal Palace a magnet for foreigners from all parts of the world: "no building in modern times, up to that point, seems to have had the Crystal Palace's capacity to excite people," and it became "London's most cosmopolitan zone, crowded at any given time with Americans, Frenchmen, Germans, Russians, . . . Indians, even Chinese and Japanese" (238). Modernization as routine, however, stemmed paradoxically from some of Paxton's greatest innovations. Berman traces the monotony of suburban developments and office parks, as well as cheap, shoddy building practices, directly back to the modular construction and prefabricated parts first introduced at the Crystal Palace.

In contrast to Berman's vision of the Crystal Palace as a site of multiple meanings for modernity, a powerful but one-dimensional reading has gained acceptance among critics and historians of postmodernity. This reading focuses on the Great Exhibition's role in producing the dominant visual economy of consumer capitalism. Inspired by Walter Benjamin's unfinished Arcades Project, an impressive group of scholars have argued that the Crystal Palace was the origin of a host of visual techniques that contributed to the increasing abstraction and disembodiment of the society of the spectacle.[27] Thomas Richards traces the origins of consumerism to the "new way of seeing things" instituted at the Great Exhibition, which he calls "the first world's fair, the first department store, the first shopping mall" (18, 17). These practices included spectacles that isolated the object from its context, constructed an abstract field of comparison among unrelated things, classified exhibits according to a rationalized system, fostered a style of distracted attention characteristic of the flaneur, and produced a totalizing account of the world. Together they helped create "a new kind of being, the consumer, and a new strain of ideology, consumerism" (5). Other critics have added to the list of visual practices that should be traced back to the exposition. Tony Bennett, in a discussion of what he calls the "exhibitionary complex," asserts that a "distinctively new ensemble of disciplines" descended from the exhibition's "display of architectural projects for the improvement of social conditions in the areas of health, sanitation, education, and welfare" (147). Susan Buck-Morss sees the "origins of the 'pleasure industry'" in the international fair because it "taught to derive pleasure from the spectacle alone" (85). Andrew Miller adds visual passivity and objectification of both viewer and thing viewed.

This is an important body of research, and I find its conclusions persuasive within the domains of experience it canvasses. But the Great Exhibition influenced other things besides the visual.[28] The noise of the crowds had profound effects, as did the later musical concerts at Sydenham Park, where the Crystal Palace was moved in 1854.[29] Paxton's innovations in ventilation affected the humidity, circulation, and condensation patterns of the atmosphere. Commentators—worried about the influx of working-class visitors on shilling days—noted that the smell of the crowds was less discernible than anticipated. Interior temperature, which had been a concern of early critics of the glass structure, proved entirely acceptable. Sensory and material effects other than the visual can be located in the Great Exhibition, and they have had ramifications in important realms of experience.

To complement Berman's reading of Paxton's legacy for the modern age, I would like to initiate a similarly multifaceted reading of his legacy for the contemporary world. Paxton's odd relationship with the Duke should make him newly interesting to critics who are challenging received notions about Victorian sexuality and class relations. His environmental consciousness will strike a chord in theorists of ecological urban planning. In building the Crystal Palace, Paxton not only saved the trees that were enclosed in its transepts but also transplanted others to different parts of the garden (he pioneered techniques for moving adult trees of amazing size). His rock gardens and lakes aimed for a natural effect, different both from formal eighteenth-century gardens and from Romantic wildernesses with picturesque ruins. His city parks in Liverpool, Birkenhead, Halifax, and Glasgow were wooded spaces with winding circulation roads enabling complete access for both pedestrians and carriages (Frederick Law Olmstead traveled to England to study Paxton's designs). Interior environments were just as important. He produced new techniques not only to reduce condensation but also to cut down or increase solar heat, to reduce noise pollution (during construction as well as after the building was complete), and to help air circulation. His engineering methods emphasized improvisation and interdisciplinary connections. He borrowed structural principles from botany, anticipating the movement known today as "biomimicry" (Benyus). He thought in terms of multi-use structures and was eager to repurpose or refunction space as well as building materials.

There is a risk in dwelling on these connections, however. It is the risk of losing sight of the heterogeneous past and substituting in its place a new monolithic image. Merely replacing one interpretation of Paxton with another version more congenial to contemporary tastes leaves intact traditional assumptions about the unity of historical experience. A "contemporary" Paxton is no more adequate than the Victorian or Modern stereotypes, and the incompatible presence of all three in the historical field shows the limits of period-bound cultural analysis. *Victoria regia* and the Crystal Palace do not cease to be episodes in important Victorian and Modern narratives just because they can also be read as outtakes from the story of the Millennium Dome. The multiple currents running through these cultural sites are compelling because they are both wayward tributaries of modernity and postmodernity, and part of the mainstream of nineteenth-century life. Paxton remains odd no matter where one locates his historical affinities. Peter Carey saw this oddity even as he saw its relevance for postcolonial Australia, too. The ability to hold multiple perspectives in this fashion helps defamiliarize yesterday as well as today. When the oddity of one age becomes acceptable in another, the critic has the opportunity to see both times in a new light.

This prospect is what makes the methodological risk taken by historians such as Carter, Gilroy, Ginzburg, and Walkowitz worth hazarding. The "cognitive wager," in Ginzburg's terms (32), is that one can combine a sense that "reality is fundamentally discontinuous and heterogeneous" with "an explicit rejection of the skeptical implications" of postmodernism (27). It is a risk these four historians all embrace in one way or another.[30] The payoff for success is a new understanding of both past and present. This double commitment—to historical knowledge and to a self-reflexive perspective on that knowledge—is exactly the cognitive wager at stake in a historical cultural studies.

My turn has come to roll the dice. Let me venture, then, on a description of the sort of historical practice needed for the future of cultural studies. As I see it, this practice has three broad features.

First, cultural studies should not shy away from tracing long historical relationships between the past and present. In doing so, however, it must attend equally to both the anomalous and the analogous. Continuity is a part of historical experience, but it exists side by side with zones of difference, areas of discontinuity and rupture. Like a geologist, the cultural historian must be aware that historical sedimentation occurs unevenly, in clumps rather than uniform layers, and that some strata of experience may not be present in all social spheres. When confronting the past, the task of cultural studies is to outline the temporal and spatial boundaries of particular cultural practices, where they begin and end, how they overlap with or contest rival forms of cultural experience, and what they reveal about the diverse spaces of culture today.

Second, traditional modes of periodization are inadequate to account for either the zones of difference that punctuate the past or the lines of continuity that stretch into some parts of today's world (but not others). Constructing periods is an essential component of historical thinking, but periods themselves have no reality outside of the context in which they appear. They are heuristic constructs that may be invoked to help with a particular topic—say, nature for the Romantics—but may only get in the way of thinking about other kinds of questions, such as women in science during the 1830s. Since each of these topics falls into the domain of culture, to account for them one needs to understand periods as flexible but dispensable cognitive instruments.

Third, a historical cultural studies should value alternative modes of writing, compositional practices that sometimes depart from linear structures. To capture the multiplicity of relations that link (and divide) past from present, the critic needs all the formal resources possible. Multiple perspectives, intertextuality, self-reflexivity, palimpsest structure, and recursive narratives can help one respond to the complexity of cultural history. One needs writing strategies that are equal to the uncanniness of history, the anachronistic, the untimely, the thick knots of connection. One needs the resourcefulness of a bricoleur and the irreverence of a hacker.

Let me take up each of these features in greater depth.

(1) This book concentrates on historical relations that fall outside the dominant patterns of cultural development. These dense nodes of connections are hard to recover and harder still to name, for our categories of understanding often fail to encompass them. Raymond Williams has attempted to account for aspects of a culture that do not conform to the dominant paradigm by calling them "residual" or "emergent." But important aspects of cultural experience, which are marginal to mainstream culture, cannot be comprehended by these two categories either. Some subcultures are not residual, for they do not nostalgically hold on to the past, but neither are they emergent, for they do not result in a new social formation in the future. Moreover, Williams's terms function within a deterministic Marxist scheme of history, and it is difficult to employ them without invoking the entire totalizing framework of Marxism. How does one characterize phenomena in the nineteenth century that had undeniable connections to literary, scientific, industrial, and economic developments at the time; that had an afterlife in prominent features of contemporary culture; but that remained "recessive" for long spans of time and should not be seen as determining the present? Answering this question is a central aim of this book.

A more recent model for describing recessive cultural traits appears in N. Katherine Hayles's important study *How We Became Posthuman* (1999). Hayles proposes two terms drawn from archaeological anthropology for use in intellectual history: *seriation* and *skeuomorph*. Seriation charts are used by anthropologists to record the way artifacts—say pottery styles—change over time. According to Hayles, "The figures that customarily emerge from this kind of analysis are shaped like a tiger's iris—narrow at the top when an attribute first begins to be introduced, with a bulge in the middle during the heyday of the attribute, and tapered off at the bottom as the shift to a new model is completed" (15). Seriation charts are valuable ways to indicate that cultural forms have periods of greater and lesser primacy, but their implicit evolutionary logic limits them as a model for some historical tasks. When Hayles describes how "conceptual fields evolve," she portrays a more seamless development than is always the case: "challenges can give rise to a new concept, which results in another generation of artifact, which leads to the

development of still other concepts" (15). Skeuomorph names a related phenomenon, a cultural form that has become outmoded but that lingers on
vestigially in a later object. "A *skeuomorph* is a design feature that is no longer
functional in itself but that refers back to a feature that was functional at an
earlier time" (Hayles 17). This latter term has a psychological dimension,
which harks back to functionalist conceptions of culture. A skeuomorph
"calls into play a psychodynamic that finds the new more acceptable when
it recalls the old that it is in the process of displacing and finds the traditional more comfortable when it is presented in a context that reminds us
we can escape from it into the new" (17). This overt functionalism, like the
earlier evolutionary view of change, circumscribes the usefulness of this
term as well. If the former portrays development as more seamless than is
always the case, the latter casts cultural survivals as more of a soothing presence than is sometime true.

Because I admire Hayles's book and because we share an interest in technology's place in contemporary culture, it behooves me to be clear about
how my goals differ from hers. Hayles's evolutionary and psychosocial models of historical change work well in recording the development of a tightly
knit set of ideas: the concepts of cybernetics and informatics that emerged
from the Macy Conferences following World War II and subsequently
helped shaped widespread cultural assumptions about the disembodied nature of information, to take Hayles's own examples. Hayles's models inform
the history of the twentieth-century digital computer that I shall examine in
chapter 8. And they support, from a different angle, the argument in chapter 2 that nineteenth-century sound technology could have given birth to a
more "embodied" conception of online communications. Hayles and I both
maintain that cultural interpretations of technologies are not given or determined in advance. Sometimes the dominant conception of an innovation
is not the best choice from among its potential range of meanings. This conviction leads us to investigate roads not taken, avenues that might still lead
to unexpected resources for our society. We part company only in investigating different kinds of historical phenomena. Whereas Hayles maps the
routes negotiated (and foreclosed) within a relatively coherent field, my
study focuses on the breaks and disjunctions, the lost possibilities, that prevent one from conceiving of the past as a single unified field.

It is telling that the metaphor of road or map will not serve the purposes
of this study unless the metaphor is qualified along the lines Paul Carter suggested. Carter's distinction between explorers' idiosyncratic maps and geog-
raphers' universal maps, which aim at "authoritative completeness" (Carter
xxiii), captures my exploratory and ad hoc relationship to the theoretical
tools I employ.[31] Better still is a word like "zone," which emphasizes the contingent field of relevance one is charting. Margaret Cohen and Carolyn
Dever have defined the value of this term for cultural critics: "The notion of
zone . . . suggests a structure produced through the intersection of other
structures that are coherent formations in their own right. A zone is a limi-

nal formation at the confluence of independent formations; it both belongs to these formations and constitutes a distinct whole of its own" (2). Doing historical cultural studies means situating a text or practice within the zones of force that alter and are altered by it. In this model, historical zones of relevance shift in size, shape, and duration; they disappear and reappear over time; and they vary in importance depending on the critic's purpose for undertaking the inquiry.

Instead of evolutionary, functionalist, or deterministic models of history, I enlist more provisional methods. This study uses a range of figurative and theoretical constructs that give salience to history's concealed junctures without reifying them into new master narratives. I work with terms such as "odd," "uncanny," "anachronistic," and "untimely." I try to think of their resonance in lives today using theoretical concepts such as prolepsis, recursion, sedimentation, circuitry, and zone. More important than the individual labels, however, is a self-critical sense of how the words and models one chooses are implicated both in the description of the past and in contemporary debates that shape the present. Self-reflexive perspectives are crucial to the project.

Michel de Certeau's seminal work *The Writing of History* (1975) recommends a self-reflexive stance as one way of remaining true to the uncanniness of history. De Certeau argues that history not only begins by differentiating past from present but, more important, that the principal categories of historical understanding replicate this founding rupture. History's status as a form of knowledge depends upon recognition of difference: "In the realm of history, an endless labor of differentiation (among events, periods, data or series, and so on) forms the condition of all relating of elements which have been distinguished—and hence of their comprehension" (36). Difference precedes the act of relating. This recognition, however, is continually imperiled by the success of history in making the dead past come alive. Hence historical knowledge possesses an uncanny dimension. "The dead souls resurge," de Certeau writes, "within the work whose postulate was their disappearance" (36–37). This uncanniness, however, does not invalidate history's claim to be a form of knowledge, for the very oddity marks a difference from received interpretations. Recapturing the past may be a primary motivation for writing history, but the "pastness" of the recovered time is constituted only by an insistence on division. Otherwise, history distorts the image of yesterday with contemporary prejudices or plays false to the complexity of today with unconscious identifications and facile analogies.

Perhaps the best name for this kind of self-reflexive awareness is the literary. Historians who foreground their own writing strategies are often accused of being overly literary. But sometimes the most adequate response to cultural anachronism lies in the methods of literature. An idea or form, for example, might be important in its time without giving birth to any descendants. At a still later moment, however, this same form may reappear, returning to haunt a new epoch with its spectral afterlife. Literature can respond to such untimely manifestations not only cognitively but also formally by embodying recurrence in a self-reflexive structure. Tom Stoppard writes eloquently in his play *Arcadia* (1993) of how the possibilities one culture has let fall can resurface in another: "The missing plays of Sophocles will turn up piece by piece, or be written again in another language. Ancient cures for diseases will reveal themselves once more. Mathematical discoveries glimpsed and lost to view will have their time again" (38). Stoppard suggests that literature, not history, is best equipped to understand such uncanny reappearances. But cultural studies needs to come to terms with them too. Without some way of responding to the return of lost cultural possibilities, both the present and the past are impoverished.

Like Stoppard, whose work will be a focus of chapter 4, I see the relationship between science and literature as a particularly rich field for exploring questions of historical disjunction and uncanny return. Since the Romantic era, science and literature have been out of sync, moving according to incompatible rhythms. Consequently, each produces odd effects when brought into the company of the other. Take the peculiar distortions that occur in period concepts when science or technology enters the picture. Scientific rationality is central to most accounts of modernity or modernization, but it is marginal to the main literary and artistic currents of Modernism. Today, however, things have changed. Science is not nearly so out of place in discussions of postmodernism. In fact, technology's place in contemporary culture has grown so extensive that formal definitions of postmodernism as an aesthetic or style of writing take a back seat to versions that stress the cultural transformations wrought by social and scientific innovations. The result is the spread of the "culture wars" onto a new front, the "science wars" that have raged in recent years.

(2) Problems of disjunction and reemergence necessarily raise the issue of periodization. In this book I am forced at every turn to confront orthodox accounts of literary and cultural history. For good (and not so good) reasons, periods have played a foundational role in the institution of literary studies. Period distinctions not only guide many scholars' thinking about texts but also organize numerous departmental and professional affiliations, many of the journals in which scholars publish, the conferences they attend, and the courses they teach.

Traditional histories divide Anglo-American culture into a fixed sequence of epochs. The most interesting schemes attempt to correlate social and economic conditions with literary and artistic norms. In a simplified but recognizable form, the sequence of periods runs like this: English culture begins with the feudal social structures of the medieval age; moves into the Renaissance, now widely called the early modern period because of its pivotal role in fashioning the modern self; experiences the growth and diffusion of modern principles such as democracy, empirical science, and secularization in the Enlightenment; is interrupted briefly in the aesthetic domain by the counter-Enlightenment impulses of Romanticism; is restored in the early twentieth century by the twin forces of high Modernism in the arts and modernity in the bureaucratic, technological, and economic spheres; and is swept away in the last few years by the advent of postmodernism, a cultural transformation affecting all aspects of life in the economically advanced sectors of the world. No interesting thinker endorses this historical scheme in the reductive terms I have laid out. But these are the categories most often at stake when writers today confront the question of periodization.[32]

A particularly influential model of periodization is the Marxist account by Fredric Jameson. Offering his study *Postmodernism, or, The Cultural Logic of Late Capitalism* (1991) as a "periodizing hypothesis" (3), he streamlines the transition from the Enlightenment to postmodernism by basing his sequence of periods on Ernst Mandel's model of the three fundamental stages of capitalism. Jameson argues that the dominance of realism, which for him embraces empirical assumptions and sociopolitical attitudes, corresponds to the first, "market" stage of capitalism; Modernism, which follows, is the cultural dominant of the second, "monopoly" stage, also described as the age of imperialism; and finally, postmodernism is the cultural logic of "late or multinational or consumer capitalism" (35–36). This has proven to be a powerful synthesis, and it has done much to restore credibility to the periodizing impulse behind literary history.

Jameson's synthetic vision gains still more power from its integration of genre theory into the larger scheme. In an earlier book *The Political Unconscious: Narrative as a Socially Symbolic Act* (1981), Jameson advocated a return to genre studies, because he viewed genre as providing the missing link between individual texts and collective social formations. A genre such as comedy or romance serves this function by encoding in a symbolic form—i.e., in conventions both pleasurable to audiences and intuitively recognizable—the assumptions of a group and a period. Hence for Jameson "genre is essentially a socio-symbolic message" (*Political Unconscious* 141). Understanding this feature of genre enables the critic to engage in what I regard as the two most important activities of literary history: describing periods and accounting for historical change. The first activity stems directly from the concept of a symbolic message. If conventions inscribe the desires, beliefs, and fears of a particular society, then the dominance of a genre, such as realism in the nineteenth century, forges a link between literature and society as a whole—in Jameson's terms, between the realist novel and market capitalism. The second activity, exploring cultural change, is facilitated by the fact that the symbolic message of a genre does not die out when it is transposed into a different era. Using an example from musicology, Jameson notes the different connotations that folk dances take on when they are transplanted into an aristocratic form such as the classical minuet or, later, appropriated for nationalist purposes in Romantic symphonies. He calls the persistence of generic motifs in a later epoch "sedimentation" and argues that attending to the role of such sedimented traces in the new work can make a genuine cultural history possible. "The ideology of the form itself, thus sedimented, persists into the later, more complex structure as a generic message which coexists—either as a contradiction or, on the other hand, as a mediatory or harmonizing mechanism—with elements from later stages" (141).

In the final pages of *Postmodernism* Jameson returns to this conception of genre, but with a pessimistic twist, pointing to the randomness and confusion of generic messages today as one of the signs that the postmodern has forgotten how to think historically. In contemporary culture

> the movement from one generic classification to another is radically discontinuous, like switching channels on a cable television set; and indeed it seems appropriate to characterize the strings of items and the compartments of genres . . . as so many "channels" into which the new reality is organized. (*Postmodernism* 373)

If contemporary culture has erased the significance of genre distinctions, then the sedimented history to which they once bore witness vanishes into the indiscriminate joys of surfing, whether through television channels or, in recent years, the World Wide Web.

Jameson's doubt about the ability of our culture to think historically is belied by the impressive body of literature and films this book surveys, works that suggest that today's culture is increasingly learning how to engage with its multicultural past. These works reveal that even the most radical genre surfing in fiction, film, television, journalism, comics, and commercial enterprises have not managed to obscure the sedimented traces of diverse cultural histories. Jameson's pessimism on this score arises from his determination to have periods correspond to fixed, all-encompassing descriptions of reality. Given such totalizing aims, he can allow mixed generic messages to have only the effects that he mentioned: contradiction or harmonization. If not recuperable in either of these ways, then radically discontinuous generic traces signify confusion, the loss of historical consciousness. They cannot be allowed to call into question the coherence of the period description itself, for even contradiction, according to Jameson's Marxist model, is always included dialectically in the original description. But challenging the coherence of period descriptions can be crucial to making visible minority experience.

By contrast, my view of periods as heuristic tools suggests that the best way to respond to incompatible cultural residues is to reconsider the initial period description. If period concepts are conceptual tools that enable critics to investigate a finite set of questions about historical experience but preclude other questions from being asked at all, then sometimes they will prove inadequate to the task at hand. When that occurs, one must frankly acknowledge the limitations of one's instruments and cast around for another method of proceeding. This process does not mean jettisoning the received period term altogether, for the category was the only thing that allowed one to see something was missing in the first place. Equally, this process does not entail proliferating new, ever more narrowly defined period designations, like some Ptolemaic cosmologist intent on adjusting the cycles of the planets to make them fit an unruly reality. The current scheme of periodization is satisfactory for many important endeavors. The concept of modernity, for example, remains a useful way of focusing attention on problems such as visual abstraction and anomie, even if it obscures other, equally important questions, such as the existence of embodied relations to technology or of alternative female and queer sexualities. Joan Kelly made this same point about an earlier historical moment in her influential essay on feminist history, "Did Women Have a Renaissance?" Instead of eliminating periods, on one extreme, or proliferating periods, on the other, I have chosen to interrogate the existing categories, deploying them where they seem appropriate but investigating their gaps and inadequacies, probing the areas of historical experience they tend to conceal. This practice might be termed a self-reflexive approach to periodization.

The urgency of this method is powerfully illustrated by Paul Gilroy's objections to the way in which the concepts of modernity and postmodernity exclude important aspects of black experience. In *The Black Atlantic: Modernity and Double Consciousness* (1993), Gilroy maintains that "the African diaspora, the practice of racial slavery, or the narratives of European imperial conquest may require all simple periodisations of the modern and the postmodern to be drastically rethought" (42). He points to the existence of archaic, premodern modes of social organization on the slave plantation and to the radically different history that emerges from a past punctuated not by changes in the cosmopolitan centers of London, Paris, and New York but by the rupture of the middle passage, by the fight for the abolition of slavery, and by the struggles of acculturation and reprisal that followed the Civil War in the United States. For black intellectuals such as W. E. B. Du Bois, Frederick Douglass, and Richard Wright, "the modern world was fragmented along axes constituted by racial conflict and could accommodate non-synchronous, heterocultural modes of social life in close proximity. Their conceptions of modernity were periodised differently" (Gilroy 197). Attending to this alternative time-consciousness allows one to recover modes of experience hidden from traditional history. Gilroy's examples include black countercultures of music and dance, utopian social projects embedded in black religious experience, modes of everyday life and economic opportunity opened to blacks by the Atlantic sailing culture, and diverse political strategies of resistance that could simultaneously invoke modern ideals of reason and universal humanity, and reject modern assumptions about rationality and progress in favor of an apocalyptic eschatology, prophesying freedom come the Jubilee. To comprehend the true character of these alternative practices, one must see how they both relied on and departed from modernity. In Gilroy's words, "The periodisation of the modern and the postmodern is thus of the most profound importance for the history of blacks in the West" (44).

(3) A self-reflexive stance toward historical period may be dramatized by performative and experimental writing strategies. A personal voice, narrative, multiple points of view, recursive loops, and irony tend to emphasize the improvisational character, the ad hoc nature of one's conceptual apparatus. Writing that enacts the cultural phenomenon it analyzes bears a particularly strong self-reflexive stamp. Like Carlo Ginzburg, who borrows formal techniques from experimental fiction without vitiating the truth claims of history, I adopt literary strategies in the hope of demonstrating in practice what I maintain in theory: that the literary has both cognitive and affective roles to play in the apprehension of the past. Many of the chapters in this book participate formally in the genre shifting and recursivity they discuss. Others highlight the incongruity of a parallel by staging comic juxtapositions.

Most fundamental to this project, however, is the use of narrative in a critical discourse about narratives. Telling stories, plotting surprises for the reader, introducing exemplary characters from literature, history, or popular culture, building arguments by indirection, accretion, flashback, recognition, climax, and denouement draw attention to the constructed nature of one's inquiry. These narrative and formal strategies diminish the impression that historical truth flows from a neutral, omniscient standpoint.

Narrative history has its own controversial history, of course. The grand narrative pretensions of nineteenth-century historiography have been viewed with suspicion for most of the twentieth century. More recently, Lawrence Stone provoked debate by announcing the "revival of narrative" in historical studies. Today, postmodernism has made metanarratives the bête noire of critical practice. The problem with narrative in traditional history, however, is not narrativity itself but the adoption of a single, all-encompassing perspective. When narrative is understood as inevitably partial, contingent rather than authoritative, it discloses the limits of its own historical practice. It allows the historian to trace discrete areas of continuity, explore disjunctive sequences, bring to life a particular state of affairs, without pretending to a global perspective that can assess all history within a universal point of view. The partiality of narrative provides a specific position from which to base a criticism of experience. A historical cultural studies needs both narrative's power to create a world that can make critique persuasive and narrative's opposite power—its self-reflexive potential—to dramatize the limits of that world.

Judith Walkowitz provides a fine example of this way of using narrative in cultural history. In *City of Dreadful Delight: Narratives of Sexual Danger in Late-Victorian London* (1992), she takes as her subject the warring narratives that helped construct a particular social world. Beginning with stories about Jack the Ripper, she shows that late-Victorian London was a site of multiple, competing representations of women's place in the public realm. There were violent fantasies of female sexual vulnerability—cautionary tales for transgressive women—side by side with rival narratives that plotted new forms of agency for women. These alternative narratives featured new social actors such as women entertainers, women consumers, female philanthropists, women in civic life, women dealing with sexual harassment, and—in the buzz words of the time—the "new woman."

In order to highlight this contested terrain, Walkowitz contrasts the huge variety of narratives about gender and sexuality circulating in 1880s London with the present-day creation of a single, unified image of that time. This contemporary simplification is symbolized by Madame Tussaud's 1980 display of Jack the Ripper in her famous wax museum. "Tussaud's Ripper street adheres to a certain invention of the Victorian past" (4), an invention that plays false to the actual diversity of the late-Victorian metropolis. Walkowitz establishes that the earlier period not only contained rival plots for women but also that the Ripper narrative was itself "a far less unified and bounded production than the depiction offered by Tussaud's installation" (5).

Several things make *City of Dreadful Delight* exemplary for someone interested in developing a historical cultural studies. To begin with, there is the way its subject matter implicitly comments on its method. By highlighting the contingent and contested nature of cultural narratives, Walkowitz draws attention to the situated status of her own use of narrative. In addition, she connects late-Victorian and late-twentieth-century culture, but she views the differences, not just the similarities, as analytically significant. Finally, she understands the continuities that do exist between the two time periods as entailing consequences for her scholarly method and her subject position as a feminist, because, she admits, the Ripper story was part of a "formative moment in the production of feminist sexual politics" (2). Feminist narratives today, no less than "new women" narratives at the end of the nineteenth century, respond to contexts outside their own theoretical field of articulation. In sum, Walkowitz's book stages its own altered assumptions about narrative, dramatizing in its content the methodological premises that support its research. Such an approach inscribes within itself a reference to its own principles of construction.

Recognizing that narratives are partial and contingent; that storytelling has performative effects that may work in the service of counterhegemonic goals, not just on behalf of dominant norms; that the power to construct versions of things has a wide variety of productive social uses—recognizing all these aspects of storytelling permits the critic to return to narrative as part of a self-reflexive and historical cultural studies.

Just over a month into the year 2000, the New Millennium Experience Company provoked another crisis of British national confidence by firing the head of the Millennium Dome and hiring a 34-year-old Frenchman as her replacement. Pierre-Yves Gerbeau, formerly an officer at Disneyland Paris, not only came from across the Channel, he spoke English with a French-American accent. A desperate remedy, to be sure, but something drastic had to be done, because the Millennium Dome, after the euphoria of its opening ceremony, had become a laughingstock, ridiculed by Prince

Charles as well as by numerous articles in the press. Attendance was far lower than was required for the Dome to recoup its costs, and there were complaints about uninspired exhibits, long lines at the popular attractions, and high prices. No sooner had M. Gerbeau been hired, however, than it was discovered that his credentials were not as impressive as had been announced (was he a vice president or merely a director of operations in charge of parking and maintenance?). The press immediately christened him "Mickey the Gerbil" and refuted claims that he was the "whiz-kid" who had saved Euro-Disney. A few days later, rumors surfaced that the Millennium Dome had hired the wrong man entirely, mistaking Gerbeau for a much more senior executive at Disneyland Paris—one Jean-Marie Gerbeaux— because of confusion over the silent x at the end of his name. There were calls in Parliament for Tony Blair's government to come clean about its role in the change of management, and Lord Falconer, minister for the Dome, issued a strong press release defending the decision. All in all, British pride had sustained another blow.

Much to everyone's surprise, the Millennium Dome immediately became much more successful. Attendance rose dramatically—by March, more people were visiting it each week than had come during the entire month of January—and revenues were suddenly ahead of projections. What had wrought this miracle by the Thames? Was "Mickey the Gerbil" not an apprentice after all but a genuine sorcerer, whose Franco-American spell had changed Britain's millennium folly into a magic kingdom? No one knew, least of all the press, which marveled at how briefly Gerbeau had been at the helm and how few changes had actually been made. The only explanation *The Guardian* could come up with was that people responded to image rather than substance. These days, an air of swagger is more important than hard-won expertise. Comparing Gerbeau to Chauncey Gardiner, the simpleton gardener in the novel *Being There* who is elected president on image alone, the paper decided: "There is a parable here about business confidence—the man with the missing x turns out to have factor x" (Lawson).[33]

If Gerbeau's smoke-and-mirrors rescue forms a postmodern parable, fit for today's image-conscious society, Paxton's earlier rescue of the Great Exhibition from the fiasco of its original building design formed a Victorian parable fit for that supposedly more heroic age. The story has always been told as a triumph of the self-made man over nearly impossible circumstances. It is the centerpiece of the Paxton legend, and I have saved it for last. It goes like this. Prince Albert and the other members of the Royal Commission issued an invitation for architectural proposals to design a building for the exhibition. The Building Committee received 233 proposals, but none was judged satisfactory. In their place the committee recommended a design of its own, a massive and hideous brick structure designed by Brunel that provoked howls of outrage when it was first published in the papers. Many people were concerned at the enormous cost; others protested the environmental damage that would be caused by constructing such a huge building out of bricks; another group recalled that the public had been promised a temporary and removable structure, but that bricks and mortar were neither; and finally, the well-to-do neighbors of Hyde Park cried out in anguish over the loss of the huge trees that would be destroyed during construction. Joseph Paxton, however, saved the day, and he did it with one of those prodigious bouts of ingenuity and hard work for which he—and his age—were to become famous.

One day while sitting as chair of a committee of the Midland Railway charged with trying an employee for an infraction of company rules, Paxton began to sketch out on a sheet of blotting paper the plans of the building that would become the Crystal Palace. Before the meeting was done, he had finished an entire draft of the structure (and, incidentally, fined the workman). The deadline of the competition had passed, but Paxton, nothing daunted, prepared complete architectural drawings in a few short days and petitioned the Building Committee to reconsider its decision. As luck would have it, Paxton carried his finished plans up to London on the train with one of the members of the Royal Commission, the great railway engineer Robert Stephenson, who was a personal friend. The article from *Household Words* mentioned earlier tells the story of how Paxton unrolled his plans before his friend in the railway car and then, taking the dinner he had not had time to consume earlier from his coat pocket, ate and smoked a cigar (against train regulations) while Stephenson examined the proposal. What followed was a rush of petitions and emergency meetings, a letter campaign in the press, and a frantic scramble to produce an estimate of construction costs in under twelve days.

Paxton's proposal cost much less than the Committee's building, and his structure could be disassembled and hauled away. The prefabricated modular parts meant that it could be assembled in under four months, with little damage to the surrounding park grounds. In the end, of course, Paxton's design was chosen, and then to top everything he succeeded in bringing the project to completion on schedule. At the opening ceremony Queen Victoria herself wanted to be introduced to the remarkable man who had given a local habitation (and a nickname) to her husband's dream. The image of Paxton walking at the head of the Opening Day procession, leading the column of royalty and dignitaries on a tour of his domain, is a memorable representation of Victorian manhood. The kind of spectacle it provides has overwhelmed other, more intimate representations of Paxton, just as the focus on visual spectacles generally has obscured features of the Crystal Palace that were out of sync with dominant trends.

After the exhibition concluded, Paxton was knighted for his efforts, concluding a storybook tale of a man's rise from humble origins. Sir Joseph Paxton had begun life as a runaway, like so many children in Dickens, then became a garden boy, but received no formal schooling of any kind. From these lowly beginnings he rose to accomplish all the things I have discussed, and more: head gardener of Chatsworth, renowned botanist, architect of the Crystal Palace and other buildings, innovator in the field of engineering, esteemed landscape designer, author of four books (two on gardening, two on botany), editor of three different magazines in these fields, director of a large railroad, Liberal member of Parliament, and very wealthy man.

Thus the Victorian tale goes, and every word of it true. But as I have shown, there are other truths about Paxton too. The Victorians worked hard to turn real stories of this kind into myths about themselves, and people have been too quick to accept them as the whole story—at first because these myths served the ideology of Victorian progress and empire; later because they served the need of the early twentieth century to mock their grandparents' belief in heroism and self-help; and now because they serve the purposes of a booming market for nostalgia or because they play the conventional "heavy" to critics bent on constructing a subversive counter-history. My point is, we still relish such tales, even if only to debunk them for their class privilege and cronyism.

Let me end by juxtaposing two brief stories that I prefer. They are both about visits to exhibitions. Together with the story of Paxton at the head of a parade of dignitaries, they form a triptych of Victorian men on display, figures at an exhibition. All three have different, complex relationships to the contemporary world, relationships of the kind that will be explored in the rest of this book. These two remaining stories both conclude with a man seated in the midst of a garden under glass. The first comes in the form of an illustration that appeared in *Punch* in 1851, during the debate over what to do with the Crystal Palace once the Great Exhibition had closed (Figure 1.3). The picture shows a portly Englishman, perched on a chair in the Win-

ter Gardens, which Paxton had proposed to establish in the soon-to-be empty Crystal Palace. The gentleman is reading Paxton's most popular book, *Flower Garden,* and he is smiling contentedly under his outlandish hat. At his elbow is a lily tank, another symbol of the guiding spirit of the master gardener. This jovial man is a figure of fun, and he clearly amuses the two scruffier citizens who peer at him from the fronds. This "John Bull" is a Pickwickian Paxton, foolish and full of good humor. Except for the corpulence, the portrait is not inappropriate to Paxton himself. It speaks to the way in which the English liked to think that a cultivator of flowers embodied their national spirit.

FIGURE 1.3
"John Bull in His Winter Garden."
Punch (August 16, 1851).

The second story exists largely in my imagination, but it springs from a real detail about Paxton's last days. Shortly before his death, the great horticulturist

FIGURE 1.4
Lily pond at the feet of the Egyptian
statues in the Crystal Palace, Syden-
ham Park. Matthew Digby Wyatt,
*Views of the Crystal Palace and Park,
Sydenham* (London: 1854).

was taken to a flower show at the Crystal Palace in Sydenham Park. Confined
to a wheelchair, he was too frail to endure for long the greetings of his many
friends and well-wishers. This visit was his last to the glass house that had
made him famous and his last to the profuse blossoms he had spent his life
nurturing. He was forced to leave early, his health too feeble to allow him to
finish touring the show. Perhaps before he left he asked to sit alone among
the flowers for a few minutes to regain his strength. I imagine him asking the
attendant to wheel his chair over to the great lily pond in the north transept
(Figure 1.4). There, under the giant reproductions of Egyptian funerary statues, he might have rested awhile, gazing at the floating leaves. It is an image
of gentle old age, the man of flowers dwarfed by statues in a strange garden.
Despite the *faux* Oriental trappings, the water lilies themselves are not exotic. Nothing so rare as *Victoria regia* could survive without the unique features he had installed in his Lily House. They are ordinary plants. Still the
deep green of their large round leaves is soothing. It pleases him to be able
to remember their names.

Two

Hazlitt, Austen, Hardy, and James

A bell rings. Another message. The voices in the machine resume their insistent chatter. So many words, streams of code, flowing through the machine on his desk. He will be doing other things, moving about his small room with the inattentive composure of a person at home in his own world, when the bell chimes. He cannot ignore it.

One morning—day had broken after another all-night session—he receives notice of a wedding to take place on the line. Sarah Orten of Pittsburgh is marrying Thomas Welch of Cincinnati, a person she has never met face-to-face, their relationship having developed on the network. Everyone on the line is invited to attend the ceremony. Most mornings at this hour the clamor is incessant, messages banging away, interrupting one another, breaking short and resuming, a chaos of signals that only an experienced hand can interpret. But today the network falls silent, waiting for the words that will unite the couple in lawful wedlock. Afterward, a chorus of good wishes pours across the wires. It makes the man in his small room feel happy. He likes knowing he is wired to a vast community of people, strangers perhaps in real life but linked by the proliferating relays of their communications network. Imagine his feelings when he reads in a trade publication some months later that Sarah Orten has been duped. Tech crimes of this sort are becoming all too common. The anonymity of the network had enabled Thomas Welch to conceal from his white, upper-middle-class wife that he was a man of color and (what the paper seemed most to resent) a barber. Sarah Orten sued for an annulment, and the courts granted her request. The man shakes his head and turns the printed pages of his journal to the next story. Later he taps out words of his own to a person on the line he has never met. He is a night telegraph operator, and the year is 1883.

Carolyn Marvin, a social historian of communications technology, mentions this case in her important study *When Old Technologies Were New* (93–94).[1] The facts of *Orten* v. *Welch* are recorded in the November 22, 1884, edition of *The Electrical World*, and the terms I have used to retell the case are drawn from this and other nineteenth-century publications about the telegraph. My purpose in telling this story is to introduce the first comprehensive information network, the electric telegraph, which originated more or less simultaneously in both Britain and the United States in 1837 and spread so rapidly that virtually all the towns and cities of England were linked by the end of the 1840s, a feat that foreshadows the astonishing growth of the Internet over the last decade. Like the Internet, the telegraph was a point-to-point system, allowing two-way communication between individuals, not a one-to-many or broadcast system such as radio, film, and television, the media most often studied in communications theory.[2] Marvin claims that the modern era "starts with the invention of the telegraph, the first of the electrical communications machines, as significant a break with the past as printing before it" (3), but few theorists of modernity have evinced interest in this technology. This often overlooked precursor to the Internet raises two critical issues.

First, the origin of the telegraph in the 1830s separates it from most other electrical technologies, which came into widespread use only in the final decades of the nineteenth century. As a result, the telegraph presents a distinctive historical problem, one that complicates many common assumptions about modernity and postmodernity (including Marvin's appealing but too simple belief that the telegraph inaugurated the modern era). For example, it calls into question important assumptions that underlie Friedrich A. Kittler's account of the "new discourse network," which he sees arising "circa 1900" as a result of "Edison's two great innovations: film and the gramophone" (*Discourse Networks* 229).[3] The fact that the telegraph scarcely appears in Kittler's influential work is both a consequence of the historical problem it presents for his argument and a source of a major shortcoming in his theory. As I shall show, Kittler's focus on modern media as recording and "storage mechanism[s]" leads him to neglect their communicative functions (*Discourse Networks* 229). This exclusion of communication (and of all communications technologies—not only the earlier telegraph but also those other inventions "circa 1900," the telephone and the wireless) results in a fundamental misconception of the relationship of technology to the senses.

In its historical dimension, my project parallels that of Jonathan Crary, who finds in technological developments of the 1830s grounds for challenging the received history of Modernist art. Crary argues that a fundamental reorganization of the observing subject takes place in the early decades of the nineteenth century and that to understand this shift one must look not merely at painting and other visual arts but also at optical devices such as the stereoscope that "operate directly on the body of the individual" (7). The telegraph, too, operated on the bodies of its users, but its effects were very different from those of optical technology. The telegraph turns out to have a surprising connection with the stereoscope, but it is the difference not the similarity between these two technologies that poses the greatest challenge to accounts of modernity.

In brief, the special historical problem of the telegraph is this: Although the nineteenth-century technology strikingly foreshadows later communications networks, it was experienced at the time in a very different way. The physical impact of sound in the instrument's operation contrasts with the disembodiment often thought characteristic of the modern encounter with information. My contention is not that sound is inherently more embodied than sight but that our experience of both sight and sound is historically constructed. Hence the problem concerns how different technologies relate to a conceptual framework, not the practical matter of whether one is more user friendly than another. The absence of sound technology from most models of modernity calls into question the global applicability of the period term, just as did the absence of African-American experience for Paul Gilroy. Sound technology is another example of a type of cultural experience that is not encompassed by any of Raymond Williams's three categories: dominant, residual, or emergent. Like Paxton's achievements, acoustic technology was on the cutting edge of scientific innovation in its day; hence it cannot be thought of as residual. But it cannot be called emergent either, because a new social formation did not, in fact, emerge from this discrepant experience. Despite its importance in the nineteenth century, the voice in the machine remains odd, a discordant experience, not conformable to the regime of modernity.

Second, the telegraph brings to prominence a curious struggle that has run throughout the 150 years in which there have been electric data networks. This struggle is between visual and aural scanning of signals. The telegraph was the site of a prolonged debate over the comparative advantages of "sound-reading" versus instruments that incorporated a recording apparatus for taking down messages in visible form. A vast array of "recording telegraphs" were patented over the course of the nineteenth century; the list anticipates (and was the inspiration for) many later writing machines, including not only the typewriter that Kittler studies but also the teletype, braille embossing machines, and chemically treated paper systems. Despite this ingenuity, aural data processing won out. To the extent this struggle has been studied at all, it has generally been viewed as a conflict among rival media—phonograph, radio, and the "talkies" on the one hand; print, silent film, and the computer screen on the other hand. The history of the telegraph, however, reveals ways in which the conflict is internal to early communications technology.

This insight becomes increasingly important as advances in information delivery make it possible for the end user at a computer terminal to transform the data stream into signals readable by any of the senses—sight and sound preeminently, but with the advent of virtual reality, touch, taste, and smell too. Unfortunately, failure to consider the difference between acoustics and optics in communications networks has distorted much contemporary thinking about media. Kittler will serve as my most detailed example of this widespread problem. In the introduction to *Gramophone, Film, Typewriter,* where he muses on the future of information systems, Kittler asserts that the digitization of all data "will erase the very concept of medium" and reduce "sound and image . . . to surface effects, known to consumers as interface. Sense and the senses turn into eyewash" (1–2). Such predictions are a variant of what N. Katherine Hayles has identified as the "erasure of embodiment" in the computer age, so that information is conceived of as a "kind of bodiless fluid that could flow between different substrates [media] without loss of meaning or form" (xi). The history of the telegraph confounds such assumptions by showing that information, which even in the nineteenth century could be decoded optically *or* acoustically, had profoundly different impacts depending on how it was apprehended. The choice of "interface" for the telegraph had effects on the body, which influenced both the meaning and form of the message. If visual data processing seemed to reinforce the growing abstraction of modern life, acoustic processing produced odd sensations that ran counter to normative trends.

This oddity is registered in the literature of the period. A number of interesting, largely neglected texts treat the role of sound devices in the communications network of their day, and they explicitly associate an engagement with acoustic technology with other forms of deviance, political, social, and sexual—but chiefly sexual. The physical connection between distant interlocutors seems to elicit thoughts of relationships that escape the increasing dominance of modern visual modes of surveillance and control. The sexual association first becomes prominent in a series of sensation novels of the 1860s, such as Mary Braddon's *Lady Audley's Secret* (1862), whose plots turn on the striking effect of telegraphy; then in detective fiction, particularly that by Arthur Conan Doyle;[4] and finally in a series of telegraph-obsessed texts from the end of the century, including Stoker's *Dracula* (1897) and two novels I shall examine at more length, Hardy's *A Laodicean* (1881) and James's *In the Cage* (1898). In James's story the oddity surrounding the machine's voice receives another name. There, the effects produced in the telegraph office are called not "odd" but "queer."

As the story of *Orten* v. *Welch* illustrates, the technological vocabulary surrounding the telegraph surprisingly anticipates today's cyber-babble. "Communications network," "information," "relays," "code," "wired," "face-to-face," "tech," even the "web"—these terms, and others equally familiar, crop up in the earlier discourse. But the familiarity of this nineteenth-century episode reaches beyond vocabulary to encompass larger social anxieties. Marvin reports on countless articles and stories from the last century concerned with the kind of issues that are making headlines today: the dangers of sexual predation over the wires, fears of uncontrolled social mobility made possible by the anonymity of the new technology, threats to the family, new forms of white-collar crime, the possibility that communications technology would be available only to the rich, and increasing government surveillance over the lives of citizens.

Equally, the kind of utopian claims about communications technologies that one hears everywhere today were easily as prominent in the last century. Here is language from a Commerce Committee report in Congress on Samuel Morse's new invention. The telegraph, this report gushes, will

> amount to a revolution unsurpassed in moral grandeur by any discovery that has been made in the arts and sciences, from the most distant period to which authentic history extends, to the present day. With the means of almost instantaneous communication . . . space will be, to all practical purposes of information, completely annihilated. . . . The citizen will be invested with . . . the [attributes of God], in a degree that the human mind, until recently, had hardly dared to contemplate. (Vail 77–78)

This congressional report was issued in 1837, when no practical telegraph lines had been laid in the United States and when the speed of data transmission was far from "instantaneous," even by the standards that were to prevail in the next decade.

Comparisons with the deity soon became a standard trope of the celebratory literature surrounding the telegraph. A poem published in the October 1858 issue of *The Atlantic Monthly* celebrating the (short-lived) triumph of the first Atlantic telegraph cable exhorts the shores of the new world to "hear the voice of God!"—"The angel of His stormy sky / Rides down the sunken wire," bringing a message of peace.[5] "Close wedded by that mystic cord" the continents will clasp hands "beneath the sea," spelling the final end of human conflict, "The funeral shroud of war!" This message of brotherhood is fused with imperialist rhetoric common in nineteenth-century technological discourse:

> Through Orient seas, o'er Afric's plain,
>   And Asian mountains borne,
> The vigor of the Northern brain
>   Shall nerve the world outworn.

Prescott's history of the electric telegraph (1860) boasted that the peoples of every Christian nation could answer in the affirmative the question God put to Job: "Canst thou send lightnings, that they may go, and say unto thee,

Here we are?" (Prescott 214). In *The Ocean Telegraph to India* (1870), Parkinson compares the engineers on the Great Eastern, which laid the cable through the Persian Gulf, to Moses standing on Mount Sinai (269–71).

The congruence between the birth of the telegraph and the coming of the information age is strong. Vocabulary, anecdotes, and social responses separated by more than a century and a half seem eerily alike. As a step toward thinking about this historical conjuncture, let me draw attention to a little-known essay about early-nineteenth-century communications systems written by William Hazlitt.

The Letter-Bell," composed in the last months of Hazlitt's life and published in 1831, shortly after his death, is an odd, digressive meditation on the charms of memory and on fidelity in the face of historical changes of the most wrenching sort—technological, to begin with, but also political. At the beginning of the essay, Hazlitt is at his desk composing sentences about the brevity of human life when suddenly his train of thought is interrupted by the sound of a bell outside in the street, a "loud-tinkling, interrupted sound" (377), which in those days announced the passing of the mail carrier. The sound throws him into a reverie, taking him back to the precious days of his youth. Notice the emphasis on the somatic qualities of the sound—striking the ear, vibrating to his brain—and on the active power of these vibrations to pierce and wake the subject:

> As I write this, the *Letter-Bell* passes: it has a lively, pleasant sound with it, and not only fills the street with its importunate clamour, but rings clear through the length of many half-forgotten years. It strikes upon the ear, it vibrates to the brain, it wakes me from the dream of time, it flings me back upon my first entrance into life, the period of my first coming up to town, when all around was strange, uncertain, adverse—a hubbub of confused noises. (377)

The postal service, then as now, was a global communications network, with links to Europe, India, Africa, the Americas, and other regions of the globe. During the last years of the eighteenth and the early decades of the nineteenth century, the British Post Office underwent an enormous expansion of its bureaucracy, systematization of its methods, and regulation of its activities.[6] In *Practicing Enlightenment* Jerome Christensen relates this rationalization of the system to the increasing powers of both government and commercial surveillance, powers nicely encoded in the ambiguous eighteenth-century usage of the word *intelligence* to mean both newsworthy communication and espionage (190–93). Christensen's argument depends on a parallel between state-sanctioned powers of postal surveillance (the right to open mail) and intelligence techniques employed by members of an increasingly powerful cartel of eighteenth-century publishing houses. Hazlitt, a sympathizer with the French Revolution, was keenly aware of the relationship between postal surveillance and both state and commercial restrictions on his ability to publish political dissent. Why, then, was one of his last essays devoted to a nostalgic celebration of this very system?

The answer lies in the particular technology he chose to commemorate—the Letter-Bell. Although the postal system of his time had comparatively few technologies to aid in the distribution of messages, those it had were viewed as harbingers of a modernity that Hazlitt, along with many of his peers, once had hoped would foster revolution and democracy. Those technologies included a new system of postal roads, a fleet of vehicles, a routing grid, a pricing structure, and centralized receiving stations. Lest you are tempted to turn up your nose at this system, let me just mention that in Hazlitt's London, personal letters were routinely delivered six to eight times a day, while business letters could arrive as often as twelve times a day. Modern efficiency, however, is something that hard experience had taught Hazlitt not to celebrate. Instead he organized his ruminations around perhaps the most evanescent of the technologies the Post Office possessed: an audible signal, which was used to indicate the availability of a gateway to the network.

The Letter-Bell heralded the letter writer's momentary chance to access the system, for the pillar-box on the street corner would not be introduced for twenty-one years, by Anthony Trollope (postal worker and novelist). Of all the features of the mail system, it is the signal bell that seizes Hazlitt's imagination. About a decade later the same signal would be grafted onto the telegraph to announce an incoming message; late in the nineteenth century the same signal would become a feature of the telephone; and, today, the same signal chimes in one's computer terminal at the arrival of a message, if that feature is enabled in one's e-mail program. The sound of these signal bells is the voice of the communications network itself, a sound produced by the interactions of a vast information system stretching around the globe even in Hazlitt's day. The bell is the network's very own sound, a voice conveying the network's (not the user's) message.

In a happy phrase, Hazlitt calls these bells "*conductors* to the imagination" (380, italics in original). They not only spark the imagination but function as relay switches as well. Hearing their "importunate clamour" breaks the circuit of attention that connects him to the present and shunts his mind into memories of "half-forgotten years." These memories are precious to him not merely because of their personal associations but also because, for many trying years, they have been the only place where the spirit of the French Revolution has continued to survive. This bitter reflection prompts Hazlitt into one of his characteristic diatribes against Wordsworth and Coleridge for betraying their former faith in liberty.

Cowards and recreants—these are the kindest words Hazlitt can find now for his former compatriots. "What would not these persons give for the unbroken integrity of their early opinions?" Hazlitt asks, and then, as if the thought of unbroken connections brings him up short, he returns to his topic of the Letter-Bell. The transition seems as abrupt as it is hyperbolic:

This is the reason I can write an article on the *Letter-Bell,* and other such subjects; I have never given the lie to my own soul. If I have felt any impression once, I feel it more strongly a second time; and I have no wish to revile or discard my best thoughts. . . . I do not recollect having ever repented giving a letter to the postman, or wishing to retrieve it after he had once deposited it in his bag. What I have once set my hand to, I take the consequences of. . . . I am not like the person who, having sent off a letter to his mistress, who resided a hundred and twenty miles in the country, and disapproving, on second thoughts, of some expressions contained in it, took a post-chaise and four to follow and intercept it the next morning. (378–79)

As he writes these lines in 1830, Hazlitt's constancy is being vindicated, for the July Revolution in France connects the closing days of the author's career to its beginnings in the glorious days of the first French Revolution. But the abrupt movement from one topic to another in this passage seems to undercut the very unity of the subject about which he boasts (perhaps overmuch). In the space of a few sentences Hazlitt moves from assertions of political fidelity, to reflections on the changing mail system, to anxious comments about taking the consequences of his actions, to a ludicrous portrait of sexual vacillation. What connects these topics? More important, where does this anxiety about punishment come from, and why does the sound of a postman's bell lead him to insist on his romantic integrity?

These questions prompt one to take seriously Hazlitt's claims that his very identity is intertwined with the communications system of his youth and that changes in this system require adjustments in the way he conceptualizes himself. The overinsistence on constancy—political, emotional, and somatic—arises from the odd position in which the ringing of the Letter-Bell puts him. For the essay charts a strange inversion in his response to the "loud-tinkling" bell. In the present, the sound "flings" him into reveries. When it "strikes upon the ear," it turns his thoughts inward. In the past, though, the bell used to wake him from his dreams. Years ago, Hazlitt confesses, "the Letter-Bell was the only sound that drew my thoughts to the world without" (379). The signal that today assures the subject of its "unbroken integrity," yesterday served to admonish its waywardness. The same sound "vibrates to the brain" with strangely opposed effects.

This is how Hazlitt is constant to himself—by growing into the opposite of what he once was. This is how he manages to feel the same impression more strongly a second time—by inverting it. I do not mean to say that Hazlitt's political convictions have changed; far from it. But something had to change to make sure those convictions remained the same. The Letter-Bell becomes the mark of this inversion in the subject. It symbolizes the fugitive adjustments of the independent subject as it struggles to preserve itself under a modern regime of surveillance. The mail system as a whole had betrayed Hazlitt's hopes that communications technology would increase democracy. Only the Letter-Bell revives in the author his earlier fond dreams. What makes its "loud-tinkling, interrupted sound" an appropriate sign, in this context, of the lengths one must go to remain constant to one-self is the odd relation of sound technology to other aspects of the communications network, a deviance just becoming apparent in Hazlitt's time.

The last sentence of Hazlitt's essay turns from memories of old letter-delivery systems to what seems like an anachronistic reference to the telegraph. The author died seven years before the electric telegraph was invented, so how is it possible for him to write: "The telegraphs that lately communicated the intelligence of the new revolution to all France within a few hours, are a wonderful contrivance; but they are less striking and appalling than the beacon-fires (mentioned by Aeschylus), which, lighted from hill-top to hill-top, announced the taking of Troy, and the return of Agamemnon" (382)? It is possible because the telegraph to which Hazlitt referred was not the electric telegraph. It was an optical semaphore network established by Claude Chappe in Paris in 1794.

The fascinating history of Chappe's telegraph is told in Gerard J. Holzmann and Björn Pehrson's *The Early History of Data Networks* (1995). Although the semaphore telegraph is nearly forgotten today, it provided continuous communication service among 29 cities in France until 1855. At its height the network had 556 telegraph stations covering some 3,000 miles, and messages sent from Paris could begin arriving at Calais in just four minutes. The stations customarily consisted of a squat tower on the top of which was mounted a metal pole equipped with two wooden beams, which could be manipulated like semaphore flags to convey the letters of the alphabet (Figure 2.1). Each station was staffed by two or more operators, one to watch for incoming signals through a telescope, the others to relay the message to the next station on the line by pulling cords connected to the mechanism on top of the tower. The French were so enamored of this optical system that they lagged behind Britain and the United States in the introduction of the electric telegraph, a communications gap that plagued their country well into the twentieth century. Years after the change to the electric telegraph, France delayed adopting the international Morse code, preferring instead to operate the electric system with an optical code based on Chappe's semaphore.

Even less well known is the fact that England also established a network of semaphore stations beginning in 1795. The British system, sponsored by the Admiralty Office, initially consisted of fifteen stations running from London to Deal. The network was extended in 1796 with ten additional stations stretching south from London to Portsmouth. There was a tower on the Portsmouth line located less than two miles from the cottage in Chawton where Jane Austen lived from 1809 until just before her death in 1817. The world of Austen's fiction may seem far removed from advances in communications technologies, but in point of fact the new telegraph system im-

FIGURE 2.1
Chappe's Semaphore Telegraph

pinges on the lives of two of her heroines—Fanny Price and Anne Elliott—who have loved ones in the British navy. In 1806 the line was extended again, with stations leading from London 200 miles southwest to Plymouth, and the year after that Yarmouth was added to the network. In all, the Admiralty built sixty-five telegraph stations and operated the system continuously until 1816, two years after the publication of *Mansfield Park*. Following Trafalgar, the telegraph adopted the semaphore code made famous at that battle by Nelson's signal: "England expects that every man will do his duty."[7] The system was temporarily abandoned in 1816, when the threat of war diminished. But a new semaphore telegraph line between London and Portsmouth went into operation in 1822 and functioned without interruption until 1847, despite the construction of an electric telegraph line between those two cities in the early 1840s. Mobile semaphore telegraph units were used in the Crimean War (1853–1856) and the U.S. Civil War (1861–1865). (Figure 2.2)

None of the characters in Austen's fiction ever sends or receives a telegram—nor did Austen herself—because the British Admiralty reserved

FIGURE 2.2
Mobile Semaphore Telegraph. Alexis
Belloc, *La télégraphie historique depuis
les temps les plus reculés jusqu'à nos
jours* (Paris: Fermin-Didot, 1888).

the telegraph line strictly for official naval business. But Austen's characters
are nonetheless touched by this technology. An illustrative instance occurs
midway through the second volume of *Mansfield Park,* when Fanny Price's
brother William, who is a midshipman on board the *Antwerp,* returns to England. Although Austen does not mention it, the news of the *Antwerp*'s arrival
would have been flashed to London via the telegraph and there conveyed to
the newspapers that competed to publish the latest shipping news. Consequently, Henry Crawford, who to please his uncle had for years "taken in the
paper esteemed to have the earliest naval intelligence" (242), has every reason
to expect that he will be the first to tell Fanny the happy tidings of William's
arrival. Henry could have trusted in the papers in London being apprized of
the docking of a ship in Portsmouth within five minutes of its dropping anchor. His satisfaction at his own cleverness in snooping through the shipping
news in order to be the first to discover the "intelligence" of William's arrival
indicates how germane the ambiguity of that word is to Austen's novel.

As it happens, Fanny has just that morning received a letter from
William telling her the news directly, but the circumstances that enabled a

letter to reach Mansfield Park from Portsmouth more rapidly than the newspapers from London apparently require special explanation: "She had a letter from [William] herself, a few hurried happy lines, written as the ship came up Channel, and sent into Portsmouth, with the first boat that left the Antwerp, at anchor, in Spithead" (241).

Henry's disappointment is the consequence of complex interactions among varied communications media. The intelligence reaches Mansfield Park through two different routes, which between them employ technologies ranging from pen, paper, alphabetic code, a boat, and a mail coach, to the semaphore telegraph, Trafalgar code, optical equipment, a news gathering organization, printing press, and another mail coach. Henry's surprise is an early manifestation of sensations that are common enough today—so common, perhaps, that one has trouble appreciating their distinctive structure. These sensations acquire their impact from the conditions of communicating across great distances, in brief intervals of time, with the aid of advanced technologies. The news of William's arrival is an information event that alters one's relations to time and distance.

Questions about information networks emerge most frequently in the novel in the Portsmouth chapters, no doubt because naval matters lead to dealings with telegraphs, shipping news, promotion lists, letters to influential officials, orders, and schedule changes. As an important seaport, Portsmouth itself might be thought of as principally a node in a system of commercial, military, and information exchange. Its harbor is a transit point connecting London with a growing empire, and much of the activity of the city is dedicated to servicing the vessels that pass through this way station and in relaying their contents to other destinations inland. Like operators in semaphore telegraph stations, who do not originate the messages they send down the line, Portsmouth derives much of its livelihood from serving as an intermediate link in a more extensive chain. Few of the commodities that arrive at the harbor—and still less of the strategic intelligence—are destined to remain there. Hence one may read Austen's Portsmouth as partly a commentary on mediation, as a symbol of how technological change in the system affects the circulation of both goods and information.

This is especially true of the strategic intelligence concerning love affairs that Fanny receives during her visit home. The final destination of the messages concerning Fanny's Mansfield friends is seldom Portsmouth, and there is an incongruity in these messages having to be routed through the humble Price establishment at all. This incongruity emerges each time Mary Crawford writes to Fanny for information about Mansfield Park. When Tom falls ill, for example, Mary uses Fanny as a conduit for acquiring news concerning Edmund's chances of becoming an eldest son. Fanny is appalled at Mary's lack of sympathetic feelings, but Fanny is amazed as well at her sudden importance in the communications loop: "Here was another strange revolution of mind! . . . With all the uneasiness it supplied, [Fanny's position at least] connected her with the absent" (386–87). But connectivity has an ambiguous

value. The cost of this new importance is a further reduction of her autonomy and personal worth—she becomes a node, a relay point, in an intricate
information network, which eventually extends, via newspaper accounts of
scandal in her family, to encompass strangers living in distant cities.

Portsmouth was significant for reasons beyond commerce and intelligence during this period. Perhaps its most famous attraction was the naval
dockyard, which was the principal manufacturing site for the British Navy.
The naval works there were renowned throughout England, and tours of the
shipbuilding yards were a highlight of most visits to the city. Jane Austen
toured the yards, looking for impressions that would connect her with her
sailor brothers, as did Maria Edgeworth and Sir Walter Scott, among countless others. The chief engineers at the Portsmouth naval works were Marc
Brunel (father of I. K. Brunel, Paxton's competitor) and Henry Maudslay
(the most gifted toolmaker of his age, who plays a role in the story of Babbage's Difference Engine). Brunel and Maudslay were so harassed by the
crowds of tourists that they asked for fences to be put up to keep out the
upper classes.

One of the things that made the dockyard famous was the revolutionary system of manufacturing introduced by Samuel Bentham, inspector
general of naval works from 1795 to 1812. Samuel, the older brother of Jeremy
Bentham, was the true inventor of the panopticon, a circular building with
a central surveillance tower that the younger Bentham publicized as a
scheme for prison reform. Samuel conceived the principles of the panopticon while working in Russia on Prince Potemkin's estate, as a way to super-
vise unskilled serfs in advanced manufacturing processes. When put in
charge of the Portsmouth naval facility, Bentham quickly discovered that the
same principles of rationalization and surveillance of the labor force were,
in his view, sorely needed. A pioneer in systematizing labor practices, he
introduced efficiency measures—the so-called Portsmouth system of manufacture—which arranged machines and workers in a production line, anticipating by more than fifty years the widespread use of assembly lines in
British manufacturing (Cooper 192). Bentham also cajoled a reluctant labor
force into giving up their longstanding right to carry home "chips" of wood
in favor of accepting true hourly wages.[8] He tricked the yard into accepting
steam-powered engines in the manufacturing process under the pretense of
needing a dock pump, and he, along with Brunel and Maudslay, patented
numerous woodcutting and metalworking machines, which cut the labor
force in half and reorganized the laborers who remained along "scientific"
principles—that is, according to their position in the manufacturing process
rather than their rank in a traditional trade guild (Cooper 194).

Bentham's panoptic arrangement for disciplining workers reveals the
direct connection between technologies of vision and the emerging disciplinary regime of modernity, a theme that Michel Foucault, among others, has
made a prominent part of the contemporary critique of Enlightenment values.[9] For Foucault, the panopticon revealed the way in which the Enlighten-

ment quest for knowledge went hand in hand with large-scale techniques for social control. If the Crystal Palace has become the touchstone for accounts of nineteenth-century spectacle, the panopticon has served as the complementary archetype for critics of modern disciplinary society. The former looms large in discussions of commodification, objectification, and visual passivity; the latter stars in discussions of surveillance and normalization. But both contribute to what Foucault calls the "unimpeded empire of the gaze" (*Clinic* 39).

The persuasive power of these two critical traditions has been great. Their very success in documenting the nineteenth-century origins of modern technologies of vision, however, has obscured the existence of countercurrents within the same period. There were voices who dissented from the growing hegemony of sight, voices whose discordant message needs to be heard. But these voices should not be confused with another trend, the postmodern critique of vision that Martin Jay has recorded in such illuminating detail. In *Downcast Eyes* (1993), Jay surveys both the "privileging of vision" (69) in the modern era and the backlash against vision in twentieth-century radical thought, from Impressionism to poststructuralism and postmodernism. Further, he anticipates the point I am making here by stressing the existence of what he calls "countercurrents to Enlightenment ocularcentrism" during the Enlightenment itself (98). As Jay shows, eighteenth- and nineteenth-century objections to the dominance of vision do not necessarily herald the particular emphases of postmodern thought. Austen, for example, objects to visual technologies of surveillance without also rejecting Enlightenment assumptions about the centrality of moral vision or the relationship between lucidity and truth.[10]

Austen's characters visit Samuel Bentham's dockyard in Volume III of *Mansfield Park,* and Fanny and Henry Crawford rest for a while on what may have been one of the very "chips" that Bentham was struggling to reform out of existence. Austen records the economic dislocation, the out-of-work dock loungers who were a consequence of Bentham's reforms. It is startling to contemplate the fact that Austen herself witnessed firsthand the social consequences of one of the first efforts to rationalize manufacturing in England. She toured one of the primary visual regimes of modernity, a panoptic system of supervision. Such a realization plays havoc with customary period assumptions—the prison reforms Dickens inveighed against visible in dockyards toured by Regency high society in Austen's day.

Perhaps even more interesting is the way Fanny's experience in Portsmouth connects the topic of surveillance with England's communications network. All the characters in the novel are adept at using the postal system for gathering intelligence.[11] Fanny scrutinizes every message for clues regarding the romantic developments she fears between Mary and Edmund. Mary, for her part, uses every communication to post strategic bulletins in support of her own and her brother's matrimonial schemes. The motif of surveillance culminates when the society column of a London newspaper brings early word of the scandal breaking over Henry and Fanny's cousin Maria Rushworth. Fanny is shocked not only by the event itself but by the means of its communication: "when her father came back in the afternoon with the daily newspaper as usual," Fanny was "far from expecting any elucidation through such a channel" (427). "Channel" here refers both to the medium—a public newspaper—and to the circuitous path the information travels: London to Portsmouth to her father to her. Confirmation has to wait for a communication directly from Mansfield, three posts later, when the "sickening knock" comes and "a letter was again put into her hands" (430).

Fanny's three months in Portsmouth educate her about some of the unpleasant consequences of being connected to loved ones only through the modern communications network. Critics have sometimes noticed Fanny's achievement at the end of the novel of a limited power of moral censure, a position of superiority that allows her to view and pass judgment on the actions of the other characters. The Portsmouth chapters, however, clarify the difference between such personal oversight—the sort of care or "cure" that Edmund comes to accept as his duty as a curate[12]—and the spying, informing, and misinforming that reaches her through the post. In Portsmouth, Fanny is placed in the debilitating position of enjoying the best intelligence the network can afford (she is the only character who receives communications from all sides) but of having virtually no ability to do anything but worry. The causes of this helplessness are overdetermined: it comes from her economically dependent status, her innate timidity, and her gender, among other things. But the sense of paralysis, the "sort of stupefaction" (429) that overwhelms her in Portsmouth, is also a result of her position as a node in an emerging information network. Every increase in Fanny's connectivity only emphasizes her inability to do anything with the information she obtains. This is an early intimation of one of the familiar drawbacks of communications at a distance. It creates a subject who, as Austen says, "might now be said to live upon letters, and pass all her time between suffering from that of to-day, and looking forward to to-morrow's" (417).

With the arrival of the electric telegraph in 1837, many people hoped that the paradoxical effects of a network that seemed both to connect and to debilitate the subject would be mitigated. This hope stemmed primarily from the marvel of speed: the appearance of "instantaneous" communication led (as it still does today) to the fantasy that distance has been annihilated. Division itself—both within and between subjects—is eliminated in the illusion of being "in touch" with the other. In the case of the electric telegraph, however, it was not only the speed but also the tactile and acoustic sense of connection that stimulated this belief. The strongest adherents to this view of the telegraph were the operators themselves. They associated the physical nature of the link they felt with other people on the line with the sound-reading methods that they pioneered.

The conflict between optical and acoustic systems of communications, which surfaced in Hazlitt's essay and which played itself out over twenty years of French policy debate, was a topic of contention among U.S. and British inventors too. Although Samuel Morse patented a sound-reading system, the Morse Telegraph Company at first vigorously fought the sound system, even issuing regulations forbidding its use. In less than a decade, however, the Morse company rule had been reversed and operators were required to receive by sound. Recording telegraphs required two employees, an operator who translated aloud the dots and dashes marked on the receiving paper and a copyist who took dictation. Operators soon found that while listening to the tapping of the instrument they could take down messages with fewer mistakes and that sound-reading freed their eyes and hands for writing. Sound-reading spread more rapidly in the United States than in Britain, perhaps because the rhythmic drumming action of striking downward on a key reinforced the somatic link between sound and signal. The British Needle Telegraph, invented by William Fothergill Cooke and Sir Charles Wheatstone—and later their ABC instruments—were operated by twisting levers to the side with the wrist. The Needle Telegraph, which was a recorder, was the dominant apparatus in Britain into the 1860s and was still employed on most private lines as late as 1888, when it began to be replaced by the telephone. Operators of these British instruments eventually learned to read the clicks of the needle by ear too, and the practice became dominant.

The role of sound in telegraphic communications was regarded by contemporary observers as one of the most startling features of this new technology. One early sound-reader is described as having "visions of sound" (Townsend 18). This telegraphist, who lays claim to being the "first practical sound-reader of the Morse alphabet," is compared, in the standard metaphor, to Moses: "What a wonderful time, labor, and money saver the sound system has proved to be, and how grateful the world should be that the keen ear and rapid penmanship of [this operator] enabled him to become the Moses of the situation!" (20). An anonymous poem begins, "Hark! the warning needles click," revealing the instrument in question to be a British Needle Telegraph. The poem goes on to taunt the ancient Greek gods in its refrain: "Sing who will of Orphean lyre, / Ours the wonder-working wire!" (qtd. in Prescott 232–33). Every nineteenth-century book on the telegraph contains sections on the wonders of reading by sound. One characteristic author exclaims: "Of all the mysterious agencies of the electric telegraph, there is nothing else so marvelous as the receiving intelligence by sound" (Shaffner 456).

Receiving intelligence by sound"—or communication—is what separates the telegraph from the later media technologies Friedrich Kittler considers. According to Kittler, the gramophone and film "store acoustical and optical data serially with superhuman precision" (*Discourse Networks*

245). The telegraph (hardly mentioned by Kittler) communicates. Of course, the telegraph stores data in the process of communicating, and gramophones and films communicate as well as record. Kittler, however, dismisses the possibility of "so-called communication" (*Discourse Networks* 229), on both historical and theoretical grounds. The historical point involves the twentieth-century preoccupation with noise, randomness, nonsense: "Circa 1900 noise was everywhere" (*Discourse Networks* 219). The theoretical point flows from Kittler's adoption of Lacanian psychoanalytic terms—the Imaginary, Symbolic, and Real—to characterize all the conditions one needs to consider in an information system:

> The gramophone empties out words by bypassing their imaginary aspect (signifieds) for their real aspects (the physiology of the voice). . . . Film devalues words by setting their referents . . . right before one's eyes. . . . To use Lacan's methodological distinction between symbolic, real, and imaginary, two of these three functions, which constitute all information systems, became separable from writing circa 1900. The real of speaking took place in the gramophone; the imaginary produced in speaking or writing belonged to film. (*Discourse Networks* 246)

If Kittler's conceptions of the gramophone and film banish the possibility of communication, the nineteenth-century idea of "receiving intelligence by sound" instantiates communication in every word, even by the exacting standards of modern communications theory. Claude Shannon's theory of the five functions of communication, which is foundational for its field, maps well onto this account of the telegraph as an acoustic technology: *receiving* emphasizes a "receiver," a device that "reconstruct[s] the message from the signal"; *intelligence,* by stressing understanding, points to both an "information source which produces a message" and a "destination [in] the person (or thing) for whom the message is intended"; *by* suggests a "channel" through which the message flows; and *sound* names "a transmitter which operates on the message in some way to produce a signal suitable for transmission over the channel" (Shannon 5–6). It is significant that Shannon's name appears nowhere in Kittler's book, a surprising omission in a work that considers the advent of "noise" as a decisive event in modernity. Just two years later Kittler tries to remedy this omission in the "Afterword to the Second Printing" of *Discourse Networks.* There he invokes Shannon's five functions of communications but without considering their bearing on his model.[13] Throughout his second thoughts on *Discourse Networks* Kittler is careful to stress that media technologies do more than store information: "An elementary datum is the fact that literature (whatever else it might mean to readers) processes, stores, and transmits data"; and again: "Archeologies of the present must also take into account data storage, transmission, and calculation in technological media" ("Afterword" 369–70). All the same, the book itself concentrates on only one of these activities, storage. The other two—processing and transmitting—rarely enter the earlier analysis.

Kittler's emphasis on media as recording technologies leads to short-comings in his theoretical model that attending to communications technologies like the telegraph (or the later telephone and wireless) might have prevented. Perhaps the most significant feature of the gramophone and film, for Kittler, is the serial record they make of the real. The marvel of these inventions is their ability "to record the singularity and seriality of a progression of sounds or images" (*Discourse Networks* 115). They are analogue devices that capture the real, noise and all, one sound or image at a time. "For the first time in history, writing ceased to be synonymous with the serial storage of data. The technological recording of the real entered into competition with the symbolic registration of the Symbolic" (*Discourse Networks* 229–30). By this last phrase Kittler indicates the way symbolic systems such as language encode data in terms of what Lacan calls the Symbolic, the larger social network of meanings that structure the subject. As Kittler explains a few pages later, "Edison's invention was not called a phonograph for nothing: it registers real sounds rather than translating them into phonemic equivalencies as an alphabet does" (*Discourse Networks* 232). Such translation makes writing closer to a digital than an analogue method of recording reality. Writing, like the telegraph and the computer, stores information about the world in a symbolic code. Thus the gramophone and film break the monopoly once "granted to the book," as Kittler puts it, "a monopoly on the storage of serial data" (*Discourse Networks* 245).

In addition to the gramophone and film, Kittler considers a third technology, the typewriter. This device also stores (and communicates) information in symbolic form, although Kittler only talks about its manner of storing data as marks on a page. Symbolic in the same way that writing is symbolic, the typewriter dislodges the old discourse network for a different reason from the two analogue recording technologies. The disturbance arises from the typist's relationship not to the Real (gramophone) or the Imaginary (film) but to the "symbolic registration of the Symbolic." The two analogue recording methods functioned temporally: they captured time in its passing. The typewriter unsettles not because of its obvious temporal property—speed—but because of its spatial organization of keys and letters. This argument, counter-intuitive on its face, is pursued with ingenuity that makes it at least plausible: "Spatially designated and discrete signs— that, rather than increase in speed, was the real innovation of the typewriter" (*Discourse Networks* 193). It is hard to believe that increased speed was not the salient feature of typewriting, but Kittler is right to emphasize the way in which the artificial spatial arrangement of keys dispels the grand illusion of handwriting, which was that writing effected a "continuous transition from nature to culture." Instead writing becomes an act of "selection from a countable, spatialized supply" (*Discourse Networks* 194). The end result is that the typewriter abstracts body from word, the individual from the writing process. In Kittler's most quoted phrase, "Underwood's invention unlinks hand, eye, and letter" (*Discourse Networks* 195).

"It is always the same story in the discourse network of 1900," Kittler asserts (*Discourse Networks* 356), but in fact this is not true. The story differs depending on where one looks. Neither the telegraph (digital) nor the telephone (analogue) fits comfortably in the story Kittler tells. Like the typewriter, the telegraph registers its data in a symbolic form, and it certainly dispels the illusion of a "continuous transition from nature to culture." Yet the telegraph links hand, ear, and letter with remarkable power. It is one of the most sensory of all language machines. The urgent pounding of its key is still a symbol of news flashes long after the technology has been displaced by other instruments: telephone, fax, e-mail, and cell phone. The tactile and acoustic sense of connection remains strong despite the fact that the telegraph, like the typewriter, encodes data via spatially discrete signs. In some respects, space is even more integral to the operation of the telegraph, for a spatial measure (length) names the constituent elements of the telegraphic code—dots and dashes.

As one would expect, there is still less congruence between the telegraph and either the gramophone or film. Despite the serial nature of the telegraph's operation, it does not "store acoustical and optical data serially with superhuman precision" (*Discourse Networks* 245). In fact, the telegraph is an inefficient storage medium. Since the Morse code is a closed book to most people (a point that plays a role in the Hardy novel discussed next), storing information on one of the numerous "recording telegraphs" invented during the nineteenth century would require translating from code back into alphabetic language. Hardly an advance on writing as a storage mechanism. What the telegraph does best is transmit data. It sends and receives intelligence by sound.

One might explain the telegraph's poor fit with Kittler's account of modern media by designating it a "transitional" technology. This strategy, however, faces several barriers. First of all, the telegraph did not really serve as a *transition* to these particular media. It did not lead to the gramophone or film, nor was it replaced by them. It did serve as an inspiration for the typewriter, but only via aspects of the telegraph that never proved practical—the various attempts to use keyboards for input and printing devices for output. Further, the telegraph coexisted happily with all three of the other technologies. Finally, other communication technologies around 1900—preeminently the telephone—have as much in common with the telegraph as with the gramophone, and more than with the typewriter and film. Instead of thinking of the telegraph as a transitional technology for the discourse network circa 1900, one might plausibly conclude that it overleaps that network and finds its place in the communications paradigm that emerged with the advent of the computer.

The telephone does not fit Kittler's model either. The incompatibility of the telephone becomes clear in Kittler's only sustained reference to the device. Kittler is discussing a passage in Freud where the psychoanalyst advises physicians on how to listen receptively to their patients. In an extended analogy, Freud compares the communicative transaction between analyst and patient to what takes place in telephony:

> To put it in a formula, he must turn his own unconscious like a receptive organ towards the transmitting unconscious of the patient. He must adjust himself to the patient as a telephone receiver is adjusted to the transmitting microphone. Just as the receiver converts back into sound-waves the electric oscillations in the telephone line which were set up by sound waves, so the doctor's unconscious is able, from the derivatives of the unconsciousness which are communicated to him, to reconstruct that unconscious, which has determined the patient's free associations. (Freud, qtd. in *Discourse Networks* 283)

The patient's unconscious transmits messages, which the analyst's unconscious must receive and then convert back into intelligibility. Freud's "formula" is far closer to Shannon's model of communication than Kittler seems to notice. Considered from today's perspective, Freud's passage combines a psychoanalytic account of the role of the unconscious in communication with the insights of contemporary communications theory. Kittler, however, focuses solely on the absence of any conscious exchange of meaning. "All conscious 'communicating' between the two counts only as a keyed rebus transmitted from one unconscious to the other. Its manifest sense is nonsense; Freud the telephone receiver picks out the parapraxes that would be mere debris under a postulate of sense" (*Discourse Networks* 284). True enough, but Kittler still seems concerned about the uneasy fit between Freud's formula and his model. Hence he concludes by discarding Freud's analogy in favor of a comparison with one of his own favored media: "Freud's telephone analogy does not go far enough. Although it avoids the traditional recording device of writing, psychoanalysis works like a phonograph that in its developed form couples electroacoustical transducers with memory. Only sound recorders can register spoken typographic errors (an oxymoronic concept in itself)" (*Discourse Networks* 284). Where Freud spoke of what the unconscious "communicated," Kittler speaks only of the power of a recording device.

Rather than thinking of the telegraph as a "transitional" stage on the road to modernity, one should conceive of it—and of all technological media—as mobilizing certain potentials out of a range of possibilities, all of which are internal, to a greater or lesser extent, to media qua media. Every medium actualizes a different combination of these potentials in its own distinctive manner. Earlier generations knew as much when they devised terms like *ut pictura poesis* to describe literature's power to paint or called orchestral music "tone poems." By concentrating on "technological data storage circa 1900," Kittler pays short shrift to media's other capacities ("Afterword" 370). This causes problems for both his history and his theory.

Thomas Hardy, a writer trained as an architect and attentive to the science of his time, knew a great deal about the various potentials of technological media. In *A Laodicean* (1881), Hardy structures several pivotal events around the rival effects of optical and acoustic technologies—photography and architectural drawings, on the one hand, and the telegraph, on the other. The novel's heroine, Paula Power, is a young heiress who has had a telegraph installed in her home, a castle of ancient date. She is a sound-reader, who "applied her ear to the instrument" (42) to take down messages, even though the receiver would most likely have been one of Wheatstone's ABC instruments. Like Hazlitt, Hardy personifies the bell as the voice of the machine itself: "The telegraph had almost the attributes of a human being at Stancy Castle. When its bell rang people rushed to the old tapestried chamber allotted to it, and waited its pleasure" (52). Even the wires, "the musical threads which the post-office authorities had erected all over the country," are notable for their sound effects when the wind makes them "hum as of a night-bee," something Hardy mentions more than once: "The wire sang on overhead with dying falls and melodious rises . . . while above the wire rode the stars in their courses, the low nocturn of the former seeming to be the voices of those stars" (21).

Whereas Hardy systematically links the heroine and her female friend to the telegraph's music, he connects all of the men in the novel—and especially the villain—with visual technology and the production of images. Somerset, the hero, is an architect, and the son of a famous artist; Captain De Stancy, his unworthy rival in love, employs trumped-up knowledge of the castle's paintings to gain access to the heroine; and Dare, the melodramatically drawn villain of the piece, is a photographer who doctors a photo so that the hero falsely appears drunk. The power to manipulate the visual domain through technological mediation symbolizes a masculine aggression whose aim is the possession of the heroine's body and castle. The difference between the hero and his two adversaries lies only in the motive for his desire, not in its objectifying nature. Although Somerset's motive is love, Captain De Stancy's lust, and Dare's avarice, they are united in wanting to take legal possession of what they see.

A Laodicean is one of Hardy's least-read novels, perhaps because it is among his oddest. Uncertain of tone, it is part novel of ideas, part gothic, part comedy of modern manners, and part love story, yet there are fascinating touches in this work of a sort one seldom finds elsewhere in the author's canon. Most of them occur early in the novel, in passages that connect the ambiguous sexuality of the heroine to Hardy's theme of the "clash between ancient and modern" (34). "Laodicean" means someone with uncertain con-

victions. The title's overt reference is both to Paula's wavering religious beliefs and to her divided loyalties to past and present, her love of antiquity
and the "ultra-modern" (17). Paula, however, wavers in her sexuality too. The
few critics who have written on this novel complain of her inability to make
up her mind about which man she will marry. As J. M. Barrie drily comments: "She engages to get engaged to an architect who must not kiss her.
Then she engages to get engaged to a soldier" (165). An anonymous writer in
the *Saturday Review* is more exasperated: "In *A Laodicean* the author showed
us very queer people doing very queer things, which seemed the odder because the background against which the characters stood out was that of life
in a country house, and the characters themselves were of such a kind that
it was imprudent to assign to them precisely the oddities which the author
did assign" ([unsigned review] 97). Perhaps because of the assumption that
it was imprudent to discuss this kind of queerness among the upper classes,
the reviewer does not go into the oddity of Paula's sexuality. All the same, the
book's vacillating plot, with its confusions of genre and tone, corresponds to
Paula's queerness, and the heroine's reluctance to kiss, much less marry, either man is based on something more than the stereotype of "feminine"
fickleness.

The reverend who compares Paula to the biblical city of Laodicea de-
nounces her as *"neither cold nor hot"* (18, italics in original), but the warmth
of her feelings for another woman, Charlotte, is never in doubt. A neighbor
gives the clue early on: "Now that's a curious thing again, these two girls
being so fond of one another," and adds, "they are more like lovers than
girl and girl" (50). Later, Paula herself shows some of her feelings in a comment on a statue of a recumbent woman: "'She is like Charlotte,' said Paula.
And what was much like another sigh escaped her lips," then she "drew her
forefingers across the marble face of the effigy, and at length took out her
handkerchief, and began wiping the dust from the hollows of the features"
(111). Charlotte is equally revealing. As she speaks of Paula, "a blush slowly
rose to her cheek, as if the person spoken of had been a lover rather than a
friend" (35).

Paula's same-sex bond destabilizes a number of elements in the novel,
including the ostensible love plot, which revolves around Somerset's rivalry
with Captain De Stancy. It destabilizes, as well, some of the usual markers of
gender. One minor character describes Paula's beauty as "middling," except
at that time of the day when she engages in her favorite pastime, working out
in a private gymnasium that she built on her property. Then "she looks
more bewitching than at any" other "because when she is there she wears
such a pretty boy's costume, and is so charming in her movements, that you
think she is a lovely youth and not a girl at all" (169). Somerset responds to
something different but equally disturbing to his assumptions about gender.
Although Paula seems "becomingly girlish and modest" to him, her "composure"—what one might read as her immunity to *his* attractions—has a
queer effect not only on her looks but also on himself: "Somehow Miss Power

seemed not only more woman than [Charlotte], but more woman than Somerset was man" (68). Far from repelling him, however, Paula's power to *un*man him seems to stimulate his desire. At one point he watches Paula caress Charlotte—"she clasped her fingers behind Charlotte's neck, and smiled tenderly in her face"—and his response is to reflect: "It seemed to be quite unconsciously done, and Somerset thought it a very beautiful action," an action that "so excited the emotional side of his nature that he could not concentrate on feet and inches" (84–85). His arousal at watching the women embrace seems to compensate him for finding himself "to be the victim of an unrequited passion" (85).

By far the most striking scene in the book involves another instance of male voyeurism. The malevolent Dare succeeds in arousing Captain De Stancy's desire for Paula only by taking him to spy on her exercises through a chink in the wall of her private gymnasium. The dynamics of sight in this act are complex. As De Stancy watches Paula, Dare and a third man watch him. The men, all of whom are plotting against Paula's well-being in different ways, clarify their places in the conspiracy through their different voyeuristic positions:

> "Is she within there?" [the third man asks].
> Dare nodded, and whispered, "You need not have asked, if you had examined his face."
> "That's true."
> "A fermentation is beginning in him," said Dare, half-pitifully; "a purely chemical process; and when it is complete he will probably be clear, and fiery, and sparkling, and quite another man than the good, weak, easy fellow that he was."
> To precisely describe Captain De Stancy's look was impossible. A sun rising in his face, such was somewhat the effect. By watching him they could almost see the aspect of her within the wall. (174)

The conspiracy links heterosexual desire with vision itself. At every stage of their pursuit, the conspirators' plans involve the visual domain. Their plot requires not only the doctoring of a photograph, as I mentioned, but also the forging of fraudulent architectural drawings for plans to restore the castle to its feudal glory. In the scene at the gym, the scopic aggression of voyeurism reveals directly the way in which the various desires of these three men objectify Paula, making visible "the aspect of her within the wall." It also displays the homosocial bond that underwrites the heterosexual competition for the body and estate of a woman. As Captain De Stancy stares at Paula through the wall, and two other men stare at him, the narrator asks rhetorically: "What was the captain seeing?" Then, in case anyone has missed the role of vision in Paula's violation, answers his own question: "A sort of optical poem" (172).

The association of optics with masculine aggression, in this text, is balanced by the symmetrical counter-association of the telegraph—and acoustics—with a queer space, within which Paula's resistance to violence is disguised as "feminine" indecision and delay. As the only two main characters who can read the telegraph's sounds, Paula and Charlotte hold intimate converse with one another across great distances, more than once about Somerset while he is standing in the room where the message is being received, feeling excluded by his inability to understand the instrument's clicks: "There was something curious in watching this utterance about himself, under his very nose, in language unintelligible to him" (42). Somerset's word "curious" understates the oddity, the queer effect, of the telegraph in Hardy's novel. The open (but to him secret) telegraphic code the women use is the correlative of the open secret of their affection. Sound-reading is both the symbol and, at times, the actual medium of a bond that excludes the normative expectations of society, and excludes as well the objectifying desires of the men who want to possess her for themselves. The evanescent quality of the telegraph's music, which leaves no permanent record of its passing, reflects Paula's precious but transient independence. For a brief period, this rich, young, unmarried woman manages to pursue her own, not the world's, desires. In the end, the memory of this time will be like an echo of a distant sound.

In the second half of the novel, a series of contrived and melodramatic events brings the heterosexual love plot to a conclusion with Paula's marriage to Somerset and Charlotte's retreat to a nunnery, no less. But the final pages of the book are given over to memory and ambivalence. Recalling the reverend's denunciation of her as neither hot nor cold, Paula whispers these less-than-reassuring words in her new husband's ear: "What I really am, as far as I know, is one of that body to whom lukewarmth is not an accident but a provisional necessity" (428).

Hardy's choice of the telegraph to represent the queer effects of Paula's desires may present difficulties of comprehension to contemporary readers, who associate advanced communications technology with disembodiment. Baudrillard has famously argued that in the "era of hyperreality," when all functions are "abolished in . . . the ecstasy of communication," the "body, landscape, time all progressively disappear" (128–31). Mark Dery describes well the "wraithlike nature of electronic communication—the flesh become word, the sender reincarnated as letters floating on a terminal screen" (1). Such was not how the first electric communications network was experienced. Nineteenth-century observers were fascinated by the fact that telegraphic signals could be read by any of the senses, a claim that shows up in book after book. For example, one writer tells of repairmen who commonly read the wires with their tongue "by placing one wire above and the other wire below it" (Shaffner 464); another author explains how operators would hold ends of wire in each hand and read the signal "by means of the passage of shocks" through the body (Prescott 341). John Hollingshead, writing in Dickens's *All the Year Round*, recounts how the coming of telegraphs to local pubs enabled an enterprising innkeeper to provide a "glass of ale and an electric shock for four-pence" (106).

One cause of this perceived difference between the two communications technologies is the differing somatic itineraries of sight and sound under modernity. As Guy Debord, among others, has maintained, sight is "the most abstract of the senses" and hence, most "adaptable to present-day society's generalized abstraction" (17). Debord emphasizes that in the society of the spectacle sight has been separated from the other senses and elevated to "the special place once occupied by touch" (17). By contrast, the conditions of modernization have made sound appear to retain a closer connection with the sense of touch, in part because the body's role in producing sound waves has not been eliminated in daily life by technology. The subject experiences this activity of production in a strained vocal cord, a gasp for breath, a hoarse throat or dry mouth after prolonged speech, the sibilance of the lips in a whisper, the thrust of the solar plexus in a grunt. Similarly, the manual operation of the telegraph worked against the abstraction of sound from the tactile realm. Even today computer manufacturers design keyboards to produce a clicking noise in an effort to link, through the agency of sound, the fingers' actions to the letters materializing on the screen.

I do not mean to romanticize the job of working in a telegraph office. From the middle of the nineteenth century onward the central stations in large cities like London and New York achieved a degree of regimentation depressing to contemplate, and the rationalization of this workplace particularly capitalized on the increasing gendering of the labor force.[14] Indeed, more than one cultural critic has suggested that nineteenth-century communications technologies such as the telegraph, typewriter, and telephone played a decisive role in moving women into the office.[15] Thus Trollope, in his story "The Telegraph Girl," describes his heroine at her labors with "eight hundred female companions, all congregated together in one vast room" (265). Sound technologies did not escape the process of modernization and, in fact, played their own part in the regimentation of the work environment (witness the role of steam whistles in factories).

What I do claim, however, is that our understanding of sound has been historically constructed so as to make it appear less abstract than vision and thus less integral to the development of modernity. Debord is right when he claims sight is more adaptable than sound to modernity's demand for abstraction, if one recognizes that the subject's experience of sight *and* sound is historically conditioned. Nineteenth-century acoustic technology reinforced rather than severed the connection between signs and the senses, particularly sound and touch. Unlike nineteenth-century optical technology, which transformed particular objects into abstract images the better to circulate as commodities, the voice in the machine operated to connect one somatic experience with another. By consolidating the sensory effects of the signal, sound technology appears to intensify rather than abstract. Hence the remarkable power of sound to provoke memories—in Hazlitt's words, to "ring clear through the length of many half-forgotten years." Who today has not felt this power when listening to an old song on the radio? The same aural effect lies behind one of the hyperbolic claims in Hazlitt's essay: "If I have felt any impression once, I feel it more strongly a second time." The memories evoked by sound seem to intensify, not diminish, with the passing of time.

One can clarify this difference by comparing an optical technology like the stereoscope, which Crary calls the "most significant form of visual imagery in the nineteenth century, with the exception of photographs" (116), with sound-producing technologies from the same period. As it happens, Sir Charles Wheatstone, who was knighted for his role in inventing the telegraph, also was coinventor of the stereoscope. This apparent coincidence is not as surprising as it may at first seem. The link between his optical, acoustical, and electrical researches was wave theory. Wheatstone, son of a musical instrument dealer, began his research career by investigating the properties of acoustical waves. At the age of nineteen, he created a sensation in London by exhibiting a musical instrument called the Enchanted Lyre, in which a replica of an ancient lyre was hung from the ceiling by a thin cord and was made to play musical pieces for hours on end without any apparent human intervention. This exhibition turned out to be a serious scientific demonstration of the ability of sound waves to travel more readily through solids than air. The lyre was connected to the sounding board of a piano in a room above, and the sound was propagated down through the wire. Wheatstone's publication of his results was the first of many contributions to acoustical wave theory that are still regarded as seminal. His contributions to optical research are even more highly regarded: he and Sir David Brewster are credited with uncovering the principles behind binocular vision.

Wheatstone's stereoscope illustrated the way in which binocular vision functioned by radically separating the images seen by each eye. Since the viewer could observe the two different images positioned on opposite sides of the instrument, the illusion of three-dimensional synthesis created by the stereoscope made clear that the visual field was constructed out of discrete parts. By breaking down the principles behind binocular vision, the stereoscope, in Crary's words, "discloses a fundamentally disunified and aggregate field of disjunct elements" (125), a disclosure that signals a break with classical principles of perspective around which the observing subject had been organized for centuries. Thus Wheatstone's stereoscope was "based on a radical abstraction and reconstruction of optical experience" (Crary 9).

Wheatstone's Enchanted Lyre and his later kaleidophone did not have the effect of disclosing the radical abstraction of sensory experience. In fact, his acoustical experiments consistently underscored the relationship between physical contact and the propagation of sound. His instruments demonstrated for audiences "the *augmentation* of sound which results from the connexion of a vibrating body with other bodies capable of entering into *simultaneous* vibration with it."[16] Wheatstone would have been perfectly justified in drawing the opposite lesson from his experiments. After all, the vibrations were not simultaneous but rather were produced by the waves propagated from one vibrating body subsequently striking another. But the conclusion that seemed evident to him (and most people in the nineteenth century) was that two bodies were vibrating in sympathy with each other. In one demonstration he showed that a wire held in the air next to a flute could not transmit the sound, but if the wire touched the side of the instrument, music would be produced at a distant sounding board. In another, he proved that "the sounds of an entire orchestra may be transmitted," although dimly, because of the air intervening between the sounding board and the music. All the same, Wheatstone wrote, "The effect of an experiment of this kind is very pleasing" ("Transmission" 58–59).

The telegraph, in similar fashion, was perceived as connecting people to one another, and the experience of communicating by wires was one of amazing immediacy, even though the signal was terribly slow by today's standards. The phrase "annihilating distance" turns up over and over again in publications about the telegraph, but as the word itself indicates, the technology actually made distance internal to the signal. The word *telegraph,* which preexisted the electrical apparatus now associated with the term (witness Chappe's semaphore system), means "writing at a distance"—and that is exactly what it did. The signal produced by a machine at one location was produced again by a machine at a distance. Hence there is no intrinsic reason why the experience should not have been one of thrilling dislocation, like the disembodied sense of "thereness" felt by many in cyberspace. The way in which sound seemed to consolidate and intensify sensory experiences, however, militated against this interpretation of the technology. Listening could have the effect of splitting the subject—between past and present, say, as in Hazlitt's essay—but the impression was one not of diminishment but superabundance.

All of these somatic effects—intensification and immediacy, combined with a sense that distance has been internalized, brought inside the subject, resulting in a split but oddly augmented identity—are on view in what is perhaps the most successful treatment of the telegraph in English literature, Henry James's *In the Cage* (1898). This fascinating story revolves around an unnamed female telegraphist who regards herself as the "contact" (James 178) through which an entire communications network flows. She works in a small station in a grocery, separated off by a wood-and-wire cage, with an appropriately named instrument at its center—the "sounder" (174). As Jennifer Wicke has pointed out, women such as the telegraphist "mediate exchange. Communication flows through them, telegraphically or otherwise enhanced."[17] This enhancement is explicitly described in electrical terms: "The great thing was the flashes" that come from her "contact with the human herd" (178), flashes that fire each of her senses in turn:

> As the weeks went on there she lived more and more into the world
> of whiffs and glimpses, she found her divinations work faster and
> stretch further. It was a prodigious view as the pressure heightened,
> a panorama fed with facts and figures, flushed with a torrent of colour
> and accompanied with wondrous world-music. (186)

The telegraphist is an early version of Donna Haraway's cyborg, a woman
wired into the information network, the interface between a vast technological network and a human system of customers and exchange.

James fully registers the oddity of the telegraphist's position, what he calls
"the queer extension of her experience, the double life that, in the cage, she
grew at last to lead" (186). "Queer" is apt, given the sexual ambiguities opened
up by this story. Eve Kosofsky Sedgwick first drew attention to James's use of
this word in another late story, "The Beast in the Jungle" (Sedgwick 172).
Since then, Eric Savoy has traced the historical context for *In the Cage* back
to the homosexual scandals of the 1890s, particularly the Cleveland Street
Affair of 1889 – 1890, which centered on the incriminating testimony of telegraph boys and "the Post Office's anxiety about the operations of its 'particularly sensitive telegraph branch.'"[18] If "queer" is apt, "extension" is equally
apropos, given the way in which the telegraph seems to bring distance inside
the subject, allowing it to incorporate two positions without contradiction.
For the telegraphist, the sense of a "double life" does not invalidate convictions, the way the photographic double exposure in Hardy's novel did.
Rather it has the odd effect, so common in James, of both multiplying and
intensifying experiences: hence "there were more impressions to be gathered
and really—for it came to that—more life to be led" (178).

Since *In the Cage* has lately begun to attract the attention that it de-
serves,[19] I concentrate on the neglected somatic dimension of the telegraph
network—and on a related sexual motif. The dangers of the telegraphist's
sexuality have sometimes been referred to the suggestion—toyed with at
several points in the story—of prostitution and blackmail. Savoy nicely
illustrates how these topics represent "James's displacement of *fin-de-siècle*
homosexual panic into the narrative economies of heterosexual transgression" (287). What has not been noticed is that the displacement, in one crucial instance, moves in the other direction—from the heterosexual to the
homosexual register. Much of the plot concerns the telegraphist's knowledge of an adulterous intrigue between an upper-class gentleman, Captain
Everard, and a married woman, Lady Bradeen. Although the telegraphist, in
the course of her work, meets Captain Everard often enough to fall obsessively in love with him, she is alone with the recipient of his secret telegrams
only once. Lady Bradeen, who has come into the station to send a wire, makes
a mistake in the private code that she and her lover have devised, a slip that
could potentially expose their affair. The telegraphist catches this slip and, to
the amazement of the sender, supplies the missing word. This act, of course,
transgresses all the rules of the telegraph service, for the woman behind the

counter is supposed to be a neutral, expressionless, transparent interface. James treats it as one of the climaxes of the story: "It was as if [the telegraphist] had bodily leaped—cleared the top of the cage and alighted on her interlocutress" (213). Even before this transgressive act, however, the scene has had a queer dimension.

When she first sees Lady Bradeen, the telegraphist finds that her feelings for Captain Everard make his lover an intensely interesting object: "The girl looked straight through the cage at the eyes and lips that must so often have been so near his own—looked at them with a strange passion" (211). The homoerotics of this kind of transference are familiar, although fiction more often chronicles two men triangulating their love for one another through a mutually desired woman. "She was with the absent through her ladyship," James remarks, then adds a further twist, "and with her ladyship through the absent" (211). So intense is this "strange passion" that, in a bewildering reversal, her desire for the man appears as if it had been stimulated by her response to the woman rather than vice versa: "But, gracious, how handsome *was* her ladyship, and what an added price it gave him that the air of intimacy he threw out should have flowed originally from such a source!" (211).

The encounter indeed represents a "queer extension of her experience," one that reproduces the oddness of the telegraph in its very structure. To be with the sender and receiver at the same instant, to feel physically present at two ends of a communications circuit—such was the way many nineteenth-century subjects experienced the "sounder." This somatic effect, discussed now in a number of different contexts, does not fit neatly with other, more "modern" aspects of James's London, such as the commodification of language in the telegraph office. If the transformation of words into commodities is the most modern feature of James's story, as several critics have maintained (Bauer and Lakritz; Wicke "James"), then the telegraphist's queer relation to this process vexes the story's own relation to modernity. James undoubtedly means to capture the modern tendency toward abstraction when he describes the telegraphist counting and reckoning the cost of the words in the messages she transmits. But this process of commodification fails to encompass every aspect of the woman's situation. Mr. Mudge, the telegraphist's stolid fiancé, makes the point unintentionally. He wants her to view her relationship with customers in more rather than less commercial terms. He does not like "to see anything *but* money made out of his betters" (203). This wish, James wryly comments, is the "straight" view of her position. "Yet [Mr. Mudge] was troubled by the suspicion of subtleties on his companion's part that spoiled the straight view. He couldn't understand people's hating what they liked or liking what they hated" (203), which is exactly the perverse way in which the telegraphist experiences her situation.

The telegraph operator's queer position in James's story corresponds to the odd, still unassimilated position of the telegraph network in the regime of modernity. Marvin claims that, "in a historical sense, the computer is no more than an instantaneous telegraph with a prodigious memory, and all the communications inventions in between have simply been elaborations on the telegraph's original work" (3). The first part of her claim has the merit of highlighting (by its audacity) the way in which the telegraph overleaps some of the media that came between then and now, but what a difference a "prodigious memory" makes. The second part of her claim, however, shows the problems with her linear conception of the history of technology. I hope to have shown that later communications inventions have a more complicated relation to the telegraph than mere elaboration. The telegraph, that long-neglected technology in histories of modernity, offers an alternative site for thinking about language machines. It has an odd relation to other communications networks, and an odd relation to the usual story of modernity.

Kittler's work shares with Marvin's the virtue of steadfastly insisting on the need for a comparative historical approach. In his Afterword, Kittler maintains that "information networks can be described only when they are contrasted with one another" (370). This insight pertains to the cultural study of technology as well. The dominant role of optics in modernity can be understood—and its limits and gaps defined—only by contrast with the rival course of acoustics over the last two centuries.

In recent years writers, sound artists, and audio engineers have begun to stress the importance of acoustic experience in the modern world. The coming of digital media, from CDs, to digital sound for movies, to the Internet, appears to have sparked much of this interest in thinking about the poetics and technology of sound. National Public Radio now airs a fascinating short-feature program, *Lost and Found Sound,* that resurrects unusual recordings of the sounds from distant years, and the Whitney Museum in New York recently held its first exhibition of sound art, "I Am Sitting in a Room: Sound Works by American Artists 1950–2000." Mia Lipner, a media theorist and performance artist who is blind, pleas in an interview for the importance of "Hearing the Net," and her audio performance piece, *Requiem Digitatem,* dramatizes her contention that "not everyone learns or processes information visually" (Young and Senft). Innovative Web sites devoted to sound, such as Sonarchy.org, have sprung up, and a special issue of *Women and Performance* has been devoted to the topic of "Staging Sound: Feminism and Re/production."

In 1997, the same year a shorter version of this chapter first appeared in *Language Machines,* two other works on sound and literature were published, marking what I hope is a new trend in cultural studies. Adalaide Morris edited *Sound States: Innovative Poetics and Acoustical Technologies,* the first collection of critical articles on this topic,[20] and Wai Chee Dimock published a provocative essay in *PMLA,* "A Theory of Resonance." The twin aims of this latter essay—"to honor the claim of the ear against the primacy of the eye in the West" and to displace "synchronic" approaches to literature in favor of a "diachronic historicism" that tracks "the dynamics of endurance and transformation that accompany the passage of time" (1060–61)—are very close to the project this book pursues.

Dimock's work is so useful for a historical cultural studies that I must say a few more words about her essay before concluding this chapter. In Dimock's view, "A theory of resonance puts the temporal axis at the center of literary study" because the "traveling frequencies of sound" suggest a way to think about the "traveling frequencies of literary texts: frequencies received and amplified across time, moving farther and farther from their points of origin, causing unexpected vibrations in unexpected places" (1061). In other words, the ungraspable motion of sound models literature's status as a changing phenomenon, what she calls, following the philosopher W. V. Quine, a "nonintegral object" (1064). The literary contains as part of its very definition the capacity for historical change: "a text can remain literary only by not being the same text. It endures by being read differently" (1064). Dimock's account of the "nonintegral survival" (1064) of the literary accords completely with the goal of attending to the manifold ways in which past cultural developments may disappear for a time and return again to haunt the present in an altered form. In the case of sound technology, the lost potential for conceiving of information in material and embodied ways may be recovered by the multimedia capacities of digital technology, which can enable users to "hear the net," the way telegraphists once heard and felt the wire.

In the next chapter, I trace "unexpected vibrations in unexpected places," to borrow Dimock's phrase, by marking the parallels between two distinctive cultural formations. The place of science in literary culture is shifting today, and the emerging configuration bears comparison with an earlier moment, the undisciplined scientific milieu of the early nineteenth century. I will argue that the changing relationship between science and literature in the contemporary world revives cultural possibilities lost from view, or from hearing, during the approximately 150 years that have intervened.

This perspective on culture institutes a "nonintegral" concept of historical continuity. Links to the past may be meaningful without being linear or causal. This perspective returns me, as well, to the question of sound technology's odd place within modernity. As should be resoundingly clear, the best way to understand these odd relations is not by shifting the putative origin of modernity thirty, forty, or even fifty years earlier. Such adjustments merely relocate the boundaries of the modern period and leave intact the larger assumptions about its unity and comprehensiveness. If modernity both inhabits and is deployed in response to a dominant scopic regime, then attending to the subject's experience of acoustic technology may help make audible queer modes of social experience not assimilable into the grand narratives of the twentieth century.

UNDISCIPLINED CULTURES

Peacock, Mary Somerville, and Mr. Pickwick

Mr. Panscope, the chemical, botanical, geological, astronomical,

mathematical, metaphysical, meteorological, anatomical, physiological,

galvanistical, musical, pictorial, bibliographical, critical philosopher ... had

run through the whole circle of the sciences, and understood them all

equally well.

—Thomas Love Peacock, *Headlong Hall*

At the time when Thomas Love Peacock was composing his first novel, *Headlong Hall* (1815), the intellectual who claimed to be acquainted with all areas of science was a figure visible enough to be worth satirizing. To qualify, this person had to have mastered not just the fields recognized as science today—chemistry, botany, geology, and so on—but also areas that would now be classified as humanities: philosophy, music, art, and literature. Back then, the "whole circle of the sciences" included more than just natural philosophy. Peacock is thought to have modeled Mr. Panscope on Samuel Taylor Coleridge, although the resemblance is not as strong as the later portraits in *Nightmare Abbey* (1818) and *Crotchet Castle* (1831). Still, choosing Coleridge as the original for a man who had run through all the sciences shows how fuzzy the line dividing poet and naturalist could be at that time. In truth, there were men—and in one notable case, a woman— for whom such a portrait would be only slightly exaggerated. Charles Babbage, John Herschel, William Whewell, and Mary Somerville, to name just the most prominent personages of the day, compassed in their studies a large arc of the circle of sciences, including belles lettres and the fine arts. Herschel published verse translations of Homer; Whewell translated Schiller's poetry and wrote on German church architecture; and Somerville debated whether or not to devote herself to a life of painting rather than scientific endeavors. Until well into the nineteenth century, people interested in natural philosophy would not have thought of themselves as savants on any other terms (the title of "scientist" was not even coined until 1834).

In the early decades of the nineteenth century intellectuals participated in a relatively undisciplined culture. For example, a robust mixture of science, literature, showmanship, and speculation brought novelists, society figures, and natural philosophers together in Charles Babbage's drawing room for weekly soirees. Babbage's evening parties may be taken as emblematic of the place of science in his world: science was very much a part of culture, an aspect of the larger intellectual life, not a separate sphere reserved for specialists. In those days, an interest in geology, say, or electromagnetism was a legitimate avocation for gentlemen, and the majority of the members of the Royal Society were not scientists at all but aristocrats and gentry with no scholarly pretensions in natural philosophy even by the standards of their own time. Sir Walter Scott, to choose the example of a literary figure, served a term as president of the chief scientific society in Scotland. When one of his heroines, Diana Vernon from *Rob Roy* (1817), describes her reading preferences, they strike her male listener as rather advanced for a lady, but they accurately mirror the predilections of a well-read person at the time when Scott's and Peacock's novels were composed: "Science and history are my principal favorites," says Diana, "but I also study poetry and the classics" (92).

The journals of the period catered to this same mixture of interests. Periodicals carried scientific papers side by side with political articles, poetry, and criticism—not just the major quarterlies such as the *Edinburgh Review* (f. 1802) or *Quarterly Review* (f. 1809), but also monthlies like *Blackwood's Edinburgh Magazine* (f. 1817) and even some weekly papers. The titles of competing weeklies convey the blend that was sought: *The Literary Gazette; and Journal of Belles Lettres, Arts, Sciences &c* (f. 1817) and *The Athenaeum Journal of Literature, Science, and the Fine Arts* (f. 1828). This last, while remaining devoted to literary reviewing, also became an authoritative voice on scientific matters. The list of its contributors of original articles serves as a roll call of distinguished scientific figures from the first part of the century.[1] As one historian of science has stressed, it is more accurate to speak of science *in* culture at that time than of science *and* culture (Cannon). The gulf between people with scientific leanings and those with other cultural tastes was not nearly so great as it became in the twentieth century.

By calling the scientific culture of Babbage's day "undisciplined," I want to evoke several meanings of the term. The culture of this period was not merely wild and free spirited, it was also subject to few of the disciplinary conventions that were to come to govern twentieth-century professional life. The sciences were not yet fully established academic disciplines, characterized by autonomous faculties, regular curricula, separate examinations, and specialized journals. Savants did not think of themselves as mastering discrete fields, and their careers did not conform to the patterns associated with modern professions. Formal training, certification of expertise, professional societies, peer review, institutional support, and disciplinary publica-tions—these hallmarks of the modern profession had not spread widely through the sciences. Of course, professionalism was in the air, particularly in areas such as law, literature, and political economy, but the movement to-ward professional norms varied from one discipline to another.[2] The phys-ical sciences were behind areas such as the law, and the biological sciences lagged still further.

The comparative lack of disciplinarity at this period has its appealing features. One was the indistinct line between entertainment and serious en-quiry that I will explore in the next chapter, a blurring that made the nine-teenth-century equivalent of hacking possible. Later in this chapter I shall return to the topic of scientific shows in order to discuss the influence of dis-ciplines in codifying these events into their modern shapes as experimental demonstrations, public lectures in institutional settings, and spectacles de-signed to enhance the social prestige and political power of the emerging scientific professions. Another appealing aspect of an undisciplined culture was the lively interchange between engineering and science. For most sa-vants, the division between pure and applied research was not so great as it was to become later in the century.[3] As I have demonstrated, Joseph Paxton was able to make significant contributions to fields as diverse as botany, ar-chitecture, engineering, and urban design, and Wheatstone's career was an-other example of this versatility. Perhaps most striking is Babbage's research, which spanned boundaries rarely crossed today. Practical engineering and technical feats—such as designing stage lighting for theaters, contriving and operating a device to measure railway vibrations, and manufacturing a working model of his calculating machine, the Difference Engine—came from the same head that produced advances in pure mathematics, statistical theory, geology, and operations research. Such an undisciplined range of in-terests is a far cry from the specialization necessary to modern science.

I draw attention to this earlier historical moment in order to lay the groundwork for a comparison with developments in contemporary society. As I shall argue in chapter 8, the relations among disciplinary formations are shifting today. The hold of the modern disciplines and professions does not seem as firm as it once did. There are many people these days for whom the assumptions of professional authority and the claims of intellectual auton-omy no longer compel allegiance. It seems plausible that a convergence is occurring among many fields, bringing about a newly undisciplined culture. Julie Thompson Klein's study of interdisciplinarity in contemporary society presents compelling evidence that in the 1990s "knowledge is increasingly interdisciplinary and boundary crossing commonplace" (5). The transfor-mation taking place now, at the turn of the millennium, by no means revives the distinctive cultural circumstances of the early nineteenth century, but there are things to be learned from the comparison nonetheless. One of the premises of this study is that knowing more about earlier historical forma-tions can illuminate what is distinctive about one's own.

Fortunately, a sophisticated account of the undisciplined culture in the nineteenth century has been developed recently by historians of science, as well as by a few literary scholars. Pathbreaking books such as Susan Faye Cannon's *Science in Culture* (1978), Jack Morrell and Arnold Thackray's *Gentlemen of Science* (1981), and Richard Yeo's *Defining Science* (1993), as well as penetrating shorter studies by George Levine, Harriet Ritvo, Simon Schaffer, Alison Winter, and others, have produced a critical awareness of the class, education, religious, and gender constraints that were unfortunate concomitants of the intellectual free play of the time. These works demonstrate the importance of responding to both the dangers and the opportunities presented by this fascinating cultural moment. In line with this project, the next section of this chapter focuses on the scientific career of Mary Somerville, in order to suggest how the undisciplined culture of her day helped her become the most prominent woman of science in the entire nineteenth century, and also to suggest what happened to her career when scientific research began to grow more professionalized.

By the 1830s the unruly scientific milieu that produced Somerville—as well as Babbage, Herschel, Whewell, and the other savants who were her friends and admirers—was just beginning to break up. One may take the founding of the British Association for the Advancement of Science (BAAS) in 1831 as a symbolic turning point in the development of the modern configuration of scientific disciplines and the consequent disappearance of England's relatively undisciplined culture. The drive to professionalize the sciences did not gain a full head of steam until the 1860s, which saw the founding of *Nature* and the Darwinian controversies, but the early efforts toward scientific reform came about during the ferment leading up to the first Reform Bill.[4] Babbage's demand for increased professional rewards for scientists in his book *The Decline of Science* (1830), as well as the unsuccessful campaign that same year to elect Herschel President of the Royal Society (rather than the King's brother, the Duke of Sussex, who had little interest in science), were other signs of incipient professionalism. Ironically, Somerville vigorously supported the reform movement within the Royal Society, and Babbage played a role in promoting the British Association, the institution that would do more than anything else at the time to discipline scientific study. The sad truth is that these two extraordinary intellectuals helped create the conditions that would ultimately marginalize the kind of science they practiced. The unanticipated consequences of their efforts on behalf of professionalizing science had devastating effects on their careers.

In 1831, the same year that the British Association held its first meeting in York, Thomas Love Peacock published the last work of fiction he would write for nearly thirty years, *Crotchet Castle*. During the years that had intervened between his first and sixth novels, his delight in satirizing the latest scientific vogue had not diminished, but the target of his satire had changed significantly. Rather than a Mr. Panscope, who understood all the sciences and arts equally well, Peacock highlights a new kind of figure, the narrow specialist, who cares about nothing outside of his tiny corner of the intellectual universe. There is Mr. Firedamp, the meteorologist, who is obsessed with draining malarial swamps; Mr. Henbane, the toxicologist, who does nothing but experiment with antidotes for poisons; Dr. Morbific, the physician, who tells everyone he meets that infectious diseases do not exist; and Mr. Philpot, the geographer, who thinks only of charting the headwaters of distant rivers. Coleridge reappears in this text under the guise of Mr. Skionar, but now he is not a master of all fields but a transcendental poet, who confuses everyone with his impenetrable speeches about Kant and the philosophy of intuition. Peacock was prescient in his understanding of the direction scientific culture was moving. Although the differentiation of disciplines was nowhere near its modern form in 1831, the signs of this future were on display for those who could read them in what Peacock terms the "'astounding progress' of intelligence," or more simply, "the march of mind" (132).

Mary Somerville was once the First Lady of science. From her arrival in London in 1815 to her departure for the continent in 1838, where she spent the last thirty-four years of her life in obscurity, she blossomed into the most eminent female mathematician and astronomer in the world. Respected as an equal by English and French savants, she moved at the center of a London social world that included renowned poets, artists, scientists, and aristocrats. The woman who sat with the Pope on a sofa in the Vatican, attended the coronations of both George IV and Queen Victoria, stayed with General Lafayette in Paris, talked poetry with Ugo Foscolo and opera with Rossini, knew both James Fenimore Cooper and Washington Irving, was intimate friends with Maria Edgeworth and Joanna Baillie, visited the studio of Turner, had her paintings praised by Hugh Blair and her feminism by John Stuart Mill, had an island named for her by the explorer Parry, was feted for a full week at Trinity College, Cambridge, by the entire science faculty, was the friend and colleague of Herschel, Babbage, and Faraday, introduced Charles Lyell to his future wife, and was the mentor of Ada Lovelace—this modest, shy, deeply generous person could say what few other women of the century could, that for nearly twenty years she was more illustrious for her scientific achievements than for her social position.

Her first book was a translation with commentary of the difficult contemporary masterpiece of astronomy, *Mécanique céleste* by Pierre Laplace. Few mathematicians in England at the time could comprehend this work, far less explain its results to the cultivated audience that existed for science. Laplace commented that Somerville "was the only woman in England who could understand and who could *correct* his works," but the compliment could not have been extended to many men either (qtd. in Patterson 41). Her volume, *The Mechanism of the Heavens* (1831), was praised in a long, thoughtful essay by Herschel in the *Quarterly Review* and received equally favorable treatment in the *Edinburgh,* the *Monthly Review,* and the *Literary Gazette.* Only the *Athenaeum* dissented, in an attack apparently motivated by personal grievances, from the consensus that this work was "luminous," "beautiful," and "profound" (qtd. in Patterson 84). No one breathed a word at this time about the volume being derivative or mere exposition. In fact, Henry Brougham, who had originally encouraged Somerville to undertake the project for his Society for the Diffusion of Useful Knowledge, turned it down as being too abstruse for his intended readership. When John Murray, the publisher of Byron, Austen, Scott, and Lyell, accepted the work, he knew that this 703-page treatise was too serious a contribution to mathematics to produce much in the way of sales. Although all the reviews commented on the gender of its author, Herschel's essay stressed that nothing "beyond the name in the title-page" identified it as "coming from a female hand" (qtd. in Patterson 86).

Like Austen before her, Somerville had to struggle against the constraints on female authorship. Her first husband, who died after three years of marriage, disapproved of her interest in mathematics. Fortunately, her second husband, the doctor William Somerville, encouraged her studies in every way he could. He eagerly invited scientific figures to their house, joined scientific societies so that he could bring home materials from libraries to which his wife was denied admittance, helped arrange for the publication of her manuscripts, and rejoiced at her every success, with no apparent sense of jealousy or competition. All the same, the task of writing was not easy for this woman. Like so many of the female intellectuals Virginia Woolf memorialized, Somerville had no room of her own in which to pursue her studies, and she had to fit them into the odd gaps in the day between tending to children, running the household, making visits, and receiving guests. A passage in her autobiography on the trials of authorship sounds remarkably like a well-known description in Austen's letters of the novelist hiding her manuscripts from unexpected visitors. Somerville writes:

> I rose early and made such arrangements with regard to my children and family affairs that I had time to write afterwards; not, however, without many interruptions. A man can always command his time under the plea of business, a woman is not allowed any such excuse. . . . I learnt by habit to leave a subject and resume it again at once, like putting a mark into a book I might be reading; this was the more necessary as there was no fire-place in my little room, and I had to write in the drawing-room in winter. Frequently I hid my papers as soon as the bell announced a visitor, lest anyone should discover my secret. (*Personal Recollections* 163–64)

Other passages describe her efforts to teach herself Latin and Greek and master advanced mathematics without any formal instruction. She did receive assistance from a number of distinguished mathematicians who encouraged her in person and answered her questions by mail, with patience at first and mutual profit in the end.[5] Still, she remembered all her life her struggle to gain admission to Lyell's lectures at King's College, London, and the irony of her statue being displayed in the Royal Society, which would not admit her as a member. In her eighty-ninth year she affirmed: "Age has not abated my zeal for the emancipation of my sex from the unreasonable prejudice too prevalent in Great Britain against a literary and scientific education for women" (*Personal Recollections* 345).

Her second book was the work that established her international renown. *On the Connexion of the Physical Sciences* (1834) considers a daunting array of scientific knowledge. It discusses the most up-to-date ideas in all the fields then encompassed by the notion of physical sciences and demonstrates the many ways in which they "are united still more closely by the common bond of [mathematical] analysis which is daily extending its empire, and will ultimately embrace almost every subject in nature in its formulae" (*Connexion* 413). This position was radical at the time. To understand its significance, one should associate it with the campaign of the self-styled "Analyticals" at Cambridge—Herschel, Babbage, and George Peacock (no relation to Thomas Love)—who fought to reform English mathematics along the lines of continental analysis. Promoting such a position not only aligned Somerville with the advanced party of science in her day, it also revealed her militant Liberal sympathies in politics and her reformist stance in the debates then raging over scientific professionalism.[6] This point about Somerville's work has been insufficiently acknowledged, even among historians of science.

Somerville remained a passionate reformer in political, scientific, and religious matters throughout her life, from her girlhood boycott of sugar to protest slavery in the West Indies to her advanced positions opposing religious bigotry and favoring animal rights (*Personal Recollections* 45–46, 124, 363). The link between such reformist sympathies and the scientific perspective Somerville shared with her analytical friends seemed abundantly clear to traditionalists in the Royal Society. Four years earlier conservatives had associated calls to restrict membership in the Royal Society to men who actually did science with the social unrest sweeping the country and had even compared Herschel's campaign for the presidency with hayrick burning.[7] Peacock, the novelist, picked up on this association with his customary discernment. When at the end of *Crotchet Castle* Captain Swing appears at the head of a mob, the conservative Reverend Folliott proclaims that the "march of mind" has brought this trouble to their doors: "It has marched into my rick-yard, and set my stacks on fire, with chemical materials, most scientifically compounded" (242). Although anything but incendiary in tone, Somerville's masterly demonstration of the powers of analysis ought to be recognized as a reformist act of cultural politics. To take such an intellectual position was inevitably to participate in the culture wars of her time.

Instead of viewing *The Connexion of the Physical Sciences* as an intervention in a debate about science in society, scholars have wrestled with an entirely different question: whether the book should be considered an original contribution or a work of popular science. Some literary critics have been tempted to recuperate the work by reevaluating the genre of popular science itself, following the lead of scholars of nineteenth-century sentimentalism in claiming that particular genres have been undervalued because they were associated with women. This strategy seems mistaken here, for it perpetuates a common misunderstanding about the genre of Somerville's work. *The Connexion of the Physical Sciences* should not be associated with popular science but with a genre Richard Yeo has named "metascientific commentary" (8), an important enterprise at this period, which produced such treatises as Herschel's *Preliminary Discourse on the Study of Natural Philosophy* (1830) and Whewell's *The Philosophy of the Inductive Sciences* (1840).

Somerville herself inadvertently raised the issue of popularization about her own work. In her dedication to the Queen, she expressed the hope that her book would make science "more familiar to my countrywomen" (*Connexion* 2), motivated, I suspect, by a feminist impulse to get more women involved in the sciences. Her publisher Murray, however, seized on the hint and advertized the volume as being written for women and young people. In later editions the publisher continued to advertize the work's simplicity and emphasized that the new illustrations would enhance its appeal to the nonscientific reader. Hence the book eventually became associated with volumes of scientific self-improvement for women and children composed by best-selling authors such as Jane Marcet and Harriet Martineau. As historians of science have recently argued, however, Somerville's book differed greatly in genre from such self-help books (Myers; Winter, "Calculus" 207–10). Whereas Jane Marcet, like other authors of self-improvement literature, employed the dialogue form to make her *Conversations on Chemistry* appealing to the daughters of the middle class, Somerville's book was composed in the style of a philosophical treatise, even though she took care to make the explanations clear to people without advanced mathematics.

William Whewell's highly positive review in the *Quarterly* characterized her book as a "popular view of the present state of science" (55), but it went on to recognize the volume as weighing in, in the manner I described above, on current debates about science. Hence Whewell, one of the leading authors of the first half of the nineteenth century, used the occasion of this review to write what has turned out to be one of his best known pieces. In it, he coined the term "scientist," using the word for the first time in print as an umbrella term to describe anyone who was engaged in one of the proliferating branches of natural philosophy. (He was responding to Coleridge's objection, in an address to the 1834 meeting of the BAAS, to the use of "philosopher" for this purpose—a debate combining lexicography and turf protection that would have made an amusing episode in a Peacock novel.) It is ironic that Whewell should choose this occasion to propose his new term, for Somerville would soon be the very kind of figure excluded from the ranks of real scientists, but her "masterly" command of all the "branches" and "subdivisions" of fields that were rapidly becoming "estranged from each other" prompted him to search for a word that could apply equally to all (Whewell 55, 59).

Richard Yeo, in a book about Whewell's own career as a commentator on the state of science, makes a point that is relevant to Somerville's work as well:

> There is some doubt whether "popularization" is an adequate term to describe the public discussion of science that occurred in this period. In the twentieth century, popularization is conceived as a communication of expert scientific knowledge to a lay audience; but this notion of a clear distinction between expert scientist and lay audience is inappropriate in the early Victorian period. Many accounts of science, in periodicals and encyclopaedias, were aimed at practising scientists as well as a wider, lay readership. Moreover, in the first half of the nineteenth century public discourse on science served at least two purposes: it not only conveyed scientific discoveries to the public, but also legitimated science as a part of cultural discourse. (Yeo 38, references omitted)

For this reason, Yeo has suggested the genre of "metascientific commentary" to describe the kind of serious public engagement with science characteristic of Whewell and, I would add, Somerville. The term captures the way in which their project resembles the modes of cultural criticism common in today's intellectual discourse. One way of understanding the achievement of Somerville's work is to acknowledge that she, like Whewell, "was seeking to influence the way in which science, its method, epistemology, and values, was defined and promoted" (Yeo 8).

Perhaps the largest metascientific contribution of *The Connexion of the Physical Sciences* was in promulgating a particular vision of the boundaries of the physical sciences. Because of its extraordinary coverage of fields, Somerville's book at first glance appeared to be the kind of circuit around the whole circle of sciences that Peacock had satirized in Mr. Panscope nearly twenty years before. Its actual achievement, however, was very different. At a time when defining and categorizing the individual sciences was recognized as an essential philosophical task, Somerville's book succeeded in forging a consensus on the range of topics that would for many years comprise the physical sciences. Patterson is informative on this point: "Scientific readers—even the most expert—accepted her view that the physical sciences encompassed astronomy (both physical and descriptive), meteorology, physical optics, heat, sound, physical geography (and a bit of incidental geology, always of the latest sort), mineralogy (and some crystallography), electricity and magnetism" (129). Somerville established the unity of a discourse that would shape research for half a century to come.

Yet by the 1840s Somerville's own role as an authoritative voice in contemporary scientific debates had ended. Most commentators have attributed her loss of influence to biographical circumstances: her husband's financial troubles and his subsequent health problems, which led to their removal to Italy, where they would live for the remainder of their lives. There is no doubt that these factors were important in marginalizing Somerville from the mainstream of English science. But even in 1834, the year of her greatest triumph, she already could perceive that the professionalizing of modern science would leave little room for her participation. Years before any of her husband's reverses, the signs of change were visible to her, as one can discern in her reaction to the early meetings of the British Association.

William Somerville was one of the 121 "Friends of Science" who were invited to the first meeting of the BAAS in 1831, and his wife would have been welcomed as a spouse, but they did not attend. In 1832, when the second meeting was being planned for Oxford, the question of "Ladies Tickets" arose, specifically in regard to Mary Somerville. William Buckland, the president-elect, wrote to one of the chief organizers:

> Everybody whom I spoke to on the subject agreed that if the Meeting is to be of scientific utility, ladies ought not to attend the reading of the papers—especially in a place like Oxford—as it would overturn the thing into a sort of Albemarle dilettanti meeting instead of a serious philosophical union of working men. I did not see Mrs Somerville, *but her husband decidedly informed me that such is her opinion of this matter,* and further I fear that she will not come at all.
> (qtd. in Morrell and Thackray 150; Buckland's italics)

Buckland was wrong about her opinion of this matter, but his fear came to pass: she did not attend. Accepting the explanation of Somerville's husband at face value, Buckland never considered the possibility that her reluctance to attend might have deeper motives.[8] The fact is, she did not believe that women should be excluded from scientific gatherings, as her determination to hear Lyell's lectures at King's College indicated. Despite her commitment to women in science and despite repeated personal invitations to her from her admirers at Cambridge to be present at the third meeting there, she again refused to attend. Whewell wrote to her, enclosing a circular announcing the meeting and reassuring her that the wives of several scientists would be there. Somerville could not but notice that she was being grouped with the (nonscientific) wives of her learned friends. At Cambridge, ladies were admitted only as spectators to the general assemblies and evening parties; they could not attend the working sessions of the individual disciplines. In 1834 friends once again pressed her to attend the annual convention, this time to be held in Edinburgh. Francis Jeffrey appealed to her and her husband as Scots to support the event, but yet again, she would not come.

Scholars have taken these invitations as a mark of the esteem in which Somerville was held by her peers, which they certainly were, but the invitations also subtly conveyed another message. They announced the creation of a new professional arena in which she could not participate. By demarcating this professional space, they gave early notice of the demise of the undisciplined culture which had nurtured her. This does not appear to have been their intention, but personal esteem and generous motives can exist side by side with institutional exclusions, something even friends like Whewell failed to perceive. The new barriers to her participation were structural rather than personally invidious, but they could not be missed. Somerville's delicacy in the manner of refusing these invitations convinced Buckland and others that she agreed that women should be barred from the discussions of the British Association, but the pattern of her entire life suggests otherwise. No one in England was more eager to hear and discuss the latest scientific intelligence than Mary Somerville.

Ironically, most of the founders of the British Association were part of the advanced party in science with which Somerville was allied. Somerville herself had supported the earlier campaign to have Herschel elected president of the Royal Society. When that failed, she sided with Babbage's party in the "Decline of Science" debate. Babbage's goals in that polemic amounted to a full-scale justification of professionalism in science. Stating baldly that the "pursuit of science does not, in England, constitute a distinct profession, as it does in many other countries," he outlined the chief "advantages which attach to professions" (*Decline* 10–11). These advantages included virtually all the elements contained in the modern definition of a profession: a code of ethics enforced by internal sanctions; peer review of scientific results; disciplinary publications; mechanisms for lobbying the government for support of pure research; awards and titles for excellence; and an ethos of dedication and selflessness. These ideals had an understandable appeal to Somerville, but she could hardly have foreseen the consequences of their widespread adoption in England. Even Babbage, who spent much of his life promoting these ideals, did not anticipate the ways in which they would marginalize the hybrid form of engineering and pure science that he practiced.

As professional, institutionally supported science began to spread, Somerville found her achievements increasingly relegated to the realm of the popular. This was a complicated and uneven process, involving changes in other sectors of the culture too. For example, the popularizing publications of Brougham's Society for the Diffusion of Useful Knowledge were only one of several trends in publishing that contributed to a separation of literary spheres into journalistic writing, on the one hand, and professional, specialized research articles on the other. (Peacock called Brougham's enterprise the "Steam Intellect Society" [*Crotchet Castle* 133–34], linking his mission of education for the masses with the newly developed steam press; later publishing developments included Cheap Editions and railway books, which differentiated audiences not only by economic class but also by taste and education.) These trends helped create the independent genre of "popular science," into which Somerville's books could be retrospectively categorized. Somerville acquiesced in this retrospective pigeonholing of her work, preferring to issue updated editions of *Connexion of the Physical Sciences* on these altered terms rather than let it go out of print. Although the book went through ten revised editions—and even appeared posthumously—the volumes from 1842 onward clearly had the status of elementary introductions rather than of original interventions in a changing scientific culture.

Many years later, as she watched the eruption of Mt. Vesuvius from her home in Naples, Mary Somerville was to remember the days when she was the First Lady of science in England. The night of the eruption in 1872 her daughter woke her so that she would not miss any of the sight. Somerville writes eloquently of the loud thunder of the roaring mountain, which she could hear despite her deafness; of the smoke and steam, rising in a pillar more than four times the height of the mountain, then spreading out at the summit horizontally across the top of the sky; of the "constant bursts of fiery projectiles, shooting to an immense height into the black column of smoke, and tinging it with a lurid red" (*Personal Recollections* 367–71). She was ninety-two at the time, only a few months from her death, but she still wrote every morning, and her fascination with the volcano reflected her lifelong passion for geology. With her daughter she traveled to Santa Lucia, immediately opposite the mountain, to be in a better position to follow the course of this great natural event. When, in the third day of the eruption, darkness fell over the streets, and people opened umbrellas to shield themselves from the rain of fine black sand, she did not share the panic that spread among many of the residents but continued at her post in the window. For, as she reports in virtually the last words of her memoir:

> Though far advanced in years, I take as lively an interest as ever in passing events. I regret that I shall not live to know the result of the expedition to determine the currents of the ocean, the distance of the earth from the sun determined by the transits of Venus, and the source of the most renowned of rivers, the discovery of which will immortalise the name of Dr. Livingstone. (373)

I end with the scene of Somerville at Vesuvius because it is connected in my mind with a novel Susan Sontag published in 1992, *The Volcano Lover.* This elegant work of historical fiction will prove fascinating to anyone who wants to experience the atmosphere of a scientific dilettante in the cultural backwater of nineteenth-century Naples. The connection with Somerville, however, is not very direct. Sontag's novel focuses on Sir William Hamilton, husband of Emma Hamilton, who became notorious as Admiral Nelson's mistress. Hamilton died in 1803, nearly forty years before Somerville moved to Naples. Yet Sontag's portrait of Hamilton's amateur scholarly research in the fields of geology, antiquities, and art, during his long tenure as British ambassador to the Kingdom of Naples, fits the image that people acquired of Somerville in the years after her retirement. Like Hamilton, her chief intercourse with the world she had left behind was through correspondence or through entertaining the occasional eminent visitor who deviated off the beaten path of the continental tour to take in her adopted city. In *Personal Recollections* Somerville describes climbing Vesuvius and walking around the crater despite the heat and danger from a recent eruption, a favorite occupation of Hamilton. In the same passage, Somerville describes smuggling a bronze statue of Minerva out of Pompeii and enshrining it in "a small but excellent collection of antiques which I still possess" (125), another biographical feature she shares with Hamilton, who was a noted collector of ancient statuary and vases. When *The Volcano Lover* describes Hamilton eagerly awaiting "the new books on ichthyology or electricity or ancient history that he had ordered from London" or communicating a paper on one of his scientific investigations to the Royal Society (23, 119), it helps me imagine what it must have been like for a powerful mind such as Somerville's to be virtually forgotten by the mainstream of scientific culture.[9] Let me underline one point, though: Mary Somerville was never an epicurean dabbler in art and science like Hamilton. Only the letters of thoughtless tourists in Naples who visited this charming old English lady who had been famous in her day could convey the impression that her scientific attainments were of that quaint, old-fashioned type.

There are other reasons to bring up Sontag's novel. One is her long-term interest in both literature and science; another is her skill in relating these interests to an earlier time period. From the beginning of her writing career, Sontag has been a model for the way an intellectual in today's world can maintain a stake in both scientific and literary culture. A bold literary theorist in the early essays collected in *Against Interpretation* (1966), she subsequently explored the cultural resonance of biomedical issues in books such as *Illness as Metaphor* (1978) and *AIDS and Its Metaphors* (1988)—all the while continuing to publish novels and short stories. In *The Volcano Lover* she juxtaposes science and artistic culture within the contours of a historical fiction. A bit like Peter Carey in *Oscar and Lucinda,* Sontag draws attention to the temporal shifts in her text, changing time periods without transition, sometimes even in the same paragraph. She creates a temporal palimpsest, layering scenes from different eras—late-eighteenth and nineteenth-century Naples, New York city in 1992, the eruption of Vesuvius in A.D. 79—one on top of another. She ends the novel with four monologues in which characters speak not only of the events they have lived through but also of things that happened long after their deaths. One character even compares herself as a nineteenth-century woman writer with "the author of this book," Susan Sontag (419).

This self-reflexive play turns the space of historical reconstruction into a fluid, allusive medium. It displays exactly the kind of literary reflexivity that can benefit cultural studies. Yet the text is responsive to the historical record, remaining true to what is known about its characters. Sontag seems to be drawn to William and Emma Hamilton for some of the same reasons that motivate my research—the promise that such odd, off-centered figures will prompt critics to think again about how the past and present intersect. It is, for me, a promise that Mary Somerville's story redeems.

On the opening page of Dickens's first novel, *The Pickwick Papers* (1836–1837), scientific organizations like the British Association for the Advancement of Science are made the butt of satire, gentle and affectionate in tone, but directed at the very same targets as Peacock's satire in *Crotchet Castle* (1831). Literary history has taught readers to separate a "Romantic" writer like Peacock from the "Victorian" Dickens, but the latter got his start in the early 1830s, before Victoria ascended the throne and while Peacock was still a personage to reckon with. Dickens published Peacock's delicate, Wordsworthian essay "Recollections of Childhood" in *Bentley's Miscellany,* which the young aspiring novelist was editing at the same time he was writing *Pickwick,* and Dickens began that novel with jabs at both the British Association and the Society for the Diffusion of Useful Knowledge. The story opens with an excerpt from the minutes of the fictional Pickwick Club, as recorded in its official "Transactions." The high point of this meeting is the communication to the Association by its General Chairman, Samuel Pickwick, of a grandiosely titled paper, "Speculations on the Source of the Hampstead Ponds, with some Observations on the Theory of Tittlebats" (*Pickwick* 67). This paper on comically trivial subjects is enthusiastically received, and the assembled members of the club forthwith vote their leader a commendation for his immense contribution "to the advancement of knowledge, and the diffusion of learning" (*Pickwick* 67). Like his then-more-famous contemporary Peacock, Dickens was attuned to the changing scientific climate; but like the man who would become his friend in the next decade, Charles Babbage, Dickens did not foresee the consequences to an undisciplined culture of the professional status and disciplinary societies that he advocated.

Both Dickens and Babbage were tireless campaigners for professional societies. Babbage was a founding member not only of the British Association but also of the Analytical Society, the Astronomical Society, the Cambridge Philosophical Society, the London Statistical Society, and more. Dickens, for his part, vigorously supported the creation of the "Guild of Literature and Art." His initial plan was for a "Provident Union of Literature, Science and Art," for which he drew up a prospectus. When this plan bore no fruit, he joined with Bulwer-Lytton to found a society that would honor writers and artists of distinction. On behalf of their proposed Guild, Dickens sponsored benefits, lent his name to petitions, and gave numerous speeches about the importance of putting the practice of letters on a professional footing. At the same time, he agitated for the reform of the Royal Literary Fund, a society that he felt was demeaning because it functioned as little more than a charitable organization for indigent writers. In Peter Ackroyd's words, Dickens's "dislike of amateurish organisation[s]" like the Literary Fund prompted him to strive "to change its charter and make it genuinely a professional organisation dedicated to the rights of authors" (Ackroyd 733,

731). Both of these causes were of a piece with Dickens's other crusades to re-form international copyright law and to establish new business models for the distribution and marketing of literature. The novelist pushed for the professionalization of the author's trade, even though he also delighted in the unruly popular culture such modern practices would supplant.

The first part of *Pickwick Papers* appeared in April 1836. By this point in the decade, attacking the annual meetings of the BAAS had become a staple of journalistic practice, somewhat like the ritual skewering of the Modern Language Association convention in *The New York Times* today. Dickens's treatment of the subject, however, differed significantly from most of the ar-ticles in the periodical press. Criticism of the Association first arose in con-servative journals. As Morrell and Thackray point out, John Henry Newman and his associates at the *Oxford University Magazine* accused the BAAS in 1834 of being "zealous missionaries intent on converting their audiences to their views" (161), views which Newman saw as inimical to High Church principles. Lockhart, editor of the Tory *Quarterly Review,* also attacked the society as undignified, and one of his reviewers objected to the absence of titled gentlemen at the Bristol meeting, a reminder that British Association scientists had been leaders in the effort to reform the aristocratic Royal So-ciety. None of these critics focused, as Dickens and Peacock did, on the link between scientific trends and the new institutions that they encouraged.

Only Cruikshank's burlesque in *The Comic Almanack* for 1835, which was a direct inspiration for Dickens, returned to Peacock's priorities, mocking "Henry Broom" and the "Society for the Confusion of Useful Knowledge," as well as other institutions that would become well-known targets of Dickens's later fiction.[10] Cruikshank's two-page parody of the Association's "Proceed-ings" not only lampooned the pretensions of individual scientists but also satirized science's role in applying "the 'do-as-little-as-possible' principle, to the state engine"; promoting the methods of the "New Poor Law Commis-sioners"; and aiding Chancery to prove "that what has a beginning does not necessarily always have an end" (*Comic Almanack* 36–37). The idea that sup-posedly "pure" research had implicit ties to state institutions and policies is an important perspective shared by Cruikshank, Peacock, and Dickens.

It is often said that Dickens had little interest in science, but this error—and it is a large one—stems from the habit of thinking of the novelist pri-marily as a mid-Victorian writer. The great scientific controversies over Darwinism in the 1860s and 1870s, which dominate cultural histories of Vic-torian science, stimulated theological and philosophical debates about de-terminism and the origin of life. Such topics bring to mind George Eliot or Hardy, not Dickens. Unfortunately, these debates have loomed so large in our imagination of Victorian science that it has been hard to perceive other forms of engagement with scientific questions.[11] Yet Dickens maintained a keen interest throughout his career in three aspects of science, a point that has been overlooked because none of his concerns figured prominently in evolutionary thinking.

First, Dickens was interested in the physical sciences, which may be taken to encompass the areas Somerville covered in her second book, particularly magnetism, theories of heat, and electricity. These interests came together in the novelist's personal experiments with mesmerism, but they surface in his fiction as early as *Pickwick,* as I shall shortly demonstrate, and continued throughout his career. Second, Dickens was equally concerned with the science of engineering and the mechanical arts, which can be seen preeminently in his fascination with the railroad but also in the attention he paid to other engineering feats, such as the Crystal Palace, London's central Post Office, and steam ships, to name only a few. As mentioned earlier, the mechanical arts had not been separated off from the pure sciences in the first half of the century, and the British Association devoted Section G of its annual meetings to the field of "Mechanical Science." Significantly, Daniel Doyce, the mechanical genius of *Little Dorrit* (1855–1857), seems to have been modeled on Babbage himself.[12] Third, Dickens was concerned about the changing institutional settings of science, a topic he heard about directly at dinner parties and other gatherings, where veterans of the science wars of the 1830s held forth about the continuing need to professionalize their fields. Like Babbage, Dickens did not perceive the contradiction between his advocacy of professionalism and his disdain for the state policies it fostered, particularly in the area of education. Nor did the novelist anticipate the effects of professionalism on the kind of showmanship and theatrical stunts in which both he and Babbage reveled.

All three of these interests inform Dickens's Mudfog papers, occasional pieces satirizing the BAAS, which the novelist published in *Bentley's Miscellany.* Dickens's "Full Report of the First Meeting of the Mudfog Association for the Advancement of Everything" appeared in October 1837, while *Pickwick* was still running in monthly parts. Such favorite Dickensian topics as mesmerism and the mechanical arts are on display, but the novelist's attention to the new institutional arrangements for science is what sets this substantial piece and its successor, published the following year, apart from other newspaper squibs attacking the British Association. Few scholars have paid much attention to the Mudfog papers. Those who have mainly concentrate on the raillery at the expense of individual scientists: the novelist gives them names like Professor Snore, Doze, and Wheezy and mocks their pomposity and love of gormandizing.[13] The most important feature of these papers, however, is their extensive imitation of the organization and procedures of the scientific society itself, something that can be found in no other satire of the Association. Dickens's focus on these new disciplinary structures is underscored by his repeated references to the incorporation of science into state bureaucracies, as well as into the organization of private charitable and educational institutions.

The fictional Mudfog Association is divided into sections devoted to the distinct scientific specialities, just as was the British Association.[14] In Dickens's parody, Section A reports on developments in "Zoology and Botany."

The section is largely devoted to a paper deploring the "moral and social conditions" of a London flea circus and advocating the creation of "infant schools and houses of industry" for these potentially useful creatures. By applying "sound principles" to the education of fleas, the "productive power of the country" could be immeasurably increased (521). The opposition between a circus and productive industry, of course, looks forward to Dickens's treatment of these same themes in *Hard Times* (1854), as does the zoologist's proposal to regulate this "species of theatrical entertainment" with an eye to placing it "under the control and regulation of the state" (521–22). The foreshadowing is even clearer in Section C, "Statistics." There one of the papers offers statistical proof of the "lamentable" taste among grammar school children for nursery rhymes, fairy tales, and novels, and the scientist prescribes the remedy of "storing the minds of children with nothing but facts and figures" (527).

One might wonder what attacks on political economy and utilitarian educational policies are doing in a satire on the British Association. Unlike today, however, such areas of inquiry enjoyed the status of "hard" sciences. For Dickens, as for the majority of his contemporaries, natural philosophy was understood to encompass them both. The modern division between the social and the natural sciences was yet another boundary that had not been firmly established. That is why Peacock, too, saw political economy as a big part of what was wrong with the trend toward modern scientific professionalism. Peacock's utilitarian character Mr. MacQuedy calls political economy "the science of sciences," and even his rival savants, who predictably dispute his claim to preeminence, do not find it strange to think of his field as equivalent to their own specialties of chemistry, geography, and medicine. His conservative opponent the Reverend Folliott makes the same assumption when he blames Henry Brougham's utilitarian Society for teaching chemistry to rick burners and the "scientific principles" of housebreaking to common thieves (*Crotchet Castle* 138, 243). In Dickens's Mudfog Association, political economy is as much at home in the section on "Zoology and Botany" as in that devoted to "Statistics," and all are granted equal status as sciences along with "Anatomy and Medicine" and "Mechanical Science."

Readers must adjust their expectations in still another way to understand Dickens's comic handling of science. Dickens's attitude toward the British Association, as well as his treatment of Mr. Pickwick's scientific interests, should be put in the context of his delight in popular entertainment. Dickens loved a good show, and the squabbling of learned men, the experimental displays, the crowds of spectators jockeying for seats, the lavish dinners, the expeditions to inspect bridges, tunnels, and other engineering projects, and the pageantry of the closing ceremony all made for good theater. Dickens's satire is affectionate, and his pleasure in mocking the scientific society is exceeded only by his gratitude for its putting so much buffoonery on display. He did not pause to straighten out how all his positions fit together. He liked professionalism *and* theatrics. He approved of the increasing disciplinary stratification of culture *and* wanted to be part of a society in which everyone was connected to everyone else by bonds of understanding and good will. He was fascinated by technological progress *and* angered by the social dislocation caused by the very engineering projects he praised. He disdained the institutional bureaucracies that applied "scientific principles" to the education of children and the care for the poor, *and* he gave speeches advocating government support of almost any new provincial institution, trade group, or author's society that asked for his help. The point is not Dickens's inconsistency: he was scarcely alone on this score. The point is how he—like Somerville, Babbage, and many others—responded to the conflicting attractions both of an older, undisciplined scientific culture, which provided a robust atmosphere of freedom and iconoclasm, and of the emerging modern disciplines, which provided mechanisms for the support of intellectual and creative inquiry.

In "The Spirit of the Age" (1831), John Stuart Mill famously proclaimed his time "an age of transition" (6). Science was only one of the things in flux. Another was the nature of popular entertainment. The example of Dickens reveals that the changes in popular entertainment were connected to the transformations occurring in other cultural arenas, such as science. According to Paul Schlicke, the 1830s saw a transition between older participatory forms of entertainment and modern, commercialized spectacles:

> The old rural pastimes of the people, which had been benignly tolerated by the gentry as integral to a social stability based on traditional lifestyles, were increasingly eroded, and by the 1830s very little had emerged to take their place. The great urban fairs, having long since lost their commercial function, were susceptible to determined efforts to suppress them, and the greatest of them, Bartholomew Fair, was effectively put down by civic fiat in 1840. . . . Most modern historians are convinced that the nadir of English popular culture was reached during the 1830s, the very time Dickens began writing about it. . . . In the long term, there was a decisive shift away from gregarious, participatory activities towards large-scale spectator entertainments such as music-hall and professional sport. (Schlicke 4–5)[15]

Both modes of entertainment were present in the annual meetings of the British Association. Gregarious, participatory exhibitions vied for the attention of conventioneers with carefully planned modern spectacles. The 1836 meeting at Bristol strikingly illustrates the conflict between these kinds of public events. The two most remarked-upon occurrences that year were William Buckland's ludicrous imitation of prehistoric birds, during one of the geology sessions, and the formal ceremony, witnessed by 10,000 spectators, to lay the foundation stone for I. K. Brunel's suspension bridge over the Avon gorge at Clifton. Each performance was engrossing in its own way.

The Literary Gazette describes the former like this: "Dr. Buckland then delivered an amusing lecture on fossil remains of animals in England; described birds much bigger than mammoths, that had left their foot-marks on the sands thousands of years ago; and by gesticulating the march of the cocks and hens of that remote era, caused much laughter among the spectators" ("British Association" 568). Buckland was known for such undignified stunts. He would do almost anything to dramatize the power of science or to debunk superstition. Stephen Jay Gould remarks that "Few scientists are so full of fun and color that their anecdotes outlive their ideas," then proceeds to tell the story of how Buckland proved that supposed "martyr's blood" in a cathedral was actually bat urine by "kneeling down and having a lick" (99). In his Bridgewater Treatise, one of eight scientific defenses of God commissioned by William Whewell, Buckland revealed the majesty of the divine plan by describing the ichthyosaurus's excretory functions. For years Buckland's son believed that his father's description of the ichthyosaurus's intestinal tract and his habit of imitating paleolithic creatures on stage had provoked a famous cartoon by Henry De la Beche, depicting a future Professor Ichthyosaurus lecturing on the extinction of humanity (Figure 3.1). Although historians of science have now established that Lyell, not Buckland, was the subject of the satire, one understands how the confusion could

FIGURE 3.1
Professor Ichthyosaurus.
Francis T. Buckland, *Curiosities of Natural History* (New York: Rudd and Carleton, 1859).

have arisen: the mixture of high spirits and real learning was the hallmark of Buckland's considerable scientific prestige (Rudwick; Gould 99–104).

The groundbreaking ceremony for Brunel's bridge, three days after Buckland's performance, was a much more elaborate affair. The staging of this event involved transportation arrangements for numerous dignitaries, hot air balloons and music to entertain the common spectators, speech making, and an elegant breakfast for 300 afterward. The newspapers all remarked on the exceptional pageantry, a far more calculated spectacle than the highjinks of Dr. Buckland. Morrell and Thackray phrase the contrast succinctly: "In Buckland's hands knowledge was buffoonery; in Brunel's it was domination" (159). Although Morrell and Thackray slight the cultural value of Buckland's showmanship, they analyze astutely the way in which the BAAS increasingly mobilized the power of the modern spectacle to promote its own professional ends:

> In subsequent years, technological spectacles were provided routinely. Accompanied by a band, cannons, flags, and the shouts of thousands, the Association's savants celebrated the opening in August 1838 of the Durham Junction Railway with its Victoria Bridge, of which one arch was the largest in Europe. . . . In 1841 at Plymouth, the battleship Hindostan was lifted by wedges before being launched "amidst the cheers of assembled thousands" who tacitly understood the combined appeals of science, invention, patriotism, imperialism, and maritime domination. Technological spectacle carried a message about the power, the majesty, and the progressiveness of science. (160)

Let me clarify the distinction I am drawing. The spectacles described above became part of the modern organization of the social sphere that culminated in what Guy Debord calls the "society of the spectacle." In Debord's use of the term, *spectacles* are an integral part of the modern bureaucratic nation state. Both governmental and commercial spectacles buttress the administrative organization of society. Located in a range of modern institutions, both official and commercial—from museums, international exhibitions, commemorations, and state-sanctioned holidays to mass media, the entertainment industry, professional sports, advertising, and marketing— modern spectacles are characterized by a vertical integration and coordination in the visual realm. They are a piece in the growing dominance (but not complete mastery) of the scopic regime of modernity, discussed in the prior chapter. Shows, on the other hand, more closely resemble the kind of "gregarious, participatory activities" Schlicke located in the fairs and rural markets that had largely disappeared in England by the1840s.

I borrow the word "shows" from Richard D. Altick's wonderful *The Shows of London,* in which he chronicles this same vanishing popular culture in an urban setting. Altick's study traces the decline of these urban shows, during the first half of the nineteenth century, and their gradual replacement by more formal institutions such as the museum. One of the final episodes in his history is the Great Exhibition of 1851, with which this book began. Although there were countercurrents to the modern spectacle throughout the century—including other influences at the Great Exhibition itself—the Crystal Palace is now generally seen as a key point of origin for Debord's "spectacle society." In the early decades of the century, by contrast, there existed a vibrant underworld of popular exhibits, assembly rooms, cabinets of curiosities, circus acts, and menageries. Scientific displays and lectures took their place in this netherworld alongside art and sculpture, theatrical performances, natural wonders from distant lands, and outright tricks and cons. The Royal Institution had its beginnings in the lecturing culture that thrived in this area, talks delivered for money by both savants and charlatans. Wheatstone exhibited his Enchanted Lyre in one of these Albemarle rooms, and it took in a respectable gate. Scientific apparatus, such as Wheatstone's lyre, kaleidophone, and stereoscope, were called without any condescension "philosophic toys," a term that captured the spirit of the earlier show culture. Babbage adored visiting Spring Gardens and Astley's as a boy, where philosophic toys competed for attention with clockwork automata and magic shows, and he attributed his fondness for science to the displays of his youth. Even as an adult, Babbage could be found browsing with fascination through the disappearing remnants of such displays.

The tension between these two cultures shaped the early years of the BAAS. Note that Buckland, the same man who worried that the admission of ladies to the formal sessions of the society would turn it into an "Albemarle dilettanti meeting," was the savant who strutted like prehistoric cocks and hens in his geology lecture. Babbage, too, preferred the unruly side of the British Association to its staged mass spectacles. He was the first to suggest having an "exhibition of manufactures at each meeting" (qtd. in Morrell and Thackray 79), and he always enjoyed the exhibits of philosophical toys. Yet during these same years formal scientific demonstrations, staged in university lecture halls and the Royal Institution, were displacing rudimentary showmanship. The newer form of experimental demonstration, whose procedures were codified in exactly this period, were disciplinary spectacles rather than "marvel" shows. The new demonstrations drew crowds to the lectures of Humphry Davy and Michael Faraday and, in the process, aided in consolidating the authority of professional science.[16] The disciplining of formerly unruly shows was crucial to establishing scientific knowledge as neutral, objective, and reproducible—and as the purview of the trained, professional scientist.

Dickens's beloved savant, Samuel Pickwick, is anything but a trained professional. His "discoveries," however, are forced to make their way in an emerging disciplinary culture. Like William Hamilton, the amateur of science who figures prominently in Sontag's *The Volcano Lover*, Mr. Pickwick's scientific interests extend widely—from geography and zoology (viz., the mighty Hampstead Ponds and the tiny tittlebat) to archeology and philology, which are the fields at stake in the fourth monthly part of *The Pickwick Papers,* issued just before the British Association opened in Bristol for the meeting discussed above.

In Part IV of *Pickwick* Dickens recounts his hero's discovery of what he believes to be an ancient stone bearing a curious inscription. Antiquarian investigations, let me repeat, were compassed within the circle of sciences not separated off as classics or philology. Mary Somerville, for example, saw philology as related to the physical sciences. In her *Connexion of the Physical Sciences* she went out of her way to show that astronomy could aid in the interpretation of hieroglyphics (105–6), and she was present when her friend Thomas Young, famous for his interpretations of the Rosetta Stone, determined the date of a papyrus from the configurations of the heavens in an Egyptian horoscope (*Personal Recollections* 131). Dickens probably had the Rosetta Stone in mind when he narrates Mr. Pickwick's comic efforts to interpret the following inscription:

+

BILST

UM

PSHI

S.M.

ARK

After enormous study Mr. Pickwick composes a pamphlet "containing ninety-six pages of very small print, and twenty-seven different readings of the inscription" (227–28). For this labor of ingenuity, the great man is elected an honorary member of seventeen scholarly societies, both in England and abroad. But his triumph is short-lived. A member of his own Pickwick Club has the presumption to doubt this antiquarian discovery and actually goes to the village where the stone was found to interview the man who formerly owned it. As a result of these investigations, the traitorous Pickwickian writes a pamphlet declaring the inscription to be the handiwork of a nearly illiterate, but still living villager and the message to read: "BILL STUMPS, HIS MARK" (228). The response to this revelation is overwhelming:

> Hereupon the virtuous indignation of the seventeen learned societies, native and foreign, being roused, several fresh pamphlets appeared; the foreign learned societies corresponded with the native learned societies; the native learned societies translated the pamphlets of the foreign learned societies into English; the foreign learned societies translated the pamphlets of the native learned societies into all sorts of languages; and thus commenced that celebrated scientific discussion so well known to all men, as the Pickwick controversy. (228–29).

As a scientist, Mr. Pickwick straddles two eras, and (poor man) he is mocked for his participation in each. The Pickwick controversy not only pokes fun at the absurdities sometimes produced by the older, amateur forms of erudition but also parodies the more recent explosion in the number of scientific societies. Between 1810 and 1840, the number of scientific associations grew fourfold.[17] The consequences of this growth were to affect many aspects of modern science, not least the role that learning would play in Britain's imperial enterprise, something Dickens rarely loses sight of when he writes about science.

Disciplinary societies and the circulation of knowledge to remote parts of the "civilised globe" (647) play a part in the final bogus discovery portrayed in the novel. Chapter 39 tells the story of a "scientific gentleman," who was interrupted in his composition of a philosophical treatise by a brilliant light gliding through the air outside his window. The actual origin of this wondrous phenomenon lies in Mr. Pickwick's use of a dark lantern to assist one of his fellow club-members in a romantic escapade. But the scientific gentleman is convinced he has stumbled upon a new electrical phenomenon that will immortalize his name. The diligent researcher ventures outdoors to determine, by empirical observation, the exact composition of these marvelous flashes, whereupon he is knocked on the head by Mr. Pickwick's servant, Sam Weller. Undeterred in the cause of science, the gentleman makes his name by demonstrating,

> in a masterly treatise, that these wonderful lights were the effect of electricity; and clearly proved the same by detailing how a flash of fire danced before his eyes when he put his head out of the gate, and how he received a shock which stunned him for a quarter of an hour afterwards; which demonstration delighted all the Scientific Associations beyond measure, and caused him to be considered a light of science ever afterwards. (649)

In all his representations of science Dickens satirized rather than celebrated the behavior of savants. His sense of the ludicrous, however, responded to something genuinely awkward about their changing cultural position. The comedy identified real areas of concern that were implicated in some of the largest social problems of the day. When the novelist returned to these same interests in later works, the transition to a modern disciplinary culture was more advanced and the ties to state institutions more visible. Thus the critique of political economy's influence on education and the treatment of the poor is more unremitting in "The Chimes" (1844) and *Hard Times.* Equally, Dickens's most sustained treatment of a mechanical engineer, Daniel Doyce in *Little Dorrit,* is dedicated to showing how a government agency, the Circumlocution Office, frustrates every effort of an enterprising scientist to serve the common good.

In Dickens's speeches, weekly journals, and other novels, he frequently attended to questions of science, invariably with the same consciousness of the institutional ramifications of new technology. If Dickens had a strong investment in finding a scientific basis for spontaneous combustion and was curious about the fossil evidence for the Megalosaurus that stalks the open-ing paragraph of *Bleak House* (1853), he coupled such concerns with a larger vision of the judicial and health care systems that he believed were crushing England's poor. He may have named a character in "The Haunted House" (1859) after John Herschel, "the great astronomer: than whom I suppose a better man at a telescope does not breathe" (273), but he also used the same instrument as a symbol of what is wrong with institutionalized "telescopic philanthropy." The grave robber who procures corpses for illicit sale to anatomy classes in *A Tale of Two Cities* (1859) makes his living off the older scientific culture that existed during the French Revolution, when the novel was set. By contrast, *Nicholas Nickleby* (1839) makes reference to the newer, state-sanctioned anatomy schools, which under the Anatomy Act of 1832 could legally dissect the corpses of executed criminals. Many other examples might be adduced. A full study of Dickens and nineteenth-century science would be worth undertaking someday. For now, suffice it to say that Dickens bore witness to a shift in the place of science in the modern world, a shift that created a division between the two cultures that may only now be closing.

The next chapter continues exploring the undisciplined world of Dick-ens and Babbage, beginning with Babbage's fascination with a mechanical automaton and looking at his invention of the Difference Engine, the first digital computer. The focus shifts, however, to emphasize the historical problem of anachronism. What does it mean that people in the 1840s shared preoccupations that are widespread today, preoccupations with computer technology, artificial intelligence, and the boundary between human and machine? Contemporary novelists, playwrights, and literary theorists have attempted to come to terms with such surprising affinities, turning to the genres of alternative history and time travel, and proposing that the concept of anachronism itself is an important but neglected form of historical expe-rience. Hence the next chapter will look closely at two highly praised con-temporary texts, William Gibson and Bruce Sterling's novel *The Difference Engine* and Tom Stoppard's play *Arcadia*.

Four

Babbage and Lovelace in *The Difference Engine* and *Arcadia*

Midway through William Gibson and Bruce Sterling's *The Difference Engine* (1991), a historical science fiction set in nineteenth-century England, an automaton startles the protagonist Edward Mallory by whirring to life in the parlor of a foreign-service operative. The figure is a carved Japanese doll, fashioned entirely of bamboo, horsehair, and whalebone. It is lifelike enough to be mistaken for a kneeling lady, although stereotypes of the submissive Asian woman contribute to the deception. The urbane secret agent appears at ease with such marvels, so Mallory, who is jealous of his reputation as a scientist, recovers his composure with a show of expertise: he places the automaton in the context of other mechanical figures, comparing it to "one of those Jacquot-Droz toys, or Vaucanson's famous duck" and observing that it moves with the precision of a "Maudsley lathe" (168).[1] The habit of associating windup figures and clockwork dolls with the latest precision engineering from the workshops of Henry Maudslay, who got his start with Marc Brunel in Samuel Bentham's dockyards, is an accurate reflection of early-nineteenth-century scientific culture. The automata of Jacquet-Droz and Vaucanson were only the most famous predecessors of countless mechanical toys that were displayed side by side with inventions such as Maudslay's lathe, Brunel's block-making machinery, Wheatstone and David Brewster's stereoscopes, Faraday's electromagnetic apparatus, and Babbage's calculating machine, the Difference Engine.[2]

Most of these scientific men were themselves fascinated by automata. Wheatstone, as I observed in chapter 2, wrote a paper on machines for generating artificial speech, which begins with the history of automata and discusses the notorious hoax of Wolfgang von Kempelen, whose "mechanical" chess player concealed a midget in its base (Wheatstone, "Review" 351). Babbage delighted in inviting guests to see his own automaton, a twelve-inch figurine he named the Silver Lady, which "attitudinized in a most fascinating manner" (Babbage, *Passages* 12). Brunel, Brewster, Wheatstone, and Faraday—as well as Ada Lovelace and Charles Dickens—all attended evenings at Babbage's house in which the Silver Lady was the featured entertainment and traps were sometimes laid for the unwary.

Games and tricks played a more prominent role in early nineteenth-century science than many realize. Lifelike mechanical figures were on the playful end of a continuum of scientific stunts and shows that ranged from harmless tricks like Wheatstone's "Enchanted Lyre" to more disreputable schemes and criminal deceptions. The illicit end of the continuum was visible in 1836, when two bankers from Paris were caught manipulating the semaphore telegraph in order to send advanced information about shifts in the stock market to a confederate in Bordeaux (Holzmann and Pehrson 75–76). The bankers introduced a secret code of their own into the optical signals of the telegraph by means of a preplanned pattern of errors. Like hackers today, the people who defrauded nineteenth-century communications systems made advances in cryptography and informatics that were often incorporated in the next generation of technology.

The bankers' manipulation of the semaphore telegraph is an early instance of what is today called "hacking," the diversion of communications resources for sport or profit. Hacking, however, has many connotations, some extending well beyond the communications world to include "any scam or clever manipulation," any bravura display of technological expertise.[3] The contemporary practice of hacking has generated its own subculture, full of flamboyant personalities, trickery, rivalries, and factions. With this cultural parallel in mind, it is easy to see many nineteenth-century technological marvels as imbued with the spirit of hacking, particularly those that involve computers, artificial intelligence, or communications. The mechanical devices of the previous century troubled the human/machine interface, just as do today's electronic devices. The greater the potential for unsettling this boundary, as in automata displays, the more open the field for "hackers," broadly conceived. Gibson and Sterling's *The Difference Engine* provides a clue: this novel not only hacks into nineteenth-century history but also extrapolates from that era's fondness for scientific tricks of all kinds. In an undisciplined culture, which did not make a rigorous distinction between showmanship and science, rogue pleasures played a role in the advancement of knowledge.

Babbage's automaton was one such rogue pleasure. As a child, Babbage had been fascinated by an exhibition of machinery in Hanover Square.

When the exhibitor entices the young boy up to the attic to view "still more wonderful automata" (Babbage, *Passages* 12), the scene takes on a hint of illicit eroticism, which frequently seems to creep into accounts of mechanical figures, from E. T. A. Hoffmann's "The Automaton" (1814) and "The Sandman" (1815) to Ray Bradbury's *Something Wicked This Way Comes* (1962) and Thomas Pynchon's *Mason & Dixon* (1997). In the attic the boy sees two naked "female figures of silver," whose "eyes were full of imagination, and irresistible" (*Passages* 12). In Babbage's hands the boyhood story swerves away from any hint of corruption and becomes a portent of his future scientific curiosity. But years later, in 1834, he chances upon the attitudinizing lady at an auction, and the excitement returns. He purchases the figure, repairs all the mechanism with his own hands, and recruits female friends to design clothing and coiffure. The whiff of eroticism returns too, now blended with Orientalist attractions: Babbage dresses the Silver Lady in a turban, pink satin slippers with silver spangles, and a tightly wound robe of Chinese crepe. This exotic outfit provokes animated discussion among his friends and leads Babbage to make a sexual double entendre at the expense of a lady who thinks the figure too slightly clad (*Passages* 273–74).

In a final scene involving his automaton, Babbage contrasts a gay circle of English friends delighting over the graceful movements of the Silver Lady with two serious foreigners, studying the operation of the Difference Engine, which was on display in an adjacent room of his house. Babbage takes a grim satisfaction in this contrast as a parable of how the English neglect his great invention while foreigners appreciate its significance. Willy-nilly, the two mechanisms have become a test for unwary visitors, another common side effect of automaton exhibitions. The result, on this memorable evening, is an ironic inversion that partakes of what Freud called the *unheimlich,* the uncanny sensation aroused when something foreign or strange changes places with something familiar and domestic. The irony lies in the fact that only foreigners recognize the importance of what is supposed to be the special province of the English—science, engineering, steam-driven machines—while "three or four of [Babbage's] most intimate friends," in the drawing room of his home, are captivated by pleasures that are not only exotically Orientalist but vaguely sexual to boot (*Passages* 319–20).

Dickens may have been thinking specifically of his friend Babbage when he satirized a scientific proposal for constructing "automaton figures" (544) in the "Full Report of the Second Meeting of the Mudfog Association For the Advancement of Everything." As I noted in the prior chapter, Dickens's reports on the "Mudfog Association" are parodies of the scientific society Babbage was instrumental in founding, the British Association for the Advancement of Science. The proposal for constructing automata occurs in a section of the report titled "Display of Models and Mechanical Science," one of Babbage's areas of greatest expertise. Dickens irreverently suggests using the mechanical figures to establish an "automaton police" (545) for the convenience of carousing young noblemen who liked to knock the block off of the occasional constable. Dickens seems to find something grotesque in the very idea of automata. His satire dwells on the perverse fascination of the prosthetic, nicely rendered in George Cruikshank's illustration "Automaton Police Office," which emphasizes detachable limbs and heads (Figure 4.1). His satire also establishes a link between the mania for mechanical science and the concurrent effort to reorganize the production of knowledge along "scientific" lines. Both are artificial aids, prosthetic devices, that transform the human world in valuable, if sometimes coercive, ways. No surprise, then, that the first use Dickens imagines for such automata is the establishment of new forms of police.

The trick involving the Japanese doll in Gibson and Sterling's *The Difference Engine* captures the spirit of both Babbage's evening gatherings and Dickens's "automaton police." There is no reason to think that the novelists are alluding specifically to either source, but Mallory's encounter with Japanese ingenuity fuses the contrasting attitudes found in Babbage and Dickens. The sexual undercurrent, the sense of uncanniness, the Orientalism—explicit in Mallory's patronizing talk of English engineering and empire—even the link with new forms of police, pick up on motifs prominent in the two nineteenth-century accounts. The novel uses Japan rather than

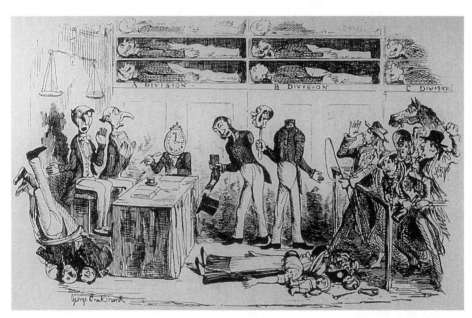

FIGURE 4.1
George Cruikshank, "Automaton
Police Office and the Real Offenders."
Bentley's Miscellany 4 (September
1838): 227.

China as an emblem of the Oriental Other, an updating in line with the geopolitical priorities of the 1990s, but Japan did figure in Victorian culture, and playful anachronisms such as a reference to the post-World War II Japanese economic miracle seem appropriate to the novel's blend of social commentary and alternative history. One of the merits of *The Difference Engine* is that it tends to evoke such paradigmatic nineteenth-century scenes with skill.

Gibson and Sterling's exuberant hacking of nineteenth-century science finds a precedent in the era's own willingness to mix science and entertainment. Their novel reflects the spirit of an age when the boundary between science and the rest of culture was not so firmly established. The novel, however, stops short of unsettling its own boundaries. In the decision to conform to the conventions of a science-fiction thriller, the authors limit the implications of their "hack." The novel ends up affirming the alliance between technology and traditional Victorian assumptions about women, empire, and the police that its irreverence about other historical pieties would seem to reject. The ideological confusion of the novel can be brought out by comparisons with two other texts: an important nineteenth-century precursor, Benjamin Disraeli's *Sybil* (1845), and a play by Tom Stoppard that invokes many of the same nineteenth-century scientific ideas. Stoppard's *Arcadia* (1993), a thoroughly self-reflexive production, extends the hacking spirit to its own dramatic conventions. The result is a text that performs tricks with contemporary as well as nineteenth-century assumptions about gender, science, and literature.

What is the relationship between contemporary hacking and nineteenth-century scientific pranks? Do today's rogue intellectual pleasures spring from the same impulses that motivated the transgressive shows in Babbage's drawing room? If so, then perhaps the unsavory aspects of nineteenth-century hacking should give pause to those who rely on transgression itself to produce alternative forms of knowledge. On the other hand, perhaps hacking with history, of the sort a historical cultural studies needs, can find its rationale in a history that often produced knowledge through hacking. This notion would suggest a justification beyond those usually offered by postmodern theorists—the loss of faith in scientific norms of objectivity, for example, or a belief in the inherent fictiveness of all writing—for considering self-reflexive and literary approaches to the past as legitimate modes of knowledge.

Gibson and Sterling's *The Difference Engine* starts with an intriguing idea: it rewrites Benjamin Disraeli's *Sybil,* an industrial novel about the reconciliation of the classes, as a historical fantasy that traces the roots of today's information society back to Victorian England. The authors, best known as the originators of cyberpunk fiction, take Babbage's invention of a computing machine in 1822 as warrant for imagining the advent of the computer age more than a century before its time. Their novel presents the Victorian era as a full-blown information order, complete with massive databases on citizens, surveillance apparatus, photo IDs, credit cards, rapid international data transmission via telegraph, and scientific societies that serve as unofficial intelligence arms of the military. Idiosyncratic as their historical conceit sounds, it participates in a thriving subgenre of science fiction known as "steampunk," which includes Rudy Rucker's *The Hollow Earth* (1992), Neal Stephenson's *The Diamond Age* (1995), and George Foy's *The Shift* (1996).[4]

Gibson and Sterling's novel is fun—at least in places. It is amusing to read of John Keats, consumptive former medical student, as a pioneer of the silent cinema; of the Reverend Wordsworth and Professor Coleridge, leaders of a successful Pantisocratic community in America; of Lord Engels, the Manchester textile magnate; of Lord Byron, Prime Minister of England, and of his daughter, Lady Ada Byron, queen of a loose confederacy of hackers called "clackers," because of the sound made by the mechanical parts in their steam-driven computers. The variations on Disraeli's novel are clever as well. Sybil Gerard, the idealistic daughter of a Chartist agitator, does not marry her aristocratic suitor Charles Egremont but is seduced and abandoned by that ambitious politician; she becomes the lover of a minor character from Disraeli's novel, Mick Radley, who here is involved in international espionage and computer software theft. Events in Disraeli's novel, both large and small, are effectively transmogrified for the contemporary plot. The riot at Mowbray Castle in *Sybil,* for example, becomes a vast Luddite uprising in London in the later novel, and offhand references to horse racing in the first two chapters of Disraeli inspire a key episode at the races, this time of steam-powered gurneys. The latter incident provides Gibson and Sterling with a vivid way of introducing Ada Byron's gambling and laudanum habits, which are based on historical sources.

The scientific developments in *The Difference Engine* are not so far-fetched as they might seem, either. All of the information technologies portrayed by Gibson and Sterling existed in some form or other during the reign of Queen Victoria. Babbage is credited by most historians of technology as having been the first person to conceive of a computer. In 1821, frustrated by the multitude of errors in standard mathematical tables of astronomical positions and tidal charts, which were laboriously calculated by hand, he exclaimed, "I wish to God these calculations had been executed by steam!" One year later, he had not only drawn detailed plans for a mechanical calculator, which he named the Difference Engine, but also constructed and exhibited a working model for a London show. The Royal Society awarded Babbage a gold medal for his efforts, and he embarked on a many-year project to build a full-scale version of his machine. The finished engine would have contained approximately 25,000 moving parts, manufactured to such precision that the first task was inventing entirely new machine tools and lathes, a task undertaken by Joseph Clement, who had been trained in the workshop of Henry Maudslay. The project was supported by the Duke of Wellington and received generous but irregular funding from the government—perhaps qualifying as the first government research-and-development program—but it was plagued by numerous delays, including Babbage's commitment to other scientific endeavors and a protracted dispute between Babbage and Clement.[5] The technical difficulties of the Engine were not insurmountable: for the bicentenary of Babbage's birth, engineers at the Science Museum in London successfully built a fully operational Difference Engine, using only tools and materials that were available in the 1830s.[6] By the time Babbage's project was abandoned in 1842, more than £17,000 of government funds and £20,000 of his own money had been expended. By contrast, the first steam locomotive was built in 1831 for less than £800. Babbage viewed the failure to complete the Difference Engine as the central tragedy of his life.

This failure did not prevent Babbage from designing an even more ambitious machine, the Analytical Engine, which is the true ancestor of today's computer. "If the Analytical Engine had been built," writes J. David Bolter, "it would indeed have been the first computer" (33). All the essential components of a digital computer were present in the 1833 design: punch cards for input of data, internal memory storage, a central processing unit (called, in Babbage's industrial-age vocabulary, the "mill"), and printed output. This second design is the one actually featured in Gibson and Sterling's novel, although they use the name of his earlier, more famous invention.

In the few years since its publication, *The Difference Engine* has garnered some remarkable praise from sources as diverse as Ridley Scott, director of *Blade Runner,* Stewart Brand, creator of *The Whole Earth Catalog,* and scholars writing in *Contemporary Literature, ANQ,* and *Victorian Studies.* In this last journal, Herbert Sussman nicely illuminates the way in which the novel rewrites Disraeli's *Sybil* but strangely reads the book as an optimistic celebration of the coming of the personal computer, whose decentralizing impulse has the potential to disrupt the emerging panoptic regime of modernity. This reading misses the way in which visual technologies of surveillance dominate the imagery, structure, and resolution of the narrative. For Brian McHale, *The Difference Engine*'s value lies in its postmodernism: like other contemporary metafictions, it represents "a new way of writing historical fiction or, better, a *new way of 'doing' history in fiction*" (222, italics in original).

The effusive praise and serious critical attention that the novel has received largely gloss over the book's pervasive misogyny and its long middle section that glorifies the violent exploits of Mallory in what amounts to a conventional science fiction shoot-'em-up.[7] The story follows the violent plot form of the technothriller, a genre that relegates women to sexual appendages of the hero or to threatened objects of technological stalkers and government conspiracies. The women in *The Difference Engine* play one or both roles but do little else. Mallory recalls with a shudder "rutting" with a "rank" Cheyenne woman on his geological expedition to America (197); his encounter with a London prostitute emphasizes the "exquisite thrill of disgust" (237) and is full of demeaning references to the smells of her sweat, urine, and "cunt" (223). Elsewhere, the thought of contraceptive devices for women—nineteenth-century versions of the diaphragm and sponge— "made his gut lurch" because "Mallory could not avoid the dark imagining of coitus involving these queer objects" (303).

Sybil Gerard and Ada Byron, the only women with more extensive parts in the plot, occupy the other conventional role, that of threatened objects of stalkers and conspiracies. As in popular cinematic technothrillers such as *Terminator* 2 (1991) and *The Net* (1995), Sybil's resourcefulness aids in her escape from the clutches of her pursuers; even so, her wheelchair-bound form is still under aerial surveillance, some fifty years later, by the cameras of the "trans-Channel airship *Lord Brunel*" (1). Ada Byron, despite her computer genius, depends on men throughout to rescue her from her excesses. Moreover, neither character escapes persistent sexual slurs: Sybil is a "fallen" woman and a "politician's tart" (228), while Ada Byron is characterized as "the greatest whore in all of London. . . . She fucks whoever she pleases, and none dare make a peep about what she does. She's had half the House of Lords, and they all tag at her skirts like little boys" (232). This revelation prompts another shudder of repulsion from Mallory: "He knew that Lady Ada had her gallants, but the thought that she let men have her, that there was shoving and spending, prick and cunt in the mathematical bed of the Queen of Engines. . . . Best not to think about it" (233, ellipsis in original).

These episodes might be read as critiques of upper-class Victorian attitudes toward sex were they not also reminiscent of the treatment of women's sexuality in Gibson's *Neuromancer* (1984) and its cyberpunk sequels.[8] The historical record suggests that Ada Lovelace had several lovers, but the insistence on misogynistic imagery in relation to woman after woman seems excessive, a quality of the narrative voice more than an effort to characterize Mallory. When sex is the subject, *The Difference Engine* loses all its knowing irony in relation to the prior century. Instead, it adopts uncritically some of the worst aspects of the futuristic action thriller. The congruence between this predominantly male genre and Victorian patriarchal attitudes reveals that, in regard to sexuality at least, this novel perpetuates rather than interrogates nineteenth-century stereotypes.

The more serious claim for the importance of *The Difference Engine* lies in its postmodern approach to history. Critics have rushed to assimilate this novel's ironic rewriting of the nineteenth century, often invoking the postmodern genre that Linda Hutcheon labels "historiographic metafiction."[9] Gibson and Sterling's fictional transformation of the past accords well with postmodern arguments about the constructed nature of all historical knowledge. For example, McHale's assertion that the novel represents a "new way of 'doing' history" implies the postmodern corollary that history itself is a form of fiction.

When assessing this novel's relation to history, however, its affinities with a second, indigenous strain of science fiction should not be overlooked.

This popular tradition is sometimes called "alternative history" or "parallel worlds," and its most celebrated exemplar is Philip K. Dick's *The Man in the High Castle* (winner of the Hugo Award for 1962), which imagines what the United States would have been like had Germany and Japan won World War II. (Dick would later write *Do Androids Dream of Electric Sheep?* [1968], the novel on which *Blade Runner* was based.) The tradition stretches further back, however, particularly when combined with the paradoxes of time travel.[10] Perhaps the most influential of such tales is Murray Leinster's "Sidewise in Time" (1934), but other notable examples include Robert A. Heinlein's "By His Bootstraps" (1941) and "All You Zombies—" (1959), Ray Bradbury's "A Sound of Thunder" (1952), Ward Moore's *Bring the Jubilee* (1953), in which the South won the Civil War, Fritz Leiber's Cold War parable *The Big Time* (Hugo Award, 1958), Keith Laumer's *The Other Side of Time* (1965), Larry Niven's "All the Myriad Ways" (1968), Harry Harrison's *Tunnel Through the Deeps* (1972),[11] and, most recently, Michael Crichton's *Timeline* (1999).

Attending to *The Difference Engine*'s roots in popular science fiction helps locate its historical assumptions more precisely. The notion of alternative history raises anachronism, in the literal sense of something out of its proper time, into a methodological principle. There is nothing wrong with such a procedure: it underwrites the intellectual paradoxes of parallel-world fantasies, and it may be the vehicle for astute social commentary. It should be recognized, however, that anachronism is a fundamentally Romantic attitude toward history, as Jerome Christensen has demonstrated. Christensen argues that willful anachronism marks the revolutionary character of Romanticism as a social movement: "*committing* anachronism romantically exploits lack of accountability as unrecognized possibility" ("Romantic Movement" 455). Whether in the form of medievalism, nostalgia, prophecy, or apocalypse, English Romanticism explores the untimely as a visionary alternative to the existing world. Christensen emphasizes the political potential of this investment, calling anachronism a "politics of the future" ("Romantic Movement" 475). For both conservatives, such as Burke and the later Coleridge, and radicals such as Blake, Hazlitt, and Percy Shelley, the untimely did have a political edge. But escapism—Christensen's "lack of accountability"—has been the specter that haunts Romanticism's social projects even more than its literary visions. "Romantic" or "visionary" are epithets still used today to belittle ideas deemed noble but foolishly impracticable. The charge of escapism, of course, bedevils science fiction, too: it is a criticism even the finest achievements of the genre have had trouble evading. For all its dangers, then, anachronism describes an approach to history common to both Romanticism and science fiction. Christensen might be discussing *The Difference Engine*, not the Romantic movement, when he concludes: "its historicity [is] the willful commission of anachronism after anachronism linked by bold analogy" ("Romantic Movement" 476).

Anachronism names the narrative consequences of hacking with history. To hack the nineteenth century in a literary work means altering the temporal order of events, deliberately creating anachronisms in a representational world. The problem of accountability raised by such hacking, however, needs to be assessed on two different levels: the mimetic and the proleptic. Parallel-world science fiction invites scrutiny primarily in mimetic terms, despite the fact that the mimesis in such novels is of an alternative reality. No matter how wild the anachronisms, the mimetic success of a work in this genre is usually clear to the initiated—the SF fan—and with good reason. The conditions of *vraisemblance* are fairly strict. In keeping with the genre's emphasis on time travel, let me chart these mimetic conditions across four dimensions. Two of these dimensions concern the relationship of anachronism to what readers think they already know: the past and the present. (1) To be interesting, anachronism must establish a creative relationship with the received wisdom about a period. Variations, however ingenious, must have a logic or plausibility that stems from accepted features of the past. (2) Anachronism should suggest intriguing perspectives on the contemporary world. Whether as cautionary fable, satire, or allegory, the anachronisms of alternative history implicitly comment on present conditions. The other two dimensions concern matters that may be largely unknown to the audience: (3) alternative history often highlights obscure or suppressed historical actors—those on the losing side in wars, whether of ideas or of armies; women, minorities, the poor, the otherwise silenced; people considered mad in their day; the young, the old, the infirm; even animals and other nonhumans (consider the partnership between dogs and robots in Clifford D. Simak's *City* [1952], the dolphins and computers in Ted Mooney's *Easy Travel to Other Planets* [1981]). (4) There is the matter of internal consistency. Whatever its liberties with external events, an alternative world must appear credible according to its own terms.

Proleptic anachronisms raise a different set of concerns. Prolepsis comes from the Greek for "anticipation." In rhetoric it is a method for anticipating and thus answering a potential objection to one's argument. In everyday language, prolepsis is a form of hyperbole that anticipates a result before it has occurred, as when sportscasters proclaim after an apparently decisive play: "It's all over now but the shouting." In poetry, prolepsis is the use of an adjective to anticipate the result of a verb: "He fouls the sick air." None of these senses of prolepsis really raises the issue of *vraisemblance*. Instead, the emphasis on anticipation and answering, prediction and consequence, indicates an orientation toward the future, an action in the present designed to intervene at a later moment. Hence the problem of accountability for prolepsis is ethical and political—that of assessing the integrity of a desired outcome, not of producing a consistent mimesis. Prolepsis makes present a future state of affairs by hacking with time.

The charge of escapism only seems to arise when readers feel that mimetic consistency is the main thing at stake. By contrast, argument or agreement are the responses prolepsis tends to elicit. Failed prolepsis provokes ethical or political disagreement—often violent repudiation—but not the simple dismissal, the shrug of the shoulders, that accompanies escapism.

Let me demonstrate using Disraeli's *Sybil,* the book that serves as a departure point for *The Difference Engine.* Disraeli's novel has often been praised for its mimetic accuracy in depicting the "condition of England," a country divided into two nations, the rich and the poor. Critics, however, have just as often rejected its proleptic politics.[12] Disraeli first came to prominence in the 1840s as the advocate of a platform founded entirely on anachronism: the Young England movement. In *Sybil* Disraeli expounds his notion that the only way to revitalize the Conservative Party is by returning to the principles that governed class relations in a (mythical) time when England was young. In the days of yore, the aristocracy of England were not tyrants but "the natural leaders of the People" (334). That day will come again, and soon, but only when England awakes from the delusive dreams of equality that have animated the past two hundred years of political debate and are fueling the Chartist movement of Disraeli's day. Hence Disraeli's anachronistic movement displaces a recent with a more distant past in order to conjure a desired future. Whig philosophy, he claims, masquerades as freedom, but it actually results in an "oligarchical system" (354) in which a coalition of newly rich industrialists and middle-class tradesmen dominate the country. True equality will come only when England restores the grandeur of its aristocracy. "The future principle of English politics will not be a levelling principle. . . . It will seek to ensure equality, not by levelling the Few but by elevating the Many" (354). Disraeli's character Egremont claims to bask in the light of another time, a future that revives a vanished past: "You deem you are in darkness, and I see a dawn. The new generation of the aristocracy of England are not tyrants, not oppressors, Sybil, as you persist in believing. Their intelligence, better than that, their hearts are open to the responsibility of their position" (334).

The Difference Engine attempts to repudiate Disraeli's political vision, not least in Gibson and Sterling's cynical account of class relations, summed up in the ugly way they have Egremont treat Sybil. Unfortunately, the novel's anachronistic politics presents difficulties too. One can learn much about the two novels by comparing the handling of the uprisings in the respective narratives. Disraeli is at pains to distinguish two kinds of subversive agents: *insurrectionaries,* such as the mob's drunken leader (mockingly called the Liberator after Daniel O'Connell), outside Chartist agitators, and the profiteer, Mick Radley; and *rioters,* who are members of the local community, driven to desperate means by penury and unendurable working conditions.[13] Disraeli's sympathies are with the latter, even though he thinks they are duped by their leaders, and he portrays their hardships with accuracy as well as compassion. Gibson and Sterling's novel contains no equivalent group, no sympathetically portrayed workers or rioters motivated by unendurable injustice. The London uprising is led by a "Frenchified race-track dandy" (187), who has adopted the Luddite name of Captain Swing and fomented revolution as part of his personal plot to achieve world domination (a science fiction convention that appears gratuitously during the climactic battle scene). This Captain Swing is treated no more sympathetically in *The Difference Engine* than the Captain Swing who was mocked by the conservative Reverend Folliott in Peacock's *Crotchet Castle*. His chief assistant is a vicious murderess, Florence Bartlett, whose "Medusa glare" (304) goads a deluded band of followers to ever more savage acts of violence.[14]

What is disturbing about this battle scene is the acquiescence to the rigid limits of an action genre. If the authors' unruly spirit had seemed to revive for a contemporary audience an early-nineteenth-century irreverence toward discursive boundaries, the embrace of technothriller conventions reestablishes the familiar modern subservience of values to science. Irony and rogue pleasures, witty tricks and traps for the unwary, are once again relegated to the domain of culture, and science resumes its place as the partner of the modern technological state. Mallory and his allies crush the insurrectionaries with an awesome display of high-tech military might, including computer guided artillery, automatic weaponry, and a prototype streamlined vehicle.[15] This triumphalist conclusion contradicts the novel's larger critique of society, in which state powers of surveillance increasingly invade all aspects of its citizens' lives. In a novel intent on hacking history, this celebration of technological warfare and secret police is disturbing. It is as if the hackers have become agents of the modern police.

The political message of this conclusion seems as anachronistic as any of the novel's technological marvels, but the politics points not to the future but to the past. If computer databases and streamlined cars come from our time, the political attitudes come straight from Babbage's drawing room. The novel's climax is a throwback to the days when English engineering and empire reigned supreme, when few challenged the marriage of technology and the police, and when masculine power and the erotics of vulnerable femininity were widely approved norms. The anachronism is mimetic of Victorian attitudes that the novel's ironic stance would otherwise seem to have left behind. Its militaristic escapism makes a poor conclusion to the project of hacking the nineteenth century.

Do the partial failings of Gibson and Sterling's experiment, like those of Disraeli's, imply a more general inadequacy in anachronism as an approach to history? Not necessarily. Babbage's invention of the computer one hundred years before its time indicates the need for a conception of history that registers the untimely. Ways of responding to lost threads of the past, to forkings in history that seemed to have vanished with little trace, are crucial to the historical enterprise.

Ada Byron, only legitimate child of George Gordon, Lord Byron, is a precocious woman of nineteen, full of aspirations for greatness in some field of science or mathematics (it hardly matters which), and protégée of Mary Somerville. One month before Ada Byron's marriage to William King, later Lord Lovelace, she receives an invitation to Babbage's house to view his Silver Lady. Babbage's flirtatious note dilates on the charms of his automaton, its turban and new dresses, but Ada Byron sees through the trap—Babbage's usual test for visitors—and saves her admiration for the Difference Engine in the next room. A friend records her reaction: "While other visitors gazed at the working of this beautiful instrument with the sort of expression, and I dare say the sort of feeling, that some savages are said to have shown on first seeing a looking-glass or hearing a gun . . . Miss Byron, young as she was, understood its working, and saw the great beauty of the invention" (De Morgan 89). The only automata this young woman cared about were mathematical; she dreamed of commanding regiments of numbers, "*harmoniously* disciplined troops;—consisting of vast *numbers* & marching in irresistible power to the sound of *Music*" (qtd. in Toole 292, italics in original).

Ada Lovelace, née Byron, is a more interesting figure than her portrayal in *The Difference Engine* would suggest.[16] Her story graphically illustrates the many barriers women confronted in attempting to engage in scientific enterprises during the last century. Despite these barriers, she became a close associate of Babbage, Somerville, Wheatstone, Brewster, Faraday, and Dickens, and she went on to write the most penetrating account of Babbage's Analytical Engine published during the nineteenth century. Fortunately, a raft of biographies and encomia have appeared in recent years (no less than five books, as well as shorter portraits in many studies of the computer revolution), which can counter the portrait drawn by Gibson and Sterling. Lovelace's reputation, however, is not of primary concern here. What is more interesting in the current context is how one approaches figures whose "untimeliness" makes their very lives seem anachronisms.

Babbage's invention of the computer is an example of untimeliness that rarely fails to astound. Lovelace's life and writings present a more complex case. She has no original discovery to her credit, and recent claims that she wrote the first computer program depend upon drawing an analogy between software code and her diagram of how the (unbuilt) Analytical Engine would go about calculating Bernoulli numbers. Yet there are elements of her story that seem oddly out of sync with her time. Daughter of Lord Byron and wife of the Earl of Lovelace, mathematically gifted and intensely ambitious, a bold and often fanciful writer, equally at home with renowned scientists and with literary figures such as Dickens, Harriet Martineau, and Anna Jameson, wealthy yet embarrassed by gambling debts, talented musically, sexually independent, often hostile toward the duties of motherhood— she crosses boundaries, confounds roles, mixes genres, fields, and interests in ways that seem almost contemporary in their freethinking, gender bending, and anticipation of today's technoculture. Yet she was not a feminist in any current sense of the term, not a bluestocking, not a crusader for philanthropic causes, not a sectarian, not an ideologue of any recognizable sort.

She simply does not fit any of the customary categories—either of her age or of our own. If she contradicts the usual image of an upper-class Victorian woman, she equally fails to conform to the few roles we have imagined for women who were "ahead of their time."

History of science has no useful vocabulary for discussing untimely figures such as Babbage and Lovelace. They are not "pioneers" of the computer age (as has sometimes been claimed) because their contributions were forgotten or ignored, playing virtually no role in the (re)invention of the computer in the 1940s. The first digital computers strikingly resemble Babbage's sketches and Lovelace's account of the Analytical Engine, but twentieth-century researchers derived none of their ideas from this long-forgotten machine. Alan Turing and John von Neumann, who turn up later in this book, had no detailed knowledge of their nineteenth-century predecessors.[17] The Romantic vocabulary of "unrecognized genius" or "visionary" does not fit for the opposite reason. Babbage received enormous recognition in his own time, and Lovelace, too, successfully published in a scholarly journal and was accepted by her scientific peers. Melodramatic phrases such as "inspired madman," "idiot savant," or "born too early" are still less applicable. The only words that seem appropriate come not from history but from literary discourse. Babbage and Lovelace can be said to "foreshadow" or "anticipate" later scientific developments, even if their works had no causal role to play in the eventual discoveries. Such descriptions are accurate only if the words retain their figurative status. As pure prolepsis, these words capture the way Babbage and Lovelace realized a desired future in the past until the literality of their present reasserted its dominance. Historians, of course, use words such as "foreshadow" and "anticipate" all the time. But they use them for local effect; they use them to underline the irony, pathos, or wonder of history. Unless a causal line can be traced, unless there is evidence of influence, anticipation is usually more a curiosity than an object of serious inquiry.

The most intriguing attempt to deal with the untimely figure of Ada Lovelace comes not from computer historians (and certainly not from Gibson and Sterling) but from the playwright Tom Stoppard. In *Arcadia* (1993) Stoppard draws extensively from the biography of Lovelace to fashion the character of Thomasina Coverly, a mathematically precocious girl of thirteen (sixteen at the conclusion of the play).[18] The drama is set entirely in the drawing room of the Coverly estate, even though it juxtaposes events separated by more than 150 years. The first story, set in the early years of the nineteenth century, mixes a conventional Regency farce—involving the young poet Byron, adulterous trysts, a jealous husband, and two threatened duels—with poignant glimpses of Thomasina's brilliance and yearning. The second story, set in the present, might be called an academic farce; it concerns the descendants of the Coverly family, still in possession of their country house, and two rival scholars who have come to investigate the very events portrayed in the nineteenth-century scenes. The play raises many of the issues that have animated this discussion: it shows Thomasina discovering scientific concepts years ahead of their time and creates deliberate anachronisms on stage—a tortoise appears in both time periods, a character in 1809 eats an apple left on the table during the twentieth century, and a coffee mug and a laptop computer remain on stage during nineteenth-century scenes.[19]

Although the dates of the nineteenth-century events (1809, then 1812) correspond to the years when Ada Lovelace's mother, Lady Byron, was entertaining Lord Byron's marriage proposals, Thomasina's personality and her mathematical ideas clearly stem from Lovelace rather than her mother. The correspondences are numerous. In the play Thomasina initiates a romantic affair with her tutor, Septimus Hodge, on the night before her seventeenth birthday; Ada Byron, as it happens, was caught in a romantic entanglement with her tutor around her seventeenth birthday.[20] Thomasina's governess bears the same name, Briggs, as the one Ada had during the period of her affair, and the girls share a talent for drawing and a love of waltzing, which both learn at sixteen (Moore 33). Thomasina is given to enthusiastic bursts of ambition, which echo passages in Lovelace's letters. When Thomasina says playfully to Septimus, "You will be famous for being my tutor when Lord Byron is dead and forgotten" (37), she repeats a boast of Lovelace, who wrote in a letter to Babbage: "I do *not* believe that my father was (or ever could have been) such a *Poet* as I shall be an *Analyst*" (qtd. in Toole 156–57, italics in original). In another letter Lovelace muses about fame coming to her only after her death (qtd. in Toole 112), and Stoppard has one of his characters comment about Thomasina, "She was dead before she had time to be famous" (76).

The most significant parallels lie in the area of mathematics. Stoppard has his thirteen-year-old prodigy anticipate three important ideas: recursion, the second law of thermodynamics, and contemporary chaos theory, including fractal geometry.[21] In interviews the playwright attests to having mined a number of recent popular science books, particularly James Gleick's *Chaos* (1987), and it is easy to track down the exact passages in Gleick and other contemporary works (notably Douglas R. Hofstadter's *Gödel, Escher, Bach* [1979] and Stephen Hawking's *A Brief History of Time* [1988]) from which Stoppard has adapted speeches. What has not been noticed, however, is that Stoppard's characters also repeatedly echo passages from Lovelace and Babbage in the course of explaining Thomasina's mathematical intuitions. Babbage's most famous line about his Analytical Engine concerns its ability to use the conclusion of one equation as the starting point of the next; his colorful description of this recursive operation is that the Analytical Engine is capable of "eating its own tail."[22] Thomasina uses much the same analogy when she tries to explain what an iterated algorithm is to her tutor: "It eats its own progeny" (77). In the twentieth-century scenes Valentine Coverly is using his laptop computer to create an algorithm that would model the changes in the grouse population on the estate over the last one hundred years. His project, which depends on ideas developed only in recent decades, when computer modeling made chaos theory conceivable, echoes Babbage too: "This thing works for any phenomenon which eats its own numbers . . . it's a natural phenomenon in itself. Spooky" (45–46).

Valentine's comment about recursion being a spooky natural phenomenon gestures toward the mathematics of cellular automata, prominent in contemporary artificial life (AL) research, in which recursive routines take on a life of their own. Lovelace's image of numbers as living entities—disciplined troops—certainly should not be taken as anticipating the idea of cellular automata, but it makes one wonder what mathematical vistas might have been opened by a functioning Analytical Engine. Without such a machine, calculating iterated algorithms was virtually insane, as Valentine explains to the responsible historian in the play, Hannah Jarvis:

> HANNAH: Why? Because they didn't have calculators?
> VALENTINE: No. Yes. Because there's an order things can't happen in. You can't open a door till there's a house.
> HANNAH: I thought that's what genius was.
> VALENTINE: Only for lunatics and poets. (79)

Even though Lovelace never had a computer, she did have the idea of the computer, and the idea was enough to prompt her to speculate about AI. In the "Notes" she published on the Analytical Engine she suggests that Babbage's invention opens up for the first time "the idea of a thinking or of a reasoning machine" (Lovelace 273). Its power would enable a mathematics that "*weaves algebraical patterns* just as the Jacquard-loom weaves flowers and leaves" (Lovelace 273, italics in original). A leaf, it turns out, is the pattern Thomasina chooses to weave with her first iterated algorithm. "I will plot this leaf and deduce its equation," Thomasina tells her uncomprehending tutor (37). It will take Valentine, the twentieth-century chaos researcher, to explain what Thomasina (and Lovelace?) could have meant:

> If you knew the algorithm and fed it back say ten thousand times, each time there'd be a dot somewhere on the screen. You'd never know where to expect the next dot. But gradually you'd start to see this shape, because every dot will be inside the shape of this leaf. It wouldn't *be* a leaf, it would be a mathematical object. But yes. The unpredictable and the predetermined unfold together to make everything the way it is. It's how nature creates itself, on every scale, the snowflake and the snowstorm. (47)

Lovelace chooses a leaf because she is in the habit of seeing numbers as revealing the secrets of nature itself. Stoppard undoubtedly chose the leaf because of the prominent role it plays in most books on chaos theory (see Gleick 238). But Thomasina shares Lovelace's dream of a mathematics of the natural world. In a parody of Fermat's Last Theorem, Thomasina writes in the margin of her mathematics primer: "I, Thomasina Coverly, have found a truly wonderful method whereby all the forms of nature must give up their numerical secrets and draw themselves through number alone. This margin being too mean for my purpose, the reader must look elsewhere for the New Geometry of Irregular Forms discovered by Thomasina Coverly" (43). Thomasina's faith that "nature is written in numbers" (37) echoes Lovelace's frequent assertion in her letters that numbers reveal the "*hidden realities* of nature" (qtd. in Toole 101, italics in original), as well as Lovelace's published declaration that mathematics alone "can adequately express the great facts of the natural world" (Lovelace 272).

Stoppard's use of historical material about Lovelace occurs in a play that insists on the paradoxical nature of both history and time. The play mocks the jealousy, pretension, and unscrupulous careerism of a historian who is shown misconstruing the very nineteenth-century scenes the audience witnesses, but it also emphasizes the paradoxes that await even the most empirical of researchers. It is not merely that false leads and burned letters make the full recovery of events impossible but that the patterns that do emerge make more sense in the present than they ever could have in the past. Faced with insights and meanings that seem to exceed the capacity of empirical history, the play switches registers and inaugurates a meditation on time. What the play offers in place of a plausible linear history is a fluid nonlinear vision of time.

This segue from the topic of history to that of temporality is characteristic of literary approaches to the anachronistic. It is a formal constituent of most parallel-world fictions such as *The Difference Engine*. Gibson and Sterling signal as much by naming the five major sections of their novel "Iterations," a name which draws attention to the recursive temporality in the text. Stoppard signals his interest in temporality by numerous small touches, including stage directions about anachronistic props, speeches about the nature of time (5, 50, 79), characters from different eras who "iterate" one another word for word, and a tortoise that evokes Zeno's paradox.[23] The most dramatic evidence of this interest, however, comes in the final scene, where the characters from the two different periods appear together. Here the farcical maneuvering over historical method is subsumed in scientific musings about synchronicity and the circularity of time.

As the play nears its end, Thomasina's tutor and the present-day chaos researcher bend over the same drawing, a diagram by Thomasina illustrating the second law of thermodynamics. The stage directions read: "SEPTIMUS *and* VALENTINE *study the diagram doubled by time*" (93). Voices double one another too, weaving a pattern of nineteenth- and twentieth-century dialogue that resonates equally well in either time. The meaning of the diagram is slowly dawning on Septimus and Valentine, but Thomasina thinks only of learning to waltz. It is the night before her seventeenth birthday, and the audience knows she is to die in a fire before morning. The adults in each century speak to one another of entropy, the slow movement of history toward an inevitable end. But Thomasina speaks of dancing and love. She is in a rush and cannot wait on history.

HANNAH: What did [Thomasina] see?

VALENTINE: That you can't run the film backwards. Heat was
the first thing which didn't work that way [. . . .] With heat—
friction—a ball breaking a window [. . .] it won't work backwards.

HANNAH: Who thought it did?

VALENTINE: She saw why. You can put back the bits of glass but
you can't collect up the heat of the smash. It's gone.

SEPTIMUS: So the Improved Newtonian Universe must cease
and grow cold. Dear me.

VALENTINE: The heat goes into the mix.

(*He gestures to indicate the air in the room, in the universe.*)

THOMASINA: Yes, we must hurry if we are going to dance.

VALENTINE: And everything is mixing the same way, all the
time, irreversibly . . .

SEPTIMUS: Oh, we have time, I think.

VALENTINE: . . . till there's no time left. That's what time means.

SEPTIMUS: When we have found all the mysteries and lost all
the meaning, we will be alone, on an empty shore.

THOMASINA: Then we will dance. Is this a waltz?

SEPTIMUS: It will serve. (93–94, ellipses without brackets in
original)

In traditional history, as in entropy, time means one thing, but in art, as
in love, it means another. The arrow points only one way, Valentine would
maintain, but *Arcadia* as a whole suggests otherwise. Events repeat themselves, even individual words return through time. Discoveries are made,
lost, made again, and their real meaning lies in the process of discovery.
"It's wanting to know that makes us matter," Hannah declares (75). This conclusion may be the only response consonant with a genuine interest in anachronism. The true historical oddity of untimely figures—of Thomasina/
Lovelace, of Babbage—is obscured if the only question becomes whether or
not they led to something in the future.[24] No matter what answer one
chooses, the question itself implies a seamless, linear conception of history
in which anything that is not demonstrably tied to a later moment is eccentric, trivial, or freakish. Stoppard, by contrast, knows that a loose historical
thread may have much to teach *because* of its being unwoven into the fabric
of history, *because* of how forlornly its frayed end sticks out from the pattern. Arguing exclusively in terms of influence and development eliminates
the possibility of messiness, nonlinear phenomena, incoherence, stubborn
unreadability. It eliminates the rogue insights and pleasures provided by a
culture that blends science, literature, and hacking.

The form of the play conveys the same message. Through its elaborate
self-reflexivity, the play strives to function as the literary equivalent of an iterated algorithm.[25] It eats its own tail, in Babbage's phrase. This self-reflexive

structure implicitly comments on the limitations of any conceptual framework, especially that of traditional history. But the structure does not deny historical meaning to the anachronism of a nineteenth-century woman who sees things before their time. Formal reflexivity is a way of making anachronism accountable, of transforming anachronism into a kind of knowledge, the knowledge of what a young woman's life might mean. By underlining the literary status of the truth it offers, self-reflexivity ensures that anachronism is taken not as mimesis but as prolepsis. This is the kind of knowledge that *Arcadia* offers in place of empirical history. This is what reflexive forms—literary works, alternative history, historical cultural studies—can reveal about untimely lives. It will serve.

Babbage's automaton and Lovelace's musings on AI participate in a long history of artificial beings, which stretches from the early nineteenth century to today's headlines. Since Mary Shelley first brought her monster to life, countless literary and scientific endeavors have featured constructs that transgress the boundary between the human and nonhuman: robots, cyborgs, androids, replicants, and clones. One could make a good case that *Frankenstein,* which is the centerpiece of the next chapter, is the most important piece of literary culture for the world of science in the past two hundred years. Frankenstein's monster establishes strong contact with the cyborgs in much recent literature, film, and theory. Its patched nerves lie hidden in the foundations of towering scientific edifices. Mary Shelley's novel closes the circuit between a mechanical automaton like Babbage's Silver Lady and the latest science fiction films, or between the Difference Engine and today's billion-dollar research programs in computer intelligence and genetic engineering.

Five

Frankenstein's Monster, Replicants, and Cyborgs

The owl of Minerva spreads its wings only with the falling of the dusk.

—G. W. F. Hegel, 1821

In Ridley Scott's *Blade Runner,* a technothriller set in the permanent twilight of Los Angeles in 2019, an owl perches in the main offices of the Tyrell Corporation, creators of the "replicants" that have set the story in motion. In a nice visual allusion, this owl takes flight through the penthouse suite, passing in front of a wall of plate glass windows, behind which a brilliant orange sun is setting. Since its first release in 1982, *Blade Runner* has been taken by critics as a vision of a particular historical epoch, the period many people today call postmodernism.[1] Its portrait of ecological disaster and urban poverty, of a visual and aural landscape saturated with advertising, of a polyglot population immersed in a Babel of competing cultures, of decadence and homelessness, of technological achievement and social decay, has appeared to many people as prescient. By bringing Mary Shelley's story of the creation of an artificial human into the era of genetic engineering and new reproductive technologies,[2] it succeeded in crystallizing some of the fears, uncertainties, and desires that surround the coming of the postmodern.

Blade Runner conveys the advent of a new age by the paradoxical means of marking its end. The flight of the owl is one of many apocalyptic touches that define for the viewer the limits of a period, the far end of an epoch just now getting underway. Hegel's words from this chapter's epigraph refer to the wisdom that comes only with hindsight, the retrospective understanding available at the end of an epoch. But how paradoxical is the movie's strategy? A period, as the word implies, is dependent on the notion of an ending, the full stop that marks a completed sentence or a bygone age. Frank Kermode drew attention to this necessity in *The Sense of an Ending* (1967), his classic study of millennialism and literature. The film's use of the owl, however, is not exhausted by the allusion to Hegel. There is something more in the image, something that unsettles its venerable standing as a sign of closure. One can identify the extra feature in a number of ways—as irony, intertextuality, simulacrum—and each of these labels invokes a familiar conception of postmodern art. Like other contemporary texts, the film relies upon a gesture that it simultaneously dismantles.

Before I indicate how the film pulls off this trick, I should say that my purpose is not to explore the deconstructive strategies of postmodernism. That task, useful as it is, has been performed often enough. My purpose is to question the scope of postmodernism by showing how its status as a period is constituted by a particular version of cultural history. This version relies on notions of unity, comprehensiveness, and closure within the historical field, concepts that the very theory of postmodernism should call into question. Moreover, the sense of unity is achieved only at the price of excluding a large body of historical actors and experiences. The postmodern, like all periods, is enabled by the exclusion of one set of historical connections and by the reliance on another, very different set of historical links. The circuits that make this theoretical creature go, so to speak, are not the only circuits etched in the last two hundred years.

The project pursued here should be seen as part of larger genealogy of postmodernism, fashioned by many hands. Genealogy, according to Michel Foucault, seeks to defamiliarize its object, eschews an era's self-representations, and points to what has been left out, what is conspicuous by its absence. The motive of genealogy is critical rather than historical: it focuses on exposing the lines of power that lie behind "the constitution of knowledges, discourses, domains of objects" (Foucault, *Power/Knowledge* 117). If one thinks of genealogy as a postmodern intellectual procedure, then it is only appropriate to turn this method on the concept of postmodernism itself, revealing how what is left out aided in the constitution of this still powerful discourse.

In the late 1950s and throughout the 1960s the term *postmodern* referred to various forms of (mostly American) literary experimentalism, ranging from the metafiction of Barth, Gass, Reed, and Sontag to the "surfiction" of Federman, Molinaro, and Sukenick.[3] Ihab Hassan was the major theorist of this phase, although Barth's essay on "The Literature of Exhaustion" and Federman's critical writings were influential. By the early 1980s postmodernism had expanded its reference to include international movements in art, architecture, film, video, and other forms of popular culture, as well as economic and social developments that were not restricted to the cultural realm at all. The concept became a tool for exploring a whole range of contemporary social practices. As an increasingly widespread intellectual discourse, which cut across the disciplinary boundaries separating literature, philosophy, sociology, anthropology, architecture, and the law, postmodernism became the unavoidable ground for engaging with a wide range of topics: the fate of modernity; the value of Enlightenment ideals of rationality and progress; the status of metalanguages or of overarching theoretical paradigms; the relationship between mass culture and "high" cultural forms; and the coming of advanced capitalism or what has been called the postindustrial society. Rather than a champion of experimental fiction like Hassan, the critics most likely to be invoked were continental theorists such as Jean Baudrillard, Jean-François Lyotard, and Michel Foucault.

This last trio serves as my reference point when I refer to postmodernism. Throughout the 1990s these were the postmodern theorists who had the most influence on cultural studies. Along with Fredric Jameson, whose book *Postmodernism, or, The Cultural Logic of Late Capitalism* (1991) prefigured his turn toward cultural studies,[4] they shaped a prominent theoretical perspective on history and periodization.

Postmodernism may now be on the wane, although one would scarcely know it from the number of books on the subject published each year. The problem of history in the study of contemporary culture, however, is still inflected by the legacy of postmodern thinking. The limits of postmodernism as a comprehensive description of the present have been established by numerous examples in the prior chapters. Here I intend to mark those limits in theoretical terms by tracing lines that connect four women who have been left out of this dominant periodizing scheme. Mary Shelley, Hélène Cixous, Donna Haraway, and Shelley Jackson share an interest in artificial creatures as vibrant as any that inhabit *Blade Runner,* but their monsters—like their "monstrous" texts—do not fit comfortably within existing historical categories.

The owl of Minerva has spread its wings. What has the power to deconstruct so evocative an image? In *Blade Runner* that power resides in a monster. At first the viewer is unaware that anything monstrous has entered the scene. As the bird settles serenely back onto another perch, a handsomely dressed woman strides into the room, introducing herself with a question: "Do you like our owl?" Deckard, a police officer played by Harrison Ford, has come to Tyrell Corp. to examine one of its new generation of replicants. "It's artificial?" he replies. Still advancing, the woman answers, "Of course it is." The camera lingers on her face, forging a link between owl and woman. The implication that both are equally artificial flickers to consciousness before being submerged in a more blatant sexual suggestion—that both are property, objects to be bought and sold. "Must be expensive," Deckard comments, the innuendo audible in his voice. The camera remains focused on the woman's face. "Very," she replies, then adds, as if to underline the association, "I'm Rachael."

The image of the owl is destabilized in at least three ways—as artificial creature, as commodity, and as woman—which in the film's terms turn out to be the same way, as monster. Shortly thereafter, the film adds a fourth source of instability by raising questions about the woman's sexuality. Deckard is asked to examine Rachael (Sean Young) to see if he can discover her status as a replicant. He gives her a test, which involves a series of questions designed to elicit involuntary emotional reactions, measured by an instrument focused on her eye. "You're reading a magazine," Deckard states, "you come across a full page nude photo of a girl." The camera remains locked on her pupil as she answers: "Is this testing whether I'm a replicant or a lesbian, Mr. Deckard?" The film immediately takes measures to contain any transgressive implications: the camera shifts to the face of Mr. Tyrell, who smiles voyeuristically; the next question calls for Rachael to assert her proprietary rights over her husband in an imagined heterosexual marriage; and later in the film, Deckard himself has an affair with her. Nevertheless, the possibility of a fourth kind of "monstrosity," that of the queer, has been established.

These four complications are significant because they represent places where postmodern discourse reveals its affiliations, establishes links to a particular version of the past by writing the history of its break with that past. Gender, commodification, the inhuman, and the queer are principal contact points, where lines of force intersect and where energy is relayed from one system to another. They are places, in other words, where the transfer from modernity to postmodernity is accomplished. Throughout the 1980s and 1990s, book after book explored one or more of these contact points to demonstrate postmodernism's break with a stable conception of identity, say, or with the universality of reason. Such highly charged nodes, however, had multiple effects. They turned out to be places where wires crossed, short-circuiting the systems, interrupting the standard flow of current.

To begin patching together an alternate circuit, let me introduce some observations on history made in 1975 by Hélène Cixous, a writer who was left out of most accounts of postmodernism.[5] In "The Laugh of the Medusa," Cixous speculates that the introduction of woman as a category in history always unsettles conventional schemes, depriving scholars of what she calls the "conceptual orthopedics" of traditional periods:

> Because she arrives, vibrant, over and again, we are at the beginning of a new history, or rather of a process of becoming in which several histories intersect with one another. As subject for history, woman always occurs simultaneously in several places. Woman un-thinks the unifying, regulating history that homogenizes and channels forces, herding contradictions into a single battlefield. (339)

More than twenty-five years after its publication, this essay seems bound to its intellectual moment. Its invocation of a "universal woman subject" (334), for example, seems at odds with today's emphasis on hybrid subjectivities, constructed by the particulars of race, sex, class, and nationality, to name just the most frequently invoked categories. But considering Cixous's essay as a production of the seventies demonstrates not only the "unifying, regulating history" that postmodernism constructed for itself but also, more surprisingly, the ways in which Cixous's ideas mirror positions found in a nineteenth-century predecessor, Mary Shelley. Interestingly, Cixous's essay manages to make contact with all four nodes mentioned above. Cixous could be describing Rachael, the figure who arrives to open up the possibility of new histories, at the very moment when the owl in flight had symbolized the closure of an epoch. Rachael "occurs simultaneously in several places," incarnating both Minerva's austere intellect and the horror of a monster like Medusa. Cixous could also be describing the effect of the film's great precursor, Mary Shelley's *Frankenstein*. Shelley's novel, which has become a much discussed text in recent years, seems to many of its best readers to occur simultaneously in several places and, hence, to be a good point to begin "un-thinking" rigid historical schemes, including, I would suggest, the scheme that helped legitimate postmodernism.

One of the oddest things about this odd and compelling novel is that it simultaneously adopts both anti-Enlightenment and anti-Romantic positions.[6] Take the novel's critique of science, perhaps its most enduring legacy. Frankenstein and his monster have become almost obligatory references in any attempt to challenge the technological pride of the modern era. The nuances of this critique, however, are still not widely appreciated. No unthinking opponent of science, Shelley was the inheritor of many of the attitudes of her mother, Mary Wollstonecraft, including the mother's Enlightenment belief in progress, the virtue of education, and the rationality of women. These positive views toward progress, including technological progress, are visible in *Frankenstein*, particularly in the first edition of 1818, alongside the indictments of scientific overreaching. Her portrait of the ideal "man of science"—Frankenstein's admired Professor Waldman—is sympathetically drawn: it combines an aversion to pedantry, dogmatism, and "petty experimentalis[m]" with frankness, good nature, and a commitment to a well-rounded, liberal approach to learning (43). In two passages that were cut from the 1831 version of the novel, the one most readers encountered until recently, Victor's father teaches him the properties of electricity by imitating Benjamin Franklin's experiment with a kite, and Victor himself works to acquire the main scholarly languages of the age and to master practical scientific advances such as distillation, the steam engine, and the air pump (34–36). As Anne K. Mellor has shown, Shelley distinguishes between "good" and "bad" science, the former epitomized by what she saw as Erasmus Darwin's respect for nature, the latter by Humphry Davy, Luigi Galvani, and Adam Walker's interventionist approaches.[7]

Still, despite these favorable assessments of science, most readers come away from the book with an overwhelming impression of the dangers of scientific hubris. What makes matters confusing is that even the Enlightenment attitudes found in the 1818 version contain critiques of scientific inquiry. The rhetoric, however, is often different from the 1831 text. Notice the balanced cadence of an eighteenth-century moralist in this warning Frankenstein gives to Walton: "Learn from me, if not by my precepts, at least by my example, how dangerous is the acquirement of knowledge, and how much happier that man is who believes his native town to be the world, than he who aspires to become greater than his nature will allow" (48). Now compare it with this typical addition to the 1831 edition that dramatizes scientific overreaching: "So much has been done, exclaimed the soul of Frankenstein—more, far more, will I achieve: treading in the steps already marked, I will pioneer a new way, explore unknown powers, and unfold to the world the deepest mysteries of creation" (1831, 241). In these additions, one finds all the Romantic motifs of madness and guilt, impenetrable mysteries, the tumult of the swelling heart, clearly marked as evidence of Frankenstein's terrible error.

A careful reader can trace both an Enlightenment and a Romantic version of each of the author's indictments of her scientist hero. Frankenstein's scientific "enthusiasm" is condemned as self-centered and isolating in the first version (46). The dangers of enthusiasm is a common Enlightenment theme, found throughout the works of Samuel Johnson or Jane Austen, to pick two writers who have rarely been identified with Shelley. In the 1831 text Shelley adds the language of madness, obsessive questing, and uncontrollable ambition. Here, in one such insertion, is Frankenstein warning Walton about scientific aspiration: "a groan burst from his heaving breast.... At length he spoke, in broken accents:—'Unhappy man! Do you share my madness? Have you drank also of the intoxicating draught? Hear me,—let me reveal my tale, and you will dash the cup from your lips!'" (1831, 232). Similar contrasts can be located concerning the sublime, an aesthetic category that is tied up with Frankenstein's scientific ambitions. Whereas in 1818 the sublime afforded "consolation," "elevated [Frankenstein] from all littleness of feeling," and "subdued and tranquilized" his grief (91), in the 1831 additions the sublime shatters boundaries and transports one beyond reason. Nature, which tends to be healing in 1818 (23, 157–58), often is described with adjectives like "savage," "imperial," and "raging" in later additions (1831, 248–49). Hence when the final text stresses Frankenstein's "fervent longing to penetrate the secrets of nature" (1831, 238), to rend the veil of this world with a violence that is identified as characteristically masculine, it associates science with a tempestuous Romantic nature.

By eliminating many positive comments about science and by exaggerating Frankenstein's Romantic spirit, the 1831 text makes it difficult to distinguish between Shelley's measured critique of nineteenth-century science and her more flamboyant denunciations of the Romantic male ego. Although related, these two dimensions of the book can be distinguished. Shelley's target was never a thoughtful natural philosophy, especially when it was balanced by other branches of learning. When Shelley takes aim at Franken-stein's research, she criticizes the excesses of an overwrought sensibility, not natural philosophy itself. The craving for immortality, the hubris of trying to rival God, a foolish regard for alchemy, or a desire to usurp women's power of creation—these passions afflict other possessed souls in nineteenth-century literature, from Faust and Cain to Melville's Ahab, and are hardly confined to mad scientists. Shelley's purpose in intensifying her rhetoric in the 1831 version is not to amplify the critique of science but to lay bare the dangers of Romantic egotism.

By distinguishing these two strands of the text, one is able to see Shel-ley's unusual historical position. Unlike most of her prominent male con-temporaries, she did not phrase her objections to Enlightenment science in Romantic terms.[8] At the same time, she did not use her resistance to aspects of Romanticism as an excuse for a conservative return to prior values, the path chosen by some of the most popular female authors of the time.[9] Shel-ley's position in relation to the principal intellectual currents of her era is so distinctive that existing categories fail to encompass it. Most critics have re-sorted to definition by negatives, just as I have in the preceding paragraphs: she is neither one thing nor another, conforms to neither this trend nor that movement. Consequently, one frequently hears of her "subversiveness" or "ambivalence."[10] Such a marginalized, embattled position is highly prized in the contemporary intellectual climate, and it is the ground on which Shel-ley's novel has entered the university curriculum. But accounts of subver-sion, like definition by negatives, always locate a work in relation to another dominant tradition. Despite the intent to undermine, the work is still de-pendent on what it would challenge.

One can see this strategy deployed at the end of an essay that has had immense influence on postmodern thought, Jacques Derrida's "Structure, Sign, and Play in the Discourse of the Human Sciences" (1966). Faced with the impossibility of describing the unnameable, Derrida chooses a signifi-cant figure to fill the void, that of a monster. Writing of the beginning of a new kind of inquiry, he includes himself among those who "turn their eyes away when faced by the as yet unnamable which is proclaiming itself and which can do so, as is necessary whenever a birth is in the offing, only under the species of the nonspecies, in the formless, mute, infant, and terrifying form of monstrosity" (293). According to Derrida, one has no choice but to turn aside, to look at something else when confronted with the un-known.[11] His gesture of turning away his eyes is the customary response to monstrosity—lifesaving, in most stories of Medusa—but it helps to estab-lish the discourse of the unnameable as the only available language of post-modernism.

Is Shelley's novel doomed to enter history only under the species of the nonspecies, a formless, mute, infant, and terrifying form? Certainly that has been the burden of much contemporary criticism, which presupposes that it can account for the terror of a work that cannot speak within the discursive norms of its period only by stressing its aporias, its places of indeterminacy, its ambivalence. But perhaps there is a different way of encountering the unnameable, a way of approaching with one's eyes open, as it were. The challenge is to find positive ways of describing the position of a work like *Frankenstein.*

For all its deconstructive intent, postmodernism's method of dealing with the unknown ends up positing it as the other of a single, unified history, a history it then designates as modernity.[12] If several histories intersect in Shelley's novel, then the more radical approach would be to acknowledge the positive character of those histories, to specify where they come together, how they contradict one another, and why they construct one monstrous creature rather than another. This approach does not mean reconciling the various, partial accounts of the past, for that would only be another way of constructing a universal history. Still less does it mean turning a once-marginal tradition into a new center, a counterhistory that is valued because of its opposition to the official heritage. (This latter gesture, to the extent that it locates the critic in Satan's party, inadvertently signals postmodernism's affinity with Romanticism.) What this approach does call for is a recognition that every history has its limits. Although these limits necessarily circumscribe inquiry, preventing certain kinds of insights, they also make other kinds of insights possible. They become a contingent foundation for knowledge. The intersection of these limits—the contact points of different histories—may create something unnameable, but that does not mean one must look away.

The advantages of specifying the positive character of different histories become apparent when one compares Shelley's novel with Cixous's "The Laugh of Medusa." Both texts use the figure of a monster as an alternative to the dominant conceptions of the visual. Both Shelley and Cixous treat the topic of looking, which Derrida brought up in a figurative way, with disturbing literalness. Both novel and essay frame the issue of sight as a matter of possessing *eyes* that see. Although the monster in Shelley's novel is hideous to look at, Frankenstein himself feels more keenly the horror of the creature looking at him. In this respect, Shelley reverses the terms of monstrosity. Frankenstein cannot bear to see the eyes of his creation watching him. Indeed, the eyes themselves seem to be the most horrid organs the creature possesses. From the first moment that Frankenstein sees "the dull yellow eye of the creature open," he is repelled by this feature, by the "watery eyes, that seemed almost of the same colour as the dun white sockets in which they were set" (52). That night, when the monster visits Frankenstein's bed chamber, what disturbs him most is the fact that the creature's "eyes, if eyes they may be called, were fixed on me" (53). Ultimately, Frankenstein has visions of monstrous eyes watching him wherever he goes: "I saw around me nothing but a dense and frightful darkness, penetrated by no light but the glimmer of two eyes that glared upon me" (179).

Mary Shelley's image of glimmering eyes plays on a similar image in her husband's poem *Alastor* (1816). When the figure of the Poet in *Alastor* dreams of "two eyes, / Two starry eyes, hung in the gloom of thought" (ln. 489–90) they are anything but dull, yellow, and watery; these "serene and azure" (ln.491) orbs lure the Poet to his death because of their ideal beauty. The dynamics are clear: the danger of the eyes in Percy Shelley's poem lies not in their power to glare down at the Poet but in their tantalizing status as objects of desire. Mary Shelley inverts these dynamics, allowing the monster to possess the power of sight.[13]

In chapter 2, I discussed Martin Jay's exhaustive study of the "antiocular bias" of postmodern thought, which Jay sees as a "metaphor for a counter-Enlightenment debunking of rational lucidity" (589). Jay comments that postmodern resistance to the hegemony of sight was anticipated only by the Romantics, who employed the rhetoric of darkness and obscure mysteries to signal their opposition to the *siècle des lumières* (107–8). Wordsworth, for example, objected to the "tyranny" of sight, calling "the bodily eye . . . the most despotic of our senses" (*Prelude* 12.128–35). Percy Shelley asserted that the "deep truth is imageless" (*Prometheus Unbound* 2.iv.116). Mary Shelley, by contrast, does not fear the power of sight—she covets it. What she resists is being reduced to the object of sight, made into the monstrosity of a display for the rapt eye.[14] Inverting these Romantic themes, however, does not return vision to the provenance of Enlightenment lucidity.

One can amplify this contrast by looking at Percy Shelley's seldom-read poem about Medusa, which has a similar perspective on monstrosity, perhaps as a result of the poet having read his wife's novel. Unpublished during his lifetime, "On the Medusa of Leonardo da Vinci in the Florentine Gallery" was assembled from manuscripts by Mary Shelley in her edition of her husband's *Posthumous Poems* (1824). In this powerful fragment, which describes a painting of Medusa's severed head mistakenly attributed to Leonardo, Percy Shelley complicates the dynamics sketched above. Although the poem focuses on "the beauty and the terror" (ln. 38) of Medusa's head, describing the way it might be seen by a viewer of the painting, by the poet, and by figures inside the painting, such as an eft, which "Peeps idly into these Gorgonian eyes" (ln. 26), its opening and closing lines stress Medusa's own power of sight, stubbornly persistent even in death. "It lieth, gazing on the midnight sky," the poem begins, and five stanzas later, is still insisting: "A woman's countenance, with serpent locks, / Gazing in death on heaven from those wet rocks" (ln. 39–40). Like his wife, Percy Shelley presents monstrous ("Gorgonian") eyes, whose strength lies in seeing as much as in being seen.

The poem is more sympathetic to Medusa than most accounts prior to Cixous's. As both Jerome McGann and W. J. T. Mitchell have observed, Percy Shelley transforms Medusa into a symbol of revolution, "a victim of tyranny whose weakness, disfiguration, and monstrous mutilation become in themselves a kind of revolutionary power" (Mitchell 712). Since the image of Medusa was widely employed by conservatives in attacks on the French Revolution,[15] a political radical such as Percy Shelley would understandably be tempted to depict her in positive terms. The poet also finds warrant for this association in the prehistory of the Gorgon, because Medusa was originally a beautiful maiden, raped by Neptune in the temple of Minerva, then turned into a monster as punishment for the "crime" of being raped. The owl on Minerva's shoulder—emblem of the goddess's wisdom—did not prevent her from taking vengeance on an innocent woman. In this disturbing myth, Medusa and Minerva become the twin faces of woman's relation to thought.

A final factor influencing the poet's sympathetic portrait of a monster may have been *Frankenstein*, which has a relation to the fragment that has not previously been remarked. Written in 1819, the year after *Frankenstein* was published, the poem, with its revolutionary subtext, resembles what Percy Shelley calls the "direct moral" of his wife's book: "Let one being be selected, for whatever cause, as the refuse of his kind . . . and you impose upon him the irresistible obligations—malevolence and selfishness" (*Prose* 283). Medusa, no less than Frankenstein's monster, was selected unfairly as the refuse her kind, and thus she turned to malevolence and selfishness. Percy Shelley's portrait of Medusa appears to comment on his wife's vision of monstrosity, particularly in the final stanza, which Mary Shelley omitted from her edition, where Medusa is called "an uncreated creature" (Additional Stanza). One wonders if Mary Shelley was prompted to leave this stanza out because of her consciousness of its bearing on her novel. Certainly the poet's conception of the "everlasting beauty" of a face where "Death has met life, but there is life in death" (Additional Stanza) romanticizes the spectacle of a dismembered female body as nothing in Mary Shelley's novel did.

Like Mary Shelley, Cixous unsettles the relationship between monstrosity and vision. Cixous challenges men to gaze directly at the monster they fear, thus mocking the familiar Freudian reading,[16] which sees Medusa as representing men's dread of castration:

> Too bad for them if they fall apart upon discovering that women aren't men, or that the mother doesn't have one. But isn't this fear convenient for them? Wouldn't the worst be, isn't the worst, in truth, that women aren't castrated . . . ? You only have to look at the Medusa straight on to see her. And she's not deadly. She's beautiful and she's laughing. (Cixous 342)

This appeal demystifies what it means to be an object of sight. Look at Medusa straight on, and you see that she won't kill you—more important, you see that you don't have to kill her.

The next step is to allow the monster to have the power of sight herself. Ovid never says whether a face that can turn men to stone has eyes that can see. But possession of sight is one of the principal things at stake in the myth.[17] One may remember that the Medusa story has an earlier chapter in which Perseus goes to the cave of the Graiae, three sisters who share a single eye, hoping to learn from them the secret of how to defeat Medusa. Perseus forces the sisters to betray the secret by stealing their eyeball when one sister takes it out of the socket to hand it on to another. Cixous switches the ownership of vision, much as Mary Shelley does, by advising all monsters to keep their eyes on the heroes who come to murder them: "Look at the trembling Perseuses moving backward toward us. . . . What lovely backs! Not another minute to lose. Let's get out of here" (342). Cixous's Medusa sees clearly enough to express desire (those "lovely backs")—and then run.

A scene in *Blade Runner* captures the interplay of vulnerability and power evoked by the possession of eyes.[18] Two of the escaped replicants, who are trying to locate their creator, stop at a genetic engineering outlet called "Eye World." While Roy (Rutger Hauer), the leader of the replicants, questions the genetic technician, the other replicant picks up two exceedingly watery and yellow eyeballs, and delicately places one on each of the technician's shoulders. The terrified worker, an Asian-American caught in an economy of specialization that prevents him from knowing the answers the replicants seek, realizes that he was the one who made Roy's eyes. When informed of this fact, Roy answers: "If only you could see what I have seen with your eyes," amplifying a prominent motif in the movie: the monster *sees.* This episode raises questions about racial stereotypes, postindustrial outsourcing of parts—here, body parts—intertextuality, and more. Another scene associates a female replicant, who is working as a snake dancer, with Medusa.[19] From the opening sequence of the film, which features an aerial view of Los Angeles at night reflected in disembodied eyes, to the pupil-dilation test that police administer to determine if a person is a replicant to the gruesome murder committed by a replicant, who pushes his thumbs through his victim's eyes, the organs of vision symbolize both the vulnerable materiality of artificial creatures and their human capacity for sight.[20]

Monsters who stare back at their would-be murderers, horrific sights with the power of seeing. What does one make of such disturbing phenomena? Cixous makes laughter, and so, at one point, does Shelley.[21] In the final chapter of the novel, Frankenstein swears an awful oath, promising to pursue the monster who has caused him so much anguish until one or the other of them perishes. This bit of Byronic posturing is greeted by an eerie sound: "I was answered through the stillness of night by a loud and fiendish laugh. It rung on my ears long and heavily; the mountains re-echoed it, and I felt as if all hell surrounded me with mockery and laughter" (200).

The current flows strong between Frankenstein's monster and Cixous's Medusa. Their laughter crackles along a circuit that has been long concealed. To test the capacity of this circuit, let me connect a third monster, one still closer to the present day, Donna Haraway's cyborg.

Published in 1985, Haraway's "A Cyborg Manifesto: Science, Technology, and Socialist-Feminism in the Late Twentieth Century" was immediately recognized in feminist circles as a disturbing challenge to some aspects of liberal, materialist, and French feminist thought. Reprinted a number of times, the focus of symposia, translated, and widely quoted, it bore a message that was virtually unique at the time. It argued that women should embrace the monstrous identity of the cyborg as an ironic political strategy for dislodging traditional images of the feminine. Making this gesture would require a willingness to explore one's complicity with technology, one's implication in the "integrated circuit" of the contemporary world. It would also mean acknowledging the fragmented, partial, constructed nature not only of one's identity but also of one's very body.

Haraway's essay makes contact with *Frankenstein* at a number of places. Both works focus on monsters because, as Haraway puts it, monsters define "the limits of community in Western imaginations" (180). Both are profoundly concerned with "taking responsibility for the social relations of science and technology" (Haraway 181). Both play on the relationship between female writing and the creation of monstrous beings. And both have developed into "ironic political myth[s]" (Haraway 149). These points of contact help one see relations between the two monsters themselves. Both Shelley's creature and Haraway's cyborg are deeply *embodied* beings. In the wake of science fiction's appropriation of the Frankenstein myth, one sometimes forgets that Shelley's creation was not a robot. As Chris Baldick puts it, the original "monster has no mechanical characteristics" (44–45). With the cyborg, the Frankenstein myth comes full circle. By dissolving the boundary between the human and the artificial, the cyborg eliminates the robotic dimension once again. With the advent of genetic engineering and cybernetic technologies, notions of artificiality have changed; the monster is no robot but a flesh-and-blood construction like ourselves. Indeed, as Haraway is at pains to point out, most people in the West today *are* cyborgs. They have internalized technology so completely that their identities have been transformed.

I can illustrate this point by moving from Haraway's utopian speculations to the mundane level of everyday existence. Think of how one's character has been reshaped by the total integration of technology with the body. Many people would be different beings without the glasses, contact lenses, or laser surgery that let them see. How would one's self-conception and behavior be changed without the availability of contraception (one form of which can be permanently implanted in women's bodies)? What about mood-altering drugs such as Prozac or body-altering drugs such as steroids and estrogen? For that matter, what about the far-older technology of vaccination? In terms of more interventionist procedures, think of people whose lives have been transformed by pacemakers, prosthetic limbs, sex-change operations, cosmetic surgery, and more. Haraway's vision is not as outlandish as it might first appear. But she would not want her manifesto domesticated; she needs her monster to remain shocking, for political reasons most of all. And it does remain shocking because of the complicity it establishes between the individual, as a cybernetic system, and the commercial, bureaucratic, and military systems against which the modern liberal subject has often defined itself.

Before I go on, let me mention a few ways in which Haraway's "Manifesto" appears to differ from its predecessor. To begin with, Haraway explicitly distinguishes her cyborg in one respect: "Unlike the hopes of Frankenstein's monster, the cyborg does not expect its father to save it . . . through the fabrication of a heterosexual mate" (151). This point forms part of Haraway's critique of the Oedipal triangle, as well as her hope for the disappearance of gender, which will be considered below. It comes back in contact with Frankenstein's monster in the next sentence, though, where Haraway asserts that the cyborg has nothing to do with the "organic family" but is an artificial creature. A second difference: Haraway's cyborg is no giant, ungainly being like Frankenstein's monster; instead, it is made possible by the miracle of miniaturization. But this change is an outgrowth of alterations in the experience of monstrosity. "Miniaturization has turned out to be about power; small is not so much beautiful as pre-eminently dangerous" (153). Hence the cyborg is not startlingly visible either. Unlike Shelley's monster, the cyborg can disorient because of its occasional invisibility: who knows what technology lies buried inside the body? But, again, this point brings Haraway back to Shelley's position. The ownership of vision becomes all the more important when new medical "technologies of visualization" make bodies "newly permeable to both 'visualization' and 'intervention'" (169).

The most important point of contact between Haraway's essay and Shelley's novel is their eccentric position in relation to established periods. On behalf of its feminist project, "A Cyborg Manifesto" distances itself from Enlightenment views of science, from postmodern critiques of those views, and in a final twist, from the main feminist attacks on both the Enlightenment and postmodernism. Let me begin with the first of these themes and work forward. In a manner by now familiar, she blames "Western epistemological imperatives" stemming from the Enlightenment for the "troubling dualisms" of "self/other, mind/body, culture/nature, male/female" and more (176–77). The science that has developed from these oppositions she labels "the illegitimate offspring of militarism and patriarchal capitalism" (151). At the same time, she refuses "an anti-science metaphysics, a demonology of technology" (181), found in some postmodern and feminist attacks on modernity. Instead she recommends taking "intense pleasure in skill, machine skill. . . . We can be responsible for machines; *they* do not dominate or threaten us" (180). Finally, she rejects those feminist critiques of postmodernism that see its interest in partiality and local knowledge as making concerted political action impossible: "We do not need a totality in order to work well. The feminist dream of a common language . . . is a totalizing and imperialist one" (173). Where this leaves her is in the midst of contradiction, which does not bother her in the least. At the center of this tangled set of positions stands the cyborg, a monstrous creature who incarnates the irony of "contradictions that do not resolve into larger wholes, . . . the tension of holding incompatible things together because both or all are necessary and true" (149).

Although Haraway, like Cixous before her, has many points of contact with Shelley, neither late-twentieth-century writer particularly resembles the other. In truth, Shelley's monster is closer to Cixous's Medusa and Haraway's cyborg than either of these later conceptions are to one another. For example, whereas Cixous assimilates all women into a universal female subject, Haraway opposes the search for an essential unity and asserts that "There is nothing about being 'female' that naturally binds women" (155). Haraway was among the vanguard of feminists in the eighties who proclaimed the value of alliance rather than identity politics and promoted an interest in partial subjects, in the kinds of agency available in border zones, in the pleasures and possibilities enabled by hybrids like her cyborg. In contrast with another theme in Cixous, Haraway does not want to base her politics on a rhetoric of victimization: "Innocence, and the corollary insistence on victimhood as the only ground for insight, has done enough damage" (157). Whereas Cixous celebrated the attractions of bisexuality, Haraway declares that the "cyborg is a creature in a post-gender world; it has no truck with bisexuality . . . or other seductions to organic wholeness." This last point may be one of the things that has made her work appealing to queer theorists as diverse as Judith Butler, Cathy Griggers, and Judith Halberstam.[22]

Cixous's distance from Haraway is indicated most graphically by Cixous's use of "orthopedics" as a negative image of what periods accomplish. Haraway values prosthetics as a sign of our posthuman condition. Periods *are* conceptual orthopedics, but recognizing that prosthetics enable all kinds of productive activities is as important as knowing that they are crutches too.

The fact that Haraway's cyborg is not a direct descendent of Cixous's Medusa points toward the value of attending to the multiple histories that intersect in a writer such as Shelley. The critic should beware of forcing different lines of connection into a monolithic counterhistory, an alternative tradition that mirrors, in its linearity and reliance on the logic of resemblance, the very tradition that omitted them in the first place. Only by tracing the separate connections back to their nineteenth-century precursor can one see the relations among these monsters that haunt the boundaries of the human.

Shelley Jackson etches all of these connections into the circuitry of her hypertext *Patchwork Girl*. Jackson's ambitious digital work takes as its premise that Mary Shelley's second monster, the female companion that Victor Frankenstein began creating but then destroyed, was secretly finished by Mary Shelley herself. The artificial creature becomes the lover of this fictional Mary Shelley, then travels to America, where she goes through numerous adventures until her death in the 1990s. Describing these events, Jackson frequently weaves quotations from *Frankenstein* into her account, creating a variegated patchwork of "original" writing and borrowed phrases, which include passages from Cixous and Haraway, as well as from L. Frank Baum, Derrida, Lyotard, and many others. Jackson's hypertext, one of the most successful efforts in this new medium, consists of 323 lexias (or screens of text), varying in length from a single sentence to some 300 or so words.[23] The lexias are joined to one another by 462 links, which create multiple pathways through the text. Like most hypertexts, *Patchwork Girl* has no proper beginning or end, but it does have numerous narrative characteristics, including characters, settings, flashbacks, recognition scenes, shifting points of view, and consecutive temporal sequences.

Because many readers will be unfamiliar with this work, I shall take a moment to describe its structure. Written with Storyspace software and published by Eastgate Systems, the premier source for stand-alone hypertexts, it is distributed on disk and equipped with maps that allow readers to visualize the structure of the crisscrossing network of lexias. The narrative core of the work is contained in two long sections.[24] The first, "Journal," contains Mary Shelley's diary of her construction of the female creature and of their initial, halting attempts at a relationship. Their bond culminates in a dramatically convincing act of lovemaking, which finely captures the characters' blend of fear and exploratory passion. The other section, "Story," is subdivided into six further parts: "M/S," which explores the love affair from the creature's point of view; "Severance," which recounts their mutual but painful decision to separate and includes a strong scene in which the creator and creation exchange skin grafts, so that each will contain a living fragment of the other; "Seagoing" and "Seance," which follow the creature across the Atlantic and narrate various adventures involving cross-dressing, an encounter with a circus freak, and the purchase of a false identity; and, finally, "Falling Apart" and "Rethinking," in which her 175-year-old body begins to break up into its component pieces. The narrative "ends" with the creature's decision to wander off into the desert of Death Valley, an effective counterpoint to the fate of Victor Frankenstein's monster, who disappears into the ice floes of the Arctic.

Flanking the narrative core, but interspersed during most reading experiences with the text, are three nonlinear sections. "Body of the Text" and "Crazy Quilt" contain meditations on hypertext writing, lyrical passages, dreams, irreverent remarks, and fragmentary musings in various voices (the author's, the creature's, the text's itself). "Graveyard," the most haunting of the sections, gives voice to the creature's individual body parts. In lexias such as "eyeballs," "lips," "left breast," and "heart," Jackson tells the stories of the dead women from whom the organs were harvested. Macabre and witty, sometimes forming tiny interpolated narratives, these passages literalize the poststructuralist dictum that the subject is always multiple.[25] Her lips, for example, come from a woman who laughed out loud at her village's disapproval. The creature inherits this trait, making her like Cixous's Medusa, who also laughs at her persecutors: "I laugh at pain, not because I'm strong, but because it's funny. My lips always get the joke. A little later, so do I" ("lips").

Her eyes give her the traits of a woman named Tituba, which was the name of a West Indian slave jailed in the Salem witch trials.[26] In common with her predecessors, the creature's eyes see more than they should, aligning her with other monsters who possess the power of vision. The figure of eyes also opens on a hidden level of Jackson's text. In a lexia that has no entry or exit, a passage unlinked to any other in the hypertext and hence inaccessible except by using the search engine provided by the software, the Patchwork Girl thanks her maker for giving her life. "Hideous progeny: yes, I was both those things, for you, and more. Lover, friend, collaborator. It is my eyes you describe—with fear, yes, but with fascination: yellow, watery, but speculative eyes" ("thanks"). This impulse to thank rather than hate one's creator marks the hypertext's largest thematic departure from Shelley's novel. The difference stems from the loving, nurturing embrace Jackson imagines her character Mary Shelley bestowing on the creature she has made.

Jackson's Mary Shelley uses a technique for creating an artificial person that more closely resembles Frankenstein's methods than the genetic engineering in *Blade Runner*. In an age of biotechnology, sewing parts together seems anachronistic, a throwback to the nineteenth century, when scientific creation of life was conceptualized in terms of assembling already existent pieces. Jackson associates this older kind of creativity with female values—weaving, collaborating, conserving, reusing. The notion of sewing internal organs into place implies meticulous care, a time-consuming total-body operation: kidneys tucked in place, intestines wound into their cavity, veins sewn one by one along their proper paths. Such patient piecework contrasts vividly with the high-tech procedures of contemporary genetics.

This contrast forms a part of Jackson's sustained critique of technoscience. Yet like Shelley before her, Jackson is no mindless opponent of science. In fact, she obviously admires what she calls the creature's "techy bent" ("am I mary"), and she draws frequent metaphors from genetics and cyborg theory. An interest in science is virtually mandatory for the affirmative pressure she puts on the Frankenstein myth. And it works well at those points where she is most true to her maternal origin—most faithful to Shelley's novel—those places where she endows her artificial creature with the pathos of life.

The intellectual coherence of this hypertext arises directly from the theoretical nexus I have been exploring, the odd collection of emphases and positions that link Mary Shelley, Cixous, Haraway, and Jackson. Jackson herself theorizes the necessity of developing alternative ways of thinking about such a nexus of temporal links. *Patchwork Girl* abandons traditional history entirely, but it is saturated with historical remainders, fragments of the past surviving into alien contexts. It captures the discontinuous sense of time passing at different rates for different beings, the paradoxes of anachronism and fragmented cultural memories. Here is a cento of passages that illustrate Jackson's alternative perspective on time and history:

> Born full-grown, I have lived in this frame for 175 years. By another reckoning, I have lived many lives (Tituba's, Jane's, and the others') and am much older. ("I am")

I am in a here and a present moment that has no history and no expectations for the future. Or rather, history is only a haphazard hopscotch through other present moments. How I got from one to the
other is unclear. Though I could list my past moments, they would
remain discrete . . . hence without shape, without end, without story.
Or with as many stories as I care to put together. ("this writing")

I don't doubt that if I had a continuous life or a block of printed past,
Proust for example, I would read it all from start to finish. There's
only one way through it and that's the way I'd go, convincing myself
that I was aligned with time. ("flow")

The present moment is furiously small, a slot, a notch, a footprint,
and on either side of it is a seethe of possibility, the dissolve of al-
phabets and of me. ("a slot, a notch")

There are many things to be said about these passages. Note the analogy
between reading hypertext (hopscotching through present moments of
text) and the creature's fragmented sense of historical continuity; note how
identity may be configured differently depending on one's temporal perspective ("By another reckoning, I have lived many lives"); note the way in
which narratives proliferate in the absence of a single, unified narrative of
history. The point I most want to underscore, however, is the way in which
the kinds of perspectives I have been exploring in this book enable new
understandings of one's relation to history. If the present moment of contemporary culture often appears cut off from everything around it, shape-
less and without story, from another perspective it may be seen as tethered
to diverse pasts by many stories. Rather than a continuous block of printed
history, with only one way through it to today, a multiplicity of pasts gives
rise to a seethe of possibilities.

A seethe of possibilities can be frightening, however. This kind of un-
certainty is monstrous to some. Multiple pasts and a diversity of present cultures may threaten the contemporary subject. Hypertext confronts these
fears (some would say exacerbates them) by embodying them technologically. When successful, it turns multiplicity to aesthetic and intellectual
ends. But hypertext is still a primitive technology and a rudimentary literary genre. Other forms of digital or hypermedia storytelling may emerge in
the near future, which will make the first efforts of hypertext writers appear
crude. Moreover, other contemporary genres such as the novel and film
often achieve similar effects. One may gain a perspective on Jackson's hypertext by comparing it with contemporary works in other media. It possesses
some of the force of Katherine Dunn's *Geek Love* (1989), a novel involving
women who have major parts of their bodies amputated. It has the repellent
fascination of David Lynch's film *Eraserhead* (1977), as well as the pathos of
the final reel of Nicolas Roeg's *The Man Who Fell to Earth* (1976), when the
alien knows he is dying. The creature's cross-dressing may remind one of

the performative flair in Jennie Livingston's documentary *Paris Is Burning* (1990), while the passages on sewing together skin may evoke similar motifs from Jonathan Demme's *The Silence of the Lambs* (1991). Finally, the sexualized play with the concept of writing on the body establishes a kinship with Peter Greenaway's experimental movies *Prospero's Books* (1991) and *The Pillow Book* (1997). Unusual as Jackson's hypertext may seem, it is hardly unprecedented in today's culture.

From my perspective, hypertext symbolizes Shelley Jackson's achievement in finding new ways to respond to discontinuous cultural legacies. Like Peter Carey, Susan Sontag, and Tom Stoppard, she has learned to account for a wide range of cultural experiences, some of which are not easily coordinated with others. *Patchwork Girl* manages to connect nineteenth- and early-twentieth-century phenomena such as Mary Shelley's writing, traveling freak shows, seances, women's quilting circles, and L. Frank Baum children's story[27] with contemporary experiences like cyborgs, computers, mestizo identities, nomadic desires, and transsexual surgery.[28] Not all of the earlier practices lead directly to their present-day cognates. They sometimes take labyrinthine paths, are interrupted, abandoned, or forgotten, only to be remembered or revived in altered contexts and for different reasons. Hypertext is one of today's methods of responding to this seethe of possibilities.

Intertextuality is another. The concept of intertextuality proposes that every text is a patchwork of allusions, a web of references ranging from explicit quotations to oblique echoes and unconscious mimicry. One of the governing tropes of *Patchwork Girl* is the analogy between intertextuality and the sutured body of the creature. The title page of the hypertext already makes this analogy central. It reads: "*Patchwork Girl; or, A Modern Monster* by Mary/Shelley, and Herself" ("title page"). The slash between the two names suggests that Mary [Shelley]/Shelley [Jackson] are not mere partners in the text but a single authorial subject, a theme that is picked up in other passages that emphasize the collaborative nature of much women's writing and of traditionally female arts like quilting.[29] In the lexia "am I mary," the creature makes this point herself: "Mary writes, I write, we write, but who is really writing? Ghost writers are the only kind there are." In another place, the creature extends the metaphor still further, equating her literary and her bodily sources. Meditating on what will happen to her at her death, she writes: "If all quotes remain tethered to their sources by however tenuous filaments, so my parts. My face will explode into fragments: eyeballs roll back to Tituba, teeth fly like sideways hail to the empty gums of Walter and Judith" ("hidden figure"). A monstrous fate.

I began my discussion by calling postmodernism a theoretical creature, one with great power on the contemporary scene and with a proportionate ability to provoke terror in some circles. In truth, all periods might justly be compared to artificial lifeforms. They lumber forth, on specified occasions, to serve their maker's ends, and their shapes often reflect the nature of

those ends as much as the true diversity of the times they strain to epito-
mize. My point is not that historical writing inevitably fails to reflect reality.
That argument, which concerns the fictionality of history, has stimulated a
vigorous debate of its own, some of which I surveyed in chapter 1, but it is
not really what is at stake here. Rather my point follows from the idea that
periods are conceptual prosthetics. As cognitive instruments, periods are
neither fictions nor realities but conceptual tools. At times one may want to
use a strategic conception of a period, much as feminist theorists have advocated adopting a strategic essentialism for political ends. Contesting postmodernism does not mean arguing about its validity as a description of the
world; it means debating the term's usefulness for asking the kinds of questions one wants answered. The term may remain a perfectly useful way of focusing attention on some contemporary problems, even if it obscures other,
equally important, questions. As Deckard says about replicants: Artificial
constructs are "either a benefit or a hazard. If they're a benefit, it's not my
problem."

If periods are cognitive tools, what kind of knowledge do they yield?
Many critics have been tempted to answer "normative" or "dominant," but
that oversimplifies the range of their usefulness. Period concepts can recon-
figure one's understanding of the past, challenging received wisdom rather
than reproducing the status quo. The more complex answer is that periods
yield *disciplinary* knowledge. They exist and function solely within the modern ensemble of disciplines, which are most visible in the academy and its
allied sectors, such as publishing, educational services, libraries, research
foundations, commercial databases, and other information industries. To
label a form of knowledge as disciplinary is not to trivialize it but rather to
indicate the kind of cultural work it undertakes. Periods are bound up with
some of today's most influential institutions and hence have pragmatic effects that are far reaching if often unnoticed. A historical cultural studies
needs to be aware of the particular domains in which its results will circulate and to be conscious of the possible ramifications of the conceptual tools
it employs.

The disciplinary ensemble described above is only a subset of the larger
organization of differentiated spheres that have structured parts of modern
society since Dickens's day. As early as *Pickwick Papers*, the relationship of
scholarly societies and specialized knowledge to other sectors of society—
governmental, imperial, commercial, and professional—was becoming clear,
as we saw in the outraged reaction of the "seventeen learned societies, native
and foreign" when Mr. Pickwick's dating of the inscription "BILL STUMPS,
HIS MARK" was challenged (Dickens, *Pickwick* 228–29). Dickens's parody
of people expending so much energy and passion on a trivial, misguided
dispute is a source of innocent humor in the novel, but the innocence of the
joke depends on the occupation being one for gentlemen with too much
leisure on their hands, like many of the amateur natural philosophers in the
early days of the Royal Society. Today, this parody of misspent energies ad-

dresses the real interests of a much larger group of people. In a society such as the United States, where for the first time in history more than fifty percent of all people are engaged in providing services rather than in agriculture or the production of goods, the circulation of knowledge becomes a vital factor in the economy.

The commodification of periods in both the nostalgia industry and academia will be the focus of the next chapter. Right now, it is important to continue pressing the nature of the different kinds of impact critical thinking might possess. As knowledge, cultural studies inevitably participates in a disciplinary environment. Under current conditions, no deconstruction, however rigorous, no new reading or theory, no critical challenge of any sort, can avoid contributing to the disciplines within which it is generated. Yet scholarly practices, like narratives, do more than generate knowledge. They establish relations, create different kinds of communities, provoke curiosity, and stimulate desires other than (or rather alongside) those for intellectual clarity. One might call this other dimension the "pragmatics" of scholarly activity. In language theory, *pragmatics* specifies how a speaker and listener are positioned in any act of communication. In the kind of act that literary criticism or history performs, pragmatics might be seen as naming the network of relations, values, ideals, and hopes constituted by a scholar's labor.

It is easy to grasp the pragmatics of storytelling and the consequences they have in other areas of life. Almost everyone will concede that the stories people tell shape who they are. Narrative plays a fundamental role in forming identities, peoples, and nations. In *The Pleasures of Babel* I explored how the pragmatics of narratives, not just their meanings, have consequences too. The relations of narrator and addressee do not just produce meanings— they create social bonds. Stories act in the world not only because of what they say but because of when and where they are heard, and by whom. Pragmatics helps explain why some stories seem proleptic and others merely escapist. The terms under which they circulate, not their content, make the difference. Pragmatics also illuminates why stories change over time even though their words may remain the same. The situation of their exchange, not the language, makes the difference. Thus narrative becomes another of those "nonintegral objects," like Wai Chee Dimock's theory of acoustic resonance, that can have a special use in an historical cultural studies.

John McGowan, whose book *Postmodernism and Its Critics* was an important contribution to the genealogy of postmodernism, has recently turned his attention to the relationship between the nineteenth century and cultural studies. In a provocative article, "Modernity and Culture, the Victorians and Cultural Studies," McGowan strives to find an alternative to the "holistic assumptions" of what he terms "zeitgeist thinking," prominent examples of which are periods ("Modernity" 8). Like me, he argues against assessing the past in relation to a defining framework, whether it be a period, an account of ideology, or a unified concept of culture. Instead, he proposes using narratives to discover "what elements of the past can mean in relation to our purposes in the present." He writes: "Instead of viewing things that appear as indices of who they (the Victorians) were and/or who we (post-moderns?) are, those things would be elaborated through stories that ponder what we might become" ("Modernity" 24). Stories "ponder" not only through their content but through the situation of their telling and retelling. Although he does not use the term, he insists on the importance of narrative pragmatics:

> Relationships and meanings are forged through various (contingent) human actions, one of which is the telling of stories in fiction and film, another of which is making interpretive arguments in criticism. In other words, the Victorians as a group characterized by certain shared features do not exist except insofar as they are produced in that similarity by a discourse that has aims on its audience. The right question is not whether the Victorians were really like that or not, but the Bakhtinian question of whom this discourse addresses (answers, contests, affirms) and to what ends. ("Modernity" 23)

Cultural studies has consistently named this dimension of its project "politics." From its beginnings, participants involved in cultural studies have aimed to intervene in the present. This political ambition has provoked much scoffing from people who cannot imagine academic work in the humanities effecting any real political change. Yet writing and scholarship always have effects, some of which are cognitive, others institutional and disciplinary, still others transactional and intersubjective. Using a word like pragmatics rather than politics would clarify the kind of social effects that might actually result from a historical cultural studies.

Combining narratives with interpretive arguments, as I have done here, underlines the connection between the pragmatics of both activities. Although the knowledge claims are radically different, both storytelling and criticism are discourses that have aims on their audiences. The status of the respective knowledge claims is something that must be assessed on another occasion. But one of the main pragmatic effects of these activities is clear. They create a form of community among those who value their aims—or who can be persuaded to find value in them.

This chapter has given a critical account of four writers linked by alternative circuits. If they form a community, it is with the readers who value their ideas and priorities more than it is with one another. (Jackson, the last in the line, a self-conscious member of this very community, is the exception that proves the rule.) Their circuit does not have the unity of a counter-history or tradition that could displace the dominant account of culture over such a long span of time. It does not form the basis of a new holistic paradigm. It takes its meanings, in a circular manner, from the pragmatic effects it produces in the present. Does this monstrous conclusion banish its meanings from the domain of thought, from the wisdom presided over by Minerva?

The owl takes wing at twilight. Hegel, a great theorist of periodization, probably was not thinking of Minerva's ancient enmity to Medusa when he wrote the aphorism with which I began this chapter. There is an irony, however, in the fact that all four writers I have considered pit their monsters against Minerva. They continue a struggle between wisdom and what wisdom once found it necessary to shut out. If one conceives of this struggle as a conflict between the closed historical circuit traced by postmodern theory and the monstrosity of what remains outside that history, then one can see why these writers represents a challenge to postmodernism. For postmodernism has often cast itself as one of the monsters too. Imagine the horror of discovering that postmodernism has been on the side of Minerva all along.

Six

Or, Dickens at the Turn of the Millennium

One overcast day in February, under the failing light of a late-afternoon sun, several curiously dressed couples were seen hurrying down the platform of the Riverfront Depot in Nashville, Tennessee. Most days of the week a group of teenagers might Rollerblade from one end of the platform to the other without endangering human life. But this evening the depot was astir: the powerful locomotive—a renovated 1952 model E8A, weighing 318,000 pounds and developing 2,250 horsepower—hissed and vibrated, pulsing with anticipation; porters beckoned anxiously to late-arriving passengers; while men in white sequined suits, with bushy sideburns and hair swept forward over their brows, escorted ladies in tight-skirted red dresses toward the elegant dining cars. One couple in particular drew the observer's attention, as they paused before a nostalgia poster of Roy Acuff's 1946 movie *Night Train to Memphis*. This couple, although dressed as creatively as the other passengers, appeared more shy than most, as though this were their first date, and perhaps a blind one at that. Hoping to discover what had occasioned the unwonted bustle at the depot, the observer moved closer; and happily, the gentleman's first words dispelled the entire mystery. Tonight the Elvis Love Train was offering another of its "Great Expectations Specials."

Every Thursday during the month of February 1994, Great Expectations Services for Singles, the nationwide video dating company, offered its members free tickets on the two-and-a-half-hour dinner excursion on the rails, a $42.95 value. An Elvis Menu of his personal favorite foods—hamburger steak, mashed potatoes, and corn bread—was available for dinner. Alas, this attractive package no longer exists. Shortly after the Elvis Love Train began running, the company received notice from Graceland that its use of Elvis's name represented an unauthorized infringement of trademark. But for a few brief weeks, inquisitive observers had the chance to view at firsthand what few perhaps had ever imagined: the courtship of Elvis and Estella.

This union brings together some of the most marketable cultural commodities from two different centuries. It nicely evokes the emotional appeal, the sentimentality, the promotional genius, the commercial crassness, and the legal maneuvering that surrounded both Dickens and Elvis in their respective eras. That it should all take place at trainside, a principal symbol of nineteenth-century technological progress, adds the finishing touch. My purpose in recording this ephemeral conjunction, however, is not to compare these very different figures but to register one instance of Dickens's continuing presence in contemporary popular culture. Like it or not, this sort of phenomenon is a way in which Dickens lives on at the turn of the millennium. A grotesque, misshapen afterlife, one might say, as unsettling as the manias that animate some of Dickens's own creations: Miss Havisham in her decaying bridal dress, or Pip fantasizing about his great expectations.

There is a logic in this afterlife, however, a logic not entirely alien to the patterns in Dickens's own stories, as my last comparison is meant to suggest. Another way of putting this point is to say that Dickens anticipates some of the characteristic features of postmodern life. The term *postmodern* should have only a heuristic value for cultural critics, as I hope my discussion in the prior chapter has established. The word can be effectively used to characterize a wide (but hardly comprehensive) set of contemporary phenomena, including theoretical positions about the impossibility of truth and the deconstruction of the subject; an ironic stance in popular media such as film, television, comics, and advertising; pastiche and eclecticism in architecture, art, and music; the commodification of everyday life; even lifestyles and belief patterns, such as the subcultural belief that Elvis is alive. As a conceptual prosthetic, postmodernism is as good a word as any to name these prominent aspects of today's culture. If Dickens anticipated some of these contemporary trends, then tracing the misshapen forms of his survival in today's world will tell readers something about themselves—and about Dickens too.

At first glance Dickens does not appear to foreshadow either the 1960s or the 1980s version of postmodernism, and he did not play any role in the articulation of either version of the theory. In terms of the literary paradigm prominent in early accounts of the movement, the Victorian novelist would not have been an obvious choice as a forerunner of metafiction. Although an acknowledged technical innovator, he was not given to elaborate self-consciousness or (intentional) self-parody. If the 1960s version of postmodernism was more formalistic and narrowly literary than the current version, Dickens's exclusion from this discourse was based on appropriately formal and stylistic concerns. The reasons that Dickens did not find a place in the post-1980s version of postmodernism are more complex, as is only befitting the more diversified references of the term. But these reasons can all be gathered under a single heading: the novelist's association with early forms of capitalism.

Both Dickens's life and his writing have long been seen as emblematic of at least two early phases of capitalism: industrial capitalism, which caught him up in its cogs at a youthful age, when he went to work at the blacking factory; and the emerging bureaucratic, managerial, or administered form of capitalism, which serves as a backdrop for late novels such as *Bleak House* and *Little Dorrit*. As is well known, Dickens's relation to both of these social formations is equivocal: to varying degrees he is their critic, agent, theorist, historian, poet, and prophet. Who has analyzed more compellingly than Dickens some of its dominant forms of consciousness: the commodity fetishism of a Krook, for example, or the alienation of a Wemmick? But who has also contributed more decisively to the spread of other forms of capitalist consciousness: the work ethic or the ideology of hearth and home? Who has exposed more savagely than Dickens the absurdity of many institutions developed under the early phases of capitalism: the workhouse, the prison, the charity school, the police, Chancery, government bureaucracies, or scientific societies? But who has also contributed more insidiously to the internalization of the very disciplinary procedures upon which these institutions rely, as his advocacy of professionalization demonstrates? Finally, who has worked more tirelessly than Dickens to invent publishing and distribution channels that would exploit the diverse markets opened up by the consolidation of a capitalist economy? Whether as critic or apologist, Dickens has deep connections with the early stages of capitalism. This fact has undoubtedly made it difficult for readers to see how he could have anything to do with a cultural position associated with advanced capitalism—postmodernism.

Once the topic has been broached, however, the mind luxuriates in the possibilities. Of course one can think of ways in which Dickens foreshadows the 1960s version. Perhaps the most obvious connection lies in the impulse to exploit "naive" or undervalued narrative conventions. Foucault has written of the importance of unauthorized knowledge procedures, such as popular narrative, in resisting the omnipresent networks of power that, he argues, increasingly characterize Western society from the nineteenth century to the present. Storytelling, particularly in popular or folktale forms, is one of Foucault's "naive knowledges, located low down on the hierarchy, beneath the required level of cognition or scientificity" (*Power/Knowledge* 82), which can serve as a resource for those people who are denied access to official culture. Lyotard, too, emphasizes the role of "narrative knowledge" in providing people with images of how to survive in the labyrinthine structures of a postindustrial society (*Postmodern Condition* 22).

Almost as obvious a connection between Dickens and postmodernism may be found in the novelist's eccentric characters. Well before the deconstruction of the subject, Dickens was presenting many figures as mere collections of humors or tics. In *The Pickwick Papers,* Alfred Jingle's telegraphic speech drew attention to the circuit of communication, the medium of the message. The speech of a later character such as Flora Finching in *Little Dorrit* is a nexus of intersecting clichés and popular languages; she is a "terminal of multiple networks," to borrow a phrase from a third noted postmodernist, Jean Baudrillard (128). Pancks, from the same novel, combines an apparent lack of interiority with bursts of strangely purposive energy. Like many Dickens characters, he exhibits what Baudrillard calls the "forced extroversion of all interiority" (132). Countless other characters in the Dickens pantomime are dispersed and decentered, to such an extent that their existence can be accounted for by a single name or trait—Bar, Bishop, maces, petty-bags, and privy purses. These allegorical types find near relatives in some of the cartoon figures of Pynchon, Barthelme, Reed, and Acker. Dickens's characters might be said to betray "an ever greater formal and operational abstraction of elements and functions," to continue drawing on Baudrillard (128). From this perspective, Dickens produces not only "modern" social phenomena, such as the liberal, autonomous self, but also "postmodern" phenomena, such as the simulacrum and the deconstructed subject.

Dickens's narrative impulse and his eccentric characters may be his most obvious links with 1960s postmodernism, but there are others that deserve mention. The disturbingly mobile nature of Dickensian desire, which seeks, as John Kucich has pointed out, "to violate the coherence and integrity of the self . . . to expend energy recklessly, in defiance of any concerns for the safety or advantage of the individual" (204), seems to anticipate the postmodern insights of Deleuze and Guattari. The carnivalesque in Dickens and the relish for parody, which turn the glamorous images of status and wealth into objects of ridicule, anticipate the central role of parody in postmodernism. Finally, the labyrinthine plots of the late novels, which bring even the most distant characters into unexpected relation with one another, might be seen as looking forward to the vast systems of connections in Pynchon. Only a thematic adjustment—from celebratory to paranoid (an adjustment that these "dark" novels seem always on the verge of making themselves)—separates the two authors' concern with hidden connections.

The links between Dickens and contemporary culture extend well beyond his foreshadowing of esoteric postmodern theory. Once one starts to look for him, this author pops up at every turn.[1] During the twentieth century, more than seventy movies were made from his works (DeBona 78)—seven of *Great Expectations* alone, including the 1998 Hollywood feature directed by Alfonso Cuarón and starring Ethan Hawke, Gwyneth Paltrow, and Robert De Niro. In the course of my inquiries, I have been told of or have seen television episodes of *The Donna Reed Show, Cheers, Wings, Quantum Leap,* and *The Simpsons* that presented takeoffs of Dickens novels. *The Paper Chase* and *Happy Days* each have segments titled "Great Expectations"; *The Twilight Zone* called one show "In Praise of Pip"; and *South Park* ran a hilarious if foulmouthed version of the novel in the last month of year 2000. On Saturday morning cartoons, Disney's *Scrooge McDuck* remains a perennial favorite. An episode of *L.A. Law* featured a case involving a stereotypical "Victorian" librarian and a young man who dropped his lawsuit against her because of a conversion experience brought on by reading *Bleak House.*

An equal number of examples can be drawn from other forms of contemporary media. Many readers will remember a singer named Tiny Tim, who made a name for himself with "Tiptoe through the Tulips." In the seventies there was a rock band called Uriah Heep (and, by the by, a Macintosh programming tool with the same name, which Neal Stephenson alludes to in *Cryptonomicon*). The Eagles' 1976 hit "New Kid in Town" tells of a boy's "great expectations," which lead even his old friends to treat him like he's something new. More recently, Tasmin Archer called her 1993 debut album *Great Expectations.* Journalism provides even better hunting grounds. A search of a magazine database turned up fifty-nine articles published in a single year that used the phrase "great expectations" in their titles, and although some of these pieces do not explicitly allude to Dickens, many of them do—such as the article on President Clinton's first one hundred days titled "Great Expectations Meet Bleak House."

Then there are the ubiquitous Dickens Web sites that I mentioned in the introduction. Dickens's appeal for the online generation encompasses the ordinary fan of Dickens's fiction; people in quest of knickknacks, clothing, and other Victoriana; students in search of help with their homework; and scholars who access the large databases devoted to his life and work. One of the first literary resources in digital form—created by George P. Landow of Brown University, several years before the World Wide Web was even invented—was *The Dickens Web* (still available on disk from Eastgate Systems, publisher of Shelley Jackson's *Patchwork Girl*). Some of the material from *The Dickens Web* has been incorporated in Landow's more ambitious online resource, *The Victorian Web.* Landow's *Dickens Page* on this site includes short scholarly articles written by many contributors on topics ranging from the novelist's biography and works to the social, political, religious, and scientific contexts of his fiction. The collaborative Web site continues to grow yearly in depth and complexity.[2]

At the other end of the spectrum is *Victorian Vanities: One Stop Shopping for Vintage Victorian Clothing,* a multimedia site that combines advertisements for the merchandise on sale with photographs of Dickens lovers in nineteenth-century costumes and brief features on topics such as "There is a bit of Pickwick in All of Us" and "Dickens and Decadence: 200 years of

Fashion" (Christopher). Despite its commercialism, the site conveys a warm, friendly sense of a community of people who love their Victorian pastime. Similarly, the "Mission Statement" of *The Dickens Fellowship,* posted on the Philadelphia branch's Web site, reveals some of the diverse motives that tempt contemporary Dickensians into cyberspace. The Fellowship was founded to promote friendship among admirers of Dickens, to preserve buildings connected with his name, and most interesting of all, "To take such measures as may be expedient to remedy or ameliorate those existing social evils which would have appealed so strongly to the heart of Charles Dickens, and to help in every possible direction in the cause of the poor and oppressed" (*Dickens Fellowship,* "Mission Statement"). If this high-minded idealism seems oddly matched with the commercialized nostalgia of many other Web sites, the contradiction is only typical of Dickens's continued attraction.

The nostalgic character of Dickens's presence in today's world is especially visible around Christmastime, when productions of *A Christmas Carol* vie for airtime on TV with *It's a Wonderful Life* and *Miracle on 34th Street.* Such nostalgia for a simpler life is by no means incompatible with commercial exploitation, as the novelist himself well knew. Scrooge is a familiar figure in magazine and TV commercials, such as the Canadian Tire jingle that runs "Spend like Santa, Save like Scrooge." In gift shops around the country, the beloved Dickens Christmas Village is a bestseller; this "collectible" shows how Dickens's creations can literally be transformed into what Wemmick calls "portable property," as Christina Rieger remarked on the electronic bulletin board VICTORIA. At the Mt. Hope Victorian Estate and Winery, near Hershey, Pennsylvania, the great novelist himself annually hosts a party of nineteenth-century notables in what is billed as a "Charles Dickens Victorian Christmas"; advance reservations may be purchased online with a major credit card. But Christmas is not the only holiday season when Dickens may turn up. The 1993 Carnival in New Orleans featured *Great Expectations* prominently. The theme of one of the parades that year was "Royal British Scribes," and the lead float depicted Miss Havisham enthroned between two bridal cakes and surrounded by members of an all-male secret society, wearing masks and bridal costumes themselves.[3]

The economic impact of Dickens is even greater in education circles, where the dissemination of his works is a matter not only of devotion but also of professional obligation. This sector is a multimillion dollar industry, which encompasses secondary school teachers, college professors, editors, publishers, book distributors, bookstore owners, librarians, compilers of online resources, and more. To speak only of the university end of the spectrum, one observes that the professional interest in nineteenth-century British literature has spawned an international network of critical journals, academic book publishers, scholarly societies, conferences, foundation grants, graduate fellowships, and salaried positions in colleges and universities.

More visible traces of the economic potential of the Dickens icon can be found on street corners and in malls all across the continent. Who has not run across antique stores called The Olde Curiosity Shoppe? Philadelphia offers a pub called the Dickens Inn, and right around the corner is another one called The Artful Dodger (this latter name turns up in Saskatoon, Saskatchewan, too). Dallas is home to one of a nationwide chain of maternity stores called Great Expectations. In the Richmond area there is a candle shop called Great Waxpectations; in Winnipeg a dessert restaurant called Baked Expectations; in Brooklyn a beauty salon called Great Hair-Spectations; in Manhattan a wine tasting called Grape Expectations. To complete the roll call of bad puns, I once saw a *Saturday Night Live* skit called "Great Expectorations" and, more recently, a sports feature about the hockey star Wayne Gretzky called "Gretz Expectations."

Now, if you are like me, you are about to shriek at the incongruity of naming maternity shops, hair salons, and restaurants after a phrase that denominates the inevitability of disappointment, of broken hearts, false hopes, and punctured dreams. This incongruity, however, is echoed and redoubled by other ironies, equally apparent but worth underscoring, such as the mixture of sentimentality and commercialism in the Dickens Christmas, or the combination in academia of idealism and love of literature with an institutional apparatus requiring professional credentialing, publication for tenure, and the annual ranking of universities by *U.S. News and World Report.* This kind of irony, I am arguing, characterizes Dickens's presence in contemporary culture. Incongruity, contradiction, the juxtaposition of mismatched signifiers and ill-assorted values—these are the tokens by which Dickens travels today. And for this reason, if for no other, Dickens is perhaps the most "postmodern" Victorian writer.

Dickens was aware that his vision went well with the commercial spirit. Many Victorian writers worked hard to make money from their fiction, but Dickens was extraordinarily fertile in devising new ways to capitalize on his imagination. Perhaps his greatest coup was his invention of a new genre, the Christmas tale. These tales were increasingly successful as specially printed seasonal books and later were carefully orchestrated to prop up circulation of the magazines he ran. These works did so much to transform the nature of the holiday that the novelist's most recent biographer has remarked that "Dickens can be said to have almost single-handedly created the modern idea of Christmas" (Ackroyd 34). Many aspects of contemporary society might surprise Dickens, but the commercialization of Christmas—and his foundational role in it—would not be one of them.

Dickens was prescient in recognizing the economic shift that was occurring in his lifetime. In the middle of the nineteenth century, England underwent a transition from an industrial economy, driven by the production of coal, iron, heavy machinery, and railroads, to a consumer economy, with its investment in advertising, marketing strategies, and household goods. As historians and cultural critics such as Martin J. Wiener, Jennifer Wicke, and Thomas Richards have demonstrated, in the decades after the Great Exhibition of 1851 a "new commodity culture dominated by advertising drew on and ultimately supplanted any alternatives to it" (Richards 1). This change helped foster a booming secondary market for Dickens's creations. In his own lifetime, Dickens saw the Little Nell Cigar, Pickwick Snuff, Gamp Umbrellas, and a host of other products bearing his characters' names; he went out of his way to visit a tavern named after his novel *Our Mutual Friend* (Dickens, *Speeches* 349). As I noted in the introduction, there was no provision for licensing such spinoffs, but Dickens understood the publicity value that came from their wide diffusion. From *Pickwick* onward, the green monthly numbers that serialized his novels carried advertisements for consumer goods ranging from foundation garments to washing machines and self-rising flour; the novelist eventually came to exercise control over what ads appeared, how they were arranged, and even what their copy should be (Wicke, *Advertising Fictions* 50). He also led the way in advertising his own works. His later novels were announced by placards on the sides of buses, billboards in railway stations, and posters wrapped around lamp posts (Ackroyd 947). Moreover, his public readings had dramatic effects on the sales of his work, which were available in the lobby after each performance. The fit was perfect: Dickens both exploited and was exploited by a burgeoning consumer economy. But consumer capitalism was only in its infancy during the novelist's lifetime. Today, one sees the full effects of this 150-year-long transformation.

The most successful contemporary venture to capitalize on Dickens's *Great Expectations* is the one with which this chapter opened, the video dating service, Great Expectations Services for Singles. With some 40 offices in cities across the country and more than 125,000 members, it claims to produce "almost two weddings a day" (Winokur 239). The enterprise is a nice model of the kind of cultural pastiche that postmodern theorists say characterizes the latest stage of capitalism. It fuses information technology with that nostalgically Dickensian name, and it charges hefty fees (often approaching $2,000) for performing a richly ambiguous personal service: supplying partners for marriage and/or casual sex. Its founder and president, Jeffrey Ullman, who conceived the idea for this multimillion dollar corporation while living in a Berkeley commune during the counterculture years (Kravitz 277), conflates venerable political rhetoric about self-determination with contemporary jargon about lifestyles and the single person. Similarly, the company's brochure jumbles together incompatible values deriving from several different epochs. Note the clash between the claims to technocratic efficiency, leisured dignity, workaholic time pressures, and a hip ability to size up strangers in this passage from a promotional letter addressed to "Dear Single": Great Expectations "is a wonderfully efficient—and dignified—way to find the kind of person you prefer to socialize with, before you agree to meet with them. So you don't waste your precious time on blind dates or with losers."[4] In a telephone interview on June 29, 1994, Ullman confirmed that the inspiration for his company's name came from Dickens, although it was the brainchild of his father, a pediatrician born in an earlier, more literate age. After suggesting the name, Ullman's father remarked that the title came into his head because he was old enough "to have gone to school with Boz"; his son, having never heard of Dickens's pen name, thought his father must be referring to Boz Scaggs. The cultural markers that adorn this dating service are scarcely less disparate than these: fledgling Victorian novelist meets blues guitarist from Texas.

Dickens's presence in the popular culture of the twentieth century has not always been characterized by incongruity. At an earlier moment, during and just after World War II, when the great "modern" values of democratic nations had been under severe challenge, Dickens's image was more serious and coherent, an instrument of cultural consolidation, not consumerist expansion. I can bring out the difference by contrasting two carefully marketed images of the author, the Classics Illustrated comic book versions of *Great Expectations*. The first version of this story was published in 1947, whereas the second, entirely new version, came out in 1990.[5] The first version rapidly became a collector's item—today a copy in mint condition sells for over $800 (Figure 6.1). Although this issue is number 43 in the series, it is the most valuable Classics Illustrated ever published because it was never reissued once it became the target of an attack in a best-selling book about comics by Dr. Fredric Wertham, *Seduction of the Innocent* (1954). Here are a few lines from Dr. Wertham's attack:

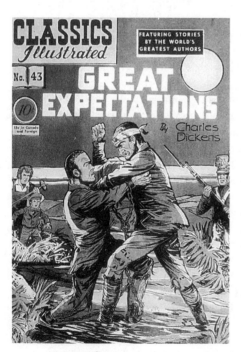

FIGURE 6.1
Classics Illustrated, 1947.

There is a comic book which has on its cover two struggling men, one manacled with chains locked around hands and feet, the other with upraised fist and a reddened, bloody bandage around his head; onlookers: a man with a heavy iron mallet on one side and a man with a rifle and a bayonet on the other. The first eight pictures of this comic book show an evil-looking man with a big knife held like a dagger threatening a child who says: "Oh, don't cut my throat, sir!" Am I correct in classifying this as a crime comic? Or should I accept it as what it pretends to be—Dickens' *Great Expectations?* (311)

A glance at the cover reveals that Dr. Wertham described the scene fairly well, as far as he went. His description of the succeeding pictures was equally accurate. My point, however, has nothing to do with violence in comic books, a topic that today seems almost quaint. Rather, I want to draw attention to the cultural markers embedded in this scene, markers of masculinity, power, legal authority, and ultimately, national identity. An honest, square-jawed blacksmith, a well-equipped soldier, and a boy dressed in his best Christmas suit witness a struggle between determined adversaries, the free and gallantly bandaged Magwitch beginning to rise above the treacherous, deservedly manacled Compeyson—a struggle between good and evil, clearly enough, with the values of a nation's men at stake.

When one turns to the 1990 version of the same story, the first thing one notices is the very different scene the artist has chosen as the centerpiece of his interpretation (Figure 6.2). The cover of a comic book is meant to grab the attention of the potential buyer, and these covers employ very different strategies for that end. Both covers dramatize formative moments in a child's life, and both emphasize the impressible young boy's status as an observer. In each, he is outside the scene, watching with rapt attention. But one is an action scene, full of violence and involving only males; the other is a scene of stasis—indeed, it symbolizes the deathly stasis of Miss Havisham—and features two female characters. The visual dynamics of watching are present in both covers, but the later version introduces a self-reflexive dimension that is missing from the earlier. The picture is an optical illusion, in which Pip appears to be looking at a painting or a tapestry, framed by the border of the carpet and by what may be a doorjamb to his left. Moreover, the spectatorial act is even more prominent, since the reader, who is positioned behind Pip's head, sees what Pip is seeing and thus shares what film theorists call the character's "gaze."

FIGURE 6.2
Classics Illustrated, 1990.

Lest one think I am reading notions of gender and self-reflexivity into a work entirely innocent of such pretensions, let me provide a bit of background on Rick Geary, the creator of the 1990 comic. Geary first gained notice as a cartoonist for the *National Lampoon,* where his strips were praised for their droll, deadpan humor and their interest in the oddity of everyday life. Prior to working on *Great Expecta-*

tions, he had published several collections of cartoons, two of which were *A Treasury of Victorian Murder* and *Rick Geary's Oddities*. After finishing the Dickens story, he produced two original comic books titled *Blanche Goes to New York* (1992) and *Blanche Goes to Hollywood* (1993), both set in the early years of this century. The choice of a female heroine and a historical setting for these quirky mysteries indicate something of his interest in the topics of both gender and history. Although both comics display his fascination with perspectives and the gaze, the second Blanche story makes this concern explicit by having the heroine come under the patronage of the movie director D. W. Griffith. (This director, it is worth mentioning, was said by Eisenstein to have learned the technique of montage from reading Dickens.) Finally, the comic also highlights Geary's political concerns, for it sympathetically recounts the struggle of the Wobblies to unionize the film industry.

What should one make of the differences between the two comics, of the shift from a male scene of power and authority to a female domestic scene of stasis with a self-reflexive concern about the dynamics of spectators and the gaze? Clearly, the masculine scenario owes much to the prevailing conventions of World War II army comics. The two muscular figures struggling on the cover evoke Sergeant Rock or Sergeant Fury more than half-starved escapees from a nineteenth-century prison ship. An even more direct influence may have been David Lean's movie of *Great Expectations,* which came out the preceding year. The comic's plot follows the movie in several places more closely than the book—particularly in the decision to leave out the character of Orlick entirely, a choice generally regarded as a major flaw in the movie (see Moynahan; MacKay; Giddings; Tharaud). Geary had no such immediate visual precursor. Perhaps, too, Geary was aware of the controversy over violence that engulfed the earlier version. Still, the 1990 comic, with its awareness of its own cultural positioning as camp, is mocking at the very points where its predecessor was earnest.

The original Classics Illustrated were marketed as being more educational than ordinary comics. That was why Dr. Wertham's critique could have such a devastating effect. Although the publisher of the contemporary Classics Illustrated gestures toward this same educational mission in his prefatory note, he spends more time touting the "distinctive, fresh and innovative" styles of his contemporary adapters. The publisher is well aware that the largest market for these $3.75 books consists not of thrill-seeking children, nor even of students looking for a crib, but of adolescent and adult comic collectors, who value this art form for its own sake. In the best postmodern fashion, Geary dispels any sense that Dickens should be treated as an object of veneration and focuses instead on the quirky and bizarre. This comic might just as well have been called, in homage to Geary's other works, *A Treasury of Dickensian Oddities*. But perhaps to a postmodern sensibility "Dickensian oddities" would have seemed redundant.

To elaborate on this contrast, let me return to David Lean's 1946 movie. This classic film has received ample attention, but one relevant question has never been addressed: Why was this director, who was to become the preeminent cinematic poet of colonialism in works such as *The Bridge on the River Kwai* (1957), *Lawrence of Arabia* (1962), and *A Passage to India* (1984), attracted to Charles Dickens? Is there a link between Lean's vision of *Great Expectations* and his later fascination with the fate of the British Empire?

In Lean's *Great Expectations,* the connection with colonialism is to be found in the depiction of Magwitch after the convict's return to England from his transportation to the colonies. The deathbed scene between Magwitch and Pip is the true climax of the movie, far more important, in Lean's rendering, than Pip's reconciliation with Joe, or even the extravagant happy ending with Estella that so many viewers have deplored. The bond between these two men generates the most intensely felt emotion in the picture, an emotion that enables the two figures to overcome all the divisions of class, education, and age. In the presence of this emotional bond, one is reminded of the other intense relationships in Lean's oeuvre between males from remote cultures: Lawrence with the Arab boys Faraj and Daud; Colonel Nicholson with his Japanese counterpart, Colonel Saito; Fielding with the Indian Aziz. This last pairing is responsible for Lean's greatest liberty with E. M. Forster's novel, the Indian and the Englishman clasping hands in friendship at the film's end. Anita Desai, Rustom Bharucha, and Millicent Bell have each denounced this bit of colonial nostalgia, but the motif is clearly crucial to Lean's vision, and it was there, in embryo, in the love between Magwitch and Pip. The fantasy is that a certain kind of bond between men of honor can overcome the violence, horrors, and injustices of this world. The genesis of Lean's fantasy came just after World War II, when Britain's hold over its colonial others had been lost. Dickens served the ends of this fantasy, providing a symbol of those qualities in the national character that might still secure the hegemony of British civilization, even if the nation's place in the new world order was permanently diminished. This strategy for promoting British self-esteem was decidedly more successful than the Millennium Dome, if the continued international appeal of Lean's films on video and DVD is any indicator.

By the 1990s, postcolonial perspectives on Australia make this particular form of colonial nostalgia unavailable to cinematic adaptors of *Great Expectations.* Alfonso Cuarón's interesting but uneven 1998 version, set in the United States at the end of the twentieth century, cuts Australia and the colonies out of the equation altogether, substituting brief references to the convict's escape to Mexico and South America, with the implication that he made his fortune in the drug trade. Ethan Hawke follows up his performance in *Gattaca* (1997), which figures in the next chapter, by portraying Pip (here renamed Finn), and Gwyneth Paltrow makes a convincing American Estella. At the same time that Paltrow has become a signature actress for the 1990s, she has also become known for her performances in movies that play with England's literary heritage (witness her title role in *Emma* [1996] and her Academy Award–winning role in *Shakespeare in Love,* released the same year as Cuarón's *Great Expectations*).

The director uses his two young stars to play Dickens's story for all the erotic charge it can yield. In a transposition that effectively captures the difference between 1990s America and Victorian England, Cuarón makes sexual longing rather than class ambition the driving force behind Finn's character. The several explicit sex scenes implicate the viewer in the film's pervasive tone of voyeurism. This effort to integrate the movie's theme with the director's choice to have Finn be an artist is hinted at by the self-referential use of imagery from Finn's drawings in the credits and then made all too obvious during the scene where Finn sketches Estella in the nude. My point in stressing the movie's voyeuristic treatment of Finn's desire for Estella is to draw out one of its great differences from Lean's version. Whereas Pip's bond with Magwitch in the 1946 movie derives its power from the boy's belated recognition of the greater love he owes to Joe, the intensity of the 1998 version stems from Finn's scopic desire to take simultaneous possession of a woman and the New York art world. Not even the presence of Robert De Niro as the convict (renamed Arthur Lustig and turned into a mob hitman) can give the convict's death scene the charge it possesses in Lean's film.

In the aftermath of World War II, Lean's reading of Dickens in terms of colonial reconciliation was less discordant than it would be today. George Orwell, writing a few years earlier, in 1940, identified the same fantasy of reconciliation between honest, straightforward men as the core of Dickens's appeal: "His whole 'message' is one that at first glance looks like an enormous platitude: If men would behave decently the world would be decent" (Orwell 417). To a contemporary novelist, however, born in one of Britain's former colonies, the message seems little less than appalling. Salman Rushdie, writing in 1984 about both George Orwell and one of Lean's later movies, *A Passage to India,* finds this fantasy to be at the core of the "zombie-like revival of the defunct Empire" (101). Rushdie calls his essay "Outside the Whale," signaling his rejection of the stance Orwell took in the title piece of his collection *Inside the Whale* (1940). As it happens, this slender volume is where Orwell's essay on Dickens appears, a Dickensian (or postmodern?) coincidence that helps locate each judgment in its respective historical moment.

Rushdie is pertinent to this discussion for another reason. He is one of several contemporary novelists who have responded to Dickens in their fiction (others include Kathy Acker, Peter Ackroyd, Oscar Hijuelos, Charles Palliser, and Graham Swift).[6] In *The Satanic Verses* (1989), Rushdie invokes a different Dickens text, his last completed novel, *Our Mutual Friend.* A climactic moment in Rushdie's narrative takes place at a party on the set of a movie version of a musical based on Dickens's work, now retitled *Friend!*

The set is a "huge re-creation of Dickensian London" (421), which condenses the nineteenth-century city so that the landmarks of Dickens's imagination lie shoulder-to-shoulder in hallucinatory proximity.[7] Real celebrities mingle with "counterfeit" guests, hired for the occasion to wear period costumes. One of the extras, a buxom maid with a map of London drawn with a magic marker on her right breast, tries to seduce Saladin Chamcha in a mock Curiosity Shop. This drunken encounter combines familiar postmodern playfulness about the indistinguishability of imitations and originals with more disturbing motifs: nationalism, xenophobia, misogyny, and racism. As she unfastens her blouse, this "cartographically bosomed stranger" (425) sings a parody of the musical's Podsnap solo, mocking the accents of foreigners in a "Rex-Harrisonian" patter and praising London as the "World's Metropolis" (424). Chamcha stands transfixed by the sight of her breast. "The metropolis summons him"—but which metropolis, the map on her breast, the Dickensian London of the set, the real London outside?—until, "giving an entirely Dickensian cry, [he] pushes his way out of the Curiosity Shop into the madness of the street" (424).

In the vocabulary of postmodern theory, Rushdie's movie set is a simulacrum;[8] but, then, Dickens's London has always been a simulacrum, an image more real than reality, one that attracted its first tourists during his own lifetime and that continues to draw them by the busload today. Such perplexities are a far cry from the "message" of Dickens in the forties. Rather than serving to consolidate a coherent national identity, this author has come to symbolize, for Rushdie, a form of madness characteristic of contemporary existence. The madness of the street stems from the fact that, in a postcolonial world, "There is no consensus about reality," to quote again from Rushdie's essay on Orwell and Lean (100). In *The Satanic Verses* London is full of incompatible realities, whether the city in question is the real one outside the movie set or the Dickensian simulacrum within.[9] But if Chamcha now experiences the streets of London as a form of madness, it is only, Rushdie seems to say, because of a logic already visible in the "roaring streets" Dickens described in the last line of *Little Dorrit*.

L ess than a decade after Peter Carey published *Oscar and Lucinda* (1988), he brought out another work of fiction set in the nineteenth century, a rewriting of *Great Expectations* from the convict's point of view. *Jack Maggs* (1997) is the most ambitious version yet of Dickens's classic. Like his earlier fiction drawing on the Crystal Palace, Carey's novel is full of temporal and spatial layers. *Jack Maggs* is a 1990s novel by an Australian living in New York; it rewrites an English novel of 1861 by telling the story of a young Dickens (renamed Tobias Oates), who is imagined composing a first novel in 1837 (the year of *Pickwick*); Oates's fictional work *The Death of Maggs* is set two decades earlier, in 1818, both because it narrates events that supposedly occurred back then and because it is plagiarized from the convict's own autobiography, which we read as the convict writes it; the convict's life story goes back still further to 1801 and tells of his Oliver Twist-like boyhood in a gang of thieves; Maggs's autobiography is meant to be an *apologia pro vita sua* to redeem himself in the eyes of Pip (here called Henry Phipps and given a decadent homosexual lifestyle reminiscent of Oscar Wilde's).

The palimpsest of times, versions, genres, and places is organized around a powerful metaphor for the kind of historical exploration Carey values. The metaphor is one of doubling. Carey presents *Jack Maggs* as an uncanny double of both *Great Expectations* and Dickens's own biography. Similarly, Carey's imaginary novelist Tobias Oakes is the double of not only Dickens but also the convict Maggs. Both Oakes and Maggs are writers; both commit murders; both conceive an illegitimate child with a sister or sister-in-law; both are tormented by the belief that this infant has been aborted; and both have "invented a respectable life" for themselves (*Maggs* 170), Oates as a husband, father, and novelist, Maggs as a prosperous Australian property owner. Carey finds a warrant for all this doubling in *Great Expectations* itself, for there Orlick is depicted as the double of Pip, the dark rival who acts out many of the violent desires Pip represses. In Carey's novel, the doubling extends to the textual level, where the reader encounters variants of the same scenes depicted in the convict's autobiography, Oates's novelization of the convict's life, and Carey's authorial narration. Most important, the doubling extends to Carey's historical project, which inverts in the process of reusing the details of Dickens's fiction and life, all in order to reveal how Victorian culture looks to one of its colonial descendants.

The metaphor for Carey's method appears explicitly in a scene early in the novel. When Maggs begins composing his autobiography, he not only uses invisible ink but also writes in mirror script. Maggs's composition is an apt symbol for the way features of the past may be hidden *and* distorted in the present. To read these invisible messages from earlier days, one often needs to take extraordinary measures. Maggs sends a small mirror along with the pages of his diary to the only reader he desires, the gentleman he has supported financially for many years. "Well, Henry Phipps," Maggs writes, "you will read a different type of story in the glass" (71). One must look in a glass, so to speak, to see the past in the present.

Great Expectations—and at last I refer to the novel by Charles Dickens—mixes cultural signs from different periods as pervasively and as incongruously as many recent texts. Joe, the simple blacksmith, for example, represents a nostalgic portrait of a figure from an earlier era, a phase of capitalism fast disappearing in 1861, when the novel was published, although not as uncommon in rural areas in 1803 to 1815, when the first volume of the novel was set. The values associated with Joe—integrity, unswerving loyalty, pride in one's craft—accrue to this residual economic order (to use Raymond Williams's term, which is perfectly appropriate here). Thus Joe's world serves as an implicit critique of the more highly developed dominant economy of London. Staging the contrast as one between country and city helps to reduce the sense of incongruity for readers. Still, the incompatibility of this ideal with mid-Victorian existence is dramatized at the end of the novel. The only way Pip can find to be true to the lessons he has learned from Joe is to spend eleven years away from the forge in his company's colonial branch in Cairo. Pip's summary of those eleven years represents the most stereotypically "Victorian" moment in the book. His only consolation, the thing that enables him to hold up his head when he thinks of how badly he has behaved, is that now he "lived frugally, and paid my debts." If the reader had any doubts about the middle-class positioning of this Victorian ethic, Pip clears them up without delay: "I must not leave it to be supposed that we were ever a great House, or that we made mints of money. We were not in a grand way of business, but we had a good name, and worked for our profits" (489).

If Joe is a holdover from a rural, pre-Victorian mode of early capitalism and Pip matures into a thoroughly up-to-date middle-class Victorian, then is there anyone in the novel who might be said to foreshadow postmodernism? I am happy to say that there is. That person is not Pip, so the answer to the question in this chapter's title must be: No. Pip might be "Victorian" or even "modern," but this earnest, frugal, self-effacing partner in a firm that works for its profits is anything but "postmodern."

I hope the reader feels the ludicrousness of this exercise: pigeonholing fictional characters with period terms is the academic equivalent of naming a dating service with a labored literary allusion, Great Expectations Services for Singles. The temporal diversity is real, however, and Dickens was as cognizant of it as a fine cultural studies critic like Paul Gilroy. The novel captures what Gilroy calls "non-synchronous, heterocultural modes of social life in close proximity" (197)—and it makes them both funny and sad.

Let me continue in this vein, whimsically nominating a different character as my representative of postmodernism. The character who has the best claim to this accolade plays a minor role in the story, but he has been a favorite with readers down through the years: Wemmick. Mr. Jaggers's clerk conflates enough incongruous cultural signs in his humble person to become a veritable icon of Dickens at the millennium. A model of businesslike decorum at the office, with his post-office mouth and his invariable advice to look after "portable property," he is an entirely different man at home, where he indulges his Aged P, shyly courts Miss Skiffins, and lovingly tends to his house and garden. The split between these two incarnations is so profound that Pip speculates that there must be "twin Wemmicks" (401). A division of this kind, between the self in its "private and personal capacity," to use Wemmick's words (310), and the public, professional self is seen often enough today but is hardly restricted to postmodernism. This kind of split was, in fact, one of the hallmarks of the "modern" self, a condition that Marx famously identified as a consequence of the worker's alienation from his labor.

If a divided self were Wemmick's only distinctive characteristic, then he would be an unusually pure representative of a single historical type, "modern man." But Wemmick's interest hardly stops there. His home at Walworth is his other claim to fame. It is a little wooden cottage, which Wemmick has transformed into a miniature Gothic castle, perfect in every detail, including mock fortifications, a moat with its own drawbridge, a flag, and a cannon, which is discharged punctually at nine o'clock each evening. He lives in a simulacrum of another era, a theme park version of feudal England. Dickens himself had already turned into comedy the postmodern notion of living in a simulacrum, which is so amusing in Rushdie and Barnes. Much like the owners of today's theme parks, Wemmick takes pride in bringing to life a cliché. He has turned his house into a literal incarnation of the saying "A man's home is his castle." His mode of existence—inside this historical replica—reproduces the economic conditions of a "freehold" (231) as far as is possible in a suburb of nineteenth-century London. As Wemmick proudly explains, "I am my own engineer, and my own carpenter, and my own plumber, and my own gardener, and my own Jack of all Trades" (230).

Inside the castle is Wemmick's prized "collection of curiosities" (231). His treasures "were mostly of a felonious character," including a forger's pen and "a distinguished razor or two" (231). The collection might be dubbed "A Treasury of Victorian Murder," as odd as Rick Geary's postmodern comic book of that name. The Aged P is so proud of his son's accomplishment that he thinks "it ought to be kept together by the Nation, after my son's time, for the people's enjoyment" (230). After visiting some of the houses preserved by the British National Trust, with their mismatched architectural styles and their (far more expensive) collections of curiosities, I sometimes wonder if they did. In short, Wemmick's home is a postmodern pastiche, a simulacrum, as misshapen and comical as Great Hair-Spectations at the local mall.

With Wemmick as a guide, one begins to notice that *Great Expectations* itself is a palimpsest of different cultural periods. In Dickens's novel, one can identify traces of at least five "non-synchronous" modes of social life, each competing with the others for cultural space: (1) the "feudal" freehold of Wemmick's castle; (2) the preindustrial capitalism of Joe's forge; (3) the "Victorian" middle-class values of Pip's mature years, with their clear connections to the fortunes of empire; (4) the "modern" alienation that splits Wemmick into twin selves; and (5) the "postmodern" world of simulacra and pastiche. They all take place in a book published in the nineteenth century, not in a work such as *Jack Maggs*. The discontinuity among these temporal layers contributes to some of the most enduring effects of Dickens's novel: the comedy of Wemmick, the narrator's retrospective tenderness toward Joe, the ethical growth of Pip, and the book's vision of the alienated condition of urban life.

Few readers before today have ever interpreted the presence of these discontinuous cultural layers as signs that there is, in Rushdie's words, "no consensus about reality." In the past, critics would single out one strand and elevate it as the master discourse of the text. Where Dickens's contemporaries saw the novel as a return to the comic types and affectionate portraits of his youthful fiction, modernist critics perceived a new, "dark" phase of social criticism, and readers of the 1940s discerned images of British national identity that could symbolically replace the loss of empire. Only at the turn of the millennium have people begun to focus on discontinuity itself, seeing in Dickens a foreshadowing of the incompatible realities of today.

L et me end this chapter by drawing some conclusions about contemporary culture's sense of history. It has become commonplace to assert that a consumer society has no historical awareness, that advanced capitalism depends upon a singleminded focus on novelty. At the same time, shoppers cruise through a landscape saturated by nostalgic references to the past, hair salons and candle stores labeled with bad historical puns. These allusions achieve their effect by being taken out of context. In most cases, they have certainly lost any literal reference to the past. They exist only as a kind of cultural malapropism, good for a brief smile, if that. Consequently, the experience of cultural dissonance has become a routine part of daily life.

Fredric Jameson has given the best account of this paradox in his book *Postmodernism.* There he describes an "ultimate historicist breakdown" but says

> we have not, for all that, ceased to be preoccupied by history; indeed, at the very moment in which we complain, as here, of the eclipse of historicity, we also universally diagnose contemporary culture as irredeemably historicist, in the bad sense of an omnipresent and indiscriminate appetite for dead styles and fashions; indeed, for all the styles and fashions of a dead past. Meanwhile, a certain caricature of historical thinking—which we may not even call *generational* any longer, so rapid has its momentum become—has also become universal and includes at least the will and intent to return upon our present circumstances in order to think of them—as the nineties, say—and to draw the appropriate marketing and forecasting conclusions. Why is this not historicity with a vengeance? (286–87)

Jameson answers his question by distinguishing between history as reification, which packages the present as a readily graspable commodity, and genuine history, which is unafraid of weighing the present in a "periodizing or totalizing abstraction" (342). The former, in Jameson's view, should be held responsible not only for the commercialization of the past but also for facile literary and cinematic genres such as historical metafiction and the nostalgia film. The latter, genuine history, opens the possibility for critique and clears a space for potentially utopian energies.

My account of the paradox differs only partially from Jameson's analysis. The difference does not arise solely from my reluctance to adopt his totalizing approach. In Jameson's hands, dialectical thinking produces explanations that combine suppleness with force, and his comprehensive scheme of history enables him to pose questions about the present that I very much want answered. The difference stems from Jameson's pessimism about the capacity of literature and film today to do more than replicate the sheer heterogeneity, the "absolute and absolutely random pluralism" for which he finds "*fragmentation* . . . much too weak and primitive a term" (371–72). Here is his description of this failure, a description that must be weighed against a reading of Rushdie or Carey, or against the other contemporary figures in this study. In postmodern culture, "different moments in historical or existential time are here simply filed in different places; the attempt to combine them even locally does not slide up and down a temporal scale . . . but jumps back and forth across a game board that we conceptualize in terms of distance" (373). Rushdie's incompatible realities, Carey's mirror script, bring greater pressure to bear on the meaning of history in today's culture than a hopscotch across a boardgame.

My understanding of the paradox begins where Jameson's does, with the experience of cultural dissonance one encounters on TV, at the mall, in cyberspace, at the movies, and between the covers of books. This dissonance represents a prominent form of historical sensibility, as common in "high" as in popular culture. Much literature, art, and architecture refers to history through devices so excessive that they seem to turn back on themselves, mocking their own efforts as if they really were only pieces on Jameson's game board. Allusion, parody, irony, and hyperbole are used to place isolated cultural details in incongruous juxtapositions, creating anachronisms that are knowing rather than proleptic or historically illuminating. This form of anachronism can be too eclectic to signify anything other than its own self-awareness. It is anachronism as white noise, signal fed back on itself to the confusion of meaning.

Anachronism can have other uses, however. The temporal slips, fragments of the past lodged oddly in the present, speak in multiple ways—most absurdly, trivially, diminishing the culture's capacity for understanding; others with the shock of mild surprise; still others with genuine and lasting power. Current theory often terms this last sort "trauma," which has the merit of registering the searing effects of historical pain that will not disappear. But the term honors modes of survival that have no voice over those that have found a way to speak. As Ruth Leys puts it, "the history of trauma is a history of forgetting" (119). Gilroy, by contrast, demands respect for forms that have managed to make themselves heard, the powerful afterlife of the black experience of slavery in contemporary music, art, dance, and literature. Toni Morrison's *Beloved* (1987) names one such survival "rememory" and captures both the difficulty and the necessity of its transmission through the multiple resonances of her phrase "not a story to pass on" (275). Cultural studies requires a language not just for haunted silence but for articulate voices. It needs a language beyond "trauma" for accessing a usable past.

"Anachronism" will not always serve. The connotations of error make that word a poor choice to describe the shattering influence of the young Beloved, say, even though her re-eruption in the life of Sethe distorts temporal boundaries. Sometimes other critical terms must be found: the monstrous, the uncanny, the untimely, the odd. Sometimes the critic must look further, adopting ad hoc words like Morrison's "rememory." Sometimes, though, as for instance in Stoppard's *Arcadia,* nothing could serve better than "anachronism."[10]

Regardless of vocabulary, it is important to acknowledge that contemporary culture *does* know how to think historically. It has complex resources for narrating and judging, perceiving and turning to account, both the past and present. To deny this truth is to hobble at the outset a historical cultural studies.

Seven

New Age Evolution, *The Gold Bug Variations*, and *Gattaca*

O n the cover of the October 1999 *National Geographic* a piglet with human DNA introduces an issue dedicated to asking: "Are we ready for the gene age?" We should be. Not since Darwin's time has there been so much public attention focused on the inherited traits of our species. During the last year of the twentieth century *The New York Times* averaged forty articles a month on the new genetics, covering topics such as Dolly the cloned sheep; newly discovered genes for breast cancer, homosexuality, and longer life; ecological and religious protests against gene tampering; insurance problems arising from genetic screening; the patenting of genes; DNA forensic evidence in criminal cases and paternity suits; the prospect of cloning a wooly mammoth; and handy recipes for cooking genetically altered food. There was Doogie, the supersmart mouse, whose memory and intelligence had been enhanced by injecting a modified gene into fertilized mouse eggs. There was the painless vaccine that one day might be delivered by rubbing DNA cream on your skin. And there was an ecoterrorist group named Seeds of Resistance, which cut down a field of genetically engineered corn in Maine, followed by the demonstrations against genetically modified food at the World Trade Organization meeting in Seattle.

During the U.S. Open tennis tournament in September, Agilent Technologies premiered a series of glossy television commercials spotlighting

166

their high-tech contributions to science.[1] One of the most effective features a montage of figures posing in blue jeans. A male voice opens with a single word—"Genes"—leading you to think you are watching an advertisement for Levi's 501, until the voiceover adds another phrase—"as in 'genetics.'"[2] Against a blank white background, intriguing images flash in rapid succession: a female model walks toward the camera, an overweight man puts his hands in his pockets, children perform hiphop moves, a pregnant woman pats her stomach, a black man with dreadlocks appears to make two children of different races grow under his hands, another African-American swings a golf club, a white man twirls circles in a wheelchair, a Native American sits motionless, an old man dances, a toddler smiles. All the while, the voiceover continues its soothing message: "Genes—they make us all alike; they make us all different. And inside our genes are the secrets to creating a world without disease."

The whole production is tied together by a winking self-reflexiveness. From the play on words with which the ad begins to the irreverent butt wiggle toward the camera at the end, the commercial toys with advertising conventions in approved postmodern fashion. This irony about its own gestures suggests that nothing is off-limits, that familiar boundaries can be rearranged at will and (as the corporate motto says) "*dreams* made real." The final words of the commercial propose the conventionality of nature itself: "So maybe, some day, genetic disease will simply . . . go out of style." The arbitrary, social nature of limits has been implicit in the visuals all along. The imaginary space of the ad displays a multicultural world where all differences are made to seem a simple matter of choice. The informality of dress and the spontaneous grace of movement are designed to put us at ease with technology. In the process, they strive to put us at ease with ourselves. Categories deemed by many to be fundamental, such as race, gender, age, disability, national origin, and sexuality, are presented as mere questions of style, like the choice to wear faded blue jeans with your shirt tail untucked. Intractable social differences have become malleable, already cured of their divisiveness. If society can be so magically transformed through a kind of recombinant image splicing, then why not the body, too? The commercial takes the good feelings inspired by a mellow multiculturalism and projects them onto a future in which the material world itself is transformed by genetic science. This attempt at social engineering, were it successful, would match anything accomplished so far by genetic engineering.

The most obvious reference to time in the ad is to a future without disease, but temporal markers inform nearly every shot. Together they constitute a distinctive attitude toward time, an attitude so pervasive today in the world of genetics and biotechnology that it might be called "genome time." What one finds in genome time is a perpetual present, which paradoxically takes an eschatological stance toward the future and replaces the past with a New Age vision of evolution. In the Agilent commercial the figures seem to live wholly in the present. They are blithe, unencumbered by their pasts. Yet the past has not been erased. Its marks are visible in the bodies themselves: lined faces, a swelling pregnancy, confinement to a wheelchair, a bare midriff starved into beauty. Age differences are prominent—as prominent as race or gender—yet their burden is miraculously light. And they bear their utopian future with equal insouciance. Narrative is almost totally absent. Figures succeed one another in rapid transition, displacing predecessors, vanishing to make way for others, but there are no consequences. The effect is paradoxical. The present becomes everything, but the past and future are not actually effaced. Instead, all times are inscribed in the present, encoded in the moment. This is the key to genome time—the present is made to contain every possible permutation of time as a suddenly legible system of signs.

I am not the first to note that genetics discourse possesses its own distinctive time sense. In a recent book on genetics and computers, Donna Haraway describes "a specific sense of time" that is "characteristic of the promises and threats of technoscience" (*Modest_Witness* 9). Relating this sense of time to Christian salvation history, she writes, "technoscience is a millenniarian discourse about beginnings and ends, first and last things, suffering and progress" (*Modest_Witness* 10). This emphasis on first and last things captures part of what is involved in genome time, but there is more.

A second feature comes from the peculiar way in which time is constitutive of the object of genetics. Ever since Erwin Schrödinger attempted to answer the question *What Is Life?* (1944) by investigating the way in which living organisms appeared to be the only things that contradicted the second law of thermodynamics, scientists have regarded temporality as an intrinsic feature of life. The great French geneticist François Jacob writes: "In contrast to most aspects of physics, biology incorporates time as one of its essential parameters" ("Time" 407). Whereas the fundamental laws of physics are time symmetric, "the arrow of time [is] required whenever life is involved. . . . It is the speciality of biology, its stamp, so to speak" ("Time" 408).[3] Time is intrinsic to the gene in complex ways, however. On the one hand, genes provide a future for both the individual and the species. A person's genotype influences many aspects of his or her development: height, weight, sex, skin coloring, facial features, propensities toward some diseases, and much more. In terms of the species, genes are responsible for evolutionary change, since genetic mutation is the mechanism by which variation occurs. On the other hand, genes bear the inheritance of the past—again for both individual and species. DNA is a replicating mechanism that preserves intact the genetic inheritance of the organism through every division of every cell. The unalterability of a person's genotype after conception is what used to be called the "Central Dogma" of genetics, a principle that states that the gene's message flows in only one direction—from DNA to the proteins that express it—and that none of the vicissitudes of later life can be transmitted backward into an individual's genetic code. This principle also has become a lynchpin of neo-Darwinism because it provides a genetic basis for rejecting Lamarckian views of evolution.

A third aspect of genome time is perhaps the most intriguing to people interested in literary theory. DNA is a sign system, a language consisting of a four-letter alphabet with three-letter codons or "words." Astonishingly complex messages can be sent with this simple code, including the instructions for generating every organism that has ever lived, plant or animal. But still more bizarre messages can be sent—any messages that the mind can conceive. A writer for the *New York Times Magazine* recently proposed translating a year's issues of the weekly magazine into the DNA of cockroaches, so that in future centuries, all the vermin in Manhattan would bear the tale of our times inscribed in their being (Muschamp 125). This fantastic suggestion indicates the way in which the genetic code is scriptable or writerly through and through. The arbitrariness of the sign is more manifest in this language than in any other, for the signifiers have no intrinsic connection to the proteins they signify, something that puzzled early geneticists, who scratched their heads over the utter lack of relation between the simple *structure* of DNA and its elaborate *function* in building life.

Biomedical scientists have embraced the analogy between language and the genetic code. Taking this metaphor seriously, however, means thinking of the genome as a self-contained sign system, with all the destabilizing consequences that entails. The unmotivated or arbitrary relation between the genetic code and the organic forms it signifies challenges the notion of a natural relation between language and reality at the fundamental level of nature itself. Thinking of the genome semiotically also challenges ordinary notions of time. In the theoretical space of the genome, the relationship between past, present, and future is arbitrary, a matter of arrangement in a synchronic system of signs. Daniel C. Dennett captures this synchronic quality when he resorts to the image of a logical "Design Space" (75) within the species's genome to explain the unmotivated character of evolutionary change. Similarly, Richard Dawkins uses terms such as "genetic hyperspace" (73) or, more colorfully, "Biomorph Land" (65) to convey the sense in which evolutionary variations, which occur in time, are always already "there," in potentia.[4] The analogy with spoken language is clear. Specific utterances (what Saussure calls *parole*) occur in ordinary linear time, but the set of all possible utterances is simultaneously present in the linguistic system (*langue*). Hence the temptation to think of genome time in abstract, spatialized terms is strong. The past and future appear inscribed, as theoretical possibilities, within the mathematical space of the code.

The convergence of literary and genetic conceptions of language is a dramatic instance of the diminishing gap between the two cultures that will be explored in the final chapter. Scientists have begun to pay greater attention to the implications of the metaphors they use. Richard Lewontin, who reviews Lily E. Kay's study of the dangers of metaphors like the "Book of Life" in the issue of *Science* that published Craig Venter's draft sequence of the human genome, advises biologists to pay attention to this kind of humanistic analysis, even if they are bewildered by her use of the "jargon of poststructuralist theory" (1263), because unexamined metaphors can influence scientific research in pernicious ways.[5] Novelists, in turn, have begun to acquire a greater understanding of genomics—not only because discoveries in this field are shaping contemporary reality but also, more fundamentally, because of the new models genomics provides for thinking about age-old literary paradoxes involving time, self-reflexivity, complexity, and self-emergent form. Some of today's best fiction writers are exploring the mysteries of the genome.

In the remainder of this chapter I will take the first steps toward sequencing the temporal structure implicit in contemporary representations of genetics.[6] Genome time comes in both utopian and dystopian variants. Strains are detectable in the work of eminent scientists from Jacques Monod to Stuart Kauffman; traits are expressed in the grandiose predictions of genome startup companies like Celera and Millennium Pharmaceuticals; its offspring populate media accounts; wild mutations flourish in science fiction; and a healthy germ line has produced some fascinating literary treatments of the new genetics. I will consider two historical fictions that uncover the nineteenth-century roots of genomics in evolutionary theory, Andrea Barrett's story "*Soroche*" (1996) and Roger McDonald's novel *Mr. Darwin's Shooter* (1998); a thriller by Greg Bear, *Darwin's Radio* (1999); a brilliant novel by Richard Powers, *The Gold Bug Variations* (1991); and a disturbing film of the near future, *Gattaca* (1997).

In the past few years numerous novels—and literary nonfiction works— have taken up Darwin's legacy in light of contemporary genomics. A surprising number of these books grant the Victorian naturalist title to their very subjects: *Darwin's Dangerous Idea* (1995), *Darwin's Black Box* (1996), *Darwin's Orchestra* (1996), *Mr. Darwin's Shooter* (1998), *Darwin's Spectre* (1998), *Darwin's Audubon* (1998), *Darwin's Radio* (1999), *Darwin's Worms* (1999), and *Darwin's Ghost* (2000). The Darwin Boom of the turn of the millennium extends beyond these obvious titles to include A. S. Byatt's novella "Morpho Eugenia" from *Angels and Insects* (1992), several of Andrea Barrett's stories collected in *Ship Fever* (1996),[7] and Simon Mawer's novel *Mendel's Dwarf* (1998). With all the media attention to genetics, an interest in evolution may hardly be surprising, but why the renewed attention to a nineteenth-century figure like Darwin (and to a lesser extent, Wallace and Mendel)? One reason for the glamour of Darwin—at least for novelists—is that he symbolizes an earlier historical moment (like our own) when science and culture seemed engaged in a single great debate about the origin of life.

Among fictional treatments of Darwin's legacy, two prominent attitudes can be distinguished. The first accepts the implications of his evolutionary theories but is critical of the class politics and imperialist assumptions underlying Victorian science. Andrea Barrett's story "*Soroche*" and Roger McDonald's novel *Mr. Darwin's Shooter* evoke forgotten figures who accompanied Darwin on the voyage of the *Beagle* in order to emphasize how marginalized people played crucial roles in history. The second attitude toward Darwin extrapolates from breakthroughs in genetic engineering to move beyond his theory and reorient his ideas toward what might be called "New Age evolution." This popular attitude is prominent in best-selling thrillers and much science fiction.

Andrea Barrett's "*Soroche*" parallels two journeys, widely separated in time, to the Portillo Pass in the Chilean Andes—one by Charles Darwin and his servant, Syms Covington, in 1835, during the voyage of H.M.S. *Beagle*, and the other in 1971, taken by the main character of the story, Zaga. Zaga is a working-class woman from Philadelphia who has married the wealthy scion of a pharmaceutical company and feels out of place in the society of his well-to-do friends. She has come to Portillo on a skiing trip, as a sort of belated honeymoon, although at the last minute she discovers that her husband's two children from a former marriage will have to make the trip with them and that she is pregnant. No sooner does Zaga arrive at Portillo Pass, some 12,000 feet high, than she is incapacitated by *soroche*—or altitude sickness—and is forced to spend her entire vacation in the hotel, entertaining herself as best she can by talking to the hotel doctor, a refined Chilean named Dr. Sepulveda, while her husband and his children ski. The doctor tells Zaga stories about Darwin's trip to Portillo Pass, derived from chapter 15 of *The Voyage of the Beagle* (1839), but Dr. Sepulveda seems most interested in recounting the history of Jemmy Button, which is an episode from Darwin's chapter 10.

Jemmy Button was one of three Fuegians who were passengers on the ship with Darwin. The Fuegians had been taken captive by Captain FitzRoy on an earlier voyage of the *Beagle* and had spent several years in London, on display as curiosities, provoking the wonder of large crowds, which included King William and Queen Adelaide, who were amused to see them bow and curtsy (Browne 234). Personally, Jemmy seemed to relish the trappings of what Darwin called "civilized man" (*Voyage* 205). Darwin described him this way: "Jemmy was short, thick, and fat, but vain of his personal appearance; he used to wear gloves, his hair was neatly cut, and he was distressed if his well-polished shoes were dirtied" (*Voyage* 207). Now aboard the *Beagle* for a second time, the Fuegians were being returned to their native land, where FitzRoy hoped they would assist a missionary in establishing an outpost of the Church of England among the "miserable, degraded savages" of Tierra del Fuego (*Voyage* 208).

The mission project rapidly degenerated into a fiasco. The three Fuegians were hardly recognizable to their families, and the gifts and supplies provided by the mission society were laughably inappropriate for the task of settling in a rugged wilderness. All the same, the missionary and the three Fuegians were left behind. A few weeks later the *Beagle* returned to find the camp destroyed and the supplies torn to pieces. The missionary was frantic to be taken back on board, but to Darwin's surprise, Jemmy Button had made up his mind to stay. Darwin speculated that deep down Jemmy wanted to come back to the ship but knew that life in England would never work. Although Jemmy seemed "thoroughly ashamed of his countrymen" (*Voyage* 209), he had been equally out of place in London. In the end, Darwin feared that Jemmy's stay in England had done him little good. A year later the *Beagle* called again at the camp where they had left Jemmy. The site at first looked deserted, but at length a canoe was seen approaching, carrying "a thin haggard savage, with long disordered hair, and naked, except a bit of a blanket round his waist" (*Voyage* 229). This man was Jemmy, who was happy to see them and was laden with gifts for Captain FitzRoy and Darwin. He had a wife now, and he did not want to go back to England; instead he seemed eager to show his friends how well he was prospering. The next day, as the ship set sail, Darwin mused: "I do not now doubt that he will be as happy as, perhaps happier than, if he had never left his own country" (*Voyage* 230).

This is the story Dr. Sepulveda tells Zaga over several long afternoons in the Hotel Portillo. Zaga is disturbed by the tale, sensing that Dr. Sepulveda means to suggest a parallel "between Jemmy's life and her own" (Barrett 100). She knows she will always be an outsider to the wealthy community in Philadelphia, just as Jemmy was only a curiosity to his English patrons. At the end of the story, Zaga's husband has died, she has given away much of his money, lost the rest in a risky investment, and she is living in the same working-class neighborhood where she was born. Like Jemmy, she finds that the members of her family view her as a stranger and are resentful at how she has squandered her money rather than given it to them. Yet somehow she is at peace with her decisions. The story ends poignantly, with Zaga, whose only child had miscarried shortly after the Portillo trip, watching her sister's baby play. The conclusion reproduces the ambiguous tones in Darwin's last comment on Jemmy Button. When Darwin reflects that his Fuegian friend "will be as happy as, *perhaps happier than,* if he had never left his own country," is he saying that Jemmy will appreciate his "savage" life more because he knows how unsuited he is for "civilization"? Or is Darwin suggesting that Jemmy has been given an opportunity to make a choice few people have about how to live out his days?

Barrett leaves the tone of her story ambiguous. She is critical of both the class bias of her heroine's society and the imperialist assumptions of Darwin's. By paralleling the two times, she exposes more effectively the social injustices of each. But she is equally interested in how the two outsiders come to terms with their respective positions. The fate of neither is determined. The openness of the story's ending stands as an implicit commentary on Darwin. The future is bound to the past, Barrett suggests, but not according to laws that one could predict in advance. The story stands as both an affirmation of temporal synchronicity and a challenge to the determinist implications of genome time.

Mr. Darwin's Shooter shares an interest in the fate of Jemmy Button with "*Soroche,*" as well as an alternating temporal structure. Like Barrett's story, McDonald's novel switches back and forth between two time periods—

1828–1839, years encompassing the voyage of the *Beagle,* and 1858–1860, when Darwin's shooter was in the last years of his life and was eagerly awaiting a presentation copy of *The Origin of Species.* Jemmy Button appears in McDonald's story, but the novel's chief concern is with Darwin's servant, Syms Covington. Covington played a surprisingly large part in collecting the material on which Darwin's theory of natural selection was based. He shot, stuffed, and preserved many of Darwin's animals and birds; collected fossils, insects, botanical specimens, and all manner of marine biology; served as Darwin's clerk and copyist; and worked for two years after Darwin's return to London, ordering the naturalist's collections. After leaving Darwin's employ, Covington emigrated to Australia, where he lived out the remainder of his life, occasionally helping his former master by collecting specimens for his later works. Very little is known about the historical Covington other than that he was born in Bedford, England, was Darwin's servant on the *Beagle,* and ended his life as the postmaster of Pambula, where he made a prosperous home and raised a large family. McDonald, however, imagines Covington as a prodigious worker, full of ambition, hungering for the smallest sign of recognition for his devoted service, yet tormented by the role he may have played in undermining the biblical account of creation.

Characteristically, Darwin does not mention his assistant's name in any of his published works. The novel portrays Covington as cruelly hurt by this neglect, but it also takes pains to set Darwin's attitude within the social conventions of his times. As McDonald says in an interview: "Darwin is an upper-class Englishman of his time dealing with his social inferiors, a definite believer in the class system" (McDonald, "Conversation" 6). Still, the stiff and distant behavior of this man toward the servant who lived with him more closely than a spouse contrasts dramatically with the relations between Joseph Paxton and his bachelor Duke (a contrast that perhaps does more to highlight the exceptional quality of the relationship discussed in chapter 1 than to indict Darwin).

What Covington wants most of all is recognition. In the face of class and education obstacles, recognition would prove his humanity, a goal that relates powerfully to the religious controversy over evolution at the time and to Covington's belief in the innate superiority of humans over the animals he kills, guts, and stuffs. Hence Covington's hurt feelings at being treated as a servant; his anger at his name not appearing in *The Origin of Species;* and the irony of the novel's title, which identifies its hero not by name but by an anonymous function—as far as history is concerned, he was nothing more than "Mr. Darwin's shooter." McDonald invents personal roots for Covington's craving for recognition, roots stemming from his childhood in a family of powerful, rambunctious older brothers, a charismatic father, and no mother (his fictional stepmother treats him flirtatiously rather than maternally). In adult life, his deepest affections are reserved for three complicated men, from whom Covington seeks only acknowledgment of his worth and humanity—John Phipps, a charismatic evangelist; Darwin, an upper-class scientist; and Dr. MacCracken, a surgeon and writer of essays in the style of Emerson (Phipps and MacCracken appear to be fictional characters; Darwin's personality and actions are based on historical research). At their first meeting, Dr. MacCracken operates on Covington to save him from acute appendicitis. The image of Covington, naked and cut open to reveal his interior organs, resonates with the many descriptions of himself gutting and displaying the birds and other animals he prepares for Darwin. It also illuminates his assertion that even if one cleaves a man in two one will not be able to see the soul within that makes him human.

The homosocial nature of Covington's craving for recognition fits in with the confined nature of life during long sea voyages in the company of men. Covington records acts of buggery on board, mentions Darwin's doubt about whether the evangelist Phipps's proselytizing to boys is sexually motivated, laughs at Darwin's blushing awkwardness whenever the subject of women comes up, and feels proud when Darwin remarks that "he'd rather missed Covington in the way of a busy, bustling wife" (*Shooter* 283). Of course these allusions to love among men exist only in the novelist's imaginative re-creation of the expedition of the *Beagle,* but the portrait effectively dramatizes the homosocial network within which nineteenth-century natural history was actually pursued. The young Darwin lived in extremely close quarters for five years with a band of sailors and explorers, and was supported by a network of older male scientists, many of whom were members of the Cambridge network featured in chapter 3. (Darwin's chief patron was John Henslow, a professor at Cambridge, who introduced his student to John Herschel, George Peacock, William Whewell, and other Cambridge savants; after the return of the *Beagle,* Darwin became a prominent member of London scientific society—he was a regular at Babbage's soirees and was elected to the Athenaeum Club in 1838, in the same group with Charles Dickens [Browne 126–27, 354].)

McDonald is more explicit than Barrett about the temporal dimension of his subject. At several critical junctures in the novel, the author mentions the vertiginous time-sense that his characters experience whenever they make geological or paleontological discoveries. Here is how one character responds to reading *The Origin of Species:* "He felt part of time with a deep contentment and understanding—*all* times past and future as well as this very particular moment" (*Shooter* 222). It would be hard to find a more precise account of genome time than this sentence, and one wonders if the compression of past and future into a vividly particular present is not anachronistically attributed to a Victorian reader by a contemporary author caught up in today's enthusiasm over genomics. Certainly, few nineteenth-century readers were suffused with a "deep contentment" at the revelations contained in Darwin's work. Darwin himself struggled throughout his expedition with the implications of what he was uncovering, and there are numerous passages in the *Voyage* that attempt to interpret the evidence in terms of divine creation. Even a passionate supporter like Thomas Huxley never felt tranquility before the dizzy vistas of time that an evolutionary perspective opened before him. Later in the novel, Covington struggles to come to terms with "what Darwin set out to prove—that limitless time made all things possible" (*Shooter* 350). In the final chapter, Covington lies on his deathbed, hallucinating that his lost companions of youth have returned—his shipmates, the evangelist Phipps, Dr. MacCracken, and Darwin—all with him at last. The chapter moves fluidly among scenes from different periods of Covington's past, mingling disparate phases of his life in one uninterrupted scene. It fills him with peace. "He never imagined that to be reconciled would be to meet with himself this way, all times present in one" (*Shooter* 360).

In McDonald's rendering, this new time sense becomes the secular equivalent of a religious state, what Darwin's Anglican tradition would describe as the "peace that passeth understanding." Here *Mr. Darwin's Shooter* verges on the spiritual or metaphysical interpretations of genome time found in much New Age science fiction. But this novel is more historically grounded in its treatment: McDonald's fiction investigates how a particular set of nineteenth-century figures would have confronted scientific discoveries that destabilized everything they had been taught to believe. Each character finds a different way of living with the knowledge that all pasts and all futures lie coiled within the present moment.

Darwin's Radio, the crossover bestseller published in the last months of 1999 by veteran science fiction author Greg Bear, is full of heated scientific debates about genetics and evolution. In one scene a high-ranking doctor in the National Institutes of Health (NIH) responds incredulously to the heroine's suggestion that the human species is about to undergo a radical evolutionary change brought about by the spread of a retrovirus similar to HIV. "What you seem to be implying," the NIH official asserts, "is a hitherto undiscovered mechanism whereby the genome takes control of its own evolution, somehow sensing the right time to bring about change. Correct?" (271). Yes—and there's more. The novel ends with the heroine giving birth to the first member of a new species, *Homo sapiens novus*.

Farfetched as *Darwin's Radio* may sound, it is only the latest example of a popular subgenre of speculative fiction that indulges in a kind of New Age evolutionary mysticism. The cyberpunk hits of Neal Stephenson—*Snow Crash* (1992) and *The Diamond Age* (1995)—revolve around viruses that code for evolutionary change, playing on the analogy between DNA code and software viruses. *Snow Crash* links this hybrid digital/DNA virus with a whole series of New Age ideas: that an ancient Sumerian religion was the source of a "neurolinguistic virus" (218) spread by cult prostitutes, that a trickster/hacker figure named Enki disseminated a countervirus through his sperm that jolted humanity out of its rut by causing the fall of the Tower of Babel (279), that Deuteronomy was a similar antivirus program or vaccine, which operated by imposing a binary logic on humanity (230, 400), and that today's "postrational" society (230) has returned to the condition of the Sumerians and needs a new hacker-savior, the appropriately named "Hiro" of the novel.[8] The evolutionary theme plays a still more prominent role in Stephenson's second novel *The Diamond Age,* which ends with the near-triumph of a society called the "Drummers," which is developing a "collective mind" (454).[9]

This utopian dream of evolutionary change has a long lineage in science fiction, dating back to Theodore Sturgeon's *More Than Human* (1953) and Arthur C. Clarke's *Childhood's End* (1953) and reaching its widest audience in Stanley Kubrick's film *2001: A Space Odyssey* (1968). The dystopian perspective on evolution dates back even further, perhaps originating in H. G. Wells's *The Time Machine* (1895), with its two mutated species, the Eloi and Morlocks, and it extends into today's ecological concerns about the rampant extinction of other species. Excitement about current-day genomics, however, has led to the "geneticization" of much science fiction.[10] Thus Nancy Kress, in her Nebula and Hugo Award winning novel *Beggars in Spain* (1993), Octavia Butler in the *Xenogenesis Series* (1987–1989), and Bruce Sterling in *Holy Fire* (1996) all focus on genetic engineering as the vehicle for speciation. Kress depicts a near future when people can choose "genemod" enhancements at will, as long as they are not inheritable, and when genetic engineering has produced a separate race known as the "Sleepless," whose mental superiority and apparent immortality provokes intense envy.[11] Butler's *Xenogenesis Series* features alien gene-traders roaming the stars in search of new species with which to splice their DNA. Both these novelists come down on the side of the emergent life form, the evolving species that Sterling calls, in a phrase that intentionally resonates with recent literary theory, the "posthuman" (138).[12]

Sterling's novel links the new genetics with poststructuralism's deconstruction of the individual. A doctor in the future's "global medical-industrial complex" (8) comments: "'Feel' is a very broad and inexact folk term. So is the term 'I,' for that matter. Maybe we can say that there will be feelings, but there won't be any 'I' to have them" (65). The analogy between poststructural and genetic deconstructions of the self is taken for granted in much recent science fiction, and it highlights the continuity between New Age pseudoscience and other aspects of postmodern culture. The analogy is prompted by the notion, discussed earlier, that DNA is structured as a language and by more recent conceptualizations of the genome by scientists in terms of chaos theory and emergent self-organizing systems. Hence one reads in the novels of self-organizing "neural nets" and species-wide forms of "distributed intelligence" (Stephenson, *Diamond* 495; Bear 84, 192), images that seem to reinforce postmodern visions of a decentered self. The analogy stems, as well, from the idea that the individual is simply a vehicle for perpetuating its genetic code, or as the familiar joke puts it: a chicken is just the egg's way of passing on its DNA. Richard Dawkins, in his writings on the "selfish gene," is the best-known proponent of this way of viewing evolution: "The true 'purpose' of DNA is to survive, no more and no less"

(*Selfish* 47). As a mere vehicle for the codes that cross it, the individual is taken apart and disseminated throughout the biosphere. Dawkins again: "The long-lived gene . . . is widely distributed in space among different individuals, and widely distributed in time over many generations. When looked at in this distributed way, any one gene can be said to 'meet' another when they find themselves sharing a body" (*Blind Watchmaker* 170).

Whether utopian or dystopian, geneticized science fiction represents a departure from traditional Darwinian theory. In *Darwin's Plots* the literary scholar Gillian Beer has argued that evolutionary ideas were deeply rooted in Victorian culture and intertwined with the nineteenth-century realistic novel in particular. Major aspects of Victorian realism such as its inclusiveness, profusion of detail, and reliance on cause and effect were common to the novel and evolutionary theory alike. By contrast, the cultural features excluded from Darwinian theory read like a recipe for the New Age synthesis of genomics and evolution. According to Beer, nineteenth-century Darwinian theory "does *not* privilege the present" (13) and does not countenance teleology or a purposive direction to evolution.[13] Further, "cloning is its contrary" (11). New Age evolutionary thinking, on the other hand, loves cloning and is teleological through and through.

The scientifically implausible premise of Greg Bear's novel *Darwin's Radio*, for example, is that the extraordinary stress of living in the present has activated a "species-level biological computer" (195) within the genome, which purposefully directs an evolutionary event. The title of Bear's work invokes Darwin only to reorient his entire theory toward a teleological conception of evolution. Bear explains the concept of "Darwin's radio" as a transposable genetic element, a so-called jumping gene, which causes mutations and ultimately alters the physical nature of an organism. The novel fancifully imagines a new evolutionary turn in humanity, caused by an infectious transposon carried in a retrovirus that communicates DNA laterally among people without sexual contact. The genetic message contained in these genes is an ancient one, dormant in the genome for thousands of years in the form of junk DNA. The resulting epidemic causes a profound evolutionary change, one parallel in its magnitude to the supplanting of the Neanderthals by *Homo sapiens*. The novel interweaves the story of a young female geneticist who has published path-breaking research on endogenous retroviruses, with that of an anthropologist who discovers in the Alps the frozen bodies of Neanderthal parents with their *Homo sapiens* infant. This aspect of the novel is obviously modeled on DNA forensic investigations done on the Tyrolean Iceman found in 1991, just as other episodes are drawn from news reports of the Kennewick Man found in 1996 on the banks of the Columbia River in Washington. These episodes of forensic anthropology enable Bear to speculate as wildly about the species' origin in a single climactic event in the past as he does about the teleological nature of the species' future.

The millennial themes visible in Bear, Stephenson, and others reflect aspects of genome time discernible in the work of some prominent scientists.

Evelyn Fox Keller devotes the central section of *Refiguring Life: Metaphors of Twentieth-Century Biology* (1995), an insightful work by one of today's foremost historians of science, to documenting vestiges of a guiding consciousness or purposive principle on the molecular level in twentieth-century biology. She calls this principle the "ghost inside the molecular machine of life" (55) and views it as a descendant of Maxwell's Demon, the imaginary being inside organic molecules that the nineteenth-century physicist James Clerk Maxwell had to postulate in order to explain how life can escape being governed by the second law of thermodynamics. For contemporary molecular biology, of course, this command and control center lies in the DNA. Jacques Monod, one of the great figures of contemporary genetics, makes much the same point about Maxwell's Demon living on in modern genetics. In *Chance and Necessity* (1970) he explains why genetics requires a teleonomic principle to complete its account of protein synthesis. The word *teleonomy* was coined in 1958 by an evolutionary biologist to denominate "end-directedness" without implying metaphysical or religious belief in a final aim. The term was quickly picked up by geneticists; Monod's translator uses it to convey the "idea of an *oriented, coherent,* and *constructive* activity" in the proteins that express DNA (45, emphasis in the original). As Monod puts it, proteins are molecular agents that "act projectively—realize and pursue a purpose" (22). "Teleonomy" purges metaphysics from purposive activity in order to find a way of talking about goal-oriented behavior at the level of the gene.

The tendency of molecular biologists to see the gene not merely as teleonomic but as the master molecule or command center of all life has been called by a number of commentators "genetic essentialism."[14] These commentators remark on the prevalence of metaphors of the genome as the Book of Man, the Code of Codes, the Holy Grail, the secret of life, the map or blueprint of all living things. The geneticist Walter Gilbert's practice in lectures of holding up a CD and pronouncing "This is you" has become virtually canonical in critical accounts of genome science.[15] As Nelkin and Lindee define it, "Genetic essentialism reduces the self to a molecular entity, equating human beings, in all their social, historical, and moral complexity, with their genes" (2). Greg Bear exaggerates this tendency toward genetic essentialism, so that even his characters crack a smile when referring to "THE MIGHTY WIZARD IN OUR GENES" and "The Master of the Genome" (195). That said, Bear's concept of a "biological computer" (195) is not so different from Monod's more sober account of a "teleonomic apparatus" (Monod 126) or from other geneticists who speak of DNA as a "'Delphic oracle,' a 'time machine,' a 'trip into the future,' a 'medical crystal ball'" (Nelkin and Lindee 7). All betray a distinctive orientation toward the future encoded in the perpetual present of the genome.

There is a relationship, I am suggesting, between the eschatological impulse in New Age evolution, even in its crudest forms, and the temporal sense implicit both in the scientific model of the gene and in the genome industry's commercial promotions. This relationship is easily as pronounced as that between Darwin's ideas and the Victorian novel. Scientific and popular cultures today are growing less insulated from one another, bringing us back toward the undisciplined cultures of the early nineteenth century. There are also interchanges between genetic ideas and the formal strategies of contemporary literature. To assess these formal influences, however, one needs to turn from popular science fiction to more experimental literary works.

In the long central chapter of Richard Powers's *The Gold Bug Variations,* the heroine Jan O'Deigh meditates about evolution, inspired by a thinker she refers to as "my friend Monod" (333). Echoing Monod's *Chance and Necessity* (1970), O'Deigh ends the chapter with a tribute to the "living, purposive program incorporated in the enzyme" (336). One word stands out in this tribute, marking it as a product of the 1990s rather than the 1970s—the reference to computer programs. The most prominent addition to the cultural representation of genetics in the last two decades has been the association between digital information and DNA code.

Today it is commonplace to discuss the genome in terms of information technology. To choose one out of countless examples, Dawkins spends an entire chapter of *The Blind Watchmaker* (1986) describing the gene as a digital memory storage device. Protesting that he is not being metaphorical, he calls genes Nature's "floppy discs" and proclaims: "DNA is ROM" (111, 117). Why? Because both DNA and Read Only Memory conform to the Central Dogma of genetics: "[They] can be read millions of times over, but only written to once" (117). In the 1950s and 1960s, however, the association between computers and biology was not widespread, despite the fact that Watson and Crick had introduced the notion of DNA as information in their landmark article on the structure of the double helix in 1953. This absence has puzzled historians of science. Horace Judson, in *The Eighth Day of Creation,* confesses to being unable to explain why geneticists overlooked the relevance of information theory to their project, since there is clear evidence that they were aware of its main ideas (242–43).

The fundamental concepts behind computers and information theory were proposed in the late 1940s. Norbert Wiener's book *Cybernetics,* published in 1948, gave wide currency to a definition of information as the opposite of noise or entropy. As Peter Galison has pointed out, Wiener developed his ideas during World War II while working on automatic guidance systems for anti-aircraft guns, where he discovered the importance of using feedback to predict the course of enemy planes. When he turned to thinking about control centers in machines, feedback loops became the key to producing what, in their different field, molecular biologists were to call teleonomy—goal-oriented behavior without conscious intention. Keller makes this point succinctly: cybernetics postulates "purposive behavior in machines, equating teleology with negative feedback" (Keller 84). This same principle of feedback was to play a crucial role in the early 1960s when geneticists began to understand how DNA "knows" when to activate and deactivate different proteins. A year after Wiener's book appeared, the mathematician John von Neumann gave the lectures that were published posthumously as his *Theory of Self-Reproducing Automata*. These lectures discussed a second concept crucial to the new genetics: the model of organisms (or automata) as self-replicating systems. Although versions of both of these ideas made their way into the early scientific literature on what was called the "coding problem" in DNA, neither of them was formulated in terms of information theory or the computer model until later.

In *The Gold Bug Variations*, Richard Powers imagines what might have happened if these two currents of thought had come together in the 1950s. The novel interweaves three distinct narrative levels, the earliest of which is the story of a year in the life of an imaginary assistant professor, Dr. Stuart Ressler, who in the course of 1957–1958, makes a series of genetic breakthroughs, which in actuality were not achieved until a few years later in the sixties. Although he does not say so, Powers clearly bases Ressler's ideas— and even aspects of his life story—on Marshall Warren Nirenberg and the experiments which were to earn him the Nobel Prize in 1968.[16] The fictional Ressler reaches his conclusions earlier than the real-life Nirenberg because of the fruitful convergence of the two fields. Powers's young geneticist reads not only early geneticists—Avery, Watson, Crick, Luria, and Chargaff—but also computer pioneers Wiener and von Neumann.

Powers's novel is long, dazzling, and difficult. The rich, highly figurative style often constructs a kind of prose poetry out of a melange of genetic terminology and computer language, as well as scholarly references from musicology, cryptography, a commentary on Poe's story "The Gold-Bug," and a fair amount of art history to boot. In an interview Powers explains the book's intricate style as an attempt to mimic through "linguistic mutation and wordplay" the generative variability and wonder of the gene: "I tried to imitate my vision of the genetic code as a punning, runaway fecundity in the book's prose. The continuous literary allusion that underwrites the prose is my attempt to join the themes of biology and language: the archive of literature as the race's high-level genome" (Neilson 20). His vision captures a current trend among geneticists themselves toward stressing the polysemy of the code. This trend has led Johannes Borgstein to propose in *The Lancet* using "A Literary Model for Cellular Mechanisms" in order to foster an awareness among scientists that genetic sequences must be interpreted at multiple levels and that the expression of characteristics is highly dependent on context (1353). Powers's multivocal style is exactly the kind of "literary model" Borgstein seeks for genetics.

The time scheme of the novel is equally complex.[17] Ressler's story of 1957–1958 alternates with the account of a love affair between two characters, a librarian named Jan O'Deigh and a graduate student in art history, Franklin Todd. The characters fall in love, move in together, and separate during a year-long period spanning 1983–1984. During this same time, Todd is postponing writing his dissertation by working with (a much older) Dr. Ressler as a computer programer for a company called Manhattan On-line. The course of O'Deigh and Todd's relationship parallels, with variations, a love affair Ressler had in the fifties, the failure of which led to his lamentable decision to renounce genetics. The story told about the middle time period culminates in an elaborate bit of computer hacking pulled off by the three main characters, which brings to a halt the banking and insurance industries in New York City. The third time-level in the novel is that of a diary O'Deigh keeps after her breakup with Todd, chronicling her solitary efforts to teach herself genetics during 1985–1986. The reader realizes at once that O'Deigh's first-person diary comprises the chapters set in 1985–1986 but only learns on the last pages of the novel that Todd has researched and written the biography of Ressler that constitutes the third-person chapters set in the fifties. O'Deigh and Todd decide to coauthor the chapters set in the middle time period, "splicing" them together (Powers's pun, 637) to make up the finished book. At every turn, the text self-reflexively draws attention to the whole topic of temporality by titling chapter subsections with phrases such as "Today in History," "A Day Without the Ever," and "The Perpetual Calendar."

This last title invokes a temporal dimension very different from the precisely recorded historical sequences of the three narratives. A "perpetual calendar" is a device for looking up the day of the week for any date on the calendar. Counting leap years, there are only fourteen possibilities, and thus a small chart can reveal the cyclical pattern of days matching up with dates throughout both past and future. This hint of a cyclical conception of time, counterpointing the quotidian histories of the characters' lives, is augmented by other aspects of the novel. Important events tend to fall on the same calendar date in each of the narratives, particularly the spring and autumn equinoxes. The running allusions to Bach's *Goldberg Variations* reinforce the idea of a temporal order based on recurring themes and variations. Equally suggestive are the many references to the natural seasons. The four seasons, like the fourfold patterns Ressler finds in Bach's *Variations,* serve to emphasize repetition rather than progress, and both are made to echo the four-letter code of DNA. The novel, which consists of thirty chapters and two arias, duplicating Bach's thirty variations and two arias, opens with a four-part poem in quatrains, which descants on the theme of cyclical time:

> Everything that ever summered forth starts
> in identical springs, or four-note var-
> iations on that repeated theme: four seasons,
> four winds, four corners, four-chambered heart
>
> in four desire-trapped bodies in the thick
> of a species-swarmed world where green thrills
> to countless change while the calendar holds still. . . . (9)

The image of a species-swarmed world springing forth from variations on the same four-note code, while the chronicle of individual histories and desires seems to hold still, dwarfed to insignificance by identical seasons, conveys the cyclical element in what I have been calling genome time. Powers's novel fleshes out, as literature and the arts best can, a fundamental but abstract insight—that the world is shaped by variations within closed systems, whether musical, linguistic, seasonal, or biological. The turn of phrase "genome time" does not appear in Powers's encyclopedic text, but it is a principle his book beautifully illustrates. The novel shows how time might look from the perspective of the gene.

The cycle of the seasons connects temporality to a second major theme in the novel: the impending threat to the natural environment. This theme arises initially from Ressler's dissatisfaction with the attitude of his fellow researchers toward science. "Science is not about control. It is about cultivating a perpetual condition of wonder. . . . It is about reverence, not mastery" (411). This critique of an instrumental attitude toward nature has been sounded often before in the twentieth century, notably in feminist science studies and in the writings of the Frankfurt school Marxists Horkheimer and Adorno. Even the choice of music as the counterweight to instrumental rationality is familiar from Adorno's writings. But Powers is anything but antiscience. The author rejects what he calls the "cynical camp of science studies," which denies the distinction between "the urge toward knowledge and the urge toward power" (Neilson 18). His character's deeper point is that "we suffer not from too much science" but from too little (325). The kind of science that Ressler would cultivate involves an understanding of complexity, interrelatedness. This desire broadens the book's critique of instrumental rationality by linking it to contemporary ideas derived from chaos theory. "Life is an immense turbulent system," Ressler asserts. "Small changes produce large swings in outcome" (410). Hence the aspect of the new genetics that worries him most is genetic engineering. Explaining the process by which deleting or adding a single gene can produce radical changes in the resulting organism, Ressler concludes: "By far the largest [risk] is ecological imbalance. Unpredictable, irreversible environmental mayhem that used to take selective breeders a lifetime to produce can now be knocked off in a dozen weeks" (409).

Several critics have singled out the environmental theme as the central message of the novel, but it is no more prominent than others: the interpenetration of historical by cyclical time; the homology among four different types of codes—genetic, computer, musical, and linguistic; the difference between meaning and mere pattern; life as a self-organizing, emergent system; the indeterminacy and final mysteriousness of living things, including the kinds of artificial life produced by artistic works and some computer programs; and, finally, the compelling need for, the unending pain of, desire. No doubt there are still more themes that could be disentangled from the rich score of this piece, but separating out one line from the composition is not the proper approach. Powers's novel itself suggests a better solution. Ressler's response to a world "that forever grows one step richer and subtler than our latest theory about it" (411) is to hope for the development of an "ecology of knowledge" (326).[18] In response to the novel the reader needs to be aware of an ecology of themes, each interdependent with the others in a complex self-organizing system.

Self-organization, in this context, represents another way to account for the appearance of order and purpose in a distributed network, whether biological or literary. In one of many passages where O'Deigh is trying to teach herself genetics, she struggles with the problem of how so many diverse creatures could arise from a simple four-letter code. Even at the level of proteins, "DNA carries just part of the instructions for these purposive, molecular machines" (370), yet these "machines," folded into the heart of every living cell, go about their multiple jobs of synthesizing other substances and replicating themselves with an almost uncanny appearance of conscious design. Her breakthrough comes when she realizes that "to manufacture breathing, searching, speaking, rule-defying life from out of constrained [inanimate] matter requires no transcendence," no concept of intention external to the process itself. "Every level of the hierarchy arises from the previous, without any need to change the rules or call in outside assistance." Instead, one must "grasp a thing . . . as the emergent interplay of parts, themselves emergent from combined performances at lower levels" (370). The conclusion O'Deigh is working toward is a principle in which all order, including the highest forms of consciousness, emerge spontaneously from complex, interdependent processes: "The machine is as self-bootstrapping, as self-*selfing* as consciousness itself. Why not? Consciousness . . . is just the self-selfing chain writ large, considering, synthesizing itself" (445; emphasis in the original).[19] The obvious corollary is that artistic works, especially in the case of allusive, multivocal texts, should be understood as self-organizing, emergent life forms. O'Deigh muses about her diary notebooks taking on a life of their own: "The notebooks I've been keeping . . . if they go on long enough, might become something new, not the thing I wanted to get at, but a live thing all the same" (518). Of course, they do become something new—they become the very work of literature one is reading.

The leap from cell to organism to consciousness to literature is breathtaking. The move, however, derives from another assumption of chaos theory, that ecosystems are fractals, possessing similar patterns of organization at every level of scale. Such "scaling," to appropriate a term from computer programers, is widespread in genetics discourse. Most of the writers discussed in this chapter—Dawkins, Dennett, Stephenson, Bear, and Powers—celebrate the wonder of this scaling in nature. Bear provides a particularly simple exposition of the idea. His heroine is wrestling with the same problem as O'Deigh—how to explain purposive behavior in complex systems:

> We don't have to posit self-awareness, conscious thought, to have
> an organized network that responds to its environment and issues
> judgments about what its individual nodes should look like. . . . The
> concept works at all levels, in the ecosystem, in a species, even in a
> society. All individual creatures are networks of cells. All species
> are networks of individuals. All ecosystems are networks of species.
> (Bear 192)

Powers's version of this principle comes late in the novel, when O'Deigh is
summing up what she has learned:

> The double helix is a fractal curve. Ecology's every part—regardless
> of the magnification, however large the assembled spin-off or small
> the enzymatic trigger—carries in it some terraced, infinitely dense
> ecosystem, an inherited hint of the whole. . . . The code is universal.
> Here, this city, me, the forest of infection on my hands, the sea of sil-
> ver cells scraped from the inside of my mouth. Every word I have, . . .
> every predication, every sculpted metaphor. (Powers 627)

Genome time, where all the differences that matter to individuals are
erased, is the perspective that makes it possible to say that consciousness and
literature are merely self-organizing processes "writ large." If every word and
metaphor she writes, every cell in the bacteria on her hands, every city and in-
finitely dense ecosystem, are just variations on a single code, then what has
become of history? Why has she labored so mightily to understand the events
of Ressler's past, or of her own life for that matter? And what has become of
the future, the future intimated by her desire for the return of Todd? The answer to these questions reveals something crucial about *The Gold Bug Variations*. For all its interest in the infinite vistas of genome time, it never neglects
the imperatives of a human time scale. Both perspectives are intricately
braided together. In contrast to the New Age evolutionary rhetoric of *Darwin's Radio*, Powers's novel insists on the urgency of historical time through
its very structure. This is the link that connects the alternating temporal
structures of "*Soroche*," *Mr. Darwin's Shooter*, and *The Gold Bug Variations*.
The layered but carefully discriminated time-periods in these three works
dramatize the importance of lives lived on their own limited, personal scale.
Those lives may be nothing in time's perpetual calendar, but their actions
have consequences all the same, which are meaningful only in historical time.

On the final pages of the novel, O'Deigh and Todd laughingly decide to
"make a baby" (638) by composing the book the reader has just finished.
"Come on," Todd says. "A few edits, a little cut-and-paste . . ." (637). This literary mode of artificial reproductive technology has been around for a long
time; even so, the self-reflexive turn produces an effective surprise, revealing
the secret of the novel's structure. The moment is satisfying yet something
of a brainteaser as well. Here are two characters *in* a story writing the story
that contains them. The text becomes a strange loop, a recursive process
without beginning or end. Hence the Aria's last line creates not just a musi-

cal repeat but a circular feedback loop: "Once more with feeling" (639). At first glance, one might suppose that the novel's recursive logic endorses cyclical rather than human time. But the ending supports both perspectives at once. For these two characters, the decision to write a book is deeply personal. It testifies to what they have learned from knowing Ressler, from nearly destroying a friend's life with an ill-advised computer hack, and from the hard course of their love. It suggests the immediate importance of Today in History. More poignantly, it bears witness to mortality. Ressler's death from cancer informs the novel from the first sentence onward. Perhaps the most eloquent testimony to a human perspective on time is the irrevocable character of this Death in History.

There is no gene for the human spirit," reads the promotional tag line for Andrew Niccol's film about a future dominated by genetic screening and genetic engineering. True enough. There are conventions, however, for the plot twists that have made this film an overwhelming favorite among doctors, scientists, counselors, and ethicists in the genetics community. Mention *Jurassic Park* (1993) to a genetics professional and you will usually be answered by *Gattaca*. The conventions that give this film so much of its style are temporal. *Gattaca*'s future is coded in the stylistic language of a terrible past. The movie evokes an ominous period, the time of National Socialism. The characters live in vast, cold, glass-and-marble structures; they cross great empty public plazas flagged with stone. Undesirable people are routinely rounded up and searched in the street. Plainclothes police wear long black trenchcoats and forties hats, iconic from countless films as the uniform of German SS officers. This style conveniently happens to be the height of retro fashion, but contemporary fascist chic is appropriate for a movie that raises the specter of eugenics.

Vincent (Ethan Hawke), the hero and narrator of the film, is born into a world in which one's entire life is determined by the inexorable predictions of genetic screening tests. He is one of the few babies conceived by the old-fashioned method, without benefit of genetic engineering. Because of his "inferior" blood, he is known as a "degenerate" (with a long "e"), another reference to the horrors of the National Socialist program. "Genoism," or prejudice based on a person's genetic makeup, is technically illegal but universally practiced. As the narrator explains: "I belonged to a new underclass, no longer determined by social status or the color of your skin. No. We now have discrimination down to a science." A genetic sample can be obtained from something as small as a fingernail clipping or single hair, the residue of a handshake or a kiss. Once a sample is obtained, the genome can be sequenced in a matter of seconds. Thanks to the actuarial tables of a probability-mad society, a person's future appears to be encoded in every cell of the body, a destiny read off from a roll of computer printout. This is a society living fully in genome time, a society that denies the openness of individual futures because of its belief in a destiny already written in the present.

The main action of the film takes place entirely within the span of a week, during the time while Vincent is waiting to leave as an astronaut on a mission to Titan. He has obtained his place on the mission through an elaborate fraud, involving the adoption of another person's "genetic identity." This makes him what is known as a "borrowed ladder," a nice touch in the script because it evokes the spiral staircase of the double helix. The cinematic time of this week is shaped and given tempo by a compelling narrative. There is a murder at the space agency, and the investigation threatens to expose Vincent's assumed identity; Vincent consummates a love affair with the heroine, Irene (Uma Thurman); an intense relationship—compounded of envy, superiority, bitterness, and love—develops between Vincent and the man whose identity he has taken; and Vincent is nearly exposed by his younger brother, a police officer assigned to investigate the murder.

As in *The Gold Bug Variations,* two conceptions of time contribute to the impact of the movie—and in this case, to thematic confusion as well. The week of dramatic action—the story time of the movie—contrasts vividly with stolen moments of tranquillity associated with the unchanging time of the gene. This contrast has contradictory effects. On the one hand, it serves to cast narrative itself as the opposite of genome time. Breathless action motifs become identified with the individual's struggle against an oppressive regime. The opposition participates in a 1990s version of the Cold War paradigm, in which the solitary rebel battles it out against totalitarianism one more time. Thus liberal individualism is invested with all the glamour of a heroic narrative—and vice versa. The struggle against an unjust eugenics state holds the audience spellbound as the clock ticks down toward the liftoff for Titan. On the other hand, the contrast oddly romanticizes the deep rhythms of genome time.

The delineation of genome time begins with the opening credits, which immediately introduce the viewer to an abnormal temporality. As the names of the actors and filmmakers appear on the screen, the four letters of the genetic code—GATC—flare briefly to prominence each time they appear in a word; then the rest of the name materializes. This is an effective emblem of the way in which the completed body of meaning is expressed from the building blocks of code. The code is deeper—more primal and less human—than the individual. Behind the letters, magnified images of nail clippings and human hairs fall in slow motion, landing with loud, hollow booms. The expansion of scale foretells the disproportionate importance such minute bodily traces will assume in Vincent's world. They are signs of the future society's technologically enhanced powers of surveillance and constraint. But the slowing of time also hints contradictorily at the utopian variant of genome time. The slow motion resonates with scattered motifs throughout the film that sound the note of a time out of time. These moments are connected with the hero and heroine's precariously snatched freedom: the two of them at dawn in a field of solar energy panels reflecting the sun and later in bed together making love. The motifs also emerge in moments of personal triumph and abandon: Vincent beating his brother by swimming out into the waves with no thought of return, Vincent lying on his back in the water staring at the stars above, and, finally, Vincent entering the long umbilical cord that leads to the womb of the space capsule. All of these images align Vincent's yearnings with the deep rhythms of the universe, with the slow, impersonal time of the gene.

Romanticizing genome time confuses not only the ideological subtext of the narrative but also the film's overt social criticism. In the first instance, confusion may actually facilitate the reassuring message that a strong person can beat the odds. The frenetic narrative glorifies individual will, but the limpid imagery identifying Vincent's dreams with eternal processes like the rising of the sun or the movement of oceans and stars suggests that his triumph is somehow inevitable, preordained. Vincent's destiny seems to lie in the stars, both literally and figuratively. The idea of triumphing over totalitarianism through willpower alone may be an ideological delusion, but the message is not made less attractive by being equated with its opposite: that each of us is united with larger impersonal forces, part of an innate necessity associated with the gene. The romanticism of this gesture also undermines the film's valuable critique of the abuses of genetics. Throughout most of the movie, the genome is invested with a terrible power. It dictates everything about a person: one's career, choice of mate, personal health, and eventual death. It contains the secret of one's fate. In the movie's terms, totalitarianism itself becomes a consequence of some inexorable logic found in the genome, for genetic makeup is what subordinates an individual to a place in the group. Phenotype is measured against an ideal genotype to produce the social hierarchy of a eugenics state. Consequently, the effort to locate Vincent's glamorous destiny in the stars undercuts the film's dystopian vision, reassuring the viewer that things will work out well in the end.

Gattaca disguises its underlying thematic confusion through its sexual subplot. Vincent's autonomous will is forged in two highly normative relationships: his rivalry with his enemy/brother and his desire for Irene. By triumphing over the genetically engineered abilities of his brother and by "getting the girl," Vincent's example suggests that heroism itself is predicated on heterosexual masculinity. This impression is strengthened by the fate of Vincent's genetic doppelgänger, Jerome (Jude Law). Jerome is a former Olympic athlete, genetically engineered for success, who became paralyzed after a botched suicide attempt when he earned only a silver medal in the games. Embittered, Jerome sells his genetic identity to Vincent, who completes the deception by surgically altering his appearance and substituting Jerome's blood, urine, hair, nail clippings, and other bodily traces for his own whenever genetic samples are required. To sustain the fraud, Jerome must disappear completely so that Vincent may assume his life. The two move in together, and a complex homoerotic relationship develops between Vincent and the disillusioned, wheelchair bound former Olympian.

Jerome's decadent world-weariness, his aristocratic manners, his incessant affected smoking, and his supercilious tone all contribute to the period flavor, invoking stereotypes of the homosexual culture of Berlin between the Wars (best known to moviegoers from the adaptation of Christopher Isherwood's *Berlin Stories,* the 1972 film *Cabaret*). The atmosphere extends to the sultry nightclub, where Vincent and Jerome exchange sophisticated banter and drink too much expensive liquor. By the end of their relationship, the two are squabbling like bored lovers, but Jerome has one more role to play before leaving the stage. When Vincent's brother the police officer tries to uncover the true identity of the person using the name Jerome, the deception is preserved only by Jerome's taking Irene onto his lap and kissing her while the brother watches. The sexual undercurrent is strong: the bond between Jerome and Vincent is "consummated" through the exchange of a shared woman, with the voyeuristic addition of tricking the rival brother to be its witness.[20]

The movie disguises its ideological confusion by being crystal clear about its sexual allegiances. Jerome and the threat of homosexuality are made scapegoats for the transgressive element in Vincent's desires. What is corrupting in the individual will is put on the shoulders of this broken man and expelled. Vincent's "heroic" desires—for Irene, for beating the system, for a destiny in space—are symbolically purged of the taint of mere egotism and made ready for their status as universal values. The last scene in the movie shows Vincent preparing to enter the long tube leading to the space capsule. As he walks down this passageway, the camera cuts back and forth to shots of Jerome, who is climbing into the glass chamber of their apartment's furnace. This act of self-immolation, the viewer understands, is both a sacrifice for Vincent and an acknowledgment of the mess Jerome has made of his life. The death-and-rebirth imagery is patent, cloying, and the suicide disturbingly participates in a homophobic scenario, in which the inevitable end for this stunted figure is self-destruction. But the sacrifice sets Vincent free. Thus the movie has it both ways: genome time is terrifying and salvific. Set free into a utopian future, Vincent steps into a time that was waiting for him all along, in his genes.

Gattaca" is the name of a space agency, founded on a set of technological and social assumptions encoded in an ideal arrangement of GATC. The compulsory character of this ideal is disturbing. How disturbing becomes evident from the fact that the original ending was cut after test screenings revealed that audiences were upset by its bleak message. According to French Anderson, the scientific consultant to the film, the original version ended with a sequence of famous people with inheritable conditions like Addison's disease, dyslexia, glaucoma, and asthma, who might not have been born had eugenic genetic screening been in place: John F. Kennedy, Jr., Albert Einstein, Ray Charles, and Jackie Joyner-Kersee. The last screen revealed the worst news: "Of course, the other birth that may never have taken place is your own" (Holden 1019). Deleting this social message helped hide the contradiction between two supposedly "timeless" ideals: Vincent's dreams and society's norms. A similar elision is at work in the Agilent commercial with which this chapter began. "*Dreams* made real" is the promise Agilent Technology offers its customers. But whose dreams? The one figure missing from the rich variations on the human form is that of a fit, healthy, white, adult male.[21] Perhaps the ugly message buried under the commercial's mellow multiculturalism is that there is one ideal form that needs no improvement. There are multiple dreams at stake, and they stand in unacknowledged contradiction. The dreams of the individual viewer may well not be those encoded in society's normative ideal.

Greg Bear's New Age evolutionism is unapologetic about embracing an ideal form for the next stage of the species's development. Darwin's "radio" signals back to the dawn of time to activate a teleological program already written in the code of DNA, and the future spreads through individuals like an incurable disease. The destiny embedded in the genome will come in the fullness of time. Confronted with the extravagant promises of some in the genetics industry—or with the equally extreme prophecies of doom from some of the industry's critics—it is important to think carefully about how the future will be born.

By contrast, Barrett, McDonald, and Powers work to rescue the future from its too facile inscription in the present. Their works imagine a future constructed out of conscious choice and public debate, a future responsive both to individual desire and to more universal imperatives. For these authors, literature's task is double. It continues to insist that individual histories matter, but it also delves into the impersonal time of the gene. Both endeavors are crucial, because at one level, genome time structures every organism on earth. The code, complete and self-sufficient, runs through and beyond the individual, reaching back to the first primordial cell and forward to whatever future the species may encounter. It is up to literature and the arts to supply the metaphors that will make the deep time of the gene comprehensible. Without losing sight of individual differences and desires, literature must devise ways to respond to a component of organic existence that is virtually immortal, that has a teleonomy of its own, and that cares nothing about identity, family, nation, race, or species. The preserve of literature is to keep both of these incompatible perspectives in play. Telling time on both the genome's perpetual calendar and history's human scale is one of the most important functions of literature today.

This dual capability demonstrates again the value of literature to a historical cultural studies. By numerous formal strategies, literature registers the timeless element in experience, even at those moments when the narrative is most local and particular. A critical approach focused on difference rather than unity needs to pay close attention to those aspects of culture that give differences their largest meanings.

Eight
CONVERGENCE OF THE TWO CULTURES
A Geek's Guide

Dickens was witness to the beginning of the two-culture split. In chapter 3, I presented Mr. Pickwick as comically trapped between an older, undisciplined culture, which mixed science, literature, engineering, and the social sciences, and a newer, disciplinary culture, which was beginning to segregate literature from science, science from engineering, and the social sciences from all the rest. Dickens's portly hero was at a loss about how to make the transition.

Today, Dickens can be said to be figuratively present when a convergence of the two cultures seems possible. Dickens appears prominently in Jon Katz's nonfiction bestseller *Geeks: How Two Lost Boys Rode the Internet out of Idaho* (2000). Katz introduces what some might consider a rare creature: a teenage computer hacker who reads literature. His book follows the fortunes of two lower-class kids who achieve success because of their technological savvy. They are members of an ever-growing group whose mastery of computers has suddenly made them "culturally trendy" (Katz xxx). They are "the new cultural elite, a pop-culture-loving, techno-centered Community of Social Discontents" (xi). Jesse, the principal hero of Katz's book, struggles to explain himself to the author through months of conversations and e-mail exchanges. The breakthrough occurs when Jesse thinks to ask Katz if he has ever read *David Copperfield*. "That's how I feel about myself,"

Jesse says. "I can't say it any better" (81). Jon Katz is the author of ten books of investigative journalism, political commentary, memoirs, and detective fiction, an occasional college professor, and a columnist for numerous magazines—a writer whose journalistic passion about obscure social outcasts has its own Dickensian quality. But it is the techie kid who invokes Dickens. Katz is not surprised in the least: "A computer geek who explains himself through Dickens is less remarkable a phenomenon than one might think. Geeks' passions often crisscross back and forth between technology and more traditional forms of culture, with unusual depths of interest in both" (83).

Such crisscrossing is the hallmark of important sectors today's society. From the young loners Katz chronicles to their successful counterparts in Silicon Valley, from role-playing gamers to the computer-special-effects wizards at movie studios, from open-source mavericks to corporate web designers, the freedom to range across diverse zones of interest and inquiry is a major source of creativity. To be passionate about technology, traditional culture, and pop culture all at once is less rare than many realize. "Journalists, educators, and pundits frequently fuss that kids like Jesse don't read or aren't well informed; in fact, they read enormous amounts of material online, and are astonishingly well informed about subjects they're interested in" (41). If most of this cultural life takes place online, "the single cultural exception was books. Perhaps as a legacy of his childhood, Jesse remained an obsessive reader. He liked digging through the bins of used bookstores to buy sci-fi and classic literature; he liked books, holding them and turning their pages" (42). As a result, this teenager "was almost shockingly bright" (10)—his notion of culture mixed philosophy, films, literature, music, technology, and politics. For Jesse, and the computer pioneers who helped produce the Internet boom of the 1990s, the idea of separating technology from other domains of culture made little sense.

The final chapter of *Charles Dickens in Cyberspace* explores a group of writers who have also discerned that the relations among science, technology, and literature are shifting. They approach the two-culture split from the other side—the literary domain—but their sense of the interconnected nature of today's culture would appeal to computer geeks, and to Dickens, too. The mixture of passions and skills they cultivate is a far cry from the specialized division of interests characteristic of culture for most of the twentieth century.

In 1959 C. P. Snow famously lamented the trend toward specialization in the twentieth century, a trend that had opened a gulf between what he called the "two cultures," science and literature. Snow framed his account in terms of his own personal experience in attempting to pursue dual careers as a scientist and a novelist, but he intended his indictment to address more general conditions of modern existence. According to Snow, most "literary intellectuals" possessed a "total incomprehension of science" and were "natural Luddites" (4, 11, 22), while most scientists were utterly ignorant of literary culture, often admitting only that they had "'*tried* a bit of Dickens,'" rather as though Dickens were an extraordinarily esoteric, tangled and dubiously rewarding writer" (12). Dickens, it seems, poses a kind of litmus test for scientists. If you can get passionate about the Inimitable, then you have some chance of bridging the two-culture divide.

The split between literature and science was not the only consequence of modern specialization that Snow deplored. Equally important was the division that had emerged between "pure and applied" science. "Pure scientists and engineers," Snow writes, now seem to live in very different worlds and hence "often totally misunderstand each other" (31). Snow's polemic succeeds in dramatizing a critique of specialization that has been widely shared by sociologists, philosophers, and cultural critics throughout the century, even if none have highlighted the specific division between science and literature more memorably than Snow. Indeed, since Max Weber, most commentators have seen the increasing differentiation of the social sphere as one of the defining characteristics of modernity.[1] The growth in the number and autonomy of the professions, the compartmentalization of academic disciplines, and the division between "pure" areas of inquiry and applied research are crucial elements in the increasing rationalization of modern society that Weber described.

Against this backdrop I want to advance the thesis that today the two cultures are converging. A change is occurring in the relationship between science, technology, popular culture, and the areas of literary and intellectual life called the "humanities." This change does not consist of a return to the particular configuration of science-in-culture of Dickens, Babbage, and Somerville's day, but the unusual historical perspective of their times can help clarify what is new in the cultural configuration emerging now. Not since the first decades of the nineteenth century, before the full development of academic disciplines, has there been such synergy between technological and other forms of imaginative creativity. Just as important is the way some engineers have begun to shape basic scientific discoveries, both in the computer field and in areas of biomedical research, particularly genomics. The line between pure and applied research blurs frequently in these areas, as does the related distinction between academic and for-profit investigations. Even after the dot-com bubble burst, these technoscientific fields remain some of the most powerful engines driving the economy, and the cultural changes they herald are spreading throughout society. Silicon Valley and Redmond are harbingers of a reorientation that has also produced biomedical entrepreneurs such as Craig Venter, formerly of Celera Genomics, not to mention the venture capitalists and IPOs that funded their work. Literary culture, broadly conceived, has a crucial place in this new economy, as it never did in the older industrial world of modernity. As experts in the analysis of information, as people long used to thinking through textual puzzles, deciphering complex verbal messages, responding to semiotic cues of all kinds, people with literary habits of mind have a unique opportunity to transform the emerging information order.

This claim about the convergence of the two cultures will not be surprising to everyone. Stefan Collini anticipated my view in his informative introduction to the 1993 reissue of Snow's essay (xliii–lxxi). Nicholas Negroponte, the director of MIT's Media Lab, also has argued that a "culture convergence" between "technology and the humanities, between science and art" is resulting from the "blend of technical and artistic" talents required by multimedia computer applications (81–83). Daniel Dennett, philosopher and theorist of cognitive studies, emphasizes how engineering is helping to break down traditional walls. Dennett maintains that the "sharp divide" Snow lamented "is threatened by the prospect that an engineering perspective will spread from biology up through the human sciences and arts" (189). He adduces Alan Turing, a pioneer of the computer who figures later in this chapter, as an exemplar of an increasingly important intellectual style: Turing was "at one and the same time [an] awesome theorist . . . and deeply practical, epitomizing an intellectual style that has been playing a growing role in science since the Second World War" (207). (Need I add that this hybrid style resembles Babbage's robust combination of interests and abilities?) A final example comes from J. David Bolter, a literary scholar who early recognized the cultural importance of the computer. Before most literature scholars had caught on, Bolter wrote that the computer "will provide the sturdiest bridge between the world of science and the traditional worlds of philosophy, history, and art. . . . It brings concepts of physics, mathematics, and logic into the humanist's world as no previous machine has done. Yet it can also serve to carry artistic and philosophical thinking into the scientific community" (xi).

To say that the two cultures are converging is not to suggest that the United States will soon enjoy a seamless, integrated culture in which literary intellectuals understand quantum theory and scientists in lab coats spend their free time reading John Ashbery and Rita Dove. It would be foolish to forecast the creation of such a holistic culture anytime soon. But that is not the kind of convergence I am talking about. Rather the convergence occurring today consists of people who live and work in an information economy being forced to confront diverse kinds of knowledge from unrelated fields in their everyday occupations. Dislocation is as much a part of this new order as integration. Downsizing and outsourcing follow in the train of this convergence as frequently as technological innovation and new digital forms of creativity. Living in an interconnected sector of the planet is having effects, for better and worse, on the way people think about problems, do research, and make decisions. The "wired world" is not just a mystification of the limited scope of the economic transformation of the 1990s; it is also a statement about material conditions that affect the ways in which knowledge is produced and disseminated. Knowledge workers, including scientists and engineers as well as people with the interpretive skills and artistic backgrounds associated with the humanities, increasingly find themselves drawing on sources of expertise from both of the two cultures. There is no less emphasis on specialization today—simply a recognition of the importance of maintaining close contact with other specialties.[2]

Ripples from this change have spread throughout popular culture. Techies, hackers, and geeks have become prominent figures in our cultural imagination. Science fiction has moved from the margins to a central place in the entertainment industries, and computer workers learn how to view the technological marvels they are constructing from the novels of William Gibson, Bruce Sterling, and Neal Stephenson. The hybrid female bodies that Donna Haraway theorized in "A Cyborg Manifesto" are brought to the screen in the pumped-up physiques of Linda Hamilton in *Terminator* 2 (1989) and Sigourney Weaver in the later *Alien* films (1986–2001), then brought to the mall by health centers and personal fitness trainers.[3] Microsoft, AOL, and Amazon.com have become as prominent in literature and popular culture as they are in the market, office, home, and frequently, courtroom. MP3, Napster, and Morpheus, which are driven as much by youth culture as by technological innovation, threaten to transform the music industry and perhaps, ultimately, the entire conception of intellectual property. And computer geeks stalk contemporary folkways, whether as the frightening monsters blamed for the Columbine massacre or as the hip antiheroes in films and television shows.

We live in an undisciplined culture again. The neat separation of domains, which was a hallmark of modernity, is under assault from all sides. Culture is politics, technology, big business, lifestyles, entertainment, education, and everything else.[4] Each of these domains, in turn, is inextricably bound up with cultural values. Hence the virulence of the culture wars of the last two decades. Disciplinary boundaries, fought for with such earnestness in the late nineteenth century and consolidated throughout most of the twentieth, seem irrelevant to many people—or worse, arbitrary and restrictive paradigms that inhibit original work. Now university presidents establish special grants to encourage interdisciplinary collaboration, particularly across different schools such as Law, Medicine, Engineering, and the Arts and Sciences. Further, the norms of professionalism are routinely viewed with suspicion. The highest ethical claims of the modern professions—to expertise, neutrality, public service, and codes of conduct—are criticized in many quarters as mere ruses to further the advancement of individual professional groups.[5] The once controversial thesis of Paul Starr's *The Social Transformation of American Medicine* (1982), which argued that the medical profession established itself only by crushing rival therapeutic models, has become a commonplace of alternative medicine gurus on daytime talk shows. The rapacity of the legal profession is axiomatic for much of society.

Alan Liu sees the "convergence between academic humanities research (the very term is symptomatic) and corporate, government, media, medical, and military knowledge work" as a defining feature of the "juggernaut of postindustrial knowledge work" (66–67).[6] While concerned that humanities students may become the "professional interpreters for an impending mental merger with the software-telecom-cable-Hollywood conglomerates" (64), he proposes that the critical ethos of literary culture may be society's best hope of challenging from within the dehumanizing features of this global economic system. For it is the new position of literary culture *within* the techno-scientific information order that presents the greatest possibilities—and greatest dangers. The hope lies in what Liu calls the "peculiarly edgy blend of aesthetics and critique once known as the literary" (68). The danger lies in the potential to be co-opted by the corporate world. To negotiate between these rival possibilities, Liu advocates a stance that resonates powerfully with my earlier analysis of nineteenth-century hacking:

> My highest ambition for cultural criticism and the creative arts, in short, is that they can in tandem become "ethical hackers" of knowledge work. . . . Many intellectuals and artists will become so like the icy "New Class" of knowledge workers that there will be no difference; they will be subsumed wholly within their New Economy roles as symbolic analysts, consultants, and designers. But some, in league with everyday hackers in the technical, managerial, professional, and clerical mainstream of knowledge work itself, may break through the ice. (68)

Ethical hacking, however, assumes the cultivation of critical judgment. If the convergence of the two cultures is to produce the "edgy blend of aesthetics and critique" Liu seeks, it will not be because "white hat" hackers, as they are known in geek circles, come by their values instinctively. In an undisciplined culture, they will be crucial members of what Hannah Arendt calls a "democratic *polis*" (149), the public space that sets the very conditions of possibility for freedom. The rebellious posture of hackers may seem to set them outside the boundaries of any *polis,* but this is an illusion,[7] and the concept of ethical hacking requires participation in a public sphere of some sort. Katz registers this necessity when he speaks of geeks' "pop-culture-loving, techno-centered Community of Social Discontents" (xi), and he suggests as well that essential, ethical forms of citizenship may take shape around alternative cultures. They do not come into being by themselves, however. As John Brenkman, following Arendt, puts it: "The citizen has to be formed, educated, socialized to the practices of participation" (119). This task is strenuous, and it becomes harder if one can find no predecessors along the way. For Jesse, Dickens was an important guide.

"For the first time ever, it's a great time to be a geek."

—Jon Katz

The first time ever. *Unprecedented. Never in history.* These kinds of phrases punctuate almost any book one picks up on the computer revolution. Katz's belief that the "rise of the geeks" is happening for the "first time ever" (xxvi) is just a tiny example of how an exclusive focus on the present may distort one's understanding *of* the present. A more disturbing example occurs in Michael Lewis's story of Jim Clark's rise to success in the world of the Internet. In *The New New Thing: A Silicon Valley Story* (2000), Lewis tells the tale of a poor high-school dropout from a small town in Texas who came to found not one but three multibillion-dollar computer companies. Lewis believes that the factors that made Clark's ascension possible are wholly unprecedented. More than that, Lewis attributes Clark's achievements to a thoroughgoing rejection of the past. Innovation occurs, in this account, because of a willingness to close one's eyes to all established rules. Clark's entrepreneurial genius ultimately becomes synonymous with his determination to annihilate the past, to forget anything that has come before. "Clark had no past, only a future" (43). "His pursuit of the new new thing depended on his curious amnesia. . . . He'd made a kind of religion of keeping only those parts of his past he needed for fuel, on his journey into the future" (261).

Lewis is an accomplished journalist whose previous book, the best-selling *Liar's Poker* (1989), gave readers a vivid glimpse inside the stock-market craze of the eighties. In this new book he seizes on Clark's unorthodox career as the key to the Internet boom of the nineties. Lewis argues that the very unconventionality of Clark's path to riches is the key to his representative status. Breaking the mold is what makes Clark typical of today's successful technology entrepreneurs.

According to Lewis, Jim Clark fits into no single professional role. He is not merely a scientist, engineer, businessman, or deal maker. He is not what one thinks of as an intellectual or a creative artist. Yet he possesses some of the skills required for each of these roles. His gift for math was recognized in the Navy, which provided him with a college education and his ticket out of poverty. He subsequently obtained a master's degree in physics and a Ph.D. in computer science, then became a professor at Stanford, but he never fit in well with academic culture. It took people like Steven Spielberg and George Lucas to recognize the importance of his research in computer graphics. The chip he designed became so important to areas such as 3-D design, virtual reality games, and cinematic special effects that people coined the term "Siliwood Valley" to describe the mental merger of Silicon Valley and Hollywood he helped pioneer. The result was his first multibillion-dollar corporation, Silicon Graphics.

His next endeavor was to see if he could bring about the merger of computers with communications technology. The platform that he and Marc Andreessen created, Netscape Navigator, blurs the line between content and medium. Is Netscape a "content provider" in its own right or is it the medium that gives one access to knowledge, entertainment, and services? A little of both, as it happens, and this ambiguity is one of many things that has contributed to the legal tangle between Netscape and Microsoft over the latter's incorporation of a Web browser in its operating system. Clark's third company, Healtheon (now known as WebMD), aimed to merge the health industry with information technology. Regardless of its ultimate success or failure, Clark has already made a fortune from its initial stock offering.[8] Being the first to fuse apparently disparate fields has been the secret to each of his triumphs.

This fact leads Lewis to emphasize how difficult it is to categorize Clark's activities. To describe him is to produce a list of the things he is not:

> He isn't doing science. He isn't engaged in what any serious thinker would call thought. Unless he makes a lot of money, he isn't even treated as a businessman. . . . On the line that asked him to state his occupation, he did not know what to write. There was no name for what he did. Searcher? . . . The searcher for the new new thing conforms to no well-established idea of what people should do for a living. He gropes. (Lewis 14–15)

Obviously, some things about Clark's success *are* unique. No one prior to the last decade has made money in precisely the same way as this person. The Internet has created surprising new business opportunities that have challenged many traditional economic theories. For some observers, including even Alan Greenspan, capitalism itself seems to have entered unfamiliar terrain. Yet there are dangers in believing that one's world has no connections to the past, that amnesia (both personal and cultural) is the key to a successful future. Beyond the obvious danger of not learning from the mistakes of the past, there is also the risk of mystifying the things that have made one's present success possible. The arrangements of power that enable many of Clark's achievements have definite historical roots, and what is distinctive about them can be properly appreciated only against the background of this history. The novelty of Clark's unorthodox penchant for boundary crossing appears greater today because the years that immediately preceded our time, the Cold War period, represented the apogee of the two-culture split. From the perspective of the early nineteenth century, Clark's ability to identify opportunities arising from the intersection of different zones of culture appears less exceptional. For all its distinctiveness, today's fluid ranging across disciplinary fields has its precedents in earlier time periods. And today's undisciplined culture, which provides the rich medium that nourishes his hybrid form of creativity, has its precedents as well.

In Lewis's "Silicon Valley Story," the failure to think historically has resulted in the construction of a myth, the all-too-common myth of heroic ambition and heroic achievement. Lewis seems mesmerized by this aspect of his subject. "Success was his chosen form of revenge" (79), Lewis writes. "He had an animal desire to have what he wanted and not to have what he did not want" (80). Later, Lewis quotes an engineer who worked with Clark at Silicon Graphics: "Jim Clark has a clarity of vision that is prompted by the purest form of greed. . . . Nothing clouds it" (119). Although this is a story of the heroic geek, rather than the titan of industry from Victorian days, the mythmaking impulse remains central to the narrative.

An essential element in most such myths is a compensatory emphasis on the price paid by those around the heroic individual. Bystanders get hurt, loved ones are left behind, and enemies are ultimately crushed. Lewis plays this card to the full. In following Clark's efforts to raise money for his enterprises, Lewis stresses that the "guy inside the venture capital firm who worked with Clark . . . was always the guy who got fired" (109). Clark, on the other hand, always made millions. The epitome of this motif is the story of Glenn Mueller's suicide.

Mueller was a venture capitalist whom Clark felt had wronged him when they were putting together the deal that created Silicon Graphics. A few years later, when Clark had left Silicon Graphics and was raising money to found Netscape, Mueller was desperate to get in on the ground floor. He repeatedly pled with Clark to allow him to invest, but Clark took great pleasure in telling Mueller that he could keep his money. Mueller would never be allowed to invest in another Jim Clark endeavor. Three days after their last conversation, Netscape was incorporated without Mueller's backing. That same day, Mueller shot himself in the head.

Lewis makes only a token effort to absolve Clark of responsibility for this death. He mentions that Mueller had been suffering from paranoid fears, and he observes that "a lot of people" tried to comfort Clark by telling him that "Mueller's suicide wasn't his fault" (84). This form of denial, Lewis acknowledges, amounts to a backdoor method of accusing Clark of the crime. According to Lewis, people reassured Clark that he wasn't responsible "because in the back of their minds they suspected that maybe Mueller's suicide *was* Clark's fault. And so did Clark" (84).

Anyone who has read a twentieth-century biography of Dickens will recognize this strategy of blame-via-denial. The story of Dickens's supposed role in the suicide of the artist Robert Seymour is one of the dramatic set pieces in most lives of the novelist. Seymour was a well-known illustrator of the 1830s who conceived the original idea for *The Pickwick Papers*. His notion was to produce a monthly publication featuring four of his drawings, centered on the idea of a gentlemen's sporting club, and to hire a writer to provide some text to accompany his artwork. Dickens, then a struggling young writer, with only *Sketches by Boz* to his credit, accepted the commission of supplying prose to accompany Seymour's drawings. In short order, however, Dickens began reconceiving the project. The novelist demanded changes, and there was a tense encounter at Furnival's Inn with the novelist, artist, and publishers all present, which resulted in Dickens's plan being adopted. Two days later, Seymour shot himself in the head.

This terrible episode has encouraged some of Dickens's detractors to compile a whole budget of charges against the novelist. His ambition, according to this line of reasoning, produced a harsh, unyielding drive for success, which resulted in harm to those who thwarted his desires in either the professional or the domestic arenas. My purpose, however, is not to evaluate either figure's personal responsibility. In the case of Dickens, such questions have been sufficiently canvassed in other places, and there is little chance that a short account can assess so imponderable a question as one person's culpability for another person's suicide. In fact, my purpose is almost the reverse. I want to draw attention to the way in which the myth of the heroic individual, with its tragic subplot, muddles cultural appraisal. Just as the drama of Mueller's suicide leads Lewis to simplify his Silicon Valley story, the sensationalism of Seymour's suicide has prevented some scholars from emphasizing the cultural transformation at stake in the battle to control the form of *The Pickwick Papers*.[9]

What is not often noticed in accounts of Dickens's struggle to impose his vision on *Pickwick* is that the issue revolved around an innovation in nineteenth-century information technology. This innovation—the use of monthly numbers to lower the price of new fiction—was as radical in its day as the changes sweeping the publishing industry now as a result of technologies such as digital books, print-on-demand, and e-texts online. It is hard to categorize Seymour's innovation: Was it a new business model (original fiction sold at a shilling a part), a new medium (part-issues in individual wrappers), or a new distribution channel for providing "content" to consumers? Did it create a new form of culture (art with some subsidiary text, as Seymour wanted, or narrative paced for monthly consumption, as Dickens insisted)? All that is clear is that Dickens grasped the potential of this hybrid innovation, whereas Seymour did not. Dickens became the most successful writer of the nineteenth century in part because he saw a relationship between his own literary impulses and this half-technological, half-socioeconomic opportunity. He did not separate one question from the other. He did not discriminate between his imaginative gifts and his entrepreneurial acumen. Or, rather, his imagination operated powerfully in both spheres.

Later in his career he seized on similar opportunities that were equally hard to categorize. Did his innovations in the magazine serialization of new fiction in his weekly publications, *Household Words* (1850–1859) and *All the Year Round* (1859–1869), represent a clever new business plan or a formal variation in literary structure? Were his annual Christmas stories a new subgenre of literature or an effort to extend his market share? What about his pioneering role in creating uniform editions of a contemporary writer or his crusade for the adoption of international copyright laws? Even Dickens's invention of the practice of giving public fiction readings could be related to these other innovations. These changes could be called "technological" in the sense that they were designed to alter some aspect of the infrastructure of the publishing industry, but they were something else as well, something "cultural." All of these projects involved crossing boundaries and bringing together domains of activity that had previously remained separate. And all greatly increased Dickens's wealth, fame, influence, and power.

Dickens's relations to technology have proven crucial to understanding some aspects of his cultural power. Critics of Dickens have sometimes failed to see how his literary gifts as a novelist were intertwined with what one might call a form of "technocultural" creativity. Dickens was consumed with his projects to transform the information order of his day. Perhaps critics have been overly willing to respect the two-culture split and hence have failed to appreciate how literary talent can be mixed up with other forms of creativity. Perhaps Dickens's undisciplined energies were scattered across too many domains to be assimilable to the modern conception of a novelist. If his technocultural innovations were not primarily "literary" in nature, neither were they "scientific" by the dominant two-culture definition of those spheres. They were too entrepreneurial, too ad hoc, too motivated by micro shifts in domains that were part market, part culture, and part media. They were a lot like the hard-to-classify enterprises of a Jim Clark today.

Let me use a decidedly tongue-in-cheek metaphor to describe the thread that runs through all of Dickens's activities: his fiction writing, editing, journalism, publishing initiatives, amateur theatricals, speeches, public readings, business decisions, and even, much of his socializing. Dickens was always searching for greater *bandwidth*. He was a superb "content provider," of course, but he was equally talented at extending the circulation of this content. His ambition was to reach every English-speaking reader on the globe, to saturate every communications market, to rig every *household* so that it could receive his *words*. He wanted his publications to be the gateway for all Victorian consumers of art and infotainment. What stimulated Dickens's creativity, what drove him to look for the new new thing, was a craving for cultural bandwidth.

"The power is shifting to the engineers."

—Jim Clark

Where power resides in an undisciplined culture is a crucial question. Trying to answer such a question in terms of heroic individual achievements (or tragic personal failings) mystifies the actual complexity of power relations during times of transition. Dickens's desire for bandwidth had consequences he did not anticipate. His restless technocultural creativity was meant to put power in the hands of artists themselves. He believed that the creative spirits of the world should be able to control the fate of their productions. He would have been the last to predict, however, that his efforts on behalf of writers would lead to the rigidly stratified system of the modern publishing industry, with its vertically organized corporate divisions that emerged in the first half of the twentieth century. The story of this later development is the subject for different book. But the lesson for this discussion should be clear. The ability to innovate does not necessarily translate into the power to control the destiny of the things one builds.

Jim Clark's failure to grasp this point can be seen in his bald assertion: "The power is shifting to the engineers" (Lewis 30). Things were not so simple in Dickens's time, and they are not any easier today. Nothing illustrates this point more effectively than current debates about how the advent of the Internet will change power relations in the twenty-first century. The most visionary of today's technological enthusiasts proclaim the dawn of a new era of political and social freedom. This libertarian utopianism puts its faith in the inherent inability of governments to control cyberspace. The decentralized, global structure of the Internet, as well as the anonymity it provides, is seen to undermine government authority. When information is free, repression cannot persist for long. Power will be dispersed to the individual user. Authority will originate from the bottom up. Or so the argument goes. Skeptics of this new dispensation present a different picture. They object to the way in which life in cyberspace might alienate people from one another and distract users from the real world. Others protest that the so-called "Information Superhighway" will bypass the majority of the world's population, which are too poor to afford access to information technology. As Bill Gates himself pointed out, vast numbers of the world's inhabitants do not even have electricity or plumbing, so what are they going to do with personal computers?

For almost a decade the debate has raged, with neither side making much headway. Only when Lawrence Lessig published his important book *Code and Other Laws of Cyberspace* (1999) did it become clear how difficult the question of power in the world of the Internet had become. Lessig argues that there is nothing about the Internet that makes it inherently "unregulable" (25). Computer code, in both its software and hardware forms, determines what cyberspace will be. Hence the values society chooses to build into the code will determine whether the Net retains a potential for freedom or becomes a space of control. The code that engineers, hackers, and software developers write will decide the future of the Net. Which would seem to suggest that Clark was right: power *has* shifted to the engineers. The reality, however, is different. Lessig makes a strong case that the needs of commerce for secure e-business transactions and for more reliable ways to identify consumers in cyberspace are exerting powerful pressures on the architecture of the Net, which will ultimately make cyberspace far more easy for governments to control. In this scenario, it is not the engineers who dictate the direction of change but a dispersed alliance among businesses, government regulatory agencies, and users themselves, who *want* the ability to buy anything they please, anytime they please, and who are unaware of (or unconcerned about) the liberties they may be giving up. This unplanned alliance is pushing cyberspace to evolve "in a very particular direction: from an unregulable space to one that is highly regulable" (25). Government and commerce may have different interests in this area, but their efforts fortuitously work in conjunction to dictate an "architecture of control" that Lessig views with dismay (30).

Lessig advocates "open-source code" as a response to the forces that are changing cyberspace into a domain of control. "Open source" means that the architecture of both computer hardware and the software programs that run on the machines are freely available to all. In contrast to proprietary code, which is copyrighted by its designer and fiercely guarded as a trade secret, open code is in the public domain. Anyone can propose modifications or correct glitches, and every suggestion must make its own way, with users being the ultimate judges of its value. The ethos of the open-source movement seems typical of the hackers this book has examined. It is irreverent yet idealistic; problem oriented and impatient of institutional restraints, yet willing to embrace the ideas of others if they seem better than one's own. It is the ethos of a Wheatstone, Somerville, Babbage, or Paxton—and it is in the spirit of Dickens's fictional engineer Daniel Doyce. To me it seems to unite some of the best qualities of an engineering approach to technology with those of a humanistic orientation. Like engineering, the open-source ethos is hardheaded, practical, and unsparingly honest: a fix either works or it doesn't, a program either performs or it crashes. Like the humanities, this movement emphasizes collaboration, disinterested service to the community, and a concern with higher social goods. In short, the open-source movement is an example of how things might work if the convergence of the two cultures comes to pass.

Open-source code figures prominently in Neal Stephenson's *Cryptonomicon* (1999), a novel I will discuss shortly. Published the same year as Lessig's book, Stephenson's massive and entertaining fiction is equally concerned to think critically about the kind of unexpected alliances that could shape the future. Both authors demonstrate the importance of finding an intellectual vantage point on new cultural alignments.

A remarkable body of literature is providing the historical perspective that is missing from Michael Lewis's book. Although not widely noted, a veritable explosion of novels, short stories, poems, and plays that engage scientific thought has occurred in the last decade.[10] Indeed, the increase in fictional explorations of scientific issues is one of the most striking literary developments at the turn of the millennium.

Of special interest is a subset of this literature, a group of texts dedicated to discovering precedents for people who love both literary and scientific culture. In what amounts to a new subgenre, these works create imaginary ancestors for their contemporary characters, analogues from history for literary people (much like the authors, one supposes) who are captivated by science and technology. In contrast to the dominant ethos of literary culture in the twentieth century, which left no place in a humanist for a love of molecular biology, say, or for the mathematics of codes, these texts provide the missing heritage for their own kind of hybrid interests. They take up the challenge of constructing an alternative past for the information age.

The characteristic feature of this subgenre is a two-generational plot, which alternates between a contemporary group of characters, generally scientists of some sort, and characters from an earlier generation. The origin of this newly popular twist on multiplot structure might lie in Thomas McMahon's first novel, *Principles of American Nuclear Chemistry* (1970), which parallels the life of an aimless, unsuccessful physicist in the 1960s with that of his father, who was a scientist on the team at Los Alamos that invented the atomic bomb. Another example is Carl Djerassi and Roald Hoffmann's play *Oxygen* (2001), which alternates between the eighteenth and the twenty-first centuries in a debate over which scientist is most deserving of a "retro-Nobel" for the discovery of oxygen: Lavoisier, Priestley, or Scheele. George Bradley's lyric meditations on science in poems such as "E Pur Si Mouve," "I'm Sorry, Einstein," and "Very Large Array" combine characters and perspectives drawn from the present and the distant past.[11]

Much better known are several works that the reader has already encountered in these pages: Tom Stoppard's *Arcadia*, in which two sets of literary-scientific characters, separated by more than 150 years, enact symmetrical dramas in the drawing room of an English country house;[12] Richard Powers's *The Gold Bug Variations*, which weaves together narratives from the 1950s and 1980s to establish a homology among computer code, the genetic code, the musical code in Bach's *Goldberg Variations*, and the poetic codes of literary language; and Andrea Barrett's prizewinning short-story collection *Ship Fever*, which juxtaposes tales of contemporary scientific researchers with those of their eighteenth- and nineteenth-century predecessors. Three other novels analyzed in earlier chapters—Gibson and Sterling's *The Difference Engine*, Susan Sontag's *The Volcano Lover*, and Roger McDonald's *Mr. Darwin's Shooter*—share the ambition of providing a heritage for contemporary science, although they do not follow the two-plot design.[13]

Other examples could be adduced, not least the novel with which I shall conclude, Stephenson's *Cryptonomicon*. Rather than extending this list, however, I propose to demonstrate how the literary status of these works generates insights about today's culture convergence that might be less salient in other accounts. My hypothesis is that a formal dimension of these literary texts—their use of two-plot structure—allows a more complex relation to become visible in historical patterns that might otherwise seem simply to mirror one another. If science and technology are the modern world's most visible tokens of the new, stories that feature scientific parallels from distant time periods provoke a strong sense of wonder. More important, they produce an idiosyncratic form of knowledge about the present. The wonder stems from discovering that people who lived in the past may have had ideas much like our own. The form of knowledge, however, comes from the realization that the same only ever reappears as cultural difference. In the course of paralleling scientific lives, these novels inevitably chronicle human differences, alterations embodied not in laboratory equipment or scientific breakthroughs but in characters, choices, and actions. Here literature's conventional (some would say old-fashioned) focus on the uniqueness of individuals is put in the service of a nonsynchronous project that undermines common assumptions about the adequacy of historical Truth. Whereas traditional history of science traces continuity *or* rupture, this body of literature gives emotional and cognitive force to *both* similarity *and* difference. This fiction encodes time as humanly meaningful by giving weight both to uncanny patterns of recurrence and to the particularity of lived experience.

Today's two-culture works suggest that at least part of Snow's complaint is no longer as relevant as it was fifty years ago—that writers know nothing, and care less, about science. The other half of the problem, that scientists and engineers are alienated from the arts and humanities, may be shifting as well, in ways that I sketched earlier and shall return to in my conclusion. Now, however, I turn to a test case for my hypothesis, a double-plot novel that portrays a breakdown of the barriers separating mathematics, engineering, music, and literature.

"He's not just any chained wretch, he is a digital chained wretch,

Marley's Ghost on the Information Superhighway."

—Neal Stephenson

Neal Stephenson's *Cryptonomicon* is the ultimate geek novel. Its two sprawling but fast-paced stories parallel the activities of Lawrence Waterhouse, a code breaker for the navy in World War II, with those of his grandson Randy Waterhouse, a computer programmer setting up an information technology (IT) business in the Philippines. The juxtaposition of their stories traces the birth of the digital computer back to a ragtag group of nonconformist code breakers in the 1940s. Stephenson accurately perceives that the interdisciplinary alliance forged by wartime conditions among humanists, scientists, engineers, the military, the intelligence services, and industry created the ideal circumstances for the conception of the computer. His novel suggests that a similar mixture of talents and interests lies behind the IT revolution today. This comparison establishes a genealogy for hacker culture, uncovering both the dangers and the opportunities that accompany its particular brand of innovation.

Stephenson's history postulates two periods of interdisciplinary ferment, separated by nearly fifty years of disciplinary isolationism. During World War II, Lawrence exploits an informal alliance among once discrete intellectual spheres. After the war, however, the long, inhospitable era of the Cold War perverts that alliance, and Lawrence responds by retreating to a university in Washington State, where he lives out the remainder of his life in obscurity. His grandson Randy, on the other hand, comes to age as the Cold War is ending. In the altered conditions of his world, Randy recognizes the impossibility of escaping from a global economy (in a university, a Philippine jungle, or anywhere else). He also recognizes the importance of hacking from within that system. The problem he faces is that the very alliance of interests that helps him and his geeky friends succeed also aids the so-called New World Order by bringing government and business interests into sync. This is Lessig's point as well. Although today's free-market ideology casts government regulation as the sworn enemy of commerce, the special conditions of the Internet revolution, according to Stephenson, are turning them into partners in the demand for technologies of control. To celebrate a freewheeling Internet culture but turn a blind eye to the way in which this same culture may inadvertently promote new forms of control will ultimately prove self-defeating. Randy, however, learns from the experience of his grandfather that neither utopianism about hacker freedoms nor paranoia about technological control is an adequate response to the moment in which he lives. He learns that one must augment one's techie skills with a keen sense of history and a critical perspective—one must develop, in short, "literary" values and techniques.

In its World War II sections *Cryptonomicon* dramatizes vividly the breakdown of disciplinary barriers that historians of science have attributed to the wartime emergency. As Julie Thompson Klein makes clear, "World War II was a major turning point" in the relations of the disciplines. It fostered "problem-focused and mission-oriented research" and enabled a "rare level of collaborative effort" not only among the scientists and engineers employed by the Manhattan Project but also among linguists, historians, sociologists, anthropologists, and others working in newly formed area studies programs that were "designed to produce knowledge about the contemporary foreign cultures of 'enemy peoples'" (174–75). Although Klein does not focus on code breaking or computer science, these activities played just as great a role in promoting the kind of "interdisciplinary problem-focused research [that] gained prominence in World War II because it answered military needs" (208).[14]

Stevenson's wartime chapters visit many of the historical scenes where fundamental breakthroughs in the development of computing took place. They also feature some of the actual historical players—most prominently Alan Turing, the British mathematician, who was one of the first people in the twentieth century to conceive of the computer. The fictional Lawrence Waterhouse encounters Turing at Princeton, where the mathematician did graduate work in 1936–1937. After the war begins, Lawrence finds himself assigned to the code-breaking team at Pearl Harbor, where he learns cryptography from a fictionalized version of the eccentric Commander Joseph Rochefort. From there, Lawrence is transferred to the British code-breaking headquarters at Bletchley Park, where he reencounters Turing, who is now overseeing the decryption machines he helped invent: Bombe and Colossus. Before too long, Lawrence is part of a commando team, whose assignment is to plant disinformation in the field to prevent the Germans from learning that the Allies have broken the Nazi's Enigma codes. He also finds himself boarding a German submarine in an incident modeled on actual wartime events (the same events that inspired the movie *U-571*, released the year after

Cryptonomicon). Ultimately Lawrence ends up back in the Pacific, where his commander—a fictional character named Colonel Earl Comstock—was, in peacetime, an executive of the Electric Till Corporation (ETC), a company suggestive of IBM. In a comically outlandish episode, Lawrence invents a fully operational digital computer, built on principles derived from his musical training on pipe organs, the design for which Comstock steals for his company. At the same time that this theft of intellectual property emphasizes the role a humanistic talent (music) might play in the multimedia computers to come, it also lays the groundwork for ETC to become a covert partner with the newly founded National Security Agency (NSA), which has already recruited Comstock as an agent.

In the novel's 900-plus pages, Stephenson is able to do imaginative justice to most aspects of the literary-scientific-engineering-military-industrial-intelligence alliance forged by the exigencies of war. Each wing of this alliance has a fictional character with his own elaborate plot line devoted to it: both Lawrence and the real-life Turing were pure mathematicians as well as unusually gifted electrical engineers (see Dennett's comment quoted earlier); civil engineering is explored in the story of a Japanese soldier Goto Dengo; the story of Marine Sergeant Bobby Shaftoe brings the military into the equation, then evolves into a portrait of the role that covert operations played in the development of cryptography from a hobby for literary gentlemen to a full-blown scientific discipline; and Comstock's machinations in the Pacific Theater provide an unpleasant foretaste of the way in which the intelligence community would begin to co-opt scientific research for the Cold War in the years to come.[15]

Alternating with the chapters set in World War II are chapters taking place in the 1990s. These contemporary sections recount the adventures of Randy Waterhouse, Lawrence's grandson, an overweight, romantically inept former gamer and Unix system operator—in short, a classic geek. Randy's life changes dramatically when he joins with his friend Avi Halaby to form an IT company they call the Epiphyte Corporation. Their efforts to get this start-up company off the ground take them to the Philippines, where a series of carefully orchestrated coincidences—reminiscent of the coincidences that structure Dickens's multiplot novels—brings Randy together with the descendants of each of the main characters from the World War II plot: Amy Shaftoe, the granddaughter of Sergeant Bobby Shaftoe; Goto Furundenendu, a civil engineer like his father; Paul Comstock, the law officer opposed to freedom on the Net; and several peripheral characters, whose roles are too minute to discuss here but whose cameo appearances are a frequent source of amusement.[16] These characters inhabit a turbulent post-Cold War culture. The speculative energy and unrestrained greed of the New World Order serve as a backdrop for the slowly emerging scheme of Randy and Avi. Their business plan turns out to have a surprising idealism at its core, a utopian motive that only gradually becomes apparent. To achieve their vision, they must negotiate a path among forces as intimidating in this contemporary setting as were the World War II enemies in their time: criminal consortiums from several countries, U.S. law-enforcement agencies, a corrupt Filipino justice system, rival venture capitalists, high-powered legal challenges, and a native insurgency movement.

The stories set in each epoch revolve around what one might call hacker conspiracies, which contain both political and aesthetic dimensions. In the World War II period, Lawrence joins with Finnish, German, and American coconspirators to steal a submarine full of looted Nazi gold in the waning days of the war. This band of intellectual nonconformists is motivated by impatience with the leaden thinking of the military bureaucracies and by their dawning realization that their discoveries will be co-opted by the postwar powers. Lawrence, a protogeek, uses his eccentricities and pranks— what would today be recognized as typical hacker style and behavior—to hide the existence of his cabal from his superiors. Randy's conspiracy involves the secret construction of a data haven in an independent kingdom on a small island off the Philippines. A data haven is a secure hideaway where the absolute privacy of customers' electronic information can be guaranteed.[17] Although the U.S. government worries that such havens would be used for money laundering, gambling, child porn, and, after 9/11, terrorism, hackers see total freedom of information as crucial to preserving individual liberties under globalization. In addition, the conspirators hope to establish an independent digital currency, backed by billions of dollars in wartime Japanese gold, which they have located in a hidden underground vault. This plan for a digital currency has as its ultimate aim freedom from all government control. Finally, Avi hopes to use the data haven to create an indestructible database filled with information to help oppressed peoples avoid future holocausts.

The novel consistently presents crypto as a "technology of freedom," to use Ithiel de Sola Pool's influential phrase. One of the World War II conspirators speculates that "if you're smart enough to break hard codes, you're automatically going to be" opposed to oppression. Even though another character immediately scoffs at this notion as "naive," Lawrence endorses it as a "leap of faith" (881), which is, at bottom, the idealistic faith at the heart of the entire book. The notion that crypto can protect freedom guides the actions of the protagonists in both time periods. Other things unite the two conspiracies: both involve illegal hoards of Axis gold, both require innovations in digital technology, and both demonstrate a subversive disregard for intellectual and political boundaries. Finally, there is the mysterious figure of Enoch Root—the only character to play a major role in both plots—who is a passionate believer in the importance of cryptography for freedom. But everyone in the two bands shares a basic antiauthoritarian spirit, a hackers' aesthetic, and a trust in the value of undisciplined free inquiry.

Although these two generations of computer hackers have much in common, Stephenson's genealogy of the information age turns out to be unexpectedly dialectical. The novel stages an internal conflict between a utopian impulse, which celebrates the freewheeling creativity of the interdisciplinary moment, and a kind of paranoia, which responds to the involvement of knowledge workers in larger structures of state power. The tug of each position counteracts the potentially overwhelming attraction of the other. If an easy utopianism, seen as much in the hackers' irreverent style as in their faith in technology, risks making them both self-satisfied and marginal to real structures of power, paranoia and a penchant for secrecy risk stifling the crisscrossing exchange of ideas so crucial to their success. The dialectical conflict of these forces generates the historical movement of the novel, a history that should prevent readers from viewing the convergence of the two cultures through rose-colored glasses.

The two generations are separated by approximately fifty years, an entire generation of discovery and struggle, which happens also to be the exact period comprising the Cold War. This missing period haunts the stories of the generations on either side. Lawrence and Turing's wartime experiments were fueled by a liberating sense that anything was possible, that no disciplinary boundary or conventional assumption would be allowed to stand in the way of the scientific breakthroughs needed to defeat fascism. Yet the reader is never allowed to forget how the postwar military-industrial complex would exploit these same discoveries for the prosecution of its crusade against communism. Colonel Earl Comstock, who steals Lawrence's ideas for ETC, tries to persuade Lawrence to join the NSA, offering him the chance to fight "our first cryptological skirmish with the Communists" (897), and years afterwards Comstock is remembered as a "Cold War policy guy—the brains behind the Vietnam War" (127). Thus the roots of Cold War paranoia were already present in the freewheeling interdisciplinary alliance behind Lawrence's discoveries. This foreshadowing of a Cold War mindset is the negative moment, the dialectical other, inside the intellectual ferment of the World War II era. It inhabited even the most joyously anarchistic moments of the earlier hacker conspiracy, for the success of their enterprises was conditioned on the wartime emergency, which brought together once distant spheres of society for a brief period of interdisciplinary creativity.

The Cold War also haunts the computer culture of the 1990s, when anticommunist ideologues are supposedly a thing of the past. Paranoia and conspiracy theories abound among many of the hackers in the novel, and although the hidden menace is not communism, the us-against-them mindset is eerily similar. The extremist fringe of hacker culture has been tainted by the violent mentality of the Cold War years in which its members grew up. In Stephenson's dialectical history, Cold War paranoia did not simply go away with the fall of the Soviet Union. Instead it lived on, infecting not only repressive government agents such as Paul Comstock but even the tactics of radical libertarians.

This haunting of each period by an intervening-but-absent time constitutes the core of the dialectic at work in the novel. The parallelism between the two represented generations—in the absence of the kind of linear causal chain that traditional history would use to explain their connection—might be expected to produce an uncanny effect, as if the past were inhabiting the present. But it doesn't. Instead, the amusing double exposure, in which characters are duplicated in their children or grandchildren, is purely pleasurable, a narrative correlative of the undisciplined high spirits that enable each generation's achievements. It is the missing period that produces a feeling of uneasiness. The burden of the Cold War years becomes more haunting for being unnarrated. And the uncanniness is transferred to the negative undercurrents in the stories on either side. The Cold War lends its oppressive aura to the hackers' paranoia, while at the same time serving as a warning against unthinking optimism.

A group of privacy freaks and encryption junkies known as the Secret Admirers represent the negative potential among the contemporary hackers. None of the main characters in Randy's corporation is a member of this group, but they all know members and tend to view their expertise as astounding and their political views as a little weird. The Secret Admirers share with their nemesis Earl Comstock the belief that a secret cabal called the Black Chamber, made up of the NSA, the IRS, the Secret Service, and their counterparts from other countries, is trying to run the world. The Secret Admirers hate the idea, whereas Comstock is completely behind it, but the world view is the same. As at the height of the Cold War, an identical belief-structure governs the actions of adversaries on both sides. No doubt some of Stephenson's readers agree with the Secret Admirers, but Stephenson betrays his own sympathies when he has Randy say: "The last thing he needs is to be hanging around with people who believe [their cause] is nothing more than a skirmish in a war to decide the fate of the Free World—a preliminary round of the Apocalypse" (726). On the last pages of the novel, when Randy and Avi are about to recover the stolen wartime gold that will insure the independence of their data haven, the Secret Admirers descend on their jungle camp in the Phillippines, making it almost impossible to work: "All of them apparently think they are present at some kind of radical societal watershed, as if global society has gotten so screwed up that the only thing to do is shut down and reboot it" (908).

One might be tempted to conclude that there are two kinds of computer people in the novel, two kinds of geeks, if you will: the reasonable and the slightly cuckoo. But that would miss the point. The craziness is internal to geek culture, just as it is to mainstream culture. This self-destructive Manicheism is a legacy of the Cold War era, which no one in the book evades entirely. The tendency to translate legitimate suspicion of control into paranoid fantasies is a displaced version of the McCarthy era mindset, and it taints the motives of everyone in the novel. Some characters are more consumed than others, but the tendency to think in us-against-them terms is the negative moment within the contemporary storyline, just as it was in the World War II plot. As in the earlier period of interdisciplinary freedom, a dialectical other inhabits the technolibertarianism of present-day geeks.

Even Enoch Root has been infected. Enoch is presented as the wisest character in the book, but he has a blind spot that implicates him in a disturbing racism. He believes that he is involved in an eternal war between Good and Evil. The fascists were the enemies once; now he is convinced that the Chinese have become the adversary. His political paranoia is explicitly linked with his advocacy of science. Enoch is a mouthpiece for one of the fundamental tenets of hacker culture: "Science flourishes where art and free speech flourish" (816). It is a doctrine that commands respect. But Enoch goes on to indict the Chinese tout court as the enemies of civilization: "If the Chinese are so civilized, how come they never invent anything?" (815). He casts his defense of scientific freedom as America's new "Manifest Destiny" (816). Enoch warns: "The next time the conflict is going to revolve around bio-, micro-, and nanotechnology. Who's going to win?" (816).[18]

Despite Enoch's paranoia, Stephenson views him—and his like-minded brethren—with amused fondness. Stephenson has been part of this "Community of Social Discontents," to recall Katz's term, and he knows its habits intimately. One of the cute motifs in the book is his division of computer people into categories based on a typology derived from Tolkien's *Lord of the Rings:* "Dwarves (steady, productive, surly) and Elves (brilliant in a more ethereal way)," as well as Wizards, who are in charge of complex networks, and an occasional Gollum, who is a slinking, devious, obsessed type (685). This typology comes into play during a confrontation between government agents intent on shutting down a computer owned by Epiphyte Corp. and an impromptu assemblage of hackers and antigovernment activists.

The scene is great fun. One cannot help rooting for the geeks, pitted against a vindictive lawyer (the Gollum) who has plagued Epiphyte throughout the novel, and an imposing array of law-enforcement officers. Stephenson is rooting for the geeks too, but this does not prevent him from registering the threatening aspects of the encounter. There is a dark undercurrent running through the antiestablishment figures, lurking just below the fellowship and high fives, which reveals how some elements of geek culture have internalized the violent impulses of the very society they oppose. Many of the hackers who arrive uninvited on the scene bear an uncomfortable resemblance to extreme right-wing survivalists and homegrown terrorist groups: "Some of these guys are wearing long coats and some aren't," but "to a man, they are carrying long weapons out in plain sight. . . . Secret Admirers—who tend to be gun nuts—have taken to going around conspicuously armed" (687). This confrontation, which develops into a near riot, ends when a group of Dwarves fries every computer chip within several blocks with a powerful "electromagnetic pulse" (693), thus rendering useless the computer the Feds are trying to seize. The government forces have been thwarted, but only at the cost of having to imitate their tactics.

The novel ends with a more hopeful scenario, however. The victory of the contemporary protagonists suggests that an alliance might be possible between the alternative energies of geek culture and the productive poten-

tialities of mainstream disciplines. This idealistic band of computer entrepreneurs triumphs because they shift nimbly between embracing the new
global economy and remaining independent of government control, critical
of the potential dangers of their own project, and aware of the historical
burden their project carries into the future. They engage in what Alan Liu
calls "ethical hacking" of the social and disciplinary spheres they inhabit.
Like the World War II group who invented the computer, this band works
both within and on the margins of the larger, global structures of the age—
big science, big business, academia, law, government, and the military-
industrial complex. Their ability to engage with these macro forces, rather
than opt out of the entire system, is essential to their success. Without a willingness to deal with the actual conditions of global power, the high-minded
idealism of their hacker ethos would be outclassed.

Stephenson chooses no less of a predecessor than Dickens to clinch this
point. Dickens has been a silent partner in the novel's two-plot structure, its
play with characters' names, and its satire of unwieldy institutions.[19] Toward
the end of the book, the great Victorian makes two appearances in propria
persona. The first is an aside about lawsuits as interminable as the one in
Bleak House, a comment that draws attention to the major role another set of
international institutions plays in the world of the novel—the legal system,
which insinuates itself into every twist and turn of the 1990s plot. The second
reference is to *A Christmas Carol.* In the epigraph with which I began this section, Stephenson portrays Randy Waterhouse as a "digital chained wretch,
Marley's Ghost on the Information Superhighway" (782). Randy, in a Philippine prison on trumped-up charges, is literally in chains, shackled in a position that forces him to use his laptop computer where his jailors can eaves-
drop on his keystrokes. The allusion again underscores the prominence in the
plot of an almost irresistible multinational power: big business. Business and
law are inescapable parts of Randy's world. He is chained to both institutions,
a digital wretch bound up in systems he would do anything to escape.

As Randy comes to understand, there is no free haven, no place where
one can escape completely from the entanglements of the world system. Instead, he must continue to work in the interstices of organizations far more
powerful than himself. He must remain a hacker, even if, at the end of the
book, he has become a very wealthy hacker. His solace is that he has learned
of others before him who have succeeded by employing the same measures.

Prophecy courts the ridicule of time, and those who dream of tomorrow
often wake to laughter. Like Stephenson, I do not pretend to know what
a convergence of the two cultures might bring, or even if current tendencies
will continue. In lieu of prophecy, therefore, I shall conclude with some remarks about how one might conceptualize such a convergence, were it to
proceed further, and about what role literature might play in the resulting
dispensation. I begin by suggesting that there exist three principal models
for the end of the two-culture split: synthesis, hegemony, and alliance.

Let me start with the rosiest and to my mind, least convincing vision. In *Consilience: The Unity of Knowledge* (1998), the biologist Edward O. Wilson proposes that a grand synthesis of all human understanding is within our grasp. The Enlightenment dream is about to be realized: "The greatest enterprise of the mind has always been and always will be the attempted linkage of the sciences and humanities. The ongoing fragmentation of knowledge and resulting chaos in philosophy are not reflections of the real world but artifacts of scholarship" (8). The basis for Wilson's optimism is his belief that science springs from the same impulse that lies at the heart of ethics, religion, literature, art, and all other humanities. "Perhaps science is a continuation on a new and better-tested ground to attain the same end" (7). Whether or not one shares Wilson's vision, it is easy to identify the literary genre in which he works. *Consilience* is an example of utopian writing, which has found a renewed market in recent years under the label of non-fiction popular science. Not only evolutionary biologists like Wilson but also gurus of Internet culture, genomics, artificial intelligence, robotics, spiritual machines, collective intelligence, and self-organizing lifeforms have revitalized Utopia for the twenty-first century.

The writings of utopian futurists lack the critical skepticism that makes Stephenson's novel more than idle entertainment. Nor do they typically exhibit the self-reflexive irony of Stoppard's *Arcadia* or the multiple resonances of Richard Powers's *The Gold Bug Variations,* to choose other examples from among two-plot works encountered here. The utopianism in Wilson's late work is missing exactly what this new genre of literature aims to supply: a vision supple enough to affirm essential ideals without minimizing the countervailing pressures that may coexist within those same ideals.

At the opposite end of the spectrum is the view that the two-culture split is no longer operative because science has achieved a virtual hegemony over all other forms of discourse. In this vision, literature and the other humanities have lost their claim to produce valid perspectives on the world and thus have become irrelevant to the real business of life. Science wins by default. The choice of the word *business* was not idle: science's power is seen as stemming from its role in the global economy as much as from any superiority of its truth claims. This is the kind of convergence Alan Liu discusses in his account of how the literary has been absorbed and "repurposed" by a culture now dominated by the needs of technoscience:

> Literature as traditionally understood no longer survives as an autonomous force. . . . Since the high point of its avowed self-possession (roughly from the eighteenth through the nineteenth centuries), literature has merged with mass-market, media, educational, political, and other institutions that reallocate, repackage, and otherwise "repurpose" its assets. (62)

There are only two roles left for humanists in this scenario: They may join the ranks of corporate knowledge workers (even if the corporation in question is a university), or they may attempt to subvert the global economy from within. In either case, prospects are bleak, as bleak as the literary genre that has responded to this future: Dystopia. The literary tradition of dystopian thinking has proved hardier than its utopian forebear, and the several futuristic visions examined in this study—from *The Difference Engine* to *Blade Runner* and *Gattaca*—level terrible charges against societies that permit science to get out of hand. These dystopian visions play an important role in contemporary culture. The import, however, of other works—from Somerville's *Personal Recollections* and Hardy's *A Laodicean* to *Oscar and Lucinda, Patchwork Girl, Ship's Fever,* and *Mr. Darwin's Shooter*—is that balancing the claims of science and literature will cultivate talents and attitudes an equitable society needs.

The final model is the one I have been building toward throughout this book. Forging alliances among disciplines, in which individuals and groups draw on diverse and shifting pools of expertise, seems like a desirable structure for convergence. In the business world, something similar has already arrived. Contemporary corporations, with their emphasis on "flexible specialization" and "project teams," have little respect for disciplinary boundaries. Emergencies appear to facilitate such alliances: World War II was one such emergency, the rapid transformation of American capitalism by IT is another, and the threat of terrorism might be a third. If this last turns out to be the case, then Stephenson's warning about the United States' tendency toward political paranoia becomes even more timely. The trick is to find ways of turning effective responses to the present emergency into permanent critical strategies. Is there a body of imaginative work that has attempted to identify such strategies? Yes—the novels, films, plays, poems, essays, and cultural-studies writing surveyed here.

Alliance building, however, is no panacea. There are as many dangers as opportunities presented by such a strategy. Evolving disciplinary norms have already undermined some longstanding safeguards of scientific research. The erosion of distinctions between pure and applied science, which has frequently drawn praise in these pages, may also render conflict-of-interest questions more troubling. Sorting out such issues will require great critical care.[20]

Whatever lies in the future, it is evident that practices and values are shifting around the very divisions that Snow described: the two cultures. The lesson I draw from Stephenson and other literary people who focus on science is that a critical engagement with technology, not withdrawal, is the best hope for what were once called humanist values. Celebrating nonconformity and disciplinary anarchism will not suffice for people who care about creating a just society. Negotiating between the advantages and the pitfalls of an undisciplined culture will require greater critical and historical perspective. And for that, what better guide than literature?

INTRODUCTION

1. Professor Matsuoka kindly supplied me with the information that his *Dickens Page* contains more than 1,000 links to other Web sites that are germane to Dickens (e-mail communication with the author, June 29, 2001). Another prominent Dickens Web site, with the very same title, *The Dickens Page,* was founded at almost the same time by George P. Landow. (Landow's electronic database, which had existed in an earlier form on disk, went up on the Web in the summer of 1995.) I discuss Landow's contributions to Dickens's presence on the Web in the last chapter of this book.

2. The few nineteenth-century novelists who rival him are Jane Austen, Lewis Carroll, Conan Doyle, Victor Hugo, and Mark Twain.

3. Most scholars of Romanticism, particularly those who focus on British authors, do not talk about their period in terms of the Enlightenment. With a few significant exceptions—such as James Engell's intellectual history of the creative imagination, Alan Bewell's work on Romantic anthropology, Jerome Christensen's book on Hume, and Marshall Brown's chapter in the *Cambridge Companion to British Romanticism*—scholars have generally not focused on the literary, philosophical, or political consequences of the British Romantics' position in (or after) the Enlightenment. There are obvious reasons for this lacuna—the Enlightenment has often seemed more relevant to developments taking place on the Continent and in Scotland—but even when critics study Wordsworth's relations with Godwin, say, or

Coleridge's with Hartley, they tend to focus on specific issues of influence and belief, rather than larger questions involving the project of modernity.

4. I take up McGowan's thesis in detail in chapter 5. Other important contributions to the project of tracing postmodernism's debts to Romantic and Victorian culture include Joel Black, Diane Elam, William Galperin, David Simpson, Orrin Wang, and all the contributors to *Victorian Afterlife*. The introduction to that volume by Dianne F. Sadoff and John Kucich is particularly useful in tracing the "Histories of the Present" at stake in this project.

CHAPTER 1

1. The Millennium Dome's failure to live up to advance publicity is discussed later in this chapter. At the end of its year-long run, the Dome was regarded as a relative disappointment. *The New York Times* reports that the 6.5 million visitors "compare favorably with other London tourist attractions, and surveys indicate customer satisfaction of 85 percent," but the Millennium Dome was a "victim of its own hyped expectations" (Hoge).

2. I was inspired to think about this comparison by an illuminating paper Ronald R. Thomas read at the 1999 conference of the Narrative Society. Thomas's discussion mentions the Crystal Palace only in its opening and closing passages, but he stresses the Millennium Dome as a symbol of England's fallen status as a world power and as the self-proclaimed "Center of Time," just as I do. I am pleased to acknowledge Thomas's priority in using this historical conceit both because it illustrates one of the themes of my book—that a historical cultural studies must consolidate and build upon other narratives—and because it stands as a pleasant reminder of the many collegial exchanges I have shared with Ron and the many other nineteenth-century scholars in the Narrative Society. The majority of Thomas's essay is concerned with another important topic, the Millennium Dome "as a culminating episode in the twentieth-century critique of the nineteenth-century science of modern geography."

3. The best of such discussions may be found in Alan Liu ("Local"), John McGowan, and the critics mentioned in n4 of Introduction.

4. In England, cultural studies traces its lineage back to Raymond Williams, who was deeply attuned to historical questions. Consequently, an account of the British movement, especially in the Birmingham Centre for Contemporary Cultural Studies where it first arose, would have to qualify many of the assertions about ahistoricism made here. The differences among British, American, and Australian cultural studies have been canvassed numerous times. Readers who are interested in the background of the movements should consult Brantlinger, Easthope, or Bathrick. For an influential collection of examples of the method, see Grossberg, Nelson, and Treichler. An overview that also challenges the method's continued deployment of a Marxist conception of class may be found in Frow. Other useful collections include Nelson and Gaonkar; Ferguson and Golding; and McGuigan.

5. Lawrence Grossberg defines cultural studies in terms of a "radical contextuality": "To say that its object of study is contextual is to say that the context is the real object of study" (143).

6. A pivotal account of this contest is Frank Lentricchia's *After the New Criticism* (1980). Other important documents in the struggle were Edward Said's *The World, the Text, and the Critic* (1983), Jonathan Arac's *Critical Genealogies* (1987), and Avram Veeser (ed.), *The New Historicism* (1989).

7. See Catherine Hall (272), MacCabe (13), Burke (191), and Steinberg (103).

8. For accounts of their practice, see Hunt's *The New Cultural History,* Burke's *Varieties of Cultural History,* and Geoffrey Eley's "What Is Cultural History?" (1995). For the difference between cultural history and cultural studies, see Steinberg.

9. See Epstein, *Radical Expression* (1994); Davidoff and Hall, *Family Fortunes* (1987); Joyce, *Democratic Subjects* (1994); Steedman, "Culture, Cultural Studies, and the Historians" (1992); Vernon, *Politics and the People* (1993); and Walkowitz, *City of Dreadful Delight* (1992), discussed later in this chapter.

10. See the essays collected in Newman, Clayton, and Hirsch, *Time and the Literary;* Elaine Scarry, *On Beauty and Being Just;* John Brenkman's "Extreme Criticism"; and Jonathan Culler's "The Literary in Theory."

11. Ruth Brown explains Lucinda's uneasiness in the presence of George Eliot as part of the novel's colonial ambivalence toward British literature, an interpretation which has some validity but does not address Lucinda's response to other aspects of British culture.

12. The most extensive treatments of Carey's use of Gosse appear in Callahan and Hassall (124–28). Petersen (114–15) and King also contain useful observations on this intertextual relation.

13. Critics have made several attempts. Ommundsen (271–72) and Huggan (49) relate gambling to the prominence of games in metafiction, which frequently uses the arbitrariness of their rules as a metaphor for the conventionality of fiction. Ashcroft notes that gambling is stereotypically regarded as a "'typical' Australian trait" and describes its role in developing a "counter-theology" (205) to the characters' inherited versions of Christianity. Fletcher also suggests reading the gambling motif as subversive of traditional Christian values (20–21). These latter seem to me to be on the right track, and their emphasis on alternative versions of Christianity accords with Dostoevsky's mystical reinterpretation of faith.

14. Dostoevsky's appearance in the library of Lucinda's mother in 1858 is an anachronism. The first translation of a Dostoevsky novel into English appeared in 1881, and there is no suggestion that Lucinda's mother knew Russian. The status of this and numerous other anachronisms in the novel will be discussed later.

15. Three critics mention the Crystal Palace in passing, spending no more than a sentence on it. One mentions in a clause that Carey may have been invoking Dostoevsky, and another uses a footnote to dismiss that suggestion. Hassall, the only critic to discuss the characters' oddness, astutely comments that Carey uses their oddness "to defamiliarise what might have been a period piece and to turn it into a searching critique of contemporary Australia" (121).

16. For an excellent discussion of Himmelfarb as the intellectual leader of the "neo-conservative romance" with Victorian political ideas, see Hadley.

17. Nussbaum's defense of literature as a repository of "universal significance" represents a very different claim from my argument that literature models ways of finding meaning and value *in* cultural difference.

18. I should note that both Nussbaum and Himmelfarb amply acknowledge this point. Each attempts to suggest ways to respond to historical difference within the framework of universal principles about the continuity of human experience. My contention is that a historical practice that reverses this priority and emphasizes difference will better serve the study of literature and culture.

19. See Altick's note, "Borrioboola-Gha, Bushmen, and Brickmakers." I thank Kurt Koenigsberger for first drawing my attention to this point. His intelligent as-

sessment of Dickens's sources for Mrs. Jellyby and the controversy surrounding her can be found in his annotations to the "Hypertext *Bleak House*," created by Nancy Metz et al., at http://athena.english.vt.edu/LIT/dickens/BleakHouse.html.

20. For attacks on postmodern approaches to history, see Windschuttle, Himmelfarb ("Postmodernist History"), and Wilson; for celebrations, see Ermarth, Jenkins (*Why History?*), and Wyschogrod. The most thorough discussions of the theoretical issues at stake are Berkhofer and Chartier. A useful collection of documents on both sides of this debate is Jenkins's *The Postmodern History Reader*.

21. Other contributions could be named, including Dominick LaCapra's most recent writings, Michel de Certeau's heterological approach (examined briefly below), and Joyce Appleby, Lynn Hunt, and Margaret Jacob's *Telling the Truth about History*. The four figures I have chosen to discuss, however, will serve to characterize the kind of historical theory that is needed to enrich cultural studies.

22. One wonders if Carey derived the idea for the celluloid episode from reading Carter's critique of the imprisoning grid of longitude and latitude (Carey 156–59; Carter 71). The narrator's mother, in *Oscar and Lucinda*, insists that the cross-hatched markings on Oscar's scrap of celluloid were the coordinates to locate his church on a map, when they were actually something far more particular and idiosyncratic: a vain attempt by a traveler (not a cartographer) to control his seasickness on the voyage over by viewing the ocean through a small frame.

23. Compare with Carlo Ginzburg's attitude toward the genres of history and fiction. In an important theoretical statement, Ginzburg traces his historical technique to a diverse set of precursors, which include fictional texts ranging from contemporary films to the novels of Proust, Woolf, Musil, Queneau, and Calvino. His point in emphasizing these sources is to suggest that professional historians can borrow the methods of fiction—as well as its critical stance toward knowledge—without collapsing the distinctions between history and fiction.

24. Lohrli, working from the office book of *Household Words*, attributes "The Private History of the Palace of Glass" (January 18, 1851) to W. H. Wills, but Margaret Darby has uncovered evidence in the archives at Chatsworth suggesting that Paxton may have written part of the essay himself, or at least corrected the proofs of the article before it went to press. In response to a query I posted to the Dickens electronic discussion list, Darby wrote: "I have worked at the Chatsworth archives and have read the proof sheets of 'The Private History of the Palace of Glass,' which have been preserved there. I have also consulted with Angus Easson of Salford University about its authorship, more specifically about whose hand supplied the emendations in the proof sheets. Dr. Easson is confident in a letter to me of November 29, 1993, that 'neither the cover-note nor the proof corrections is by Dickens or by Wills.' We might expect that they would have been written by Paxton himself, and the archivists at Chatsworth I worked with thought it might be Paxton's hand, but were not sure. Angus Easson also told me that there might have been two stages of proofs and two different hands, or even the same hand with two different pens on two different occasions" (Darby, "On 'The Palace of Glass'").

25. Darby, who generously shared with me her essay "Joseph Paxton's Water Lily" before publication, describes the mixture of imperial arrogance and scientific care that makes this tale typical of nineteenth-century botanical expeditions: "The lily's story first exemplifies the paradoxes of imperial plant hunting, in which invasiveness and dominance went hand in hand with nurture. The history of this tropical plant's journey to England is strikingly typical of the scientific and imperial motives that en-

couraged Englishmen to penetrate forbidding foreign environments in order to pluck up what grew there, often destroying whole ecosystems in the process. Having worked so hard to bring home the plants made vulnerable by this very resourcefulness, they then devoted themselves with delicate sensitivity to the plants' needs" (258).

26. Alison Booth discusses the analogy between women's education and the cultivation of hothouse flowers (47–51). Adrienne Munich considers the stir produced by *Victoria regia* as an allegory of the disturbing implications of a woman possessing Queen Victoria's power (212–17). Darby sees the image of Annie on the lily as expressing "not only women's vulnerability, but their connection to the mysteries of nature, and probably also masculine anxiety about woman's reproductive power and the need to control it" ("Joseph Paxton's Water Lily," 266).

27. I discuss Guy Debord's *The Society of the Spectacle* in chapter 2 and distinguish between the modern spectacle and earlier nineteenth-century shows in chapter 3.

28. This point might seem self-evident, but the only recent critics who have analyzed the Great Exhibition's nonvisual legacy at any length are Berman and Auerbach. It is significant that few of the other critics of the exhibition even cite Berman—his emphases fall largely outside the orthodox discourse on the Great Exhibition. Berman is also the only critic prior to Landon to have analyzed Dostoevsky's response to the Crystal Palace, a fact that makes it all the more surprising that Landon does not mention Berman's study.

29. For a discussion of the musical heritage of the Crystal Palace, see Musgrave.

30. Carter's dual commitment has already been discussed. Gilroy uses the motif of sailing, much as Carter does traveling, to capture the "variations and discontinuities in modern experience" and "the decentred and inescapably plural nature of modern subjectivity" (46), but he insists that attending to the materiality and the performative character of black experience can "partially displace [the postmodern] concern with textuality" (36). Walkowitz, too, describes late-Victorian London as a "series of multiple and simultaneous cultural contests and exchanges across a wide social spectrum" (10), but she views her engagement with questions of women's power, agency, and experience to be a corrective response to the epistemological challenges posed by postmodernism (7–8). Finally, Ginzburg not only makes the cognitive wager discussed in the text but also takes an "experimental attitude" toward issues of narrative representation and self-reflexivity. He argues that history must involve a "definite awareness that all phases through which research unfolds are *constructed* and not *given:* the identification of the object and its importance; the elaboration of the categories through which it is analyzed; the criteria of proof; the stylistic and narrative forms by which the results are transmitted to the reader" (32).

31. Susan Stanford Friedman relies on a similar distinction in the use of the term "map" in her valuable study of the encounter zones where diverse cultures in the United States come into contact with one another. Friedman's *Mappings* suggests new ways to narrate the history of a cultural field riven by difference.

32. For evidence of this assertion, consult the large literature surrounding the Habermas–Lyotard debate over the question of modernity and postmodernity, or the contributions of the other figures who have made significant advances in thinking about this same topic: Zygmunt Bauman (sociology), David Harvey (geography), Andreas Huyssen (literature), Fredric Jameson (Marxism), Gianni Vattimo (philosophy), and Robert Wuthnow (sociology).

33. Ten months later, Mr. Gerbeau had become the only figure involved with the Dome who was still viewed favorably by the press. On December 31, 2000, the day

the Dome closed its doors for good, the *New York Times* reported: "Mr. Gerbeau, 35, is the only official to emerge from the affair undisgraced, and he even ended up on a short list of year 2000 heroes phoned into the BBC this week by listeners" (Hoge A4).

CHAPTER 2

1. Marvin confuses the date of the article in *The Electrical World,* a rare slip by this careful researcher. Similar stories can be found in many nineteenth-century publications about the growth of the telegraph system. By the last decades of the century, tales of telegraph romance and telegraph fraud had become staples of journalism and popular fiction.

2. Headrick notes that the origins of broadcast media have received far more attention than those of point-to-point communication, which is the mode of technology that underlies the Internet (9). This was particularly true when I first presented this argument at the English Institute in 1995 (subsequently published in Masten, Stallybrass, and Vickers, *Language Machines* [1997]). In addition to Headrick, works that treated the telegraph included Marshall McLuhan's chapter in *Understanding Media* (217–26); James W. Carey's "Technology and Ideology: The Case of the Telegraph"; and Scott Bukatman's "Gibson's Typewriter." In the last few years research on the telegraph has begun to increase. See Morus, Standage, Gitelman, Thurschwell, Menke, and Otis.

3. In an expansion of the second half of *Discourse Networks 1800/1900* (1985), published the following year as *Gramophone, Film, Typewriter* (1986), Kittler revises this date to "circa 1880" to reflect more accurately the introduction of these technologies.

4. For an account of Sherlock Holmes's engagement with the telegraph, see Brodie.

5. This poem, "The Telegraph," is quoted in its entirety in Prescott (371–72).

6. See Robinson's chapter 12, "The Post Office during Peace and War—1784–1815," for an account of the rapid development of the postal system during this period.

7. For the cultural prominence of Nelson's signal throughout the nineteenth century and in Dickens particularly, see Clayton, "Londublin."

8. For the social consequences of Bentham's reforms, see Peter Linebaugh's excellent discussion in "Ships and Chips: Technological Repression and the Origin of the Wage." Carolyn Cooper describes the worker's privilege of scavenging chips as follows: "The 'chips' that woodworkers at Portsmouth Dockyard were by traditional perquisite allowed to take home with them for fuel had gradually grown in definition to 3 feet long, so that a 3-foot width of windows, doors, staircases, and cupboards became standard in the architecture of Portsmouth working-class houses" (194n37). Thus when Fanny reflects on the "narrowness of the passage and staircase" (*Mansfield Park* 380) on her first night back in her parents' house, she is noticing for the first time the architectural consequences of the older dockyard system.

9. See Foucault's *The Birth of the Clinic* and *Discipline and Punish.* For an extended reading of the panopticon in relation to the English novel, see Bender.

10. I discuss Austen's asymmetric relationship to other period categories employed in most literary histories in *Romantic Vision and the Novel* (59–80).

11. Mary Favret has made a similar point in connection with the distinction in Austen's work between correspondence within a local community and communications that enter into a national grid (12–14, 133–75).

12. For the role of this ethical imperative in bringing closure to Austen's narratives, see D. A. Miller's *Narrative and Its Discontents* (24–25).

13. An interest in communications theory seems to have been forced upon Kittler by his turn toward investigating computer technology. Shannon is not the only pioneer of communications theory missing from *Discourse Networks;* Alan Turing and Norbert Wiener are not to be found either. All three, however, show up in Kittler's writings once he begins to focus on "universal machines" (in Turing's famous phrase), which process and communicate, not merely record and store, data.

14. A sophisticated analysis of the role of women in the telegraph industry, particularly in the United States, is Katherine Stubbs, "Operating Fantasies."

15. See Kittler (347–68) and Wicke ("James" 147).

16. See Wheatstone, "On the Transmission of Musical Sounds" (50, my italics). Wheatstone's original interest in electricity was prompted by the desire to find a way to transmit sounds—both music and the human voice—from one city to another. As part of this effort, he published an article in 1835 describing his creation of an artificial voice or speaking machine ("Review [Of Reed Organ-Pipes, Speaking Machines, Etc.]"). William Macready, who introduced Wheatstone to Dickens in the 1840s, "recorded in his diary that on 29 April 1840 he saw Professor Wheatstone at King's College demonstrating the electric telegraph and a speaking machine which said 'Momma, papa, mother, thumb, summer'" (Bowers 33). Automata such as Wheatstone's speaking machine will be a focus of chapter 4.

17. See Wicke, "James" (148). Stubbs also notes the telegraph operator's position as a "mediating agent" in the communications network and comments on her attempts "to change her status from industrial toiler to brain worker, to move from the working-class subjection of manual labor to the bourgeois respectability of the information specialist" (8, 36).

18. See Savoy (290), quoting Simpson, Chester, and Leitch, *The Cleveland Street Affair* (18).

19. In addition to Wicke ("James"), Savoy, and Stubbs cited above, valuable recent treatments of James's story include Bauer and Lakritz; Naomi Schor (123–24); Walton (91–100); Rowe; and Nixon. In the years since this chapter first appeared, there has been renewed interest in the role of the telegraph in James's story (see Menke; Thurschwell).

20. The essays in this volume begin their story about acoustical technologies in the 1920s, no doubt because the aural record available to scholars only becomes abundant in the early years of the twentieth century. Before this collection, one could point only to a handful of works that raised the question of sound at all: Jacques Attali's *Noise* (1985), Kaja Silverman's *The Acoustic Mirror* (1988), Garrett Stewart's *Reading Voices* (1990), and Douglas Kahn and Gregory Whitehead's *Wireless Imagination* (1992). Kahn and Whitehead sum up the state of acoustical criticism in a single line: "it remains almost unheard of to think about sound" (ix).

CHAPTER 3

1. According to Leslie Marchand, "a whole history of science in the Victorian era might be written from the pages of that journal alone, for it chronicled in detail the meetings of all the scientific societies, Geographical, Astronomical, Botanical, Horticultural, and Ornithological. . . . Moreover, Dilke [the editor after 1830 and close friend of Keats] secured the outstanding scientists in each field to make the reports:

Airy, Herschel, Russell, Lindley, Yarrell, Bucher, Washington, Augustus De Morgan, Sedgwick, Playfair, and Lyell. . . . In addition, all important, and many unimportant, scientific books, from Darwin's *Voyage of the Beagle* and Lyell's works on Geology to *The Origin of Species* and *The Descent of Man* were reviewed carefully and at length in the columns of the *Athenaeum,* usually by a competent, and frequently by an outstanding, scientist. And the pages of the magazine were always open to correspondence on scientific matters and to scientific controversy" (53). Richard Yeo complains that the "'importance of science in general literate culture' has been missed by most historians of the quarterlies" (Yeo 81, references omitted) and provides a breakdown of the number of scientific contributions to the *Edinburgh, Quarterly,* and *Westminster Review* to buttress his claims (82).

2. For an illuminating account of the uneven movement toward professionalism in law and literature in this period, see Schoenfield. A more general history of professionalism in the nineteenth century may be found in Larson. The connection between professionalism and the so-called New Class of knowledge workers has been explored by Daniel Bell.

3. Brian Bowers, mentioning Faraday and Wheatstone as examples, declares: "In the 1830s it is impossible to make any distinction between people whom we would now call pure scientists and those whom we would call applied" ("Faraday" 163).

4. If numerous historians of science identify the decade of the 1860s as the era when the autonomy of modern scientific disciplines was consolidated, just as many locate the beginnings of this process in the 1830s. For arguments about the greater availability of professional scientific careers in the 1860s, see Young (126–63); MacLeod and Werskey; Fichman (105); and Yeo (32, 39). Historians who trace the first signs of this development back to the 1830s include Cannon (146); Morrell and Thackray (423–25); Winter ("Construction," 25); and Yeo again.

5. In her intelligent and thoroughly researched biography of Somerville's early years, Elizabeth Chambers Patterson goes so far as to say: "The readiness and ease with which Mrs. Somerville and her unusual interest in science were accepted by the London scientific community and the up-to-the-minute training she received from men who were at the very time creating the science of the day attests not only to the openness of scientific society to the talented and well-connected but also to the absence of any anti-female bias among scientists" (xi). Patterson is right to mention the importance of being socially "well-connected" as a factor in Somerville's ready reception in this community, and Patterson adds that scientific men at that time were "safe from economic or professional threat from scientific women," which presumably made it easier for them to be "welcoming to serious students be they male or female" (xi).

6. Hyman provides a useful discussion of the Analyticals at Cambridge, clarifying the relationship between their "militant Liberalism" and their lifelong crusade to reform mathematical science (24). He quotes Babbage and Herschel's coauthored book *Memoirs of the Analytical Society,* which argued that an abstract, arbitrary, and immutable form of mathematical notation, such as was available on the continent, would separate scientific results from extraneous ideas and nonscientific implications (25–26). This step toward disassociating science from the rest of society represents an early theoretical justification for modern disciplinary autonomy. Cannon also clarifies the "new romantic-liberal-scientific stance" (40) of these same figures in her chapter on "The Cambridge Network" in *Science in Culture.*

7. According to Babbage's figures, only 109 out of the 714 members of the Royal Society in 1830 had ever contributed a paper to the chief scientific journal of the day,

the Society's own *Philosophical Transactions* (Babbage, *Decline* 155). Somerville was the first woman to publish an original research paper in this journal.

8. Morrell and Thackray, who are excellent on most aspects of the founding of the British Association, accept Buckland's account of why Somerville did not attend and seem rather patronizing to Somerville generally. They mention her only twice in their massive history of the society, and identify her as "the wife of the physician William Somerville (1771–1860)" and author of "numerous popular texts including *Mechanism of the Heavens*" (150n252). The notion that *Mechanism of the Heavens* could be considered a "popular text" is almost absurd, since it was extremely difficult, was regarded at the time as a "profound mathematical work" (Whewell 67), was never marketed by her publisher as anything but a scientific treatise, never sold well, and was never reprinted.

9. Joanna Baillie writes to Somerville as early as 1843 to commiserate with her for being largely forgotten by London scientific circles. Baillie tells of calling on "a lady of rank who has *fashionable* learned folks coming about her, and she informed me that there are new ideas regarding philosophy entertained in the world, and that Sir John Herschel was now considered as a slight, second-rate man. . . . I suppose, you will not be much mortified to hear that your name was not mentioned at all. So much for our learning" (qtd. in *Personal Recollections* 264).

10. Late in the composition of *Crotchet Castle,* Peacock learned that Brougham had accepted a position in the government, something he had promised never to do, and that he had been knighted as a consequence. Peacock was driven to new levels of scorn for the political economist, appending a savage poem called "The Fate of a Broom" to the novel and writing a scene in which one character remarks: "Here is a declaration of the learned friend's that he will never take office," and another responds: "Then, sir, he will be in office next week" (243). Four years later in his satire on the British Association, Cruikshank was still mocking Brougham for this hypocrisy by thanking him for "be-*Knight*-ing the public intellect" (37). The problem with Brougham accepting a government post was one of conflict of interest. Brougham's society, dedicated to reform principles, could hardly be expected to adhere to policies dictated by the conclusions of a purportedly neutral science—political economy—when its leader had become Lord Chancellor in the reigning administration.

11. Most books on literature and science in the Victorian period do not even begin until the 1860s, and thus inevitably, focus on the Darwin controversies. See, for example, Gillian Beer; Tess Cosslett; Peter Allan Dale; Sally Shuttleworth; George Levine (*Darwin and the Novelists*). There are exceptions, of course. Alison Winter's book on mesmerism comes to mind. Still, the academic division of labor between Romanticists and Victorianists has had strange effects on thinking about the intersections between nineteenth-century literature and science. Critics of Romanticism have tended to investigate the topics of magnetism, electricity, and chemistry because of their relevance to the dominant figure in this area, Mary Shelley. Critics of Victorian literature have been more likely to look into botany, geology, marine biology, entomology, and the other fields that contributed to evolutionary theory.

12. Anthony Hyman, *Charles Babbage: Pioneer of the Computer* (193–95), demonstrates that Daniel Doyce was based in part on Babbage.

13. See Chaudhry for a basic account of the two papers. This article usefully identifies several of the journalistic sources Dickens used and some of the individ-

ual scientists who were targets of particular passages. Chaudhry, however, misunderstands the nature of science in the 1830s when he faults the BAAS for being "indiscriminate in its confusion between science, technology, social statistics and sheer crankiness" (111). His view that Dickens's "main satirical target" is the "vain, gluttonous quack who loved to see his name in the press" (111) may be why he thinks "Dickens's satire is superficial" (106). Chaudhry conceives of the BAAS as primarily devoted to popularizing (rather than professionalizing) science and thus misses the satire's larger significance as a response to professionalization generally. The satire of the profession of journalism, with which each Mudfog paper begins, becomes relevant to the rest of the piece if one correctly understands Dickens's interest in the antics of groups struggling (and largely failing) to establish professional norms.

14. In 1836 and 1837 the BAAS was divided into seven sections: (A) mathematical and physical science, (B) chemistry and mineralogy, (C) geology and geography, (D) zoology and botany, (E) medical science, (F) statistics, and (G) mechanical science. Dickens concentrates on the last four specialities.

15. Dickens's critics have long recognized that the novelist underwent a shift from showman to professional author after the 1830s, and particularly with the writing of *Dombey and Son* (1846). One of the best accounts of this shift is by Gabriel Pearson, who writes: "With *Dombey*, Dickens ceased definitively to be Boz, the old popular 'Inimitable,' with Boz's peculiar showman's gusto, his ringside intimacy, his mountebank's creative mendacity" (56) and becomes instead "the professional craftsman" (57). Musselwhite reframes this account of the shift in Dickens's career in terms of what he calls the "commodification of the novelist" (143–53).

16. Studying Davy's renowned lectures at the Royal Institution and his later Bakerian Lectures at the Royal Society, Greg Myers has shown how they contributed to both institutionalizing and formalizing the procedures of the scientific demonstration (47–51).

17. In 1810 there were only 15 scientific societies in all of Britain; in 1820, this number had grown to 26; in 1830, to 40 societies; and in 1840, to no less than 70 scientific organizations (Morrell and Thackray 547).

CHAPTER 4

1. Gibson and Sterling misspell "Jacquet" and "Maudslay," but the novel consistently rings changes on the lives of real nineteenth-century writers, politicians, and scientists.

2. For the origin of automata in mechanical-clock making, see Otto Mayr (21). Accounts of the elder Jacquet-Droz's writing boy and the younger Jacquet-Droz's pianoforte player, as well as Vaucanson's duck and his equally famous flute player, may be found in Anson Rabinbach (51–52, 57). Jean-Claude Beaune's "The Classical Age of Automata: An Impressionistic Survey from the Sixteenth to the Nineteenth Century" contains an illuminating typology of automata (433–34) in what otherwise is indeed an "impressionistic" survey. For a mid-nineteenth-century scientific account of these machines, see Hermann von Helmholtz, "On the Interaction of the Natural Forces."

3. See Forester and Morrison for an account of the "wide range of meanings" (77) that accrue to this term.

4. Hantke defines the genre of steampunk, relates it to postmodern historiographic metafiction, and lists numerous other examples in "Difference Engines and Other Infernal Devices."

5. A sophisticated analysis of Babbage's quarrel with Clement and its implications for modern reconceptualizations of labor appears in Schaffer, "Babbage's Intelligence: Calculating Engines and the Factory System."

6. The story of this contemporary undertaking may be found in Swade. Other modern sources on Babbage's engines are Hyman; Velma R. and Harry D. Huskey; Bromley; and Collier.

7. Sussman's article is an exception. He points out that "an orgasmic pleasure in violence affirms masculine bonds as the only refuge in an anarchic world" and that "*The Difference Engine* dwells at length on the macho derring-do of Mallory and his band of male-bonded heroes, in using the new military technologies to vanquish the 'Luddites'" (10).

8. A number of critics have leveled similar charges against cyberpunk fiction generally and Gibson's early work in particular. See Csicsery-Ronay; Ross; Sponsler; and Stockton. Tyler Stevens extends the critique of sexual attitudes in cyberpunk to include homophobia in his "'Sinister Fruitiness.'"

9. See Hutcheon, *A Poetics of Postmodernism.* In addition to McHale's "Difference Engines," see both Spencer and Tatsumi. Tatsumi also discusses the novel's orientalism.

10. Catherine Gallagher recent essay "Undoing" explores the formal and social implications of the alternative-universe and time-travel plots in today's culture.

11. Harrison's novel features both Babbage and I. K. Brunel, the engineer who completed the first tunnel beneath the Thames in 1843.

12. Thom Braun, a recent editor of the novel, charitably terms Disraeli's political interpretation of history "idiosyncratic" (499).

13. Christensen records the penchant in the political philosophy of the period for distinguishing between these two categories of social rebels ("Romantic Movement" 469–71).

14. For a diametrically opposed reading of Gibson and Sterling's Luddites, see Spencer, who argues that the novelists propose a "Luddite utopianism" (416). The disastrous course of their rebellion and the ugliness of their characterization tell against this interpretation.

15. Sussman has a good analysis of this aspect of the novel (10–11).

16. There is a problem in deciding how to refer to a figure with as many names as Ada Augusta King, née Byron, Countess of Lovelace. Traditional usage would dictate Lady Lovelace, which seems rather stiff. The great majority of biographers and critics have chosen to call her "Ada," a habit that seems as unacceptable as the old practice of calling Austen "Jane." I have chosen to use the name "Lovelace," on the model of the way people commonly denominate a lord by his title: hence, William King, Lord Lovelace, is usually referred to as "Lovelace" and George Gordon, Lord Byron, as "Byron."

17. Metropolis and Worlton have determined that only two of the inventors of the modern computer—Vannevar Bush and Howard Aiken—had any awareness of Charles Babbage's work and that this awareness did not influence their research. The best assessment of this question in regard to Aiken is by the historian of science I. Bernard Cohen, who concludes that while Aiken's admiration for Babbage was great, his actual knowledge of the Analytical Engine was superficial. Cohen writes: "Aiken's first machine (the Mark I/ASCC) suffered a severe limitation which might have been avoided if Aiken had actually known Babbage's work more thoroughly" (172).

18. Barton briefly mentioned Ada Lovelace as a possible source for the character of Thomasina in her review of the play. O'Malley notes this possibility again and summarizes Lovelace's career in "*Arcadia:* Algorithms and Echoes of Ada." In a roundtable discussion at the Mathematical Sciences Research Institute in Berkeley, Stoppard denied that he had Lovelace in mind when he conceived Thomasina, but he has often told interviewers that he read biographies of Byron while preparing to write the play (see Corbett, "Math Program Plays to Packed House"). In view of the many parallels between the two figures detailed below, it seems reasonable to conclude that Stoppard absorbed information about Lovelace's life from Byron biographies, which subsequently came in handy when writing about a mathematically precocious young woman in the nineteenth century.

19. See the stage directions in *Arcadia* (15, 35, 43, and 53).

20. See Toole (32–33) and Doris Moore (52).

21. Brief explanations of the play's use of the second law of thermodynamics and chaos theory may be found in Prapassaree and Jeffrey Kramer; of chaos theory and Fermat's last theorem in Guaspari. The most thorough treatment of chaos theory in the play occurs in Demastes (85–103).

22. See Hyman (164). Babbage's image is quoted in a multitude of popular science books on computing, chaos theory, and mathematics. For example, see Hofstadter, who credits Babbage with understanding the concept of Strange Loops and relates this idea to Babbage's interest in mechanical automata and Lovelace's interest in artificial intelligence (AI) (25).

23. Ronnick examines Zeno's paradox, as well as other Arcadian themes in the play. Hofstadter's *Gödel, Escher, Bach* contains chapters of imaginary dialogue in which Zeno, the Tortoise, and Achilles are frequent participants. For more on the Arcadian elements in Stoppard's play, see Graham.

24. A controversy rages at present about whether Lovelace is an unjustly neglected pioneer of the computer or, in Bruce Collier's words, "the most overrated figure in the history of computing" ("Preface to the Garland Edition," unpaginated). The most thorough of the debunkers is Dorothy Stein. The most passionate of the defenders are Betty Alexandra Toole, Joan Baum, and Sadie Plant. Balanced recent biographies are by Doris Langely Moore and Benjamin Woolley.

25. Melbourne makes the same point in "'Plotting the apple of knowledge': Tom Stoppard's *Arcadia* as Iterated Theatrical Algorithm."

CHAPTER 5

1. Among the many critics that treat the film's relation to postmodernism, the ones that have been most helpful for this discussion are Byers; Bukatman (*Terminal Identity* 130–37); Fisher; and McNamara.

2. Several critics have noted the film's allusions to *Frankenstein,* but the most thorough is Desser, who focuses on allusions involving the religious figures Adam, Satan, and Christ. See also Abbott.

3. My history draws on Huyssen's admirable chapter "Mapping the Postmodern" in *After the Great Divide,* the work to which I refer graduate students and colleagues who ask for clarification of the term.

4. A subsequent collection of this critic's essays was titled *The Cultural Turn* (1998).

5. Meaghan Morris comments on the exclusion of Cixous—and of Donna Haraway, to whom I turn shortly—from most postmodern theory (378).

6. Although this chapter criticizes current understandings of periods, it is frequently necessary to use established terms in order to demonstrate why they are not satisfactory. As I said in chapter 1, my goal is not to eliminate periods, which serve many useful cognitive and disciplinary functions, but to establish their heuristic character.

7. See Mellor, "*Frankenstein:* A Feminist Critique of Science." Alan Rauch makes a similar case for Shelley's sympathy for liberal physician/scientists of the sort represented by John Bell, who strove hard to save her son William Shelley, and William Lawrence, who attended Percy Shelley many years later (Rauch 250–52). In "*Frankenstein* and Radical Science," Marilyn Butler also stresses Mary Shelley's attention to the science of her times. Butler focuses on the novelist's involvement in the debates between vitalism and materialism, the latter of which was advocated by Lawrence.

8. I am thinking of such well-known animadversions on science as Wordsworth's "Our meddling intellect / Mis-shapes the beauteous forms of things:— / We Murder to dissect" ("The Tables Turned," lines 26–28) and his discussion in the "Preface" to the *Lyrical Ballads* of the "contradistinction" of "Poetry and Matter of Fact, or Science" (*Lyrical Ballads* 254); Coleridge's statement that a poem "is opposed to works of science, by proposing for its *immediate* object pleasure, not truth" (2.14); or Keats's attack on Newton for destroying the "poetry of the rainbow by reducing it to a prism" (qtd. in Haydon, 2.54–55). Two influential accounts of Romanticism and science are M. H. Abrams's *Mirror and the Lamp* (298–335) and Hans Eichner.

9. See Marilyn Butler's *Jane Austen and the War of Ideas* for an account of the conservative turn among several popular women writers. Butler argues that Austen was part of a conservative backlash against the French Revolution. Particularly with the publication of *Mansfield Park* in 1814, Austen "shared with other conservative writers, especially women moralists" an emphasis on "her heroines' subordinate role in a family, upon their dutifulness, meditativeness, self-abnegation, and self-control" (xvi). Butler adduces as examples of the anti-Jacobin backlash popular novels such as Hannah More's *Coelebs in Search of a Wife* (1809), Maria Edgeworth's *Patronage* (1814), Mary Brunton's *Self-control* (1812) and *Discipline* (1814), and Frances Burney's *The Wanderer* (1814). Whether or not one agrees with Butler's view of Austen as a Christian moralist, one can see how the conservative anti-Romanticism Butler finds in the novels she mentions differs from the anti-Romantic posture of Mary Shelley.

10. Among the critics who have offered the most powerful readings of this novel in recent decades, "ambivalence" has become a key word for describing Shelley's subject position—ambivalence about authorship (Gilbert and Gubar), "about female self-assertion" (Poovey, *Proper Lady* 116), motherhood (Homans, *Bearing the Word* 100–19; Judith Butler, "My Monster"), gender (Veeder), the imagination (Mellor, *Mary Shelley*), Rousseau (Marshall 190), and realism (Levine, "Ambiguous Heritage"). This term is essential for explaining the contradictions of Shelley's life and art. But it does not help one understand how period categories regulate literary history. Ambivalence locates contradiction in an earlier psychological or psychosocial entity (such as an author, or a structure like Lacan's Symbolic), not in the assumptions of today's historical approach.

11. Barbara Freeman, quoting the same passage from Derrida in the context of an account of *Frankenstein,* makes a related point about "theory" generally (29).

12. John McGowan, in an article I shall return to at the end of this chapter, says much the same thing about cultural studies rather than postmodernism. Cultural

studies "posits features of modernity generally seen as negative—the development of capitalism (whether monopoly or late or global) and of the bureaucratic state—and then considers the relative positioning of various groups ('subcultures') in relation to that modernity, gauging which groups are better equipped to resist it" ("Modernity and Culture" 12).

13. Margaret Homans adds a biographical dimension to these dynamics. Discussing an incident that occurred at Lake Geneva one evening in July 1816, when Percy Shelley had a vision of his wife as a monster with eyes on her breasts, Homans suggests that "Mary's sense of herself viewed as a collection of incongruent body parts—breasts terminating in eyes—might have found expression in the demon" (109).

14. William Galperin has shown that "the romantic antipathy to the visible" (26) provoked its own counternarrative, a "return to the visible" as an unthematized literality. In a discussion that valuably complements my argument here, Galperin describes this "attachment to the particular" (24) as "romanticism's unappreciated rejection of itself" (29). Mary Shelley does not figure in Galperin's study, but her monster might be read as bringing to life the nonhuman principle Galperin calls the "agency of the merely seen or seeable" (1).

15. See Neil Hertz's discussion of the Medusa motif in popular denunciations of the Terror.

16. This reading comes from Freud's essay "Medusa's Head," as well as his interpretation in "The Uncanny" of E. T. A. Hoffmann's *The Sandman,* a Romantic novel featuring a pair of plucked-out eyes. Both of Freud's essays declare images of physical mutilation to be "easily" interpreted. Threats to eyes are symbols of castration, Freud maintains in "The Uncanny," while in "Medusa's Head," he writes: "The terror of Medusa is thus a terror of castration that is linked to the sight of something" (273).

17. The possession of voice is another disputed issue in the myth. Lynn Enterline, in her remarkable chapter "Medusa's Mouth," draws attention to a female voice in the *Metamorphosis* that the reader can easily fail to hear. "In Medusa's story, Ovid imagines an avenging *os* [mouth] comparable to the *clamor* of the Bacchae—a frightening pair of lips that constitute an internal form of protest against, and revenge for, the male rhetoric of vocal animation" (79).

18. Among the many critical discussions of eyes in *Blade Runner,* see especially Silverman ("Back to the Future") and Marder. Neither connects this motif to *Frankenstein.* In Steven Spielberg's recent movie *Minority Report* (2002), based on another story by Philip K. Dick, a character played by Tom Cruise has his eyes surgically replaced to foil retinal-scanning ID devices; he carries his original eyes in a plastic bag.

19. Thomas Byers discusses *Blade Runner* in the context of the Medusa story (80–82, 88).

20. In a provocative article on *Frankenstein* and film, James Heffernan theorizes that cinema brings to the foreground the very thing the novel hides from the reader, the monster's external appearance: "By forcing us to face the monster's physical repulsiveness . . . film versions of *Frankenstein* prompt us to rethink his monstrosity in terms of visualization" (136). *Blade Runner* is one of the films that confirms this point about cinematic adaptations. Heffernan seems right to me when he stresses the novel's refusal to make the body of the monster visible. My reading suggests a reason for this omission: Shelley's antithetical desire to literalize the power of seeing rather than being seen.

21. At least one other critic has heard "the laugh of the Medusa" echoing in Shelley's text. Bette London uses the same figure to refocus attention on the spectacle of

a vulnerable masculinity in *Frankenstein*. Attending to this laughter allows the reader to refuse the "position allocated for woman," which is "to see and not to see" the fragility of the male body (London, "Mary Shelley" 265). London suggests what I am arguing here: the laugh of the Medusa raises the specter of a monster that sees.

22. Judith Butler's *Bodies that Matter* (1993) begins with an epigraph from Haraway's "Manifesto." Cathy Griggers claims that Haraway "should have a special valence for lesbians, who as a group have a history of playing with body assemblages," particularly with phallic prostheses (127). Judith Halberstam quotes Haraway's contention that "'cyborg unities are monstrous and illegitimate,'" then comments: "The cyborg monster celebrates itself as peripheral to family and to the human" (Halberstam 162).

23. George Landow proposed the term *lexia* in his influential study of this medium *Hypertext: The Convergence of Contemporary Critical Theory and Technology*. The term has since become standard in discussions of hypertext.

24. The structuralist distinction between *fabula* and *sujet* is helpful here. In speaking of the narrative core, I am referring to the chronological arrangement of events, which narratologists call the *fabula*, not the actual order, or *sujet*, of the lexias. In this hypertext, the lexias can be rearranged in many ways, and hence the *sujet* has no single order. Later, when I speak of the end of the narrative, I am of necessity referring to the *fabula* not the *suject*, whose "end" occurs only when the reader decides to cease following links through the alternative pathways of the text.

25. Here is a lexia (one of many) that endorses the poststructuralist position by quoting directly from Haraway's "A Cyborg Manifesto": "'Identities seem contradictory, partial, and strategic. . . . We find ourselves to be cyborgs, hybrids, mosaics, chimeras'" (Jackson, "identities"). Although Jackson's hypertext is unpaginated, each lexia is identified in the Storyspace maps by an uncapitalized title, which I cite parenthetically to identify the location of quotations.

26. The character of Tituba also appears in Arthur Miller's *The Crucible* (1953) and in Maryse Condé's historical novel *I, Tituba, Black Witch of Salem* (1986). In Jackson, this character underlines a theme prominent in *Frankenstein* and *Blade Runner*: that the monster is little more than a slave. *Patchwork Girl* presents this theme in more racialized terms than Shelley or Scott, for the creature in Jackson's hypertext is sewn together from the skins of people from different races.

27. Baum uncannily anticipates the nexus of associations that links *Frankenstein* with Cixous—and with the queer themes in Jackson's own hypertext. Baum's *The Patchwork Girl of Oz* (1913), the seventh of his Oz books, presents children with an animated rag-doll, who, Medusa-like, turns two people to stone by spilling a Liquid of Petrifaction on them. Her first sound, on coming to life, is uproarious laugher. When called a horrid sight, the Patchwork Girl laughs again: "'Horrid?' she replied. 'Why, I'm thoroughly delightful. . . . Of all the comic, absurd, rare and amusing creatures the world contains, I must be the supreme freak'" (Baum 57). The Patchwork Girl's defiant streak continues in a later passage, which is one of several that licenses Jackson to assimilate Baum's creation to her own queer discourse: "'Your world pleases me, for it's a queer world, and life in it is queerer still. Here am I, made from an old bedquilt and intended to be a slave. . . . I am enjoying life and seeing the world, while the woman who made me is standing helpless as a block of wood. If that isn't funny enough to laugh at, I don't know what is'" (Baum 68).

28. Marjorie Garber also sees an "anticipation of transsexual surgery" in *Frankenstein*. She cites Dr. Frank-N-Furter in *The Rocky Horror Picture Show* (1975), a

character who is described in the movie as the "sweet transvestite from Transsexual Transylvania," as evidence that the "association of the Frankenstein story with transsexualism is not as far-fetched as it may at first appear" (111).

29. Two excellent studies of the collaborative ethos in nineteenth- and twentieth-century women's texts are Bette London's *Writing Double: Women's Literary Partnerships* and Holly Laird's *Women Coauthors*.

CHAPTER 6

1. As is only appropriate for a book titled *Charles Dickens in Cyberspace,* my research has been assisted by an online discussion group, VICTORIA (listserv@iubvm .ucs.indiana.edu). In response to my query about references to Dickens in popular culture, I received wonderful, quirky, occasionally inspired suggestions. Some items I had already thought of myself, but others were completely new to me. In the next six paragraphs, I incorporate many of the references that turned up in that forum, which is archived at the excellent scholarly site *Victorian Research Web* (Leary). In addition to the postings cited individually in the text, let me acknowledge the suggestions made by Steve Bernstein, Andrea Broomfield, James Bucanek, Dennis Denisoff, Sandy Donaldson, Brad Gadberry, Sheldon Goldfarb, Libby Gruner, Kathy Holliday, Emily Jenkins, Devoney Looser, James McKeown, Deborah McMillion, Theresa Muir, Christina Rieger, Meri-Jane Rochelson, Linda Schulze, Dave Smith, Herbert Tucker, Timothy Watson, and Alan Winston. Alison McKee and Andrea Kalas responded individually to my request for assistance in locating archives of television serials.

2. Other academic Web masters who have devoted considerable energy to promoting Dickens research online include Patrick Leary, Indiana University, creator of *Victorian Research Web;* Mitsuharu Matsuoka, Nagoya University, Nagoya, Japan, creator of *The Dickens Page,* which was discussed in the introduction; Brahma Chauduri, editor of *Victorian Studies on the Web;* Glenn Everett, University of Tennessee at Martin, Web master for *The Northeastern Victorian Studies Association;* Patrick McCarthy, University of California, Santa Barbara, moderator of *The Dickens Forum;* Kirsten L. Parkinson, University of Southern California, editor of *New Books in Nineteenth-Century Studies;* the unidentified creators of *Dickens and the Waste Land of London,* a site maintained at Stanford University; and Jon Michael Varese, Web editor for *The Dickens Project* at the University of California.

3. For a reading of the political dynamics behind the 1993 New Orleans Carnival, see Vennman. Barbara Vennman generously sent me photographs she had taken of the "Charles Dickens" float. Her article also notes that one of the "oldest, private, white men's clubs" in New Orleans is the Pickwick Club (13).

4. Quoted from a promotional letter advertising Great Expectations Services for Singles, signed by Jeffrey Ullman. In a nice touch, the letter spells "Centre" the British way. It contains a "Singles Profile" on the reverse side, which includes questions about one's income, education level, marital status, and current social situation. The fuzziness about motives is encapsulated in the choices listed for "My Primary Social Goal: (1) To date a lot, (2) Having a steady relationship, (3) Marriage." Letter on file with the author.

5. I want to thank Joseph Witek for guidance and insight into the world of Classics Illustrated comic books and to the work of Rick Geary. His excellent *Comic Books as History* provided me with my first orientation to the criticism of this genre. Assistance with locating copies of the U.S. and British versions of the 1947 Classics Illustrated *Great Expectations* was provided by Dan Malan, editor of *Classics Collec-*

tor Magazine; Hollis Lawrence O'Neal of Nashville, Tennessee; and Rich Rostel of Louisville, Kentucky.

6. Kathy Acker doesn't beat around the bush when she titles her experimental fiction simply *Great Expectations* (1982). Among the many ironies of Acker's text (a work containing transexuality, rape, prostitution, and suicide), one of the more lighthearted is a parody of Wemmick's remark about "portable property" (Acker 7). For other contemporary novels that revisit Dickens, see Peter Ackroyd's *English Music* (1992), Oscar Hijuelos's *Mr. Ives' Christmas* (1995), Charles Palliser's *The Quincunx* (1989), and Graham Swift's *Waterland* (1983).

7. The scene foreshadows Julian Barnes's conceit in *England, England* (1998), mentioned in chapter 1, which involved turning the Isle of Wight into a historical theme park.

8. Rushdie shows his familiarity with the theoretical discourse of postmodernism by having another woman reproach Chamcha in the following terms: "I am an intelligent female. I have read *Finnegans Wake* and am conversant with postmodernist critiques of the West, e.g. that we have here a society capable only of pastiche" (*Satanic Verses* 261).

9. My thanks to Timothy Watson, who made this point in his thoughtful posting to VICTORIA on Dickens and *The Satanic Verses.*

10. An instance where "anachronism" sheds light on a novel about slavery is Charles Johnson's *Middle Passage* (1990). Johnson's tale of the 1830s flaunts its anachronistic use of jargon and attitudes from the 1990s to drive home the inescapable links between then and now.

CHAPTER 7

1. Agilent's inaugural TV campaign may be viewed online at <http://www .agilent.com/about/feature/tv_ads.html> (visited 12/16/99).

2. The pun must be hard to resist. Nelkin and Lindee mention a public-television catalog that "offers a 'double helix bracelet' that 'looks great with genes'" (13). Late in 1999, IBM announced a $100 million project to create a new supercomputer named "Blue Gene," whose unprecedented speed would be used to simulate protein folding. IBM, of course, has long been known in business circles as Big Blue.

3. Lately, physicists have begun to debate whether or not quantum theory still represents the universe in time-symmetric terms. For the most prominent contributions to this discussion, see Stephen Hawking, "The Arrow of Time," in *A Brief History of Time;* Roger Penrose, "Cosmology and the Arrow of Time," in *The Emperor's New Mind;* and Hawking and Penrose, "The Debate" in *The Nature of Space and Time.* Jacob takes account of this debate in his latest book, where he writes, "None of the equations of classical physics included a parameter for time. In an immutable universe where past and future were indistinguishable, time was reversible. . . . In the new cosmology, the universe, galaxies, stars, elements, and particles all acquired a history" (*Of Flies* 19).

4. Dawkins writes: "There is a definite set of biomorphs, each permanently sitting in its own unique place in a mathematical space. It is permanently sitting there in the sense that, if only you knew its genetic formula, you could instantly find it; moreover, its neighbours in this special kind of space are the biomorphs that differ from it by only one gene" (*Blind Watchmaker* 65).

5. Lewontin's admonition is not the only recommendation to take humanists seriously that appeared that week. In the issue of *Nature* that published the other

draft sequence of the human genome, the historian of science Horace Judson began his article "Talking about the Genome" with this aphorism: "We think we think with words: too often the words think us" (769). He went on to discuss the "phrases current in genetics that most plainly do violence to understanding" (769).

6. Works on representations of genetics in popular culture are beginning to emerge. See Nelkin and Lindee; Rosner and Johnson; Wald; and Dijck. Wald's article is deeply informed by literary and cultural issues; Dijck's book is the only to deal with works of literature and film at any length.

7. "The Behavior of the Hawkweeds" revisits Mendel's legacy; "The English Pupil" and "Rare Bird" feature Linnaeus; "*Soroche*" recalls Darwin on the voyage of the *Beagle;* and "Birds with No Feet" reintroduces Wallace's discoveries to the contemporary reader.

8. Since evolution depends on sexual reproduction, sex plays a large role in these novels. For a devastating account of the relations between the sexes in *Snow Crash,* see Stockton (594–98). Stockton's critique of Stephenson's portrayal of women is extensive, but she does not even get around to discussing the central role of rape in initiating the novel's desired social transformation. In the process of being sexually assaulted by the villain, a massive rank-smelling "homicidal mutant" (390), the fifteen-year-old heroine is unable to prevent herself from having an orgasm as soon as he enters her (381). Stephenson's *The Diamond Age* features gang rapes of the only major female characters, the twelve-year-old Nell, whose precocious development has been a delightful thread in the narrative, and the adult actress Miranda, whose drugged sacrifice to a ritual rape (497–99) is intended to move the species to the next evolutionary stage.

9. In the next chapter I discuss Stephenson's latest novel *Cryptonomicon* (1999) in more favorable terms. A word should be said about what is appealing in Stephenson's two cyberpunk novels. Both his earlier books display a vision of the social consequences of economic and technological change that is not only astute but imaginative. *Snow Crash* depicts a world in which nation states have lost all real power and the United States is divided into independent franchise states run by corporations, which grant citizenship and control their borders with private police forces. The energy and wit of this vision is in the lineage of a classic science fiction satire on commercialism such as Frederik Pohl and C. M. Kornbluth's *The Space Merchants* (1953). *The Diamond Age* extends this vision by imagining a new world order governed by the Common Economic Protocol, in which any group—including ethnic groups, races, lifestyle enclaves, skill collectives, or philosophical circles—may affiliate into independent self-governing units called "Phyles."

10. For the concept of "geneticization" in contemporary society, see Lippman (19), and Hubbard and Wald (65–8).

11. The geneticization of this text can be illustrated by comparing Kress's novel with Robert Heinlein's *Methuselah's Children* (1941), which *Beggars in Spain* resembles in many respects. Heinlein's long-lived race is achieved not by genetic engineering but by a careful breeding program.

12. For a sophisticated exposition of the "posthuman," see Hayles's *How We Became Posthuman,* which I discussed in chapter 1. Hayles's book also contains useful readings of Stephenson's *Snow Crash* and Greg Bear's first novel, *Blood Music.*

13. See also Levine, who likewise stresses the denial of teleology in both nineteenth-century realism and Darwinism (*Darwin and the Novelists* 18).

14. See Franklin; Nelkin and Lindee (2); and Haraway (*Modest_Witness* 147–88). Haraway relates "genetic essentialism" to another concept, "gene fetishism," which she defines as a "belief in the self-sufficiency of genes as 'master molecules,' or as the material basis of life itself, or as the codes of codes" (*Modest_Witness* 145).

15. For Gilbert's own words on this topic, see his essay "A Vision of the Grail" (96).

16. Other commentators have noticed the link between Ressler and Nirenberg (see Labinger [92] and Dewey [65–66n4]). There appear to be two main sources for many of Powers's details about the heroic age of genetics: Horace Judson's magisterial history of this period and Monod's *Chance and Necessity*.

17. Labinger presents an astute discussion of the time scheme. In addition, he illuminates the extensive musical allusions to Bach and relates them to the structure of the novel. For general discussions of the novel, see Dijck (157–62); Herman and Lernout (especially their ingenious proposal for decoding the novel's epigraph); Hurt; and Dewey.

18. Strecker makes the same point in his brief discussion of *The Gold Bug Variations*.

19. The concept of emergent self-organizing systems is most familiar today from the work of Stuart Kauffman. Kauffman published his first book in 1993, two years after *The Gold Bug Variations*, but ideas of self-organizing systems were found in the work of many chaos theorists during the eighties. See, for example, Gleick (1987).

20. Further evidence of the homoerotic subtext was made available by the DVD release of *Gattaca*. One of the deleted scenes on this disc showed a genetic counselor assuring Vincent's parents that the so-called "gay gene" had been removed from Vincent's genetically engineered brother.

21. I owe this insight to a questioner from the audience at the Narrative Society panel, "Bloodlines: Genetics, Race, and Narrative," organized by Alison Booth at the Modern Language Association Convention, December 28, 1999.

CHAPTER 8

1. Weber's analysis of the rationalization of society under modernity may be found in *The Protestant Ethic and the Spirit of Capitalism*. Among Weber's many heirs, two who base their theories of modernity on the division of society into semi-autonomous spheres are Jürgen Habermas (*Reason and the Rationalization of Society*) and Michael Walzer (*Spheres of Justice: A Defense of Pluralism and Equality*).

2. Compare with Collini, who writes: "In general terms, the most marked changes to the map of the disciplines in the last three decades have taken the apparently contradictory, or at least conflicting, forms of the sprouting of ever more specialised sub-disciplines and the growth of various forms of inter-disciplinary endeavour. But in one sense, these changes both tell in the same direction: in place of the old apparently confident empires, the map shows many more smaller states with networks of alliance and communication between them criss-crossing in complex and sometimes surprising ways" ("Introduction," xliv). Collini emphasizes two concepts that are crucial to this discussion: interdisciplinary alliances and crisscrossing networks of communication.

3. As noted in chapter 5, Haraway was another early prophet of convergence, arguing that in a world where everyone is already integrated in the circuits of technology, scientist and nonscientist alike must take "responsibility for the social rela-

tions of science and technology," which "means refusing an anti-science metaphysics, a demonology of technology, and so embracing the skillful task of reconstructing the boundaries of daily life, in partial connection with others, in communication with all of our parts" (181).

4. I present a more detailed account of these developments in chapter 1 of *The Pleasures of Babel*.

5. Jerome Christensen, writing about the need for universities to rethink their mission in an age when learning to *use* knowledge is of as much importance as acquiring knowledge, draws the same conclusions about the decay of the professional ideal. Today, "undergraduates [are] facing careers in a world where attaining a professional identity counts less than developing the versatility to remake oneself according to projects that one intermittently joins or initiates" (*Romanticism at the End of History* 181).

6. For a complementary account of this phenomenon, see Bill Readings, *The University in Ruins*.

7. Lawrence Lessig, whose work is discussed later in this chapter, makes clear that the Internet, no less than other domains of society, is governed by laws.

8. As of the last day of year 2000, the stock value of Clark's third company had declined precipitously, but it was still outperforming other tech stocks. The *New York Times* reports: "WebMD has actually weathered the dot-com crash better than many other companies" (Krugman).

9. There are important exceptions to this generalization. See, especially, John Sutherland's *Victorian Novelists and Publishers*, Robert D. Altick's *The English Common Reader*, and R. L. Patten, *Charles Dickens and His Publishers*.

10. This trend is too large to explore in a single chapter. The vogue encompasses literature dealing with computer science: Rudy Rucker's *The Hacker and the Ants* (1994) and Richard Powers's *Galatea 2.2* (1995); virtual reality: Powers's *Plowing the Dark* (2000); physics: Lisa Grunwald's *The Theory of Everything* (1991), Louis B. Jones's *Particles and Luck* (1993), Anna McGrail's *Mrs. Einstein* (1998), Michael Frayn's *Copenhagen* (1998), and Rebecca Goldstein's *Properties of Light* (2000); oceanography: Susan M. Gaines's *Carbon Dreams* (2000); chemistry: Carl Djerassi's tetralogy of what he calls "science-in-fiction"; and genetics: Philip Kerr's *A Philosophical Investigation* (1992) and Simon Mawer's *Mendel's Dwarf* (1998).

11. George Bradley's poems appear in the following books: *Terms To Be Met* (37), *Of the Knowledge of Good and Evil* (8), and *The Fire Fetched Down* (43).

12. A. S. Byatt's *Possession: A Romance* (1990) anticipates Stoppard's use of contemporary scholars as foils for a nineteenth-century plot. Although the Victorian characters are chiefly literary figures, like their twentieth-century counterparts, an important strand of the earlier characters' romance involves their interest in marine biology.

13. Sontag comes closest, interpolating the reflections of an anonymous narrator, who lives in 1990s New York. Novels that focus entirely on scientists from the past may be associated with this subgenre because they inevitably suggest an analogy with contemporary scientific developments. Byatt's *Angels and Insects* (1992), Victoria Glendinning's *Electricity* (1995), and Thomas Mallon's *Two Moons* (2000) fit this model, each in a distinctive way.

14. For historians who stress the role of military-inspired interdisciplinary research in aiding Alan Turing, Norbert Wiener, John von Neumann, and others to develop the computer, see Peter Galison, "The Ontology of the Enemy: Norbert Wiener

and the Cybernetic Vision"; Andrew Hodges, *Alan Turing: The Enigma;* and Simon Singh, *The Code Book: The Evolution of Secrecy From Mary Queen of Scots to Quantum Cryptography.*

15. Stephenson's delight in playing with names is positively Dickensian. The character Bobby Shaftoe goes to sea and returns to marry a woman he has left behind, just as in the nursery rhyme "Pretty Bobby Shaftoe." Goto is a pun on the computer programing term "GOTO." Enoch Root puns on another computer term, a system's root directory. But the name of Earl Comstock presents a more complex case. The surname *Comstock* inevitably calls to mind the zealous nineteenth-century crusader for public morality. The character's full name is identical to that of a real-life technology aide to Senator Ted Stevens. In 1998, the year before the publication of *Cryptonomicon,* Earl Comstock was a prominent spokesperson on behalf of the senator's efforts to regulate the Internet, a cause that Stephenson passionately opposes. The joke continues into the contemporary generation depicted in the novel, where one of the chief villains of the 1990s plot is the fictional Earl Comstock's son, Paul Comstock, who is cast as the Attorney General of the United States and who is said to be engaged in a personal crusade to criminalize advanced encryption techniques on the Net, a continuing subject of debate today. Stephenson, needless to say, also opposes any effort to restrict crypto techniques. While composing *Cryptonomicon,* he published a manifesto online advocating strong cryptography and open-source codes (http://www.cryptonomicon.com/beginning.html [visited December 5, 2000]). This essay has since been published as a book titled *In the Beginning . . . Was the Command Line* (New York: Avon Books, 1999).

16. In the interests of full disclosure, I should say a word about one of these minor characters because he is a parody of academics like me. Early in the novel, Randy encounters an obnoxious Yale professor who is a self-professed authority on the misnamed "Information Superhighway." This professor, Dr. G. E. B. Kivistik, defends a stereotypical version of postmodern dogmas about the relativity of values and the indeterminacy of language. Stephenson's parody of academic jargon is not very astute; in comparison with someone like David Lodge, who exposes this kind of academic posturing brilliantly, Stephenson has a tin ear. But Randy does get the better of Kivistik in a debate about the Internet by pointing out that he ought to know something about technical matters before he pontificates about the Net in the media. Nothing much more is heard about Professor Kivistik. Late in the novel, however, a baby is born to a woman in the World War II plot, who has been romantically involved with three of the main characters in that time period. Since this woman does not know which of the men is her child's father, she names him after all three: "Günter Enoch Bobby Kivistik" (851). As in other such intersections between the two plot lines, nothing overt is said about the baby's connection with the Yale professor, now in his fifties, whom Randy had encountered more than 700 pages earlier (81).

17. The concept of a data haven is being put to the test by the newly founded HavenCo, which has joined forces with the cash-strapped royalty of Sealand, a country established on an abandoned World War II British gun tower six miles off England in the North Sea. Sealand became an independent country in 1967 as a result of a lawsuit brought by a self-described "former English major," now "Prince Roy" of Sealand (http://www.sealandgov.com/history.html [visited December 16, 2000]). HavenCo, which shares many of the ambitions of Stephenson's fictional Epiphyte Corp., invokes Stephenson's precedent on its own Web site. If one browses to http://www.eruditorum.org/, which is a name of a secret society in the novel dedi-

cated to privacy and good crypto, one finds the message: "welcome to the societas eruditorum. This is not a datahaven. HavenCo is," with a link to HavenCo's actual home page, http://www.havenco.com/ (visited December 16, 2000). The existence of this corporation confirms, at least in one instance, the oft-repeated rumor that Stephenson's novels serve as the business plans for many computer companies.

18. In an extended philosophical debate with Randy, Enoch reveals that he believes that history has been nothing but an everlasting battle between Athena and Ares (801–8). Ares, the god of war, is evil because of his destructive predilections; Athena is good because, in Enoch's system, she is not only the goddess of wisdom but also of technology. She is the patron saint of hackers, and as such, is associated with other trickster gods: the Sumerian Enki, the Norse Loki, and the Native American Coyote. To readers of Stephenson's other novels, this invocation of mythology is a familiar feature. Enki, as a hacker-trickster, was a major motif in *Snow Crash.* I confess that I found that aspect of *Snow Crash* ridiculous: it smacked of adolescent pseudo-profundity, particularly in its sexist fixation on rape and its association with a similar racism. It is hard to assess Stephenson's investment in his various New Age versions of ancient mythology. In *Snow Crash* these philosophical flights seemed to be an integral part of the overall theme. In *Cryptonomicon,* they are confined to just a few passages and are subjected to critique by skeptical characters such as Randy. Stephenson has promised a prequel to this novel, set in the seventeenth century. There are hints that Enoch's *Societas Eruditorum* goes back to that earlier century and so may figure in the projected novel. If so, my hope is that Stephenson continues the critical perspective on this kind of fuzzy mythology that he has begun here.

19. Stephenson demonstrated his interest in Victorian culture at much greater length in his previous novel, *The Diamond Age* (1995), which imagined an entire society of Neo-Victorians living in the nanotech world of the twenty-first century.

20. For an example of the kind of work required, see John Guillory's penetrating examination of the disciplinary stakes raised by the Sokal affair.

Abbott, Joe. "The 'Monster' Reconsidered: *Blade Runner*'s Replicant As Romantic Hero." *Extrapolation* 34 (1993): 340–50.

Abrams, M. H. *The Mirror and the Lamp: Romantic Theory and the Critical Tradition.* New York: Norton, 1958.

Acker, Kathy. *Great Expectations.* New York: Grove Press, 1982.

Ackroyd, Peter. *Dickens.* New York: HarperCollins, 1990.

Altick, Richard D. "Borrioboola-Gha, Bushmen, and Brickmakers." *The Dickensian* 74 (1978): 157–59.

———. *The Shows of London.* Cambridge: Harvard University Press, 1978.

———. *The English Common Reader: A Social History of the Mass Reading Public, 1800–1900.* 2nd. ed. Columbus: Ohio State University Press, 1998.

Appleby, Joyce, Lynn Hunt, and Margaret Jacob. *Telling the Truth About History.* New York: Norton, 1994.

Arac, Jonathan. *Critical Genealogies: Historical Situations for Postmodern Literary Studies.* New York: Columbia University Press, 1987.

Arendt, Hannah. "What Is Freedom?" *Between Past and Future: Six Exercises in Political Thought.* New York: Viking, 1961.

Ashcroft, Bill. "Against the Tide of Time: Peter Carey's Interpolation into History." *Writing the Nation: Self and Country in the Post-Colonial Imagination.* Ed. John C. Hawley. Amsterdam: Rodopi, 1996. 194–213.

Attali, Jacques. *Noise: The Political Economy of Music.* Minneapolis: University of Minnesota Press, 1985.

Auerbach, Jeffrey A. *The Great Exhibition of 1851: A Nation on Display.* New Haven: Yale University Press, 1999.

Austen, Jane. *Mansfield Park.* Ed. Tony Tanner. 1814. Harmondsworth, Middlesex: Penguin, 1966.

Babbage, Charles. *Reflections on the Decline of Science in England and on Some of Its Causes.* 1830. Shannon, Ireland: Irish University Press, 1971.

———. *Passages From the Life of a Philosopher.* 1864. Ed. Martin Campbell-Kelly. New Brunswick, NJ: Rutgers University Press, 1994.

Baldick, Chris. *In Frankenstein's Shadow: Myth, Monstrosity, and Nineteenth-Century Writing.* Oxford: Clarendon Press, 1987.

Barnes, Julian. *England, England.* 1998. New York: Knopf, 1999.

Barrett, Andrea. *Ship Fever.* New York: Norton, 1996.

Barrie, J. M. "Thomas Hardy: The Historian of Wessex." *Contemporary Review.* Ed. R. G. Cox. Rpt. in *Thomas Hardy: The Critical Heritage.* 1889. New York: Barnes & Noble, 1970.

Barth, John. "The Literature of Exhaustion." *The Atlantic Monthly* 220.2 (1967): 29–34.

Barton, Anne. "Twice Around the Grounds: *Arcadia.*" *The New York Review of Books* 42.10 (1995): 28–31.

Bathrick, David. "Cultural Studies." *Introduction to Scholarship in Modern Languages and Literatures.* Ed. Joseph Gibaldi. New York: Modern Language Association, 1992. 320–40.

Baudrillard, Jean. "The Ecstasy of Communication." *The Anti-Aesthetic: Essays on Postmodern Culture.* Ed. Hal Foster. Port Townsend, WA: Bay Press, 1983. 126–34.

Bauer, Dale M., and Andrew Lakritz. "Language, Class, and Sexuality in Henry James's 'In the Cage'." *New Orleans Review* 14:3 (1987): 61–69.

Baum, Joan. *The Calculating Passion of Ada Byron.* Hamden, CT: Archon Books, 1986.

Baum, L. Frank. *The Patchwork Girl of Oz.* 1913. New York: Dover, 1990.

Bauman, Zygmunt. *Intimations of Postmodernity.* London: Routledge, 1992.

Bear, Greg. *Darwin's Radio.* New York: Ballantine Publishing, 1999.

Beaune, Jean-Claude. "The Classical Age of Automata: An Impressionistic Survey From the Sixteenth to the Nineteenth Century." *Fragments for a History of the Human Body, Part I.* Ed. Michel Feher. Trans. Ian Patterson. New York: Zone Books, 1989. 431–80.

Beer, Gillian. *Darwin's Plots: Evolutionary Narrative in Darwin, George Eliot and Nineteenth-Century Fiction.* London: Routledge & Kegan Paul, 1983.

Bell, Daniel. *The Coming of Post-Industrial Society: A Venture in Social Forecasting.* New York: Basic Books, 1976.

Bell, Millicent. "What Happened in the Cave?" *Partisan Review* 53 (1986): 103–10.

Bender, John. *Imagining the Penitentiary: Fiction and the Architecture of Mind in Eighteenth-Century England.* Chicago: University of Chicago Press, 1987.

Bennett, Tony. "The Exhibitionary Complex." *Culture/Power/History: A Reader in Contemporary Social Theory.* Eds. Nicholas B. Dirks, Geoff Eley, and Sherry B. Ortner. Princeton: Princeton University Press, 1994. 123–54.

Benyus, Janine. *Biomimicry: Innovation Inspired by Nature.* New York: Morrow, 1997.

Berkhofer, Robert F. Jr. *Beyond the Great Story: History As Text and Discourse.* Cambridge: Harvard University Press, 1995.

Berman, Marshall. *All That Is Solid Melts into Air: The Experience of Modernity.* 1982. New York: Penguin Books, 1988.

Bewell, Alan. *Wordsworth and the Enlightenment: Nature, Man, and Society in the Experimental Poetry .* New Haven: Yale University Press, 1989.

Bharucha, Rustom. "The 'Boom' of David Lean's *A Passage to India.*" *Before His Eyes: Essays in Honor of Stanley Kauffmann.* Ed. Bert Cardullo. Lanham, MD: University Press of America, 1986. 155–61.

Black, Joel. *The Aesthetics of Murder: A Study in Romantic Literature and Contemporary Culture.* Baltimore: Johns Hopkins University Press, 1991.

Blade Runner. Dir. Ridley Scott. Warner Brothers, 1982.

Bolter, J. David. *Turing's Man: Western Culture in the Computer Age.* Chapel Hill: University of North Carolina Press, 1984.

Booth, Alison. *Greatness Engendered: George Eliot and Virginia Woolf.* Ithaca: Cornell University Press, 1992.

Borgstein, Johannes. "The Poetry of Genetics: Or Reading a Genetic Sequence—A Literary Model for Cellular Mechanisms." *The Lancet* 351 (1998): 1353–54.

Bowers, Brian. *Sir Charles Wheatstone, FRS: 1802–1875.* London: Her Majesty's Stationery Office, 1975.

Bradbury, Ray. "A Sound of Thunder." *R Is for Rocket.* 1952. New York: Bantam, 1965. 57–68.

———. *Something Wicked this Way Comes.* 1962. New York: Bantam, 1967.

Bradley, George. *Terms To Be Met.* New Haven: Yale University Press, 1986.

———. *Of the Knowledge of Good and Evil.* New York: Knopf, 1991.

———. *The Fire Fetched Down.* New York: Knopf, 1996.

Brantlinger, Patrick. *Crusoe's Footprints: Cultural Studies in Britain and America.* New York: Routledge, 1990.

Braun, Thom. "Appendix: Disraeli's View of History." *Sybil; or, The Two Nations.* Ed. Thom Braun. London: Penguin, 1980. 499–501.

Brenkman, John. "Extreme Criticism." *Critical Inquiry* 26 (1999): 109–27.

The Bridge on the River Kwai. Dir. David Lean. Columbia Pictures, 1957.

"British Association. Sixth Meeting: Bristol." *The Literary Gazette; and Journal of Belles Lettres, Arts, Sciences, &c.* 3 Sept. 1836: 561–69.

Brodie, Robert N. "'Take a Wire, Like a Good Fellow': The Telegraph in the Canon." *The Baker Street Journal* 41 (1991): 148–52.

Bromley, Allan G. "Difference Engines and Analytical Engines." *Computing Before Computers.* Ed. William F. Aspray. Ames: Iowa State University Press, 1990.

Brown, Marshall. "Romanticism and Enlightenment." *The Cambridge Companion to British Romanticism.* Ed. Stuart Curran. Cambridge: Cambridge University Press, 1993. 25–47.

Brown, Ruth. "English Heritage and Australian Culture: The Church and Literature of England in *Oscar and Lucinda.*" *Australian Literary Studies* 17 (1995): 135–40.

Browne, Janet. *Charles Darwin Voyaging.* Princeton: Princeton University Press, 1996.

Buck-Morss, Susan. *The Dialectics of Seeing: Walter Benjamin and the Arcades Project.* Cambridge: MIT Press, 1989.

Bukatman, Scott. "Gibson's Typewriter." In Dery. 71–90.

———. *Terminal Identity: The Virtual Subject in Postmodern Science Fiction.* Durham, NC: Duke University Press, 1993.

Burke, Peter. *Varieties of Cultural History.* Cambridge, UK: Polity Press, 1997.

Butler, Judith. *Bodies That Matter: On the Discursive Limits of "Sex".* New York: Routledge, 1993.

Butler, Marilyn. *Jane Austen and the War of Ideas.* Oxford: Clarendon Press, 1987.

———. "*Frankenstein* and Radical Science." *Frankenstein.* Ed. J. Paul Hunter. New York: Norton, 1996. 302–13.

Butler, Octavia E. *Dawn.* Vol. 1 of *The Xenogenesis Series.* New York: Warner Books, 1987.

————. *Adulthood Rites*. Vol. 2 of *The Xenogenesis Series*. New York: Warner Books, 1988.

————. *Imago*. Vol. 3 of *The Xenogenesis Series*. New York: Warner Books, 1989.

Byatt, A. S. *Possession: A Romance*. New York: Random House, 1990.

————. *Angels and Insects*. New York: Random House, 1992.

Byers, Thomas B. "Kissing Becky: Masculine Fears and Misogynist Moments in Science Fiction Films." *Arizona Quarterly* 45.3 (1989): 77–95.

Callahan, David. "Peter Carey's *Oscar and Lucinda* and the Subversion of Subversion." *Australian Studies* 4 (1990): 20–26.

Cannon, Susan Faye. *Science in Culture: The Early Victorian Period*. New York: Dawson and Science History Publications, 1978.

Carey, James W. "Technology and Ideology: The Case of the Telegraph." *Communication as Culture: Essays on Media and Society*. Boston: Unwin Hyman, 1989. 201–30.

Carey, Peter. *Oscar and Lucinda*. New York: Random House, 1988.

————. *Jack Maggs*. New York: Knopf, 1998.

Carter, Paul. *The Road to Botany Bay: An Essay in Spatial History*. London: Faber and Faber, 1987.

Chadwick, George F. *The Works of Sir Joseph Paxton 1803–1865*. London: Architectural Press, 1961.

Chartier, Roger. *On the Edge of the Cliff: History, Language, and Practices*. Trans. Lydia G. Cochrane. Baltimore: Johns Hopkins University Press, 1997.

Chaudhry, G. A. "The Mudfog Papers." *The Dickensian* 70 (1974): 104–12.

Chauduri, Brahma, ed. *Victorian Studies on the Web*. Web page. URL: http://www.victoriandatabase.com/. May 20, 2002.

Christensen, Jerome. "The Romantic Movement at the End of History." *Critical Inquiry* 29 (1994): 452–76.

————. *Practicing Enlightenment: Hume and the Formation of a Literary Career*. Madison: University of Wisconsin Press, 1987.

————. *Romanticism at the End of History*. Baltimore: Johns Hopkins University Press, 2000.

Christopher, Rochelle A. *Victorian Vanities: One Stop Shopping for Vintage Victorian Clothing*. Web page. URL: http://www.victorianvanities.com/homepage/Page_1x.html. May 20, 2002.

Cixous, Hélène. "The Laugh of the Medusa." *Feminisms*. Eds. Robyn R. Warhol and Diane Price Herndl. Trans. Keith Cohen and Paula Cohen. New Brunswick, NJ: Rutgers University Press, 1991. 334–49.

Clayton, Jay. *Romantic Vision and the Novel*. Cambridge: Cambridge University Press, 1987.

————. *The Pleasures of Babel: Contemporary American Literature and Theory*. New York: Oxford University Press, 1993.

————. "Dickens and the Genealogy of Postmodernism." *Nineteenth-Century Literature* 46 (1991): 181–95.

————. "Londublin: Dickens's London in Joyce's Dublin." *Novel: A Forum on Fiction* 28 (1995): 327–42.

Cohen, I. Bernard. "Babbage and Aiken." *Annals of the History of Computing* 10 (1988): 171–93.

Cohen, Margaret and Carolyn Dever. "Introduction." *The Literary Channel: The Inter-National Invention of the Novel*. Ed. Cohen and Dever. Princeton: Princeton University Press, 2002. 1–34.

Coleridge, Samuel Taylor. *Biographia Literaria or Biographical Sketches of My Literary Life and Opinions.* 1817. Eds. James Engell and W. Jackson Bate. 2 vols. In *The Collected Works of Samuel Taylor Coleridge.* Princeton: Princeton University Press, 1983.

Collier, Bruce. *The Little Engines That Could've: The Calculating Machines of Charles Babbage.* Harvard University Dissertation. 1970. New York: Garland, 1990.

Collini, Stefan. "Introduction." *The Two Cultures.* By C. P. Snow. Cambridge: Cambridge University Press, 1993. vii–lxxi.

Condé, Maryse. *I, Tituba, Black Witch of Salem* [*Moi, Tituba, Sorcière . . . Noire De Salem*]. Trans. Richard Philcox. 1986. Charlottesville: University Press of Virginia, 1992.

Consultation Document. 1998. Web page. URL: http://www.fco.gov.uk/news/keythemepage.asp?32. May 20, 2002.

Cooper, Carolyn C. "The Portsmouth System of Manufacture." *Technology and Culture* 25 (1984): 182–225.

Corbett, Gail. "Math Program Plays to Packed House." *SIAM [Society for Industrial and Applied Mathematics] News* 32.3 (1999): 1+.

Cosslett, Tess. *The "Scientific Movement" and Victorian Literature.* Sussex: Harvester Press, 1982.

Crary, Jonathan. *Techniques of the Observer: On Vision and Modernity in the Nineteenth Century.* Cambridge: MIT Press, 1990.

Crichton, Michael. *Timeline.* New York: Alfred A. Knopf, 1999.

Cruikshank, George. "Proceedings of Learned Societies." *The Comic Almanack* (1835): 36–37.

Csicsery-Ronay, Istvan. "Cyberpunk and Neuromanticism." *Mississippi Review* 47/48 (1988): 266–78.

Culler, Jonathan. "The Literary in Theory." *What's Left of Theory? New Work on the Politics of Literary Theory.* Eds. Judith Butler, John Guillory, and Kendall Thomas. New York: Routledge, 2000. 273–92

Dale, Peter Allan. *In Pursuit of a Scientific Culture: Science, Art, and Society in the Victorian Age.* Madison: University of Wisconsin Press, 1989.

Darby, Margaret Flanders. "On 'Palace of Glass.'" Online posting. April 3, 2000. Charles Dickens Forum. dickns-l@listserv.ucsb.edu. May 20, 2002.

———. "Joseph Paxton's Water Lily." *Bourgeois and Aristocratic Cultural Encounters in Garden Art: 1550–1850.* Ed. Michel Conan. Washington, D.C.: Dumbarton Oaks, 2002. 255–83.

Darwin, Charles. *The Voyage of the Beagle.* Ed. Leonard Engel. 1860 ed. First published, 1839. New York: Anchor Books, 1962.

———. *The Origin of Species.* Ed. Gillian Beer. 1859. Oxford: Oxford World Classics, 1998.

Davidoff, Leonore and Catherine Hall. *Family Fortunes: Men and Women of the English Middle Class 1780–1850.* London: Hutchinson, 1987.

Dawkins, Richard. *The Selfish Gene.* Oxford: Oxford University Press, 1976.

———. *The Blind Watchmaker: Why the Evidence of Evolution Reveals a Universe Without Design.* New York: Norton, 1996.

De Certeau, Michel. *The Writing of History.* Trans. Tom Conley. New York: Columbia University, 1988.

De Morgan, Sophia Frend. *Memoirs of Augustus De Morgan.* London, 1882.

DeBona, Guerric. "Doing Time; Undoing Time: Plot Mutations in David Lean's *Great Expectations.*" *Literature/Film Quarterly* 20 (1992): 77–100.

Debord, Guy. *The Society of the Spectacle.* Trans. Donald Nicholson-Smith. New York: Zone Books, 1994.

DeLillo, Don. *Ratner's Star.* New York: Knopf, 1976.

Demastes, William W. *Theatre of Chaos: Beyond Absurdism, into Orderly Disorder.* Cambridge: Cambridge University Press, 1998.

DeMause, Lloyd. "The Evolution of Childhood." *The History of Childhood.* Ed. Lloyd DeMause. New York: Psychohistory Press, 1974.

Denfeld, Rene. *The New Victorians: A Young Woman's Challenge to the Old Feminist Order.* New York: Warner Books, 1995.

Dennett, Daniel C. *Darwin's Dangerous Idea: Evolution and the Meanings of Life.* New York: Simon and Schuster, 1995.

Derrida, Jacques. "Structure, Sign, and Play in the Discourse of the Human Sciences." *Writing and Difference.* Trans. Alan Bass. Chicago: University of Chicago Press, 1978. 278–93.

Dery, Mark, ed. *Flame Wars: The Discourse of Cyberculture.* Durham, NC: Duke University Press, 1994.

Desai, Anita. "The Rage for the Raj." *The New Republic* 25 Nov. 1985: 46–50.

Desser, David. "The New Eve: The Influence of *Paradise Lost* and *Frankenstein* on *Blade Runner.*" *Retrofitting "Blade Runner": Issues in Ridley Scott's "Blade Runner" and Philip K. Dick's "Do Androids Dream of Electric Sheep?"* Ed. Judith B. Kerman. Bowling Green, OH: Popular Press, 1991. 53–65.

Dewey, John. "Hooking the Nose of the Leviathan: Information, Knowledge, and the Mysteries of Bonding in *The Gold Bug Variations.*" *Review of Contemporary Fiction* 18.3 (1998): 51–66.

Dick, Philip K. *The Man in the High Castle.* 1962. New York: Berkley Medallion, 1974.

———. *Do Androids Dream of Electric Sheep?* 1968. New York: Ballantine Books, 1996.

Dickens, Charles. *The Posthumous Papers of the Pickwick Club.* Ed. Robert L. Patten. 1836–37. Harmondsworth, UK: Penguin Books, 1972.

———. "Full Report of the First Meeting of the Mudfog Association for the Advancement of Everything." *Sketches by Boz and Other Early Papers, 1833–39.* Ed. Michael Slater. The Dent Uniform Edition of Dickens' Journalism. 1837. Columbus: Ohio State University Press, 1994. 513–30.

———. "Full Report of the Second Meeting of the Mudfog Association for the Advancement of Everything." *Sketches by Boz and Other Early Papers, 1833–39.* Ed. Michael Slater. The Dent Uniform Edition of Dickens' Journalism. 1838. Columbus: Ohio State University Press, 1994. 530–51.

———. *The Life and Adventures of Nicholas Nickleby.* Ed. Michael Slater. 1838–39. Harmondsworth, UK: Penguin Books, 1978.

———. *The Life and Adventures of Martin Chuzzlewit.* Ed. P. N. Furbank. 1843–1844. Harmondsworth, UK: Penguin Books, 1968.

———. "The Chimes." *The Christmas Books.* Ed. Michael Slater. 2 vols. 1844. Harmondsworth, UK: Penguin Books, 1971. 1:149–245.

———. *Dombey and Son.* Ed. Peter Fairclough. 1846–1848. Harmondsworth, UK: Penguin Books, 1970.

———. *David Copperfield.* Ed. Trevor Blount. 1849–1850. Harmondsworth, UK: Penguin Books, 1966.

———. "Valentine's Day at the Post-Office." *Charles Dickens' Uncollected Writings From "Household Words" 1850–1859.* Ed. Harry Stone. 2 vols. March 30, 1850. Bloomington: Indiana University , 1968. 1.69–84.

———. *Bleak House.* Ed. Norman Page. 1852–1853. Harmondsworth, UK: Penguin Books, 1971.

———. *Hard Times.* Ed. Paul Schlicke. 1854. Oxford: Oxford University Press, 1989.

———. *A Tale of Two Cities.* Ed. Norman Page. 1859. London: J. M. Dent, 1994.

———. *Little Dorrit.* Ed. John Holloway. 1855–1857. Harmondsworth, UK: Penguin Books, 1967.

———. "The Haunted House." *The Complete Ghost Stories of Charles Dickens.* Ed. Peter Haining. 1859. New York: Franklin Watts, 1983. 261–84.

———. *Great Expectations.* Ed. Angus Calder. 1861. Harmondsworth, UK: Penguin Books, 1965.

———. *Our Mutual Friend.* Ed. Stephen Gill. 1864–1865. Harmondsworth, UK: Penguin Books, 1971.

———. *Collected Papers* 2 vols. London: Nonesuch, 1937.

———. *The Speeches of Charles Dickens.* Ed. K. J. Fielding. Oxford: Clarendon Press, 1960.

The Dickens Fellowship, "Mission Statement." Web page. URL: http://members .cruzio.com/~varese/dickens/mission.html. May 20, 2002.

Dickens and the Waste Land of London. Web page. URL: http://www.stanford.edu/ dept/english/victorian/dickens/. May 20, 2002.

Dijck, José Van. *Imagenation: Popular Images of Genetics.* Houndmills, UK: Macmillan Press, 1998.

Dimock, Wai Chee. "A Theory of Resonance." *PMLA* 112 (1997): 1060–71.

Disraeli, Benjamin. *Sybil; or, The Two Nations* . 1845. Ed. Thom Braun. London: Penguin, 1980.

Dostoevsky, Fyodor. *Notes From Underground.* 1864. Trans. Mirra Ginsburg. New York: Bantam Books, 1974.

Duffy, Enda. *The Subaltern Ulysses.* Minneapolis: University of Minnesota Press, 1994.

Dunn, Katherine. *Geek Love.* New York: Knopf, 1989.

Easthope, Antony. *Literary into Cultural Studies.* New York: Routledge, 1991.

Eichner, Hans. "The Rise of Modern Science and the Genesis of Romanticism." *PMLA* 97 (1982): 8–30.

Eisenstein, Sergei. "Dickens, Griffith, and the Film Today." *Film Form: Essays in Film Theory.* Trans. Jay Leyda. New York: Harcourt, Brace, 1949.

Elam, Diane. *Romancing the Postmodern.* New York: Routledge, 1992.

Eley, Geoffrey. "What Is Cultural History?" *New German Critique* 65 (1995): 19–36.

Engell, James. *The Creative Imagination: Enlightenment to Romanticism.* Cambridge: Harvard University Press, 1981.

Enterline, Lynn. "Medusa's Mouth: Body and Voice in the *Metamorphoses.*" *The Rhetoric of the Body From Ovid to Shakespeare.* Cambridge: Cambridge University Press, 2000. 39–90.

Epstein, James. "Spatial Practices/Democratic Vistas." *Social History* 24 (1999): 294–310.

———. *Radical Expression: Political Language, Ritual, and Symbol in England, 1790–1850.* New York: Oxford University Press, 1994.

Eraserhead. Dir. David Lynch. Columbia TriStar, 1977.

Ermarth, Elizabeth Deeds. *Sequel to History: Postmodernism and the Crisis of Repre-sentational Time.* Princeton: Princeton University Press, 1992.

Everett, Glenn, webmaster. *The Northeastern Victorian Studies Association.* Web Page. URL: http://fmc.utm.edu/nvsa/index.htm. May 20, 2002.

Favret, Mary A. *Romantic Correspondence: Women, Politics and the Fiction of Letters.* Cambridge: Cambridge University Press, 1993.

Ferguson, Marjorie and Peter Golding, eds. *Cultural Studies in Question.* London: SAGE Publications, 1997.

Fichman, Martin. "Biology and Politics: Defining the Boundaries." In Lightman. 94–118.

Fisher, William. "Of Living Machines and Living-Machines: *Blade Runner* and the Terminal Genre." *New Literary History* 20 (1988): 187–98.

Fletcher, M. D. "Post-Colonial Peter Carey." *SPAN* 32 (1991): 12–23.

Forester, Tom, and Perry Morrison. *Computer Ethics: Cautionary Tales and Ethical Dilemmas in Computing.* 2nd. ed. Cambridge: MIT Press, 1994.

Foucault, Michel. *Power/Knowledge: Selected Interviews and Other Writings 1972–1977.* Ed. Colin Gordon. Trans. Colin Gordon, Leo Marshall, John Mepham, and Kate Soper. New York: Pantheon Books, 1980.

———. *The Birth of the Clinic: An Archeology of Medical Perception.* Trans. A.M. Sheridan Smith. New York: Pantheon Books, 1973.

———. *Discipline and Punish: The Birth of the Prison.* Trans. Alan Sheridan. New York: Vintage Books, 1979.

———. "What Is Enlightenment?" *The Foucault Reader.* Ed. Paul Rabinow. Trans. Catherine Porter. New York: Pantheon Books, 1984. 32–50.

Foy, George. *The Shift.* New York: Bantam, 1996.

Franklin, Sara. "Essentialism, Which Essentialism? Some Implications of Reproduc-tive and Genetic Technoscience." *Issues in Biological Essentialism Versus Social Construction in Gay and Lesbian Identities.* Eds. John Dececco and John Elia. London: Harrington Park Press, 1993. 27–39.

Freeman, Barbara. "*Frankenstein* with Kant: A Theory of Monstrosity, or the Mon-strosity of Theory." *Substance* 52 (1987): 21–31.

Freud, Sigmund. "Medusa's Head." *The Standard Edition of the Complete Psychologi-cal Works of Sigmund Freud.* Trans. James Strachey. Vol. 18. 1922. London: Hog-arth P. 273–74.

———. "The 'Uncanny.'" *On Creativity and the Unconscious: Papers on the Psychol-ogy of Art, Literature, Love, Religion.* Trans. Alix Strachey. New York: Liveright, 1961. 122–61.

Friedman, Susan Stanford. *Mappings: Feminism and the Cultural Geographies of En-counter.* Princeton: Princeton University Press, 1998

Frow, John. *Cultural Studies and Cultural Value.* Oxford: Clarendon Press, 1995.

Galison, Peter. "The Ontology of the Enemy: Norbert Wiener and the Cybernetic Vi-sion." *Critical Inquiry* 21 (1994): 228–66.

Gallagher, Catherine. "Undoing." *Time and the Literary.* Newman, Clayton, and Hirsch. 11–29.

Galperin, William H. *The Return of the Visible in British Romanticism.* Baltimore: Johns Hopkins University Press, 1993.

Garber, Marjorie. *Vested Interests: Cross-Dressing and Cultural Anxiety.* New York: HarperPerennial, 1993.

Gattaca. Dir. Andrew Niccol. Columbia Pictures Corporation, 1997.

Geary, Rick. *Charles Dickens's Great Expectations.* Classics Illustrated. New York: Berkley, 1990.

Gibson, William. *Neuromancer.* New York: Ace Science Fiction, 1984.

Gibson, William, and Bruce Sterling. *The Difference Engine.* New York: Bantam Books, 1991.

Giddings, Robert. "Great Misrepresentations: Dickens and Film." *Critical Survey* 3 (1991): 305–12.

Gilbert, Sandra, and Susan Gubar. *The Madwoman in the Attic.* New Haven: Yale University Press, 1979.

Gilbert, Walter. "A Vision of the Grail." *The Code of Codes: Scientific and Social Issues in the Human Genome Project.* Eds. Daniel J. Kevles and Leroy Hood. Cambridge: Harvard University Press, 1992. 83–97.

Gilroy, Paul. *The Black Atlantic: Modernity and Double Consciousness.* Cambridge: Harvard University Press, 1993.

Ginzburg, Carlo. "Microhistory: Two or Three Things That I Know About It." *Critical Inquiry* 20 (1993): 10–35.

Gitelman, Lisa. *Scripts, Grooves, and Writing Machines: Representing Technology in the Edison Era.* Stanford: Stanford University Press, 199.

Gitlin, Todd. "The Anti-Political Populism of Cultural Studies." *Dissent* 44.2 (1997): 77–82.

Gleick, James. *Chaos: Making a New Science.* New York: Viking Penguin, 1987.

Glendinning, Victoria. *Electricity.* New York: Doubleday, 1995.

Gould, Stephen Jay. *Time's Arrow, Time's Cycle: Myth and Metaphor in the Discovery of Geological Time.* Cambridge: Harvard University Press, 1987.

Graham, Peter W. "Et in *Arcadia* Nos." *Nineteenth-Century Contexts* 18 (1995): 311–19.

Great Expectations. Dir. David Lean. Cineguild, 1946.

Great Expectations. Dir. Alfonso Cuarón. 20th Century Fox, 1998.

Griggers, Cathy. "Lesbian Bodies in the Age of (Post)Mechanical Reproduction." *The Lesbian Postmodern.* Ed. Laura Doan. New York: Columbia University Press, 1994. 118–33.

Grossberg, Lawrence. "Toward a Genealogy of the State of Cultural Studies: The Discipline of Communication and the Reception of Cultural Studies in the United States." In Nelson and Gaonkar. 131–47.

Grossberg, Lawrence, Cary Nelson, and Paula Treichler, eds. *Cultural Studies.* New York: Routledge, 1992.

Guaspari, David. "Stoppard's *Arcadia.*" *Antioch Review* 54 (1996): 222–39.

Guillory, John. "The Sokal Affair and the History of Criticism." *Critical Inquiry* 28 (2002): 470–508.

Habermas, Jürgen. *Reason and the Rationalization of Society.* Vol. 1 of *The Theory of Communicative Action.* Trans. Thomas McCarthy. Boston: Beacon Press, 1984.

———. *The Philosophical Discourse of Modernity.* Trans. Frederick Lawrence. Cambridge, Mass.: MIT Press, 1987.

Hadley, Elaine. "The Past Is a Foreign Country: The Neo-Conservative Romance With Victorian Liberalism." *Yale Journal of Criticism* 10 (1997): 7–38.

Halberstam, Judith. *Skin Shows: Gothic Horror and the Technology of Monsters.* Durham, NC: Duke University Press, 1995.

Hall, Catherine. "Discussion." In Grossberg, Nelson, and Treichler. 270–76.

Hantke, Steffen. "Difference Engines and Other Infernal Devices: History According to Steampunk." *Extrapolation* 40 (1999): 244–54.

Haraway, Donna J. "A Cyborg Manifesto: Science, Technology and Socialist-Feminism in the Late Twentieth Century." *Simians, Cyborgs, and Women: The Reinvention of Nature.* New York: Routledge, 1991. 149–81.

———. *Modest_Witness@Second_Millennium.FemaleMan©_Meets_OncoMouse™.* New York: Routledge, 1997.

Hardy, Thomas. *A Laodicean.* Ed. Jane Gatewood. 1881. Oxford: Oxford World Classics, 1991.

Harrison, Harry. *Tunnel Through the Deeps.* New York: Putnam, 1972.

Harvey, David. *The Condition of Postmodernity: An Enquiry into the Origins of Cultural Change.* Oxford: Blackwell, 1990.

Hassall, Anthony J. *Dancing on Hot Macadam: Peter Carey's Fiction.* St. Lucia, Australia: University of Queensland Press, 1994.

Hawking, Stephen. *A Brief History of Time.* Updated and Expanded Tenth Anniversary Ed. New York: Bantam Books, 1998.

Hawking, Stephen and Roger Penrose. *The Nature of Space and Time.* Princeton: Princeton University Press, 1996.

Haydon, Benjamin. *Correspondence and Table-Talk. With a Memoir by His Son, Frederic Wordsworth Haydon.* 2 vols. London: Chatto and Windus, 1876.

Hayles, N. Katherine. *How We Became Posthuman: Virtual Bodies in Cybernetics, Literature, and Informatics.* Chicago: University of Chicago Press, 1999.

Hazlitt, William A. "The Letter-Bell." *Uncollected Essays.* Ed. P. P. Howe. Vol. 17. *The Complete Works of William Hazlitt.* New York: AMS Press, 1967.

Headrick, Daniel R. *The Invisible Weapon: Telecommunications and International Politics 1851–1945.* New York: Oxford University Press, 1991.

Heffernan, James A. W. "Looking at the Monster: *Frankenstein* and Film." *Critical Inquiry* 24 (1997): 133–58.

Hegel, G.W.F. "Preface." *The Philosophy of Right.* Trans. T. M. Knox. 1821. New York: Oxford University Press, 1967.

Heinlein, Robert A. "By His Bootstraps." *The Menace from Earth.* 1941. New York: Signet Books, 1962. 39–88.

———. *Methuselah's Children.* 1941. New York: Signet Books, 1958.

———. "All You Zombies——." *6 x H.* 1959. New York: Pyramid Books, 1963. 126–37.

Helmholtz, Hermann von. "On the Interaction of the Natural Forces." *Science and Culture: Popular and Philosophical Essays.* Ed. David Cahan. Trans. John Tyndall. 1854. Chicago: University of Chicago Press, 1995. 18–45.

Herman, Luc and Geert Lernout. "Genetic Coding and Aesthetic Clues: Richard Powers's *Gold Bugs Variations.*" *Mosaic* 31.4 (1998): 151–64.

Herschel, John F. W. *A Preliminary Discourse on the Study of Natural Philosophy. A Facsimile of the 1830 Edition.* New York: Johnson Reprint Corp., 1966.

Hertz, Neil. "Medusa's Head: Male Hysteria Under Political Pressure." *Representations* 4 (1983): 27–54.

Hijuelos, Oscar. *Mr. Ives' Christmas.* New York: HarperCollins, 1995.

Himmelfarb, Gertrude. "Postmodernist History." *On Looking into the Abyss: Untimely Thoughts on Culture and Society.* New York: Knopf, 1994. 131–61.

———. *The De-Moralization of Society: From Victorian Virtues to Modern Values.* New York: Knopf, 1995.

History Zone. 1999. Web page. URL: http://GreenwichPast.com/history/. April 21, 2003.

Hodgart, Matthew J. C. "Aeolus." *James Joyce's "Ulysses": Critical Essays.* Eds. Clive Hart and David Hayman. Berkeley: University of California Press, 1974. 115–30.

Hodges, Andrew. *Alan Turing: The Enigma.* New York : Simon and Schuster, 1983.

Hoffmann, E. T. A. *The Sandman.* [n.p., 1817].

Hofstadter, Douglas R. *Gödel, Escher, Bach: An Eternal Golden Braid.* New York: Basic Books, 1979.

Hoge, Warren. "After a Year, Millennium Dome Calls It a Day." *The New York Times* 31 Dec. 2000: A4.

Holden, Constance. "Didactics of *Gattaca.*" *Science* 278 (1997): 1019.

Hollingshead, John. "House-Top Telegraphs." *All the Year Round* (1859): 106–9.

Holzmann, Gerard J., and Björn Pehrson. *The Early History of Data Networks.* Los Alamitos, CA: IEEE Computer Society Press, 1995.

Homans, Margaret. *Bearing the Word: Language and Female Experience in Nineteenth-Century Women's Writing.* Chicago: University of Chicago Press, 1986.

Hubbard, Ruth and Elijah Wald. *Exploding the Gene Myth.* Boston: Beacon Press, 1993.

Huggan, Graham. *Peter Carey.* Melbourne: Oxford University Press, 1996.

Hunt, Lynn, ed. *The New Cultural History.* Berkeley: University of California Press, 1989.

Hurt, James. "Narrative Powers: Richard Powers as Storyteller." *Review of Contemporary Fiction* 18.3 (1998): 24–41.

Huskey, Velma R., and Harry D. Huskey. "Lady Lovelace and Charles Babbage." *Annals of the History of Computing* 2 (1980): 229–329.

Hutcheon, Linda. *A Poetics of Postmodernism: History, Theory, Fiction.* New York: Routledge, 1988.

Huyssen, Andreas. *After the Great Divide: Modernism, Mass Culture, Postmodernism.* Bloomington: Indiana University Press, 1986.

Hyman, Anthony. *Charles Babbage: Pioneer of the Computer.* Princeton: Princeton University Press, 1983.

"I Am Sitting in a Room: Sound Works by American Artists 1950–2000." Whitney Museum of American Art. Curated by Stephen Vitiello. New York: January 11–16, 2000. URL: *http://www.hi-beam.net/org/whitney/janoo.html.* October 11, 2002.

Iggers, Georg G. *Historiography in the Twentieth Century: From Scientific Objectivity to the Postmodern Challenge.* Hanover, NH: Wesleyan University Press, 1997.

Jackson, Shelley. *Patchwork Girl; or, A Modern Monster by Mary/Shelley, and Herself.* CD-ROM. Watertown, MA: Eastgate Systems Inc., 1995.

Jacob, François. "Time and the Invention of the Future." *The Logic of Life: A History of Heredity and The Possible and the Actual.* Trans. Betty E. Spillmann. Harmondsworth, UK: Penguin Books, 1989. 403–25.

———. *Of Flies, Mice, and Men.* Trans. Giselle Weiss. Cambridge: Harvard University Press, 1998.

James, Henry. "In The Cage." *In The Cage And Other Tales.* Ed. Morton Dauwen Zabel. 1898. New York: Norton, 1969.

Jameson, Fredric. *The Political Unconscious: Narrative As a Socially Symbolic Act.* Ithaca, NY: Cornell University Press, 1981.

———. *Postmodernism, or, The Cultural Logic of Late Capitalism.* Durham, NC: Duke University Press, 1991.

————. *The Cultural Turn: Selected Writings on the Postmodern, 1983–1998.* London: Verso, 1998.

Jay, Martin. *Downcast Eyes: The Denigration of Vision in Twentieth-Century French Thought.* Berkeley: University of California Press, 1993.

Jenkins, Keith, ed. *The Postmodern History Reader.* London: Routledge, 1997.

————. *Why History? Ethics and Postmodernity.* London: Routledge, 1999.

Johnson, Barbara. "My Monster/My Self." *Diacritics* 12.2 (1982): 2–10.

Johnson, Charles. *Middle Passage.* New York: Atheneum, 1990.

Joyce, Patrick. *Democratic Subjects: The Self and the Social in Nineteenth-Century England.* Cambridge: Cambridge University Press, 1994.

Judson, Horace Freeland. *The Eighth Day of Creation: The Makers of the Revolution in Biology.* Expanded ed. 1979. New York: Cold Spring Harbor Laboratory Press, 1996.

————. "Talking About the Genome." *Nature* 409 (2001): 769.

Kahn, Douglas, and Gregory Whitehead. *Wireless Imagination: Sound, Radio, and the Avant-Garde.* Cambridge: MIT Press, 1992.

Kant, Immanuel. *Philosophical Writings.* New York: Continuum, 1986.

Katz, Jon. *Geeks: How Two Lost Boys Rode the Internet out of Idaho.* New York: Villard, 2000.

Kauffman, Stuart A.. *At Home in the Universe: The Search for Laws of Self-Organization and Complexity.* New York: Oxford University Press, 1995.

Keller, Evelyn Fox. *Refiguring Life: Metaphors of Twentieth-Century Biology.* New York: Columbia University Press, 1995.

Kelly, Joan. "Did Women Have a Renaissance?" *Women, History, and Theory: The Essays of Joan Kelly.* Chicago: University of Chicago Press, 1984.

Kermode, Frank. *The Sense of an Ending: Studies in the Theory of Fiction.* New York: Oxford University Press, 1967.

Kern, Stephen. *The Culture of Time and Space, 1880–1918.* Cambridge: Harvard University Press, 1983.

King, Francis. "Edmund Gosse Goes to Australia." *The Spectator* 2 Apr. 1988: 32–33.

Kittler, Friedrich A. *Discourse Networks 1800/1900.* Trans. Michael Metteer. 1985. Stanford, CA: Stanford University Press, 1990.

————. *Gramophone, Film, Typewriter.* Trans. Geoffrey Winthrop-Young and Michael Wutz. 1986. Stanford, CA: Stanford University Press, 1999.

————. "Afterword to the Second Printing." 1987. In Kittler, *Discourse Networks.* 369–72.

Klein, Julie Thompson. *Crossing Boundaries: Knowledge, Disciplinarities, and Inter-disciplinarities.* Charlottesville: University Press of Virginia, 1996.

Kravitz, Lee. "Finding the Ideal Matchmaker." *Cosmopolitan* Oct. 1988: 274–77.

Kress, Nancy. *Beggars in Spain.* New York: Avon Books, 1993.

Krugman, Paul. "Real Reality's Revenge." *The New York Times* 31 Dec. 2000: 4:9.

Kucich, John. *Repression in Victorian Fiction: Charlotte Bronte, George Eliot, and Charles Dickens.* Berkeley: University of California Press, 1987.

Labinger, Jay A. "Encoding an Infinite Message: Richard Powers's *The Gold Bug Variations.*" *Configurations* 3 (1995): 79–93.

LaCapra, Dominick. "History, Language, and Reading: Waiting for Crillon." *American Historical Review* 100 (1995): 799–828.

Laird, Holly A. *Women Coauthors.* Urbana: University of Illinois Press, 2000.

Landon, Philip. "Great Exhibitions: Representations of the Crystal Palace in May-
hew, Dickens and Dostoevsky." *Nineteenth-Century Contexts* 20 (1997): 27–59.
Landow, George P. *The Victorian Web.* 1995. Web page. URL: http://landow.stg
.brown.edu/victorian/victov.html. May 20, 2002.
———. *The Dickens Page.* Web page. URL: http://landow.stg.brown.edu/victorian/
dickens/dickensov.html. June 28, 2001.
———. *The Dickens Web.* CD-ROM. Watertown, MA: Eastgate Systems, n.d.
Larson, Magali Sarfatti. *The Rise of Professionalism: A Sociological Analysis.* Berkeley:
University of California Press, 1977.
Laumer, Keith. *The Other Side of Time.* 1965. New York: New American Library, 1972.
Lawrence of Arabia. Dir. David Lean. Horizon Pictures, 1962.
Lawson, Mark. "You Can Bank on the X-Factor." *The Guardian* March 4, 2000. URL:
http://www.guardian.co.uk/Archive/Article/0,4273,3970286,00.html. May 20,
2002.
Leary, Patrick. *Victorian Research Web.* 1996. Web page. URL: http://www.indiana
.edu/~victoria/vwcont.html. May 20, 2002.
Leiber, Fritz. *The Big Time.* 1958. New York: Ace Books, 1972.
Leinster, Murray. *Sidewise in Time and Other Scientific Adventures.* 1934. Chicago-
Shasta Publishers, 1950.
Lentricchia, Frank. *After the New Criticism.* Chicago: University of Chicago Press,
1980.
Lessig, Lawrence. *Code and Other Laws of Cyberspace.* New York: Basic Books, 1999.
Levine, George. "The Ambiguous Heritage of Frankenstein." *The Endurance of
"Frankenstein".* Eds. George Levine and U. C. Knoepflmacher. Berkeley: Univer-
sity of California Press, 1979. 3–30.
———. *Darwin and the Novelists: Patterns of Science in Victorian Fiction.* Chicago:
University of Chicago Press, 1988.
Lewis, Michael. *Liar's Poker: Rising Through the Wreckage on Wall Street.* New York:
Norton, 1989.
———. *The New New Thing: A Silicon Valley Story.* New York: Norton, 2000.
Lewontin, R. C. "In the Beginning Was the Word [Rev. of Lily E. Kay, *Who Wrote the
Book of Life? A History of the Genetic Code*]." *Science* 291 (2001): 1263–64.
Leys, Ruth. *Trauma: A Genealogy.* Chicago: University of Chicago Press, 2000.
Lightman, Bernard, ed. *Victorian Science in Context.* Chicago: University of Chicago
Press, 1997.
Linebaugh, Peter. "Ships and Chips: Technological Repression and the Origin of the
Wage." *The London Hanged: Crime and Civil Society in the Eighteenth Century.*
Cambridge: Cambridge University Press, 1992. 371–401.
Lipner, Mia. "Requiem Digitatem." Audio tape supplement for "Sexuality and Cy-
berspace." *Women and Performance: A Journal of Feminist Theory* 9.1 (n.d.).
Lippman, Abby. "Prenatal Genetic Testing and Screening: Constructing Needs and
Reinforcing Inequities." *American Journal of Law and Medicine* 17 (1991): 15–50.
A Literary Tour of Charles Dickens's Greenwich. 1999. Web page. URL: http://
greenwichpast.com/vip/writers/dickens-greenwich-tour.htm. April 21, 2003.
Liu, Alan. "Local Transcendence: Cultural Criticism, Postmodernism, and the Ro-
manticism of Detail." *Representations* 32 (1990): 75–113.
———. "The Future Literary: Literature and the Culture of Information." *Time and
the Literary.* Newman, Clayton, and Hirsch. 61–100.

Lohrli, Anne. *Household Words; a Weekly Journal 1850–1859, Conducted by Charles Dickens. Table of Contents, List of Contributors and Their Contributions Based on the Household Words Office Book in the Morris L. Parrish Collection of Victorian Novelists, Princeton University Library.* Toronto: University of Toronto Press, 1973.

London, Bette. "Mary Shelley, *Frankenstein,* and the Spectacle of Masculinity." *PMLA* 108 (1993): 253–67.

———. *Writing Double: Women's Literary Partnerships.* Ithaca, NY: Cornell University Press, 1999.

"Lost and Found Sound." National Public Radio. September 1999–2002. URL: *http://www.npr.org/programs/lnfsound/.* October 11, 2002.

Lovelace, Ada. "Notes by the Translator of L. F. Menabrea's 'Sketch of the Analytical Engine Invented by Charles Babbage.'" *Science and Reform: Selected Works of Charles Babbage.* Ed. Anthony Hyman. 1843. Cambridge: Cambridge University Press, 1989. 267–311.

Lyotard, Jean-François. *The Postmodern Condition: A Report on Knowledge.* Trans. Geoff Bennington and Brian Massumi. Minneapolis: University of Minnesota Press, 1984.

MacCabe, Colin. "Tradition Too Has Its Place in Cultural Studies." *Times Literary Supplement* 26 May 1995: 13.

MacKay, Carol Hanbery. "A Novel's Journey into Film: The Case of *Great Expectations.*" *Literature/Film Quarterly* 13 (1985): 127–34.

MacLeod, R. M., and G. Werskey. *Nature* 224 (1969): 423–61.

Mallon, Thomas. *Two Moons.* New York: Pantheon, 2000.

The Man Who Fell to Earth. Dir. Nicolas Roeg. British Lion Film Corporation, 1976.

Marchand, Leslie A. *The Athenaeum: A Mirror of Victorian Culture.* Chapel Hill: University of North Carolina Press, 1941.

Marder, Elissa. "*Blade Runner*'s Moving Still." *Camera Obscura: A Journal of Feminism, Culture, and Media Studies* 27 (1991): 77–87.

Markham, Violet R. *Paxton and the Bachelor Duke.* London: Hodder & Stoughton, 1935.

Marshall, David. *The Surprising Effects of Sympathy: Marivaux, Diderot, Rousseau, and Mary Shelley.* Chicago: University of Chicago Press, 1988.

Marvin, Carolyn. *When Old Technologies Were New: Thinking About Electric Communication in the Late Nineteenth Century.* New York: Oxford University Press, 1988.

Matsuoka, Mitsuharu. *The Dickens Page.* 1995. Web page. URL: http://lang.nagoya-u.ac.jp/~matsuoka/Dickens.html. May 20, 2002.

Mayr, Otto. *Authority, Liberty, and Automatic Machinery in Early Modern Europe.* Baltimore: Johns Hopkins University Press, 1986.

McCarthy, Patrick, moderator. "The Dickens Forum." Online discussion group. listserv@listserv.ucsb.edu. May 20, 2002.

McLuhan, Marshall. *Understanding Media: The Extensions of Man.* New York: New American Library, 1964.

McDonald, Roger. *Mr. Darwin's Shooter.* New York: Atlantic Monthly Press, 1998.

———. "A Conversation With Roger McDonald." *Mr. Darwin's Shooter.* Harmondsworth, UK: Penguin Books, 1999. 6–10.

McGann, Jerome J. "The Beauty of the Medusa: A Study in Romantic Literary Iconolgy." *Studies in Romanticism* 11 (1972): 3–25.

McGowan, John. *Postmodernism and Its Critics*. Ithaca: Cornell University Press, 1991.

———. "Modernity and Culture, the Victorians and Cultural Studies." In Sadoff and Kucich. 3–28.

McGuigan, Jim, ed. *Cultural Methodologies*. London: SAGE, 1997.

McHale, Brian. "Difference Engines." *ANQ* 5 (1992): 220–23.

McKean, John. *Crystal Palace: Joseph Paxton and Charles Fox*. London: Phaidon Press, 1994.

McLuhan, Marshall. *Understanding Media: The Extensions of Man*. New York: New American Library, 1964.

McMahon, Thomas. *Principles of American Nuclear Chemistry*. Boston: Little, Brown, 1970.

McNamara, Kevin R. "*Blade Runner*'s Post-Individual Worldspace." *Contemporary Literature* 38 (1997): 422–46.

Melbourne, Lucy. "'Plotting the Apple of Knowledge': Tom Stoppard's *Arcadia* as Iterated Theatrical Algorithm." *Modern Drama* 41 (1998): 557–72.

Mellor, Anne K. "*Frankenstein*: A Feminist Critique of Science." *One Culture: Essays in Science and Literature*. Ed. George Levine. Madison: University of Wisconsin Press, 1987. 287–312.

———. *Mary Shelley: Her Life, Her Fiction, Her Monsters*. New York: Routledge, 1989.

———. "Possessing Nature: The Female in *Frankenstein*." *Romanticism and Feminism*. Ed. Anne K. Mellor. Bloomington: Indiana University Press, 1988. 220–32.

Menke, Richard. "Telegraphic Realism: Henry James's *In the Cage*." *PMLA* 115 (2000): 975–90.

Metropolis, N., and J. Worlton. "A Trilogy on Errors in the History of Computing." *Annals of the History of Computing* 2 (1980): 49–59.

Mill, John Stuart. *The Spirit of the Age*. Ed. Frederick A. von Hayek. 1831. Chicago: University of Chicago Press, 1942.

Millennium Dome Building. 1999. Web page. URL: http://greenwich2000.com/millennium/experience/exhibition-gendes.htm. May 20, 2002.

Millennium Time-lines. 1999. Web page. URL: http://GreenwichPast.com/history/time-line/index.htm. April 21, 2003.

Miller, Andrew H. *Novels Behind Glass: Commodity Culture and Victorian Narrative*. Cambridge: Cambridge University Press, 1995.

Miller, Arthur. *The Crucible*. New York: Viking Press, 1952.

Miller, D. A. *Narrative and Its Discontents: Problems of Closure in the Traditional Novel*. Princeton: Princeton University Press, 1981.

Minority Report. Dir. Steven Spielberg. Twentieth-Century Fox, 2002.

Mitchell, W.J.T. "Ekphrasis and the Other." *South Atlantic Quarterly* 91 (1992): 695–719.

Monod, Jacques. *Chance and Necessity: An Essay on the Natural Philosophy of Modern Biology*. Trans. Austryn Wainhouse. New York: Knopf, 1971.

Mooney, Ted. *Easy Travel to Other Planets*. New York: Farrar, Straus, Giroux, 1981.

Moore, Doris Langley-Levy. *Ada, Countess of Lovelace: Byron's Legitimate Daughter*. London: John Murray, 1977.

Moore, Ward. *Bring the Jubilee*. New York: Farrar, Straus & Young, 1953.

Morrell, Jack, and Arnold Thackray. *Gentlemen of Science: Early Years of the British Association for the Advancement of Science* . Oxford: Clarendon Press, 1981.

Morris, Adalaide, ed. *Sound States: Innovative Poetics and Acoustical Technologies*. Chapel Hill: University of North Carolina Press, 1997.

Morris, Meaghan. "Feminism, Reading, Postmodernism." *Postmodernism: A Reader.*
    Ed. Thomas Docherty. New York: Columbia University Press, 1993. 368–89.

Morrison, Toni. *Beloved.* New York: Knopf, 1987.

Morus, Iwan Rhys. "The Electric Ariel: Telegraphy and Commercial Culture in Early
    Victorian England." *Victorian Studies* 39 (1996): 339–78.

Moynahan, Julian. "Seeing the Book, Reading the Movie." *The English Novel and the
    Movies.* Eds. Michael Klein and Gillian Parker. New York: Ungar, 1981. 143–54.

Mrs. Brown. Dir. John Madden. BBC, 1997.

Munich, Adrienne. *Queen Victoria's Secrets.* New York: Columbia University Press,
    1996.

Muschamp, Herbert. "Designs for the Next Millennium: Jaron Lanier." *The New York
    Times Magazine* 5 Dec. 1999: 125.

Musgrave, Michael. *The Musical Life of the Crystal Palace.* Cambridge: Cambridge
    University Press, 1995.

Musselwhite, David E. "Dickens: The Commodification of the Novelist." *Partings
    Welded Together: Politics and Desire in the Nineteenth-Century English Novel.*
    London: Methuen, 1987. 143–226.

Myers, Greg. "Fictionality, Demonstration, and a Forum for Popular Science: Jane
    Marcet's *Conversations on Chemistry.*" *Natural Eloquence: Women Reinscribe
    Science.* Eds. Barbara T. Gates and Ann B. Shteir. Madison: University of Wis-
    consin Press, 1997. 43–60.

Negroponte, Nicholas. *Being Digital.* New York: Knopf, 1995.

Neilson, Jim. "An Interview With Richard Powers." *Review of Contemporary Fiction*
    18.3 (1998): 13–23.

Nelkin, Dorothy, and M. Susan Lindee. *The DNA Mystique: The Gene As a Cultural
    Icon.* New York: W. H. Freeman, 1995.

Nelson, Cary, and Dilip Parameshwar Gaonkar, eds. *Disciplinarity and Dissent in
    Cultural Studies.* New York: Routledge, 1996.

The Net. Dir. Irwin Winkler. Columbia Pictures Corporation, 1995.

Neumann, John Von. *Theory of Self-Reproducing Automata.* Ed. Arthur W. Burks. Ur-
    bana: University of Illinois Press, 1966.

Newman, Karen, Jay Clayton, and Marianne Hirsch, eds. *Time and the Literary.* New
    York: Routledge, 2002.

Niven, Larry. "All the Myriad Ways." *All the Myriad Ways.* 1968. New York: Ballantine
    Books, 1971. 1–11.

Nixon, Nicola. *ELH* 66 (1999): 179–201.

Nussbaum, Martha C. *Poetic Justice: The Literary Imagination and Public Life.*
    Boston: Beacon Press, 1995.

O'Malley, Jr. Robert E. "*Arcadia:* Algorithms and Echoes of Ada." *SIAM (Society for
    Industrial and Applied Mathematics) News* 28.3 (1995): 7–8.

Ommundsen, Wenche. "Narrative Navel-Gazing, Or How to Recognise a Metafic-
    tion When You See One." *Southern Review (Australia)* 22 (1989): 264–74.

Orwell, George. "Charles Dickens [1940]." *Inside the Whale.* Vol. 1. *The Collected Es-
    says, Journalism and Letters of George Orwell.* 3 vols. New York: Harcourt, 1968.

Otis, Laura. *Networking: Communicating with Bodies and Machines in the Nineteenth
    Century.* Ann Arbor: The University of Michigan Press, 2001.

Parkinson, J. C. *The Ocean Telegraph to India: A Narrative and a Diary.* Edinburgh:
    William Blackwood, 1870.

Parkinson, Kirsten L. *New Books in Nineteenth-Century Studies.* Web page. URL: http://www.usc.edu/dept/LAS/english/19c/newbooks.html. June 28, 2001.

Paris Is Burning. Dir. Jennie Livingston. Off-White Productions, 1990.

A Passage to India. Dir. David Lean. EMI Films, 1984.

Patten, R. L. *Charles Dickens and His Publishers.* London: Oxford University Press, 1978.

Patterson, Elizabeth Chambers. *Mary Somerville and the Cultivation of Science, 1815–1840.* The Hague: Martinus Nijhoff, 1983.

Peacock, Thomas Love. *Headlong Hall / Nightmare Abbey.* 1816, 1818. London: Dent, 1965.

———. *Nightmare Abbey/Crotchet Castle.* Ed. Raymond Wright. 1818, 1831. Harmondsworth, UK: Penguin Books, 1969.

Pearson, Gabriel. "Towards a Reading of *Dombey and Son.*" *Dickens and the Twentieth Century.* Eds. John Gross and Gabriel Pearson. London: Routledge & Kegan Paul, 1962.

Penrose, Roger. *The Emperor's New Mind: Concerning Computers, Minds, and the Laws of Physics.* Oxford: Oxford University Press, 1989.

Petersen, Kirsten Holst. "Gambling on Reality: A Reading of Peter Carey's *Oscar and Lucinda.*" *Australian Literary Studies* 15.2 (1991): 107–16.

Piers, Maria W. *Infanticide.* New York: Norton, 1978.

The Pillow Book. Dir. Peter Greenaway. CFPress, 1995.

Plant, Sadie. *Zeros + Ones: Digital Women and the New Technoculture.* London: Fourth Estate, 1997.

Poe, Edgar Allan. "The Gold-Bug." 1843. *Poetry and Tales.* Ed. Patrick F. Quinn. New York: The Library of America, 1984. 560–96.

Pohl, Frederik, and C. M. Kornbluth. *The Space Merchants.* New York: Ballantine Books, 1953.

Pollock, Linda A. *Forgotten Children: Parent-Child Relations From 1500 to 1900.* Cambridge: Cambridge University Press, 1983.

Pool, Ithiel de Sola. *Technologies of Freedom.* Cambridge: Harvard University Press, 1983.

Poovey, Mary. *The Proper Lady and the Woman Writer.* Chicago: University of Chicago Press, 1984.

Post, Stephen G. "History, Infanticide, and Imperiled Newborns." *Hastings Center Report* 18.4 (1988): 14–17.

Powers, Richard. *The Gold Bug Variations.* New York: Morrow, 1991.

Prapassaree and Jeffrey Kramer. "Stoppard's *Arcadia:* Research, Time Loss." *Modern Drama* 40 (1997): 1–10.

Prescott, George B. *History, Theory, and Practice of the Electric Telegraph.* Boston: Ticknor and Fields, 1860.

"The Private History of the Palace of Glass." *Household Words* 11.43 (1851): 385–91.

Prospero's Books. Dir. Peter Greenaway. Miramax Films, 1991.

Pynchon, Thomas. *Mason & Dixon.* New York: Henry Holt, 1997.

Rabinbach, Anson. *The Human Motor: Energy, Fatigue, and the Origins of Modernity.* New York: Basic Books, 1990.

Rauch, Alan. "The Monstrous Body of Knowledge in Mary Shelley's *Frankenstein.*" *Studies in Romanticism* 34 (1995): 127–53.

Readings, Bill. *The University in Ruins.* Cambridge: Harvard University Press, 1996.

Richards, Thomas. *The Commodity Culture of Victorian England: Advertising and Spectacle, 1851–1914.* Stanford, CA: Stanford University Press, 1990.

Robinson, Howard. *The British Post Office: A History.* Princeton, NJ: Princeton University Press, 1948.

Ronnick, Michele Valerie. "Tom Stoppard's *Arcadia:* Hermes' Tortoise and Apollo's Lyre." *Classical and Modern Literature* 16 (1996): 177–82.

Rosner, Mary, and T. R. Johnson. "Telling Stories: Metaphors of the Human Genome Project." *Hypatia* 10.4 (1995): 104–29.

Ross, Andrew. *Strange Weather: Culture, Science, and Technology in the Age of Limits.* London: Verso, 1991.

Rowe, John Carlos. "Spectral Mechanics: Gender, Sexuality, and Work in 'In the Cage.'" *The Other Henry James.* Durham, NC: Duke University Press, 1998. 155–80.

Rudwick, M.J.S. "Caricature as a Source for the History of Science: De La Beche's Anti-Lyellian Sketches of 1831." *Isis* 66 (1975): 534–60.

Rushdie, Salman. *The Satanic Verses.* New York: Viking, 1989.

———. "Outside the Whale." *Imaginary Homelands: Essays and Criticism 1981–1991.* London: Granta Books, 1991. 87–101.

Sadoff, Dianne F. and John Kucich, eds. *Victorian Afterlife: Postmodern Culture Rewrites the Nineteenth-Century.* Minneapolis: University of Minnesota Press, 2000.

———. "Introduction: Histories of the Present." In Sadoff and Kucich. ix–xxx.

Said, Edward W. *The World, the Text, and the Critic.* Cambridge: Harvard University Press, 1983.

Scarry, Elaine. *On Beauty and Being Just.* Princeton: Princeton University Press, 1999

Savoy, Eric. "'In the Cage' and the Queer Effects of Gay History." *Novel* 28 (1995): 284–307.

Schaffer, Simon. "Babbage's Intelligence: Calculating Engines and the Factory System." *Critical Inquiry* 21 (1994): 203–27.

Schlicke, Paul. *Dickens and Popular Entertainment.* London: Allen & Unwin, 1985.

Schoenfield, Mark. *The Professional Wordsworth: Law, Labor, and the Poet's Contract.* Athens: University of Georgia Press, 1996.

Schor, Naomi. *Reading in Detail: Aesthetics and the Feminine.* New York: Methuen, 1987.

Schrödinger, Erwin. *What Is Life? The Physical Aspect of the Living Cell.* 1944. Cambridge: Cambridge University Press, 1967.

Scott, Joan W. "Experience." *Feminists Theorize the Political.* Eds. Judith Butler and Joan W. Scott. New York: Routledge, 1992. 22–39.

Scott, Walter. *Rob Roy.* 1817. New York: Dent, 1906.

Sedgwick, Eve Kosofsky. "The Beast in the Closet: James and the Writing of Homosexual Panic." *Sex, Politics, and Science in the Nineteenth-Century Novel.* Ed. Ruth Bernard Yeazell. Baltimore: Johns Hopkins University Press, 1986. 148–86.

Senn, Fritz. *Joyce's Dislocations: Essays on Reading as Translation.* Ed. John Paul Riquelme. Baltimore: Johns Hopkins University Press, 1984.

Shaffner, Taliaferro P. *The Telegraph Manual: A Complete History and Description of the Semaphoric, Electric and Magnetic Telegraphs of Europe, Asia, Africa, and America, Ancient and Modern.* New York: Pudney and Russell, 1859.

Shakespeare in Love. Dir. John Madden. Miramax Films, 1998.

Shannon, Claude E., and Warren Weaver. *The Mathematical Theory of Communication.* 1948. Urbana: University of Illinois Press, 1963.

Shelley, Mary Wollstonecraft. *Frankenstein; or, The Modern Prometheus (The 1818 Text).* 1818. Chicago: University of Chicago Press, 1982.

Mary Shelley's Frankenstein. Dir. Kenneth Branagh. TriStar Pictures, 1994.

Shelley, Percy Bysshe. *The Complete Works of Percy Bysshe Shelley.* Eds. Roger Ingpen and Walter E. Peck. 10 vols. New York: Gordian, 1965.

———. *The Prose Works of Percy Bysshe Shelley.* Ed. E. B. Murray. Vol. 1. Oxford: Clarendon Press, 1993.

Shuttleworth, Sally. *George Eliot and Nineteenth Century Science: The Make-Believe of a Beginning.* Cambridge: Cambridge University Press, 1984.

The Silence of the Lambs. Dir. Jonathan Demme. Orion Pictures, 1991.

Silverman, Kaja. *The Acoustic Mirror: The Female Voice in Psychoanalysis and Cinema.* Bloomington: Indiana University Press, 1988.

———. "Back to the Future." *Camera Obscura: A Journal of Feminism, Culture, and Media Studies* 27 (1991):109–32.

Simak, Clifford D. *City.* New York: Ace Books, 1952.

Simpson, Colin, Lewis Chester, and David Leitch. *The Cleveland Street Affair.* Boston: Little, Brown, 1976.

Simpson, David. *The Academic Postmodern and the Rule of Literature: A Report on Half-Knowledge.* Chicago: University of Chicago Press, 1995.

Singh, Simon. *The Code Book: The Evolution of Secrecy From Mary Queen of Scots to Quantum Cryptography.* New York: Doubleday, 1999.

Snow, C. P. *The Two Cultures.* 1959. Cambridge: Cambridge University Press, 1998.

Somerville, Mary. *Mechanism of the Heavens.* London: John Murray, 1831.

———. *On the Connexion of the Physical Sciences.* London: John Murray, 1834.

———. *Personal Recollections, From Early Life to Old Age, of Mary Somerville. With Selections From Her Correspondence. By Her Daughter, Martha Somerville.* Boston: Roberts Brothers, 1874.

Sonarchy. Jack Straw Productions. URL: *http://www.sonarchy.org/.* October 11, 2002.

Sontag, Susan. *Against Interpretation: And Other Essays.* 1966. New York: Picador, 2001.

———. *Illness As Metaphor.* New York: Farrar Staus Giroux, 1978.

———. *AIDS and Its Metaphors.* New York: Farrar, Straus and Giroux, 1988.

———. *The Volcano Lover.* New York: Farrar Straus Giroux, 1992.

Southgate, Donald. *"The Most English Minister . . ." The Policies and Politics of Palmerston.* New York: St. Martin's Press, 1966.

Spencer, Nicholas. "Rethinking Ambivalence: Technopolitics and the Luddites in William Gibson and Bruce Sterling's *The Difference Engine.*" *Contemporary Literature* 40 (1999): 403–29.

Sponsler, Claire. "Cyberpunk and the Dilemmas of Postmodern Narrative: The Example of William Gibson." *Contemporary Literature* 33 (1992): 625–44.

Staging Sound: Feminism and Re/Production. 2001. Web page. URL: http://www.echonyc.com/~women/Issue18/index.html.

Standage, Tom. *The Victorian Internet: The Remarkable Story of the Telegraph and the Nineteenth Century's On-Line Pioneers.* New York: Walker Publishing, 1998.

Starr, Paul. *The Social Transformation of American Medicine.* New York: Basic Books, 1982.

Steedman, Carolyn. "Culture, Cultural Studies, and the Historians." In Grossberg, Nelson, and Treichler. 613–21.

Stein, Dorothy. *Ada: A Life and a Legacy.* Cambridge: MIT Press, 1985.

Steinberg, Michael P. "Cultural History and Cultural Studies." In Nelson and Gaonkar. 103–29.

Stephenson, Neal. *Snow Crash.* New York: Bantam Books, 1992.

————. *The Diamond Age.* New York: Bantam Books, 1995.

————. *Cryptonomicon.* New York: Avon Books, 1999.

————. *In the Beginning . . . Was the Command Line.* New York: Avon Books, 1999.

Sterling, Bruce. *Holy Fire.* New York: Bantam Books, 1996.

Stevens, Tyler. "'Sinister Fruitiness': *Neuromancer,* Internet Sexuality and the Turing Test." *Studies in the Novel* 28 (1996): 414–33.

Stockton, Sharon. "'The Self Regained': Cyberpunk's Retreat to the Imperium." *Contemporary Literature* 36 (1995): 588–612.

Stone, Lawrence. "The Revival of Narrative: Reflections on a New Old History." *Past and Present* 85 (1979): 3–24.

Stoppard, Tom. *Arcadia.* London: Faber and Faber, 1993.

Strecker, Trey. "Ecologies of Knowledge: The Encyclopedic Narratives of Richard Powers and His Contemporaries." *Review of Contemporary Fiction* 18.3 (1998): 67–71.

Stubbs, Katherine. "Operating Fantasies: Gender, Class and the Technology of the Telegraph." Unpublished manuscript. Rev. from *Working-Class Women in American Literature and Culture, 1860–1940.* Dissertation. Duke University, 1996.

Sussman, Herbert. "Cyberpunk Meets Charles Babbage: *The Difference Engine* as Alternative Victorian History." *Victorian Studies* 38 (1994): 1–23.

Sutherland, John. *Victorian Novelists and Publishers.* Chicago: University of Chicago Press, 1976.

Swade, Doron D. "Redeeming Charles Babbage's Mechanical Computer." *Scientific American* 268.2 (1993): 86–91.

Tatsumi, Takayuki. "Comparative Metafiction: Somewhere Between Ideology and Rhetoric." *Critique* 39 (1997): 2–17.

Tausky, Thomas E. "Getting the Corner Right: An Interview with Peter Carey." Online http://www.arts.uwo.ca/~andrewf/anzsc/anzsc4/carey4.htm. *Australian and New Zealand Studies in Canada* 4 (1990). May 20, 2002.

Terminator 2: Judgment Day. Dir. James Cameron. Carolco Pictures, 1991.

Tharaud, Barry. "*Great Expectations* as Literature and Film." *The Dickensian* 87 (1991): 102–10.

Thomas, Ronald R. "Telling Time and Post-National Space: Plotting the Prime Meridian and the Dome of the Millennium." *Narrative: An International Conference.* Hanover, NH, 1999.

Thurschwell, Pamela. "Henry James and Theodora Bosanquet: On the Typewriter, *In the Cage,* at the Ouija Board." *Textual Practice* 13 (1999): 5–23.

Tiffany, Grace. "Our Mutual Friend in 'Eumaeus': Joyce Appropriates Dickens." *Journal of Modern Literature* 16 (1991): 643–46.

Tony Blair Unveils Millennium Products. 1999. Web page. URL: http://greenwich2000 .com/millennium/info/millenniumproducts.htm. May 20, 2002.

Toole, Betty Alexandra. *Ada: The Enchantress of Numbers: Prophet of the Computer Age.* Mills Valley, CA: Strawberry Press, 1998.

Torgovnick, Marianna. "Introduction." *Eloquent Obsessions: Writing Cultural Criticism.* Ed. Torgovnick. Durham, NC: Duke University Press, 1994. 1–4.

Towards a 'Cool Britannia'. Web page. URL: http://greenwich2000.com/millennium/ info/panel2000.htm. May 20, 2002.

Townsend, John Wilson. *The Life of James Francis Leonard, the First Practical Sound-Reader of the Morse Alphabet.* Vol. 24. Filson Club Publications. Louisville, KY: John P. Morton, 1909.

Trollope, Anthony. "The Telegraph Girl." *Why Frau Frohmann Raised Her Prices and Other Stories.* 1877. New York: Arno Press, 1981.

U-571. Dir. Jonathan Mostow. Universal Pictures, 2000.

[Unsigned review]. *Saturday Review.* 18 Nov. 1882. Rpt. in *Thomas Hardy: The Critical Heritage.* 18 Nov. 1882. Ed. R. G. Cox. New York: Barnes & Noble, 1970.

Vail, Alfred. *The American Electro Magnetic Telegraph: With the Reports of Congress, and a Description of All Telegraphs Known, Employing Electricity or Galvanism.* 1845. Rpt. in *Eyewitness to Early American Telegraphy.* New York: Arno Press, 1974.

Varese, Jon Michael, ed. *The Dickens Project.* Web page. URL: ttp://humwww.ucsc.edu/dickens/index.html. May 20, 2002.

Vattimo, Gianni. *The End of Modernity: Nihilism and Hermeneutics in Postmodern Culture.* Trans. Jon R. Snyder. Baltimore: Johns Hopkins University Press, 1991.

Veeder, William. *Mary Shelley & Frankenstein: the Fate of Androgyny.* Chicago: University of Chicago Press, 1986.

Vennman, Barbara. "New Orleans 1993 Carnival: Tradition at Play in Papier-Mache and Stone." *Theatre Insight* 10 (1993): 5–14.

Veeser, Avram, ed. *The New Historicism.* New York: Routledge, 1989.

Vernon, James. *Politics and the People: A Study in English Political Culture, C. 1815–1867.* Cambridge: Cambridge University Press, 1993.

Wald, Priscilla. "Future Perfect: Grammar, Genes, and Geography." *New Literary History* 31 (2000): 681–708.

Walkowitz, Judith R. *City of Dreadful Delight: Narratives of Sexual Danger in Late-Victorian London.* Chicago: University of Chicago Press, 1992.

Walton, Priscilla L. *The Disruption of the Feminine in Henry James.* Toronto: University of Toronto Press, 1992.

Walzer, Michael. *Spheres of Justice: A Defense of Pluralism and Equality.* New York: Basic Books, 1983.

Wang, Orrin N. C. *Fantastic Modernity: Dialectical Readings in Romanticism and Theory.* Baltimore: Johns Hopkins University Press, 1996.

Weber, Max. *The Protestant Ethic and the Spirit of Capitalism.* Trans. Talcott Parsons. 1904–1905. London: George Allen & Unwin, 1985.

Wertham, Fredric M. D. *Seduction of the Innocent.* New York: Rinehart, 1954.

Wheatstone, Charles. "On the Transmission of Musical Sounds Through Solid Linear Conductors, and on Their Subsequent Reciprocation." *The Scientific Papers of Sir Charles Wheatstone.* London: Physical Society of London, 1879. 47–63.

———. "Review [Of Reed Organ-Pipes, Speaking Machines, Etc.]." *The Scientific Papers of Sir Charles Wheatstone.* London: Physical Society of London, 1879. 348–67.

Whewell, William. "*On the Connexion of the Physical Sciences.* By Mrs. Somerville." *The Quarterly Review* 51 (1834): 54–68.

———. *The Philosophy of the Inductive Sciences: Founded Upon Their History.* 2 vols. London: J.W. Parker, 1840.

Wicke, Jennifer. *Advertising Fictions: Literature, Advertisement, and Social Reading.* New York: Columbia University Press, 1988.

———. "Henry James's Second Wave." *Henry James Review* 10 (1989): 146–51.

Wiener, Martin J. *English Culture and the Decline of the Industrial Spirit, 1850–1980.* Cambridge: Cambridge University Press, 1981.

Wiener, Norbert. *Cybernetics; or, Control and Communication in the Animal and the Machine.* 1948. Cambridge: MIT Press, 1961.

Williams, Patricia J. *The Alchemy of Race and Rights.* Cambridge: Harvard University Press, 1991.

Williams, Raymond. *Marxism and Literature.* Oxford: Oxford University Press, 1977.

Wilson, Edward O. *Consilience: The Unity of Knowledge.* New York: Knopf, 1998.

Wilson, Norman J. *History in Crisis? Recent Directions in Historiography.* Upper Saddle River, NJ: Prentice Hall, 1999.

Windschuttle, Keith. *The Killing of History: How Literary Critics and Social Theorists Are Murdering Our Past.* New York: The Free Press, 1997.

Winokur, Scott. "Matchmakers of the Nineties—From Yentas to Computers." *Cosmopolitan* June 1991: 236–39.

Winter, Alison. "The Construction of Orthodoxies and Heterodoxies in the Early Victorian Life Sciences." In Lightman. 24–50.

———. "A Calculus of Suffering: Ada Lovelace and the Bodily Constraints on Women's Knowledge in Early Victorian England." *Science Incarnate: Historical Embodiments of Natural Knowledge.* Eds. Christopher Lawrence and Steven Shapin. Chicago: University of Chicago Press, 1998. 202–39.

———. *Mesmerized: Powers of Mind in Victorian Britain.* Chicago: University of Chicago Press, 1998.

Witek, Joseph. *Comic Books as History: The Narrative Art of Jack Jackson, Art Spiegelman, and Harvey Pekar.* Jackson: University Press of Mississippi, 1989.

Woodcock, Bruce. *Peter Carey.* Manchester, UK: Manchester University Press, 1996.

Woolley, Benjamin. *The Bride of Science: Romance, Reason and Byron's Daughter.* Basingstoke, UK: Macmillan, 1999.

Wordsworth, William. *Poetical Works.* Eds. Thomas Hutchinson and Ernest de Selincourt. London: Oxford University Press, 1969.

Wordsworth, William, and Samuel Taylor Coleridge. *Lyrical Ballads: The Text of the Edition With the Additional 1800 Poems and the Prefaces.* Eds. R. L. Brett and A. R. Jones. London: Methuen, 1965.

Wrightson, Keith. "Infanticide in Early Seventeenth-Century England." *Local Population Studies* 15 (1975): 10–21.

Wuthnow, Robert. *Communities of Discourse: Ideology and Social Structure in the Reformation, the Enlightenment, and European Socialism.* Cambridge: Harvard University Press, 1989.

Wyschogrod, Edith. *An Ethics of Remembering: History, Heterology, and the Nameless Others.* Chicago: University of Chicago Press, 1998.

Yeo, Richard. *Defining Science: William Whewell, Natural Knowledge, and Public Debate in Early Victorian Britain.* Cambridge: Cambridge University Press, 1993.

Young, Cathy and Teresa M. Senft. *Hearing the Net: An Interview with Mia Lipner .* Web page. URL: http://www.echonyc.com/~women/Issue17/lipner.html. January 29, 2001.

Young, Robert M. *Darwin's Metaphor: Nature's Place in Victorian Culture.* Cambridge: Cambridge University Press, 1985.